Contents

Welcome to the guide

Welcome to the first edition of AA Best Restaurants. This brand new guide includes every single UK and Republic of Ireland restaurant with an AA Rosette and showcases the very best throughout both countries.

In the first section of the guide you'll find the 3, 4 and 5-Rosette restaurants and the AA's annual award winners, and in the following section are the restaurants that have been awarded 1 or 2 Rosettes for the excellence of their food. As always our hotel and restaurant inspectors have been travelling up and down the country, making anonymous visits to hundreds of establishments and have awarded the coveted AA Rosettes to the best places to eat. See pages 8–9 for more details on how the food is assessed and the Rosettes awarded.

The quality of the dining scene just keeps getting better and better – Best Restaurants 2018 includes 15 five-Rosette, 42 four-Rosette and 202 three-Rosette restaurants.

Award winners

Our award winners are a particularly strong group of places, chosen as best in class by our hospitality awards panel. The Restaurants of the Year for each of the home nations and London represent that crucial juncture where a distinctive concept meets the finest cooking with an emphasis this year on international influences.

Likewise, our individual award winners are all highly experienced; from the AA Chef of the Year, whose career has seen him in the kitchens of many famous and glamorous restaurants (see page 10) to the Lifetime Achievement Award recipient who having started his working life in the army, went on to become a leading light in the hosptiality industry (see page 12). The Food Service Award winner, although a venue, is a success story because of the dedication and enthusiasm demonstrated by its owners for more than 30 years (see page 13).

Toasting the very best

The AA Wine Awards (see page 16) single out three restaurants that our inspectors feel have shown a real passion for and knowledge of wine. This year, multi-Rosette restaurants play all the star roles. We've also highlighted notable wine lists throughout the guide – so look out for ♟.

Things can change

The transient nature of the hospitality industry means that chefs move around all the time, and restaurants may change ownership. As any change at the multi-Rosette level requires a new inspection to verify their award, some of these restaurants appear in the guide with their Rosette level unconfirmed at the time of going to press. Our inspections are ongoing throughout the year however, so once their award is confirmed it will be published at www.theaa.com/restaurants

The up-and-coming chefs

It's not just the established and experienced venues that are celebrated by the AA. This year sees the second AA College Restaurant of the Year award (see page 15), which is designed to mirror the main Rosette award process by highlighting the best catering college teams.

In partnership with People 1st, the AA has awarded College Rosettes in relation to food, service and kitchen management – visit www.theaa.com/hotel-services/college-rosettes to find out more.

Tell us what you think

We welcome your feedback about the restaurants in this guide, and the guide itself. So, please write in or email us at aa.restaurants@theaa.com with your feedback.

Join us online

Discover all of our Rosetted restaurants at theaa.com/restaurants

- Search by restaurant name and location.
- View the venue ahead of your visit using the restaurant galleries
- Get the latest news on all the AA's award-winning venues.
- Find AA-rated places to stay as well as recommended pubs with great food.

Using the guide

1. Location
Restaurants appear in two sections: 3, 4 & 5 Rosette restaurants and AA award winners, followed by 1 and 2 Rosette restaurants. They are listed in country and county order, then by town and then alphabetically within the town. There is an index by restaurant name at the back of the guide.

2. Map reference
In the first section of the guide each restaurant is given a map reference – the map page number and a two-figure reference based on the National Grid.
For example: **Map 18 SD49**

18 refers to the page number of the map section at the back of the guide

SD is the National Grid square (representing 100,000 sq metres)

4 is the figure reading across the top and bottom of the map page

9 is the figure reading down at each side of the map page. For Central London and Greater London, there is a map section starting on page 104.

AA regional award winners are highlighted on the maps.

3. AA Rosette award
Restaurants can be awarded from 1 to 5 Rosettes. See pages 8–9 for details.

4. Food style
A summary of the main cuisine type(s).

5. Vegetarian menu
V Indicates a vegetarian menu. Restaurants with some vegetarian

dishes available are indicated under Notes (see 13, below).

6. Notable wine list
This symbol, where present, indicates a wine list chosen as notable by an AA panel (see pages 16–17 for details).

7. Chef(s)
The names of the chef(s) are as up-to-date as possible at the time of going to press, but changes in personnel often occur, and may affect both the style and quality of the restaurant.

8. Seats
Number of seats in the restaurant and private dining room.

9 Times
Daily opening and closing times, the days of the week when closed and seasonal closures. Some restaurants offer all-day dining. Note that opening times are liable to change without notice. It is always wise to check in advance.

10. Prices
Prices are for set lunch and dinner, tasting menus and à la carte dishes. Note: prices quoted are an indication only, and are subject to change. Service charges are not included here and may vary depending on the size of the party. Most restaurants will have some form of service charge.

11. Wines
Number of wines under and over £30 (€30 in Ireland), and number available by the glass.

The Vineyard

2.─MAP 5 SU46

◉◉◉ Modern British **V** ♟ ─3–6.

01635 528770 | Stockcross, RG20 8JU

www.the-vineyard.co.uk

World-class wines and modern French cuisine in five-star splendour

When only a five-star, contemporary country house splurge will do, The Vineyard comes up with the goods: luxurious rooms, chic public areas and a glossy spa, while Robby Jenks's classy, intelligent cooking makes the place a dining destination in its own right. The foodie business goes on in an elegant split-level dining room, where a sweeping staircase sports a grapevine-style balustrade, tables are dressed in crisp white linen, and artwork jazzes up the walls. Opening the show, pink and tender quail's breasts are counterpointed with charred baby gem lettuce, tarragon purée and pistachios, or beef sirloin tartare might be helped along by horseradish, buttermilk and Granny Smith apple. Dishes gain lustre from top-class ingredients rather than off-the-wall combinations or techno trickery – main-course tenderloin and belly of suckling pig with cabbage and smoky bacon, caramelised onion purée and apple being a case in point. To finish, espresso granita arrives with blackcurrant cream and coffee sponge. Despite the name, they don't make wine at The Vineyard, but they do serve amazing wines from a world-class cellar that runs to a staggering 30,000 bottles, with around 100 available by the glass – there's even a pairing option to go with an amuse-bouche of smoked cod's roe cornet with lemon.

Chef Robby Jenks **Seats** 86, Private dining room 140 **Times** 12–2/7–9.30 **Prices** Set L 3 course £29, Set D 3 course £65, Tasting menu £75–£99, Sunday lunch £39 **Wines** 2,500 bottles over £30, 60 bottles under £30, 100 by glass **Parking** 100 **Notes** Children welcome ─7–13.

12. Parking

On-site parking or nearby parking.

13. Notes

Additional information as supplied by the restaurants including, for example, availability of Sunday lunch, vegetarian dishes (not a full menu, see 5, opposite) and their policy towards children.

Facilities for disabled guests

The Equality Act 2010 provides legal rights for disabled people including access to goods, services and facilities, and means that service providers may have to consider making adjustments to their premises. For more information about the Act, see the UK government website www.gov.uk.

The establishments in this guide should be aware of their obligations under the Equality Act.

We recommend that you phone in advance to ensure that the establishment you have chosen has appropriate facilities.

How the AA assesses for Rosette Awards

First introduced in 1956, the AA's Rosette Award scheme was the first nationwide scheme for assessing the quality of food served by restaurants and hotels.

A consistent approach

The Rosette scheme is an award, not a classification, and although there is necessarily an element of subjectivity when it comes to assessing taste, we aim for a consistent approach throughout the UK. Our awards are made solely on the basis of a meal visit or visits by one or more of our hotel and restaurant inspectors, who have an unrivalled breadth and depth of experience in assessing quality. Essentially it's a snapshot, whereby the entire meal including ancillary items (when served) are assessed. Of all the restaurants across the UK, approximately 10% are of a standard which is worthy of 1 Rosette and above.

What makes a restaurant worthy of a Rosette award?

For AA inspectors, the top and bottom line is the food. The taste of a dish is what counts, and whether it successfully delivers to the diner the promise of the menu. A restaurant is only as good as its worst meal. Although presentation and competent service should be appropriate to the style of the restaurant and the quality of the food, they cannot affect the Rosette assessment as such, either up or down. The summaries below indicate what our inspectors look for, but are intended only as guidelines. The AA is constantly reviewing its award criteria, and competition usually results in an all-round improvement in standards, so it becomes increasingly difficult for restaurants to reach an award level.

The next level

Achieving a Rosette is a huge achievement and something not to be underestimated. We are often asked by chefs and proprietors: "What is the difference between 1 and 5 Rosettes and how can I get to the next level?" We answer that it's how well a chef manages to apply advanced technique while retaining maximum flavour, and assuming an appropriate quality of source ingredients.

While we endeavour to work with the industry and promote great cooking across the UK, it is of paramount importance for chefs to always serve their market first. We recommend they don't chase awards, but see them as something to celebrate when they come along. Where, however, the winning of Rosettes is an aspiration, the simple guidelines, shown opposite, may help. Experiencing AA food tastings, enhanced food tastings or signing up to one of the AA Rosette Academies can also give further insight and guidance, but these are separate from the awards process and do not influence any assessments.

◉ One Rosette

These restaurants will be achieving standards that standout in their local area, featuring:

- food prepared with care, understanding and skill
- good quality ingredients

The same expectations apply to hotel restaurants where guests should be able to eat in with confidence and a sense of anticipation.

Around 45% of restaurants/hotels in this guide have one Rosette.

◉◉ Two Rosettes

The best local restaurants, which aim for and achieve:

- higher standards
- better consistency
- greater precision is apparent in the cooking
- obvious attention to the selection of quality ingredients

Around 45% of restaurants/hotels in this guide have two Rosettes.

◉◉◉ Three Rosettes

Outstanding restaurants that achieve standards that demand national recognition well beyond their local area. The cooking will be underpinned by:

- the selection and sympathetic treatment of the highest quality ingredients
- timing, seasoning and the judgment of flavour combinations will be consistently excellent

These virtues will tend to be supported by other elements such as intuitive service and a well-chosen wine list.

Around 10% of the restaurants/hotels in this guide have three Rosettes and above.

◉◉◉◉ Four Rosettes

Among the top restaurants in the UK where the cooking demands national recognition. These restaurants will exhibit:

- intense ambition
- a passion for excellence
- superb technical skills
- remarkable consistency
- an appreciation of culinary traditions combined with a passionate desire for further exploration and improvement

42 restaurants in this guide have four Rosettes.

◉◉◉◉◉ Five Rosettes

The pinnacle, where the cooking compares with the best in the world. These restaurants will have:

- highly individual voices
- exhibit breathtaking culinary skills and set the standards to which others aspire to, yet few achieve

15 restaurants in this guide have five Rosettes.

Announcements of awards

One and two Rosettes are awarded at the time of inspection. Three and four Rosette awards are announced twice during the year, but never at the time of inspection. Five Rosettes are awarded just once a year and never at the time of inspection.

Suspension of multi-Rosettes (3, 4, 5 Rosettes)

When a chef holds 3, 4 or 5 Rosettes and moves from one establishment to another, the award is suspended at that establishment and does not follow the chef automatically. We recommend that when a change of chef occurs, establishments let us know as soon as possible in order for us to schedule inspections.

AA Chef of the Year 2017–18

A popular and coveted title, this unique award, introduced in 1996, offers all AA Rosette-awarded chefs the chance to decide which of their peers deserves the ultimate recognition of their performance over the past twelve months.

JOHN T WILLIAMS MBE

From modest beginnings in a Tyneside fishing family to executive head chef at The Ritz, John Williams's career as a hotel chef has headed ever upwards from the time he saw one of the pioneering TV chefs, Graham Kerr – *The Galloping Gourmet* – in action and decided that cooking was the way to go. Trained on a classical cookery course at a technical college, Williams still believes in the value of learning the basics and nurturing up-and-coming talent through apprenticeships, an ethos he promotes in his role as Chairman of the Academy of Culinary Arts (ACA).

After a rookie stint in a country-house hotel in Northumberland, the siren call of the capital lured him to the Royal Garden Hotel where an inspirational 8-year sojourn with Rémy Fougère developed his craft and laid the solid classical French foundations that we still see today. Aged just 27, Williams saw his future career at the helm of a brigade in a big hotel kitchen rather than in a restaurant, securing a place amid the blue-chip tradition, heritage and history of Claridge's under the aegis of Mario Lesnik. During the 9 years in the Claridge's kitchens he was in charge of sorting out the food for Baroness Margaret Thatcher's 70th birthday. The next glossy hotel in his sights was The Berkeley before the irresistible lure of arguably the world's grandest of grand hotels, The Ritz, came in 2004.

A chef who prefers the heat of the kitchen to the sparkle of the TV studio lights, Williams counts Michel Bourdin and Brian Turner amongst his own mentors, and has consistently raised the bar for the UK's young chefs through his motivational work via the ACA apprenticeship scheme, ensuring that the weight of diners' expectations in a special occasion destination such as The Ritz will always be met.

Previous winners

Raymond Blanc OBE
Belmond Le Manoir aux Quat' Saisons,
    Great Milton, Oxfordshire

Heston Blumenthal
The Fat Duck, Bray, Berkshire
Hinds Head, Bray, Berkshire
Dinner by Heston Blumenthal,
    London SW1
The Crown at Bray, Berkshire

Michael Caines
The Coach House by Michael Caines,
    Kentisbury, Devon

Daniel Clifford
Midsummer House, Cambridge,
    Cambridgeshire

Andrew Fairlie
Andrew Fairlie at Gleneagles,
    Auchterarder, Perth & Kinross

Chris and Jeff Galvin
Galvin La Chapelle, London E1

Shaun Hill
Walnut Tree Inn, Abergavenny,
    Monmouthshire

Philip Howard
Elystan Street, London SW3

Tom Kerridge
The Hand and Flowers, Marlow,
    Buckinghamshire
The Coach, Marlow, Buckinghamshire

Jean-Christophe Novelli

Pierre Koffmann

Nathan Outlaw
Restaurant Nathan Outlaw,
    Port Isaac, Cornwall
Outlaw's Fish Kitchen, Port Isaac,
    Cornwall
Outlaw's at The Capital, London SW3

Gordon Ramsay
Restaurant Gordon Ramsay,
    London SW3

Simon Rogan
L'Enclume, Cartmel, Cumbria

Germain Schwab

Rick Stein
The Seafood Restaurant,
    Padstow, Cornwall
Rick Stein at Sandbanks,
    Sandbanks, Dorset

Kevin Viner

Marcus Wareing
Marcus, The Berkeley, London SW1

Marco Pierre White

Martin Wishart
Martin Wishart at Loch Lomond,
    Balloch, West Dunbartonshire
Restaurant Martin Wishart,
    Leith, Edinburgh

AA Lifetime Achievement Award 2017–18

The AA Lifetime Achievement Award, introduced in 2006, recognises professionals within the hospitality industry who have committed their lives to the pursuit of perfection within their discipline. Their significant contributions to the industry have made a notable impact.

PHILIPPE ROSSITER

Perhaps with a French mother who was a teacher by profession, Philippe Rossiter's career was mapped out from day one, although his route into hospitality was somewhat unorthodox. Born in the UK, Philippe was eager to join the army and was stationed across the UK and Europe, rising to the rank of Colonel and appointed to head up the Army School of Catering.

With the strong management and planning skills learnt in a structured army environment, together with his passion for the education and development of young people in the hospitality sector, it was not surprising that Philippe took on the mantle of Chief Executive of the Institute of Hospitality. During his 10 years at the Institute, he was directly involved in education provision which led to extensive links with The University of Surrey, where he was awarded an honorary doctorate; this sat naturally with his academic qualifications which include an honours degree in Hotel and Catering Management and an MBA. Philippe's time as the Executive Secretary of the Master Innholders was instrumental in driving up standards and professionalism in the hotel industry, the benefits of which we continue to see today.

Philippe 'retired' in 2012 after a long and successful career in the hospitality sector. Although a keen gardener, he was not one to simply potter about in the herbaceous borders. No, not Philippe Rossiter. At the age of 70 he is now running marathons – not just for personal enjoyment, but raising funds for key hospitality industry charities of Hospitality Action and Springboard which are dear to his heart and reflect his determination to help others succeed.

He hasn't neglected his French roots either, and spends quite a lot of time with his extended family in Normandy.

AA Food Service Award 2017–18

Introduced in 2013, this award recognises restaurants that deliver excellent standards of service and hospitality. The teams at these restaurants deliver technical service skills, and their food and beverage knowledge is of the highest standard.

THE THREE CHIMNEYS & THE HOUSE OVER-BY, COLBOST, ISLE OF SKYE

The Three Chimneys story begins back in 1984 when the place was a simple stand-alone seasonal restaurant driven by a couple's passion for Scottish food. Now into their fourth decade of continuous ownership and leadership, Shirley and Eddie Spear remain very much hands-on at the helm of their business. And that's no mean feat considering the place operates at almost full capacity, seven days a week and for 11 months of the year. They welcome over 22,000 guests annually that represent a significant boon to the local economy, and play a considerable part in building Skye's gastronomic reputation. The strength of its attraction is even more remarkable given its far-flung location: lying an hour's drive from the Skye Bridge, and with the last five miles or so by single track road, you're unlikely to be just passing by this remote foodie mecca.

The Three Chimneys has long been held in high esteem within the industry and remains a byword for superlative hospitality and service. Staff are trained to care for guests every minute of the way from arrival through to departure in a relaxed and informal manner. Head chef Scott Davies continues to maintain respect for the island's identity with his inventive approach, which draws from the Scottish and Nordic heritage of the Highlands and Islands and allows superlative ingredients the opportunity to speak for themselves, truly living up to the ethos of 'the best of Skye, Land and Sea'.

The place doesn't sit on its laurels: the last four years have seen a top-to-toe programme of refurbishment and the investment of £100k in a new kitchen to provide a state-of-the-art environment for the brigade. Shirley's lifetime work in the Scottish food and beverage sector was recognised in the Queen's 90th birthday honours list when she was awarded an OBE for services to food and drink in Scotland.

See pages 296–7

AA Restaurants of the Year 2017–18

Potential Restaurants of the Year are nominated by our team of full-time inspectors based on their routine visits. We are looking for somewhere that is exceptional in its chosen area of the market. While the Rosette awards are based on the quality of the food alone, Restaurant of the Year takes into account all aspects of the dining experience.

England winner
THE FREEMASONS AT WISWELL, WHALLEY, LANCASHIRE
See pages 102–3

London winner
ELYSTAN STREET, LONDON SW3
See pages 138–9

Scotland winner
THE DINING ROOM, EDINBURGH
See pages 270–1

Wales winner
BEACH HOUSE RESTAURANT AT OXWICH BEACH, SWANSEA
See pages 314–5

AA College Restaurant of the Year 2017–18

The AA College Rosette Scheme is designed to recognise the efforts of students, both front and back of house who are the future of the hospitality industry. The college accreditation process, provided by People 1st, recognises colleges offering exceptional hospitality training, and those that perform above and beyond as centres of excellence in a specialist field.

Winner

ACADEMY

ACADEMY AT SOUTH CHESHIRE COLLEGE
Dane Bank Avenue,
Crewe, CW2 8AB

Runners up

THE BRASSERIE AT MILTON KEYNES COLLEGE
Sherwood Drive, Bletchley,
Milton Keynes, MK3 6DR

AVENUE 141 AT FAREHAM COLLEGE
Fareham College, Bishopsfield
Road, Fareham, PO14 1NH

Foxholes Restaurant, Runshaw College – Winner 2016 – 2017

AA Wine Awards 2017–18

The annual AA Wine Awards, sponsored by Matthew Clark Wines, attracted a huge response from our AA recognised restaurants with over 1,000 wine lists submitted for judging. Three national winners were chosen.

Wales and Overall winner
YNYSHIR, EGLWYS FACH,
CEREDIGION
See pages 302–3

England
THE FIVE FIELDS,
LONDON SW3
See pages 140–1

Scotland
ANDREW FAIRLIE AT
GLENEAGLES, AUCHTERARDER,
PERTH & KINROSS
See pages 294–5

All the restaurants in this year's guide were invited to submit their wine lists. From these the panel selected a shortlist of over 230 establishments who are highlighted in the guide with the Notable Wine List symbol ♥.

The shortlisted establishments were asked to choose wines from their list (within a budget of £80 per bottle) to accompany a menu designed by last year's winner Frederic Bruges of Sketch (Lecture Room & Library).

The final judging panel included Nick Zalinski, Business Director, Matthew Clark Wines (our sponsor), Frederic Bruges, Director of Wine at Sketch and Paul Hackett, AA Hotel Services. The judges' comments are shown in the award winners' entries in the guide.

What makes a wine list notable?
We are looking for high-quality wines, with diversity across grapes and/or countries and style, the best individual growers and vintages. The list should be well presented, clear and easy to navigate. To reflect the demand of diners, there should be a good choice of varied wines available by the glass.

Things that disappoint the judges are spelling errors on the lists, wines under incorrect regions or styles, split vintages (which are still far too common), lazy purchasing (all wines from a country from just one grower or negociant) and confusing wine list layouts. Sadly, many restaurants still do not pay much attention to wine, resulting in ill-considered lists.

To reach the final shortlist, we look for a real passion for wine, which should come across to the customer, a fair pricing policy (depending on the style of the restaurant), interesting coverage (not necessarily a large list), which might include areas of specialism, perhaps a particular wine area, sherries or larger formats such as magnums.

Ynyshir, Eglwys Fach, Ceredigion (see pages 302–3)
– the winning wine selection

Menu	Wine Selection
Canapés – Vodka Martini jelly; black pudding croquette; parmesan sablés	Aperitif: Court Garden, Blanc de Noir 2010
Starter – Native oyster; poached langoustines; raw razor clams, olive oil, salt, lime; gratinated cockles, bacon and cream, leeks; salted sea bass, shiso	Katsuyama Lei, Hitombore 55%
Fish course – Arctic char, cauliflower, romanesco, almonds with Cassis beurre blanc	Georg Breuer, Terra Montosa 2014
Meat course – Whole roasted duck, blackberry bigarade, January king cabbage, Tourtière, truffle, foie gras, spinach, sauce Périgueux	Ruqqabellus, Archaeus 2012
Cheese course – Comté, white chocolate, Roquefort, walnuts, pear, smoked goats' cheese sorbet, Sancerre jelly, leek salad with honey vinaigrette	Suertes del Marques Trenzado 2014
Pudding course – Orange soufflé, honey ice cream, dry apricots, walnuts, exotic fruit sabayon	Digestif: Diplomatico Venezuelan Rum

The AA Wine Awards are sponsored by
Matthew Clark, Whitchurch Lane, Bristol, BS14 0JZ
Tel: 01275 891400
email: enquiries@matthewclark.co.uk
web: www.matthewclark.co.uk

TIMELESS ELEGANCE
FROM VILLEROY & BOCH

The perfect contours and proportions of classical Roman architecture are the inspiration behind the design of La Classica and La Classica Contura.

Sophisticated, modern and stylish, in premium bone porcelain.

SPONSORING THE AA AWARDS FOR 25 YEARS

Villeroy & Boch are proud to have presented the AA Awards since 1992.

Quality and inspiration are the defining qualities of a great restaurant. They are also the values that have made Villeroy & Boch, with its tradition of innovation dating back to 1748, the leading tableware brand in Europe. Dining with friends and family, and enjoying good food and drink together are special to all of us, and these occasions are made all the more special when served on beautiful tableware from Villeroy & Boch.

Our distinctive and original designs have consistently set the pace for others to follow and provide the perfect setting chosen by many of the world's leading chefs to frame their award-winning creations. Villeroy & Boch offer a wide range of stunning designs to suit any lifestyle and decor, and create the perfect ambience for successful entertaining and stylish family living.

AA MEMBERS SAVE 10%

As an AA member you enjoy 10% off when shopping online using this link: www.theaa.com/rewards
In addition, members of the AA also receive 10% off full price products in any of our Concession Stores on presentation of an AA membership card.

UK and Ireland customer services line: 0208-871-0011
line open Monday-Friday 9am-5pm

ENGLAND

Bedfordshire

WOBURN

Paris House Restaurant

MAP 12 SP93

◉◉◉ Modern British V

01525 290692 | London Road, Woburn Park, MK17 9QP

www.parishouse.co.uk

Impeccable contemporary cooking in a reassembled timbered house

The entrance to Paris House never fails to impress, through a grand gateway and across 22 acres of deer park in the Duke of Bedford's Woburn estate. The ostensibly Tudor manor is actually a Victorian facsimile built in 1878 for the International Exhibition in Paris, where it caught the eye of the 9th Duke, who shipped it all back from the Rue des Nations to Bedfordshire flat pack-style for reassembling. If you find yourself ambling around the gardens to sharpen the appetite for the gastronomic extravaganza that awaits, look for the bomb shelter that was built, so legend has it, as a bolt hole for Winston Churchill to chill out in while up doing work at nearby Bletchley Park.

The windows may be mullioned, but after a top-to-toe refurbishment in early 2017, the interiors set a suitably up-to-date note – think funky red chandeliers and eye-catching original artworks – for Phil Fanning's ingeniously fresh fusion ideas. Asian influences underpin the menus, which are headed in Roman numerals by their numbers of courses, starting with a fairly leisurely VI at lunch, and extending into the full-works VIII and X at dinner. Timings and techniques are spot on, and the cooking involves a high degree of invention – if you're going for broke with the

all out 10-course version, expect a succession of astonishing ideas all vying for pole position on the diner's palate. Brill might open the itinerary, with the lively accompaniments of coconut, grapefruit and turmeric, before tandoori-spiced rabbit appears with yogurt and mango chutney. Next up, a pasta-based dish matched with confit egg yolk and parmesan, all aromatised with the sensuous note of truffle might lead on to more of those Asian flavours in an idea combining crispy pork with pickled ginger and pungent kimchi. The kitchen is adept at squeezing every molecule of flavour out of the first-class ingredients, thus fish dishes might see turbot with palm heart and chou farci in a clever marine version of pot au feu, while the main meat offering combines Challans duckling with red miso and mushrooms.

A plate of artisan cheeses ripened to prime condition makes an extremely tempting optional extra before a fashionable crossover dish of parsnip pannacotta with maple, bacon and parsnip flakes segues into a brace of dessert courses, perhaps an off-the-wall medley of blackberries, olive oil, red wine and toasted marzipan, followed by an invigorating trio of poached rhubarb, white chocolate and Buddha's hand lemon, or perhaps a reinvented take on the tiramisú theme involving pear, marsala, coffee and mascarpone to close the show. The attention to detail throughout is astonishing.

Chef Phil Fanning **Seats** 37, Private dining room 14 **Times** 12–2/7–9, Closed Christmas, Monday to Wednesday, D Sunday **Prices** Dinner 8/10 course £91–£109, Lunch 6 course £43, **Wines** 99 bottles over £30, 3 bottles under £30, 13 by glass **Parking** 24 **Notes** Sunday lunch, Children welcome

Berkshire

Restaurant Coworth Park
MAP 6 SU96

◉◉◉ Modern British V ☙
01344 876600 | London Road, SL5 7SE
www.coworthpark.com

Wondrous classical cooking in Georgian splendour

The imposing white Georgian mansion house has 240 acres of Berkshire to itself, and is only a stroll from the Great Park at Windsor. Among the attractions at Coworth is a polo field, where you can book lessons if you're a newbie. After a solid day's battling at the hoops, you'll find Coworth has a fistful of different dining options, leading up to the majestic restaurant, where the organically themed decor includes oak leaves and acorns in plaster relief and an enormous copper ceiling sculpture.

The menus are in the youthfully capable hands of Adam Smith, a former Roux scholar with a distinctly classical turn of mind and wondrous technical ability. An opening dish of sautéed duck liver with peach, almonds and ginger demonstrates confident handling of combinations, and mains might take in braised turbot with asparagus and morels in Jura wine, truffled blackleg chicken with celery and mushrooms, or a bravura serving of spring lamb with its sweetbreads, artichoke and aubergine in a deeply savoury jus. Dessert could be almond mousse with caramelised Granny Smith, caramel custard, raisins, vanilla ice cream and a strong Calvados sauce, or traditional lemon tart with meringue garnish and a bewitching note of mint.

Chef Adam Smith **Seats** 66, Private dining room 16 **Times** 12.30–3/ 6.30–9.30, Closed Monday and Tuesday, L Wednesday and Thursday, D Sunday **Prices** Set L 2 course £30, Set L 3 course £35, Set D 3 course from £45, Tasting menu 7 course from £95, Starter from £18, Main from £34, Dessert £18, Sunday lunch from £45 **Wines** 400 bottles over £30, 4 bottles under £30, 18 by glass **Parking** 100

BRAY

The Fat Duck

MAP 6 SU98

@@@@@ Modern British V ♥
01628 580333 | High Street, SL6 2AQ
www.thefatduck.co.uk

A narrative concept menu from a modern legend

Heston Blumenthal's Fat Duck, and its ubiquitously telegenic proprietor himself, have entered the latter-day pantheon of culinary legend, but are also the subject of a great deal of fundamentally mistaken belief. On the latter side, many have come to believe that the cooking here is all something of an elaborate jape, its formidable cost an index of the degree to which people are prepared to be starstruck by reputation alone, even while they set about eating unrecognisable items that only bear the most indistinct relation to food. That nothing could be further from the truth is what accounts for the other half of the legend. Those who do make it here – and the waiting list and booking system are not for the faint-hearted – from all corners of the globe are regaled with a culinary performance that, with awe-inspiring consistency, transcends the known limits within most other kitchens.

Dishes arrive in gigantic seashells with electrical wires trailing from them, or perched on great white cushions floating in mid-air. A pair of ice lollies is stuck in a tray of gravel. A couple of little packets look like discarded litter on a patch of grass. There is humour of course, but only the kind that assumes we're all on the same side. What the presentations might obscure, it should be admitted, is the unimpeachable quality of their prime materials, and if Blumenthal has spoken of wanting to create the sense of thrilled anticipation one had as a child when the family set out on its summer holiday, that joy is tangible in the intensity of the flavours as much as in the entertaining menu concept that it generates. The glass box of sashimi with its shellfish foam and 'sand' of miso oil, tapioca and panko crumbs would be remarkable in itself, even without the iPod earbud that pours a soundtrack of crashing waves into your skull. A glass of rabbit consommé is served half-hot and half-cold, a bewildering moment of sensory distortion.

There are dishes, though, that look just like restaurant dishes, the most artful concept of all, when a serving of duck à l'orange is so poignantly intense, the meat so treasurably tender and flavourful, that all the surrounding narrative trickery fades away. That's ultimately what great cooking is about and, after allowing for all the theatrical ingenuity, the Fat Duck is incomparably good at that too.

Chefs Heston Blumenthal, Jonny Lake **Seats** 42 **Times** 12–2/7–9, Closed 2 weeks at Christmas, Sunday and Monday **Prices** Only tasting menu available £265 **Wines** 500 bottles over £30 **Parking** Two village car parks **Notes** Children welcome

BRAY *continued*
Hinds Head

MAP 6 SU98

◉◉◉ British ♟

01628 626151 | High Street, SL6 2AB

www.hindsheadbray.com

Heston's modern take on old-English fare with bang-on flavours

Heston Blumenthal never intended to emulate the nearby Fat Duck's culinary pyrotechnics in Bray's village boozer, but rather to offer traditional true-Brit cooking in tune with the building's 15th-century heritage, although the place is clearly packed with diners looking for a glimpse of that Blumenthal wizardry. A refurbishment in 2017 introduced a clubby lounge bar upstairs with eccentric touches in its funky decor – stained glass windows, off-the-wall taxidermy, and Persian rugs – as a backdrop to an on-trend listing of cocktails, artisan gins and no-nonsense bar snacks, while the drill in the main restaurant is a trio of monthly-changing set menus offering well-crafted versions of robust British dishes.

Starters can be as simple as pea and ham soup, presented with a touch of rustic flair and full-on flavours, or a trencherman's terrine of ham hock, pork tenderloin and leek. Main courses might bring the comforting familiarity of chicken, ham and leek pie with wholegrain mustard and mash, or you could opt for prime protein in the form of a rib-eye of Hereford beef served with Reform sauce and those legendary triple-cooked chips. To finish, there could be the nursery comfort of treacle tart with milk ice cream, or white chocolate and lemon cheesecake with biscuit ice cream.

Chef Janos Veres **Seats** 88, Private dining room 18 **Times** 12–2.15/6–9, Closed 25 December, D 1 January, bank holidays and Sunday **Prices** Set L 3 course £25, Set D 3 course £25, Set dinner 4/6 course £45/£58 **Wines** 65 bottles over £30, 11 bottles under £30, 11 by glass **Parking** 40 **Notes** Private dining 3/5 course, Vegetarian available, Children welcome

The Waterside Inn

MAP 6 SU98

☺☺☺☺ French
01628 620691 | Ferry Road, SL6 2AT
www.waterside-inn.co.uk

The Roux family's riverside restaurant four and a half decades on

It was this old English pub by the banks of the River Thames that first put Bray on the culinary map; over 40 years later, it is still a Roux family affair, and the place remains a benchmark experience for anyone who wants to know just how sublime refined French cooking can be. It's a luxurious, soul-soothing spot — white linen, green silk banquettes, the gleam of fine crystal and silverware, and the summer sparkle of the river seen from a dining room opening onto the little jetty — and under Diego Masciaga's orchestration the front-of-house performance is as polished as you'll find anywhere.

Alain Roux trades in pitch-perfect classical French gastronomy, but there are modern touches threaded seamlessly through — the lemongrass-scented chicken bouillon, for example, that accompanies ravioli and 'diablotins' of Burgundy snails loaded generously with parsley and garlic. Rock-solid culinary judgment and respect for classicism are a hallmark of main courses such as the whole braised Dover sole for two that comes with lobster mousseline, asparagus, and champagne and chive sauce, or the tender rabbit fillets partnered with celeriac fondant, glazed chestnuts and Armagnac sauce.

Alain is a master pâtissier, so this is absolutely not the place to skip exquisite desserts such as air-light rhubarb soufflé with raspberries, or a more up-to-date confection of blood orange and ginger-flavoured baked Alaska with iced bourbon whiskey parfait. Of course, none of this comes cheap, and a quiet word with your bank may be needed to make the most of the monumental wine list.

Chef Alain Roux **Seats** 75, Private dining room 8 **Times** 12 2/7 10, Closed 26 December to 1 February, Monday and Tuesday **Prices** Set L 2 course from £52, Set L 3 course £63.50-£82, 6 course dinner £160, Tasting menu 7 course £167.50, Sunday lunch **Wines** 1,000+ bottles over £30, 1 bottle under £30, 14 by glass **Parking** 20 **Notes** Vegetarian available, Children 12 years

Berkshire

The Royal Oak Paley Street

MAP 6 SU87

◉◉◉ Modern British 🍷

01628 620541 | Paley Street, Littlefield Green, SL6 3JN

www.theroyaloakpaleystreet.com

Contemporary British cooking chez Parkinson

Under the tender loving care of the Parkinson family, the Royal Oak has been reborn as an elegant village pub for our times. Its trim whitewashed frontage and modern garden, complete with waterfall, look bold and inviting, and inside, low beams and brick fireplaces retain something of the Oak's past, even while James Bennett plots a course into the realm of the culinary contemporary. There is a conscious effort to emphasise the inherent flavours of seasonal ingredients, and dishes look the part too, full of vivid natural colour and contrasting textures. Leek and potato terrine with a purée of alexanders are the inspired accompaniments to an opening serving of corn-fed chicken, while a dressed crab salad might be spiked with blood orange to point up its bracing freshness. Main courses keep one foot in the heritage British camp, so a majestic pie of guinea fowl and pork, served with mash and gravy, comes as no surprise, but there may also be garlic-crumbed cod with salsify in red wine sauce, or braised veal shin in bone marrow crust with sweetbreads, broccoli and almonds. Desserts make exciting things happen with some familiar luxuries: a baked chocolate mousse comes in a scatter of hundreds and thousands with honey ice cream, or you could wait a genteel quarter hour for a freshly baked plum frangipane tart.

Chef James Bennett **Seats** 80, Private dining room 20 **Times** 12–2.30/ 6.30–9.30, Closed D Sunday **Prices** Set L 2 course £25, Set L 3 course £30, Starter £7–£11, Main £20–£31, Dessert £7, Sunday lunch £20–£35 **Wines** 400 bottles over £30, 80 bottles under £30, 20 by glass **Parking** 70 **Notes** Vegetarian available, Children welcome

The Vineyard

MAP 5 SU46

◉◉◉ Modern British V ♟

01635 528770 | Stockcross, RG20 8JU

www.the-vineyard.co.uk

World-class wines and modern French cuisine in five-star splendour

When only a five-star, contemporary country house splurge will do, The Vineyard comes up with the goods: luxurious rooms, chic public areas and a glossy spa, while Robby Jenks's classy, intelligent cooking makes the place a dining destination in its own right. The foodie business goes on in an elegant split-level dining room, where a sweeping staircase sports a grapevine-style balustrade, tables are dressed in crisp white linen, and artwork jazzes up the walls. Opening the show, pink and tender quail's breasts are counterpointed with charred baby gem lettuce, tarragon purée and pistachios, or beef sirloin tartare might be helped along by horseradish, buttermilk and Granny Smith apple. Dishes gain lustre from top-class ingredients rather than off-the-wall combinations or techno trickery — main-course tenderloin and belly of suckling pig with cabbage and smoky bacon, caramelised onion purée and apple being a case in point. To finish, espresso granita arrives with blackcurrant cream and coffee sponge. Despite the name, they don't make wine at The Vineyard, but they do serve amazing wines from a world-class cellar that runs to a staggering 30,000 bottles, with around 100 available by the glass — there's even a pairing option to go with an amuse-bouche of smoked cod's roe cornet with lemon.

Chef Robby Jenks **Seats** 86, Private dining room 140 **Times** 12–2/7–9.30 **Prices** Set L 3 course £29, Set D 3 course £65, Tasting menu £75–£99, Sunday lunch £39 **Wines** 2,500 bottles over £30, 60 bottles under £30, 100 by glass **Parking** 100 **Notes** Children welcome

L'Ortolan

MAP 6 SU76

◉◉◉ Modern French V ♟

0118 988 8500 & 0118 988 9107 | Church Lane, RG2 9BY

www.lortolan.com

Consummate modern gastronomy in a former vicarage

Occupying a red-brick 17th-century vicarage in immaculately kept mature gardens, L'Ortolan feels a world away from Reading and the M4. It's an elegant, high-toned operation that has been a fixture in the top flight of British gastronomic destinations since the 1980s, and Tom Clarke has brought new energy and focus to the output here, offering creative, dynamic contemporary cooking with its feet firmly grounded in classical

continued

French cuisine. Harmoniously contrasting flavours are built up in flavour-packed openers such as goose liver terrine with blood orange and honey, or crab enlivened with ponzu and seaweed. Pedigree local meats are hunted down for impressive, highly detailed mains like poached breast and confit leg of guinea fowl with asparagus and wild garlic, or there may be immaculately timed fish — pan-fried stone bass, for example, with seared squid, curry and cauliflower. The innovative edge continues to desserts — rhubarb, say, given a thorough outing as a pneumatic mousse and multifarious textures alongside rosemary ice cream. The lunch menu du jour is a keenly-priced entry point, trading upwards to the à la carte or menu gourmand; if you're happy to go with the flow, there's a Surprise menu — whichever you opt for, clever little appetisers and pre-desserts are part of the deal.

Chef Tom Clarke **Seats** 58, Private dining room 22 **Times** 12–2/7–9, Closed 2 weeks Christmas to New Year, Sunday and Monday **Prices** Set L 2 course from £28, Set L 3 course from £32, Set D 2 course from £58, Set D 3 course from £65, Tasting menu £75–£105 **Wines** 210 bottles over £30, 1 bottle under £30, 17 by glass **Parking** 30 **Notes** Chef's table, Children 3 years +

Bristol

BRISTOL
Casamia Restaurant
MAP 4 ST57

◉◉◉◉◉ Modern British V ♀
0117 959 2884 | The General, Lower Guinea Street, BS1 6SY
www.casamiarestaurant.co.uk
Canalside venue for the best in contemporary gastronomy

The move in 2016 to the old Bristol General Hospital site by the canal brought fresh impetus to Casamia. For all its evidently humble derivation (My House), there's a feeling of distinctiveness and style to the place that grips you as soon as you pass through the monumental stone arch of the doorway and through the sleek glass doors. Inside, all is as contemporary as can be, the quietly industrious kitchen on view, the monochrome ambience of white-linened tables and tiled floor leavened by photographic blow ups of trees at various stages of their annual cycle. In our urban divorce from nature, there is probably still no more immediate visual indicator of the seasons than how much, if any, foliage there is on the trees, and these images indicate the organic rhythms to which Peter Sanchez-Iglesias' menu design is conformed. Four times a year, the set multi-course taster changes, reflecting what has become available. The aim is to mobilise all five senses through the medium of food, making the diner aware of every aspect of a dish, to which end exotic presentations and treatments of ingredients in accord with the latest in culinary aesthetics are to be expected, and the menu specifications, which don't give much away, leave everybody guessing until the moment the plate – or whatever its mode of transport is – arrives.

A little parmesan tartlet might be the opening gambit, before the much-prized carabineros Mediterranean prawn makes an appearance alongside a little seaweed. Sticking with shellfish for the moment, a scallop is teamed with pomelo for a sweet and sharp partnership, before intermediate courses such as salad and risotto come by. Principal fish dishes might partner brown trout with crab, and then offer lemon sole in a featherlight sabayon, before the main meat business, two separate servings of duck or spring lamb, takes a bifocal approach. Throughout these dishes, there are unexpected transformations of flavour, often achieved through resort to today's preferences for what were once preservation techniques – pickling, fermenting and salting – adding complexity, but also emphasising the innate character of the various components.

A pair of desserts rounds things off, with variations of rhubarb a sure fire bet on a spring menu, and then there are final startling tastes to see you through the closing stages – a sublimely scented take on Turkish delight, soft sweet-savoury fudge made with mushroom. Wine flights at two levels are offered, and are worth factoring into the budget, one way or the other. Tasting menus essentially don't work as well if you try to stick to one wine, or none, and the level of thought that has gone into the combinations here is crystal clear, and you'll find one revelation after another as you work your way through the courses.

Chef Peter Sanchez-Iglesias **Seats** 28 **Times** 12.15–1.30/6.30–8.15, Closed Christmas, New Year and bank holidays, Sunday to Tuesday, L Wednesday and Thursday **Prices** Set menu £98 **Wines** 165 bottles over £30, 16 bottles under £30, 34 by glass **Parking** Car park off Commercial Rd **Notes** A large table in separate area of restaurant is available for parties of 12, Children welcome

Buckinghamshire

The Artichoke

MAP 6 SU99

◉◉◉ Modern European V ♟
01494 726611 | 9 Market Square, Old Amersham, HP7 0DF
www.artichokerestaurant.co.uk

Creative and technically impressive cooking with local flavour

Laurie and Jacqueline Gear's high-flying restaurant may have its roots in the 16th century with the gnarled oak beams, bare floorboards and the capacious inglenook that constitute its framework, but the whole interior design aesthetic has been reworked in a muted, contemporary style with modern art depictions of – you guessed it – artichokes; views into an open kitchen bring yet more life and energy to the space. If you notice that things have a distinctly Scandinavian look, that's because fate propelled the restaurant along a new path a decade ago, when a fire in the neighbouring property forced it to close and Laurie used that downtime productively to put in a game-changing stint at Scandi superstar Réné Redzepi's Noma in Copenhagen.

He returned to Amersham's market square fired up with new inspiration, and The Artichoke's culinary direction has headed ever upwards. His dynamic, expertly crafted food arrives via a tasting menu (with wine flight), a veggie version, plus a carte and an excellent value set lunch. A spring version of the latter gets off to a flying start with superb breads – fluffy brioche flavoured with thyme, bacon and shallot, and Mackeson stout-flavoured wholemeal – and a terrific amuse of fennel mousse and crab purée to prime the tastebuds for a starter of sea trout

tartare with pickled turnip and radish, crunchy seed wafers and lime cream cheese. There's brilliance in the fish department too: main-course roasted cod loin comes with River Fowey mussels, chickpeas, taramasalata, crisp chicken skin and chicken broth, and to finish, the kitchen delivers a light-as-air galette of crisp pastry layered with poached pears, crème patissière and caramelised white chocolate alongside a harmonious Poire Williams sorbet. Elsewhere, components counterpoint each other cleverly in multi-faceted starters such as mustard and apple caramel-glazed bacon with apple jelly and purée, caraway pickled onion and pickled cauliflower, and there's plenty going on in complex main courses too: smoked saddle of venison might come partnered with chervil root, orange curd, pickled red onions and Brussels sprouts.

Desserts are no less creative and appealing — dark chocolate and pistachio tart, perhaps, with buttermilk sherbet and salted caramel, or go for a savoury finish with French and English farmhouse cheeses with hand-made crackers. The Artichoke is a class act in every way, with smartly-dressed staff in stone-coloured aprons providing polished and professional service, and a wide-ranging and intelligently curated wine list whose imaginative bins cover the globe in style.

Chefs Laurie Gear, Ben Jenkins **Seats** 48, Private dining room 16 **Times** 12–3/6.30–11, Closed 2 weeks at Christmas, 2 weeks in April, 2 weeks in August/September, Sunday and Monday **Prices** Set L 2 course £24, Set L 3 course £28, Set D 2 course £42, Set D 3 course £48, Tasting menu 5// course £38–£68, Starter £13.50–£14.50, Main £24–£25.50, Dessert £6.50–£8.50 **Wines** 246 bottles over £30, 5 bottles under £30, 13 by glass **Parking** On street, car park **Notes** Children 8 + years at dinner

Buckinghamshire

The Pointer
MAP 5 SP61

Modern British
01844 238339 | 27 Church Street, HP18 9RT
www.thepointerbrill.co.uk

Prime local produce in a rustic-chic dining pub

As we went to press the Rosette award was suspended due to a change of chef – reassessment will take place in due course.

The Pointer's roots extend deep into its local community. As well as being a welcoming country pub in the picturesque village of Brill near Aylesbury, it also encompasses a working organic farm with Longhorn cattle, rare-breed Middlewhite pigs and Hampshire Down sheep, a kitchen garden, as well as an adjacent butcher's shop for take-outs of its pedigree meats. The interior has an almost late-medieval feel, with heavy low beams entwined with bare twigs and exposed roughcast stone walls in the dining room, leavened by simple modern prints.

Seats 30 **Times** 12–2.30/6.30–9, Closed 1 week in January, Monday, D Sunday **Prices** Set L 2 course £18, Set L 3 course £22.50, Starter £9–£15, Main £21–£30, Dessert £8–£10, Sunday lunch £36–£49 **Wines** 74 bottles over £30, 13 bottles under £30, 13 by glass **Parking** 5 **Notes** Vegetarian available, Children welcome

---

MARLOW
The Coach
MAP 6 SU88

⊛⊛⊛ Classic French
3 West Street, SL7 2LS
www.thecoachmarlow.co.uk

Big-hearted cooking in Tom Kerridge's second pub

Just down the road from the celebrated Hand & Flowers, Tom Kerridge's second pub takes a different approach to the celebrated mothership: The Coach doesn't take bookings, so you just have to turn up with fingers crossed. It's a cosy, pubby sort of space dominated by the L-shaped pewter bar, with elbow-to-elbow tables, and an open kitchen complete with a meat fridge and rôtisserie on display. It's a busy, buzzy spot, where chefs pitch in to help the switched-on, chatty staff whisk dishes out to the tables. Head chef Nick Beardshaw was Kerridge's sous-chef at the Hand & Flowers, so you can expect food in a similar vein – big on flavour and made with top-class ingredients handled with real skill. Divided between meat and 'no meat' dishes, the menu reads like a roster of unpretentious modern pub fodder, starting with silky duck liver parfait counterpointed with fig and cherry chutney. The same generous, contemporary British tone informs main courses: perfectly-timed sea bream fillet comes with a rich stew of butter beans, trompette mushrooms and lovage, or you might go for black pudding-stuffed quail, cooked in the rôtisserie and served with Keralan moilee sauce. For pudding, top-class pastry skills are to the fore in a luscious duck egg custard tart with rhubarb ice cream.

Chefs Nick Beardshaw, Tom Kerridge **Seats** 40 **Times** 12–2.30/6–10.30, Closed 25–26 December **Prices** Starter £5.50–£15.50, Main £5.50–£15.50, Dessert £6.50, Sunday lunch from £13.50 **Wines** 14 bottles over £30, 6 bottles under £30, 20 by glass **Notes** Meals cannot be pre-booked, Breakfast available, Vegetarian available, Children welcome

The Hand & Flowers
MAP 6 SU88

◉◉◉◉ Classic French **V**

01628 482277 | 126 West Street, SL7 2BP

www.thehandandflowers.co.uk

TV chef's finely crafted country pub cooking

Food-fans will already be familiar with Tom Kerridge's regular TV work, and will probably have at least one of his cookbooks, but to get properly up close and personal, a trip to the unspoiled Georgian environs of Marlow is in order. Here the whitewashed pub with its hanging baskets and smooth contemporary makeover (there are beauty treatments if you feel you need a buff-up) is the intuitive setting for Kerridge's cleverly conceived combination of traditional British and French country cooking. Choose respectively from cheesy smoked haddock omelette or duck liver parfait with orange chutney and brioche to set the ball rolling. Main courses might present the day's fish catch in thrilling array, with cuttlefish, truffled roast artichokes, hazelnuts and wheat-beer beurre blanc, or match melting pork tenderloin with garlic sausage, a malted beignet of the cheek and pickled cabbage, with a dressing of mustard mayonnaise, for a handsome display of real meat. There's a world of nostalgic satisfaction too in desserts that take in rhubarb and custard slice with liquorice ice cream, or milk toffee tart with Old English spice and grapefruit sorbet, while a straightforward crème brûlée could be the last word in silky, creamy seduction. Booking well in advance is essential, and inevitably forward planning is required if you want to sit down to their popular Sunday lunches, in The Shed, the business now extends to a private dining room just up the road, where there's a choice of three bells-and-whistles tasting menus and a very special roast on Sundays.

Chef Tom Kerridge **Seats** 54, Private dining room 9 **Times** 12–2.45/6.30–9.45, Closed 24–26 December, 1 January, D Sunday **Prices** Set L 2 course from £25, Set L 3 course from £29.50, Starter £9.50–£16.50, Main £28.50–£39.50, Dessert £10.50–£13.50, Sunday lunch from £35.50 **Wines** 150 bottles over £30, 10 bottles under £30, 35 by glass **Parking** 20 **Notes** Children welcome

Buckinghamshire

Humphry's at Stoke Park

MAP 6 SU98

◉◉◉ Modern British
01753 717171 | Park Road, SL2 4PG
www.humphrysrestaurant.co.uk

Innovative contemporary country-club cuisine

Few of Britain's country houses come with the pedigree of Stoke Park. The 300 luxuriant acres, including restful parkland and lakes, were turned into Britain's first country club in 1908, but the building and grounds themselves reach back considerably further in time than that. In the 1790s, Humphry Repton was hired to make over 'Capability' Brown's magnificent landscaped grounds, which have since morphed into an estate of many parts, with a championship golf course (all 27 holes of it), 13 tennis courts and state-of-the-art spa. Surveying it all, the elegant domed and pillared mansion house at its centre deserves all of its five stars: the opulent interiors are splendidly preserved, and come with the full complement of fine oil paintings, antiques and all the architectural bells and whistles you would expect in a top-flight luxury hotel.

When it comes to dining, the cream of the options is Humphry's, a magnificent room, with a marble fireplace, an intricate plasterwork ceiling, a soothing decor of golds and yellows, and floor-to-ceiling windows overlooking the lake. In charge of the kitchen is Chris Wheeler, who has his job cut out to live up to the lavish surroundings and the weight of special occasion diners' expectations. But fear not, there's no doubting that his cooking is on song — he makes it his mission to ensure that your

culinary memories of Stoke Park will live long, and achieves it with innovative dishes that mobilise the full range of contemporary technique, while maintaining respect for the prime materials. Naturally, in such a high-toned setting, luxury ingredients abound – that's clear from the off in starters such as lobster and ginger bisque served with ravioli packed with moist and sweet lobster, or that stalwart of the country-house repertoire, foie gras, which is served glazed and accompanied by spicy bread, plum compôte and ginger.

Main courses effortlessly underline the kitchen's class, among them a highly-detailed composition built around pan-roasted stone bass, which arrives with various textures of cauliflower, trumpet mushrooms, and king prawn and lemongrass dumplings. Meat is also handled with dazzling attention to detail: loin, belly and cheek of pork could be matched with black pudding (made in-house, naturally), choucroute, houmous, charred baby gem lettuce and a deeply flavoured pork sauce, or beef fillet with truffled potato terrine, sherry-glazed onions, watercress purée and red wine jus. Puddings hold form with the rest of the output, perhaps passionfruit soufflé with raspberry and lime sorbet and passionfruit sauce, or consider the peak-condition English and French cheeses.

Chef Chris Wheeler **Seats** 50, Private dining room 146 **Times** 12–2.30/ 7–10, Closed 24–26 December, 1st week in January, Monday and Tuesday, L Wednesday to Saturday **Prices** Set L 2 course £25, Set L 3 course £29.50, Set D 3 course £68, Tasting menu £85, Starter £11.50–£14.50, Main £27.50–£32.50, Dessert £11.50–£12.50, Sunday lunch £35 **Wines** 90 bottles over £30, 4 bottles under £30, 12 by glass **Parking** 400 **Notes** A la carte lunch only, Vegetarian available, Children 12 years + at lunch

Buckinghamshire

TAPLOW

André Garrett at Cliveden

MAP 6 SU98

◉◉◉ Modern British, French V ☙

01628 668561 | Cliveden Estate, SL6 0JF

www.clivedenhouse.co.uk

Stunning dishes in a stately home

One of England's stateliest homes, Cliveden brings with it the sort of history that's anything but decorous. A century of racy goings-on since its tenure by the Astors lends a salacious whiff of scandal to dining in the impeccably elegant, swagged and chandeliered restaurant with its shimmering views over parterre gardens to the Thames.

André Garrett has taken to this luxurious setting like a duck to water, using finely-honed technique to deliver dazzling contemporary French dishes built on gilt-edged ingredients. The results are served up via a carte or seven-course tasting menu (there's an inspired veggie version too) if the whole table is up for it, plus a weekday lunchtime market menu that, while not quite a total steal, represents great value considering the high-flying setting.

Foie gras is a suitably decadent opening gambit, but it takes a spark of brilliance to match it with pear, granola and pistachio. Next up, locally-stalked venison is partnered by watercress, chestnut, blackberries, boulangère potatoes and grand veneur sauce, while fish is handled with equal aplomb, perhaps roast turbot fillet with braised celery hearts, chicory condiment and brioche butter. To conclude, dessert seduces with a lush chocolate workout involving ganache, Aero and crumble paired with Moroccan mint ice cream, or there's tropical notes in the marinated pineapple carpaccio, lime and long pepper.

Chef André Garrett **Seats** 78, Private dining room 60 **Times** 12.15–2.30/7–9.45 **Prices** Set L 2 course £28, Set L 3 course £33, Set D 3 course from £55, Tasting menu £85–£97.50, Starter £15–£24, Main £28–£45, Dessert £12–£14.50, Sunday lunch £60 **Wines** 575 bottles over £30, 8 bottles under £30, 10 by glass **Parking** 60 **Notes** Children welcome

MIDSUMMER HOUSE

Midsummer House is located in the heart of historic Cambridge. This Victorian Villa encapsulates Daniel Clifford's vision for culinary perfection and is home to some seriously stylish food.

Daniel Clifford's quest for culinary perfection has taken the restaurant to another level over the past 13 years; his cooking has a modern-focus which is underpinned by classical French technique offering seriously sophisticated food with dishes arriving dressed to thrill.

Upstairs there is a private dining room, and a sophisticated bar and terrace for alfresco drinks with river views. Our private dining room is the perfect location for small weddings, lavish birthday celebrations, simple family gatherings or corporate entertaining.

Midsummer Common, Cambridge CB4 1HA

Tel: 01223 369299 • **Fax:** 01223 302672

Website: www.midsummerhouse.co.uk

Email: reservations@midsummerhouse.co.uk

Cambridgeshire

Midsummer House Restaurant

MAP 12 TL45

◉◉◉◉◉ Modern British V ♥

01223 369299 | Midsummer Common, CB4 1HA

www.midsummerhouse.co.uk

Minutely considered modern cooking by the river

First-timers may be struck by the relative simplicity of Midsummer House. It's no grand mansion, but a modestly proportioned Victorian dwelling overlooking the Common, snug behind its garden wall, with a conservatory extension built out on the left-hand side. It sits beside the river on what is still common grazing land, so one mustn't be at all alarmed to see the odd herd of cows plodding peaceably by just outside, with the more expected sight of university rowing teams gliding past behind them on the Cam.

Daniel Clifford took the place on just under 20 years ago, with the intention of making it one of the city's — and indeed county's — destination restaurants, an aspiration that has been not just realised but impressively sustained over the years. The dining room is done in relaxing charcoal tones, with smart napery, crystal light fittings, and a picture window giving on to the kitchen. In recent times, the format has been simplified, the previous range of menus now refined to an eight-course core offering, with vegetarian alternative, and a further five-course option at lunch. Clifford's dishes are minutely considered, with nothing extraneous or superfluous, each one displaying evidence of the intense culinary thought

that has gone into it. It's cooking that is of course responsive to the seasons, but also has great imaginative energy, and never looks less than striking. The various elements are brought together in inspired counterpoint, as when a pairing of red mullet and octopus is given its extra dimension with 3-D accompaniments of fennel and orange, or when the widely favoured combination of beetroot and horseradish brings a new angle to a serving of roasted Anjou pigeon, which comes with a pastilla of its confit leg. Perhaps the true measure of confidence is to make an ostensibly run-of-the-mill proposition into something revelatory, so asparagus season might see an opening plate of bright green spears under flawless hollandaise with a little burnt onion for sweetness, while spelt risotto of morels and wild garlic is a masterclass in earthy pungency, and texturally unimpeachable too.

The optional cheese course is worth considering, as a glance at the royally laden trolley will confirm, and the pair of desserts to follow might begin with the famous aerated pear with blueberry and white chocolate, and go on to a dramatic face-off of passionfruit and dark chocolate, with a creamy yogurt sorbet holding the line. A wine cellar approaching 1,000 listings should furnish something for everyone.

Chef Daniel Clifford **Seats** 45, Private dining room 16 **Times** 12–1.30/7–9, Closed 2 weeks at Christmas and New Year, Sunday and Monday, L Tuesday **Prices** Tasting menu 5 course lunch £56.50, 8 course £120 **Wines** 945 bottles over £30, 17 by glass **Parking** On street **Notes** Children welcome

See advert on page 39

Cambridgeshire

CAMBRIDGE

Restaurant Alimentum

MAP 12 TL45

◉◉◉ Modern European ♥
01223 413000 | 152-154 Hills Road, CB2 8PB
www.restaurantalimentum.co.uk

Impeccable ingredients and classy cooking

In case you were wondering, the name means 'food' in Latin – this is
Cambridge, after all – but that's where any reference to classicism stops
at this dynamic modern operation. First impressions might raise a few
eyebrows: after entering via the ground floor of a modern block, the bold
red-and-black decor and laminate floors give the feel of a swanky bar or
nightclub, but the rest of a trip to Alimentum is a journey of discovery in
one of the high-flyers of Cambridge's lively dining scene.

The action is all there in front of your very eyes, thanks to an open-to-
view kitchen giving a window onto chef-proprietor Mark Poynton and his
brigade at work. The thoroughly diverting, cutting-edge style of cooking is
delivered via set-price lunch and dinner menus offering six choices at each
stage, trading upwards to seven-course tasting options, whose terse
descriptions fail to convey their complexity and multi-layered flavours.
Components are sourced ethically, and deep flavours are conjured in some
thought-provoking alignments of textures and flavours – broadly modern
European in scope, but also blending fusion references from all over the
brave new world. Every dish comes to the table looking as entertaining as
can be, with artfully composed assemblages of cubes, oblongs and
smears. Seasonality is given due respect, with trusted local suppliers

providing top-end raw materials that the kitchen combines with panache and intelligent sensitivity in starters such as smoked eel and duck liver, their richness leavened by apple and dandelion, and aromatised with truffle, or the clear Indian orientation of scallops matched with curry, apple, cumin dhal, coriander and yogurt. Main courses of assured technical refinement and creativity transmit their message with powerful immediacy, perhaps 80-day-aged beef sirloin in a muscular partnership with beef fat potatoes, veal sweetbreads, parsley and mushrooms, and game cookery also displays heaps of confidence, as when saddle of venison is plated with prunes, chestnut, blue cheese and trompette mushrooms. Fish dishes deliver true flavours in ideas such as hake with brandade, smoked leeks, mussels and red wine.

Desserts might delve into the retro repertoire for a reworking of the Black Forest theme, all lush dark chocolate and cherry, with a boozy hit of cherry beer and Kirsch, or offer a glorious parade of Francophilia via tarte Tatin with Braeburn and Granny Smith apples and lavender. Wines have been discriminatingly sourced from Europe and beyond, with many classy bottles to suit the enterprising style of the food.

Chef Mark Poynton **Seats** 62, Private dining room 30 **Times** 12–2/6–9.30, Closed 24–30 December and bank holidays, L 31 December **Prices** Set L 2 course £27.50, Set L 3 course £35, Set D 2 course £55, Set D 3 course £70, Tasting menu 7 course £60–£80, Sunday lunch £35–£60 **Wines** 144 bottles over £30, 11 bottles under £30, 28 by glass **Parking** NCP Cambridge Leisure Centre (3-minute walk) **Notes** Vegetarian available, Children welcome

Cheshire

ALDERLEY EDGE
The Alderley Restaurant

MAP 10 SJ87

@@@ Modern, Classic British **V**

01625 583033 | Macclesfield Road, SK9 7BJ

www.alderleyedgehotel.com

Dynamic modern cooking amid the Cheshire smart set

The restaurant here will reopen on 1st December 2017 after a major refurbishment.

Perched on wooded slopes above the des-res village of Alderley edge, this rather posh hotel was built originally to showcase the status of a 19th-century industrialist. The place has moved with the times and comes kitted out with dollops of style to keep the Cheshire smart set beating a path to the door. When it comes to fine dining, the conservatory restaurant grabs pole position over lush grounds and gardens, while chef Sean Sutton conjures up exciting modern British food brimming with locally-sourced ingredients, all composed with a happy marriage of flavours and textures. Choosing from a trio of tasting menus (five, seven and ten courses, since you ask) in support of the carte, you might get off the blocks with Scottish langoustines with parsnip and a workout of chicken textures, or soy-cured duck breast with Chinese cabbage and macerated fennel. At main course stage, cannon of lamb with confit new potatoes and wild garlic should keep the carnivores happy; fishy ideas might see confit hake plated with crispy squid, chorizo and cannellini beans. Desserts are as thoughtfully composed and impeccably executed as the rest of the show – a deconstructed lemon tart, say, involving lemon curd, caramelised pastry and liquorice ice cream.

Chef Sean Sutton **Seats** 80, Private dining room 130 **Times** 12–2/7–10, Closed 1 January, L 31 December, D 25–26 December **Prices** Set L 2 course £27.95, Tasting menu £54.95, Starter £11.95–£12.95, Main £22.95–£26.50, Dessert £10.95, Sunday lunch £27.95 **Wines** 300 bottles over £30, 19 bottles under £30, 16 by glass **Parking** 82 **Notes** Children welcome

CHESTER

Simon Radley at The Chester Grosvenor
MAP 15 SJ46

@@@@ Modern French V ♥

01244 324024 | Eastgate, CH1 1LT

www.chestergrosvenor.co.uk

Resourceful and innovative dining near the racecourse

As befits a hotel of the Grosvenor's standing, especially one grand enough to overlook a racecourse, there is a wealth of dining options within, but the red-hot favourite is undoubtedly the room named after its long-standing executive chef. It's a place of refined civility, where immaculate linen, table posies and confidently well-versed staff add to the sense of occasion.

Radley's food has moved with the times, and offers a comprehensive insight into the resourceful and innovative methodology of the present day. That might translate into a first course of jellied eels with fried and poached oysters, sea veg and leafy lemon purée, or a fascinating assemblage of lamb sweetbread with barbecued aubergine, soft burrata and crunchy biscotti. For main, a pairing of 'two hens' is a convocation of butter-poached black-leg chicken and native lobster with an intense scenting of Périgord truffle, while the beef offering combines charred sirloin and a bresaola of ox cheek with pickled smoked onion and black pepper. Cleverly constructed desserts include a crisp chocolate shell filled with apple dacquoise and Calvados toffee, or an interpretation of Pina Colada made with coconut blancmange and variously textured manifestations of pineapple.

For the no-holds-barred excursion through the kitchen's paces, take the eight-course tasting menu, which may begin with sweet-sour mackerel and end with charcoal-pastry pumpkin croustade, with a main course of French squab pigeon and burnt cauliflower to anchor it all. The vegetarian version is equally inventive, encompassing dishes such as mushroom brioche with whipped ceps, toasted hazelnuts and Pedro Ximenez jelly.

Chefs Simon Radley, Ray Booker **Seats** 45, Private dining room 14 **Times** 6.30–9, Closed 25 December, 1 week in January, Sunday and Monday, L all week (except December) **Prices** Tasting menu 8 course (also vegetarian) £69–£99 **Wines** 690 bottles over £30, 30 bottles under £30, 17 by glass **Parking** Car park adjacent to hotel (£10 for 24 hours) **Notes** Children 12 years +

Cheshire

PECKFORTON
1851 Restaurant at Peckforton Castle
MAP 15 SJ55

Modern British **V**

01829 260930 | Stone House Lane, CW6 9TN

www.peckfortoncastle.co.uk

Fine cooking in a grand hotel

As we went to press the Rosette award was suspended due to a change of chef – reassessment will take place in due course.

This place may look like a medieval castle, but the numeric in the restaurant's name denotes the year this mightily imposing building was finished, straight out of the imagination of a wealthy Victorian gent. Today's hotel and wedding venue does justice to the lofty ambition of its originator, with pampering treatments, events, luxe bedrooms and a host of outdoor activities on hand. The 1851 Restaurant has made the hotel a dining destination, too. The slick and stylish dining room matches the modern thinking in the kitchen, with a shimmering wall of wine bottles as you enter.

Seats 65, Private dining room 160 **Times** 12.30–3/6–9.30, Closed L Monday to Friday **Prices** Dinner 5 course £45, Sunday lunch £14.95–£19.95 **Wines** 15 bottles over £30, 30 bottles under £30, 12 by glass **Parking** 300 **Notes** Children welcome

▶ Cornwall and the Isles of Scilly

BRYHER (THE ISLES OF SCILLY)
Hell Bay
MAP 2 SV81

◉◉◉ Modern British **V**

01720 422947 | TR23 0PR

www.hellbay.co.uk

Assured cooking in a Scillies hideaway

Bryher is one of the more isolated of the Scillies, a tiny island that can be tramped on foot in not much more than a morning, following a ferry crossing from St Mary's or Tresco. Set amid gentle hillocks laden with gorse and stretching golden sands, Hell Bay is an evocatively misnamed location. The white hotel behind its picket fence looks unassuming enough, but is a beacon of culinary creativity, thanks to Richard Kearsley's assured, confident cooking. Naturally, fish is a big draw, from local mackerel with fennel pannacotta and gribiche, to mains such as the glorious seared turbot in bisque sauce, with balancing accompaniments of charred lettuce and luxurious lobster tortellini, its pasta shell of dim sum tenderness. Supplies can be pretty erratic on a small island, but West Country venison usually makes it here too, for a signature dish of the haunch in chocolate jus with turnip gratin and red cabbage. Finish with well-rendered prune and Armagnac soufflé with a rather shy Earl Grey ice cream, but good walnut and cranberry biscotti, or pineapple Tatin with coconut sorbet. Breakfasters may gather their own eggs if they wish from the chicken coop. Meanwhile, the menu on offer in the Crab Shack next door is simplicity itself – crab, scallops or mussels.

Chef Richard Kearsley **Seats** 70, Private dining room 12 **Times** 12–2/ 6.45–9.30, Closed 2 November to 17 March **Wines** 20 bottles over £30, 30 bottles under £30, 11 by glass **Parking** 5 **Notes** Children welcome

PADSTOW

⍟⍟⍟⍟ Modern British V ☻
Paul Ainsworth at No. 6
MAP 2 SW97
See page 48

The Seafood Restaurant
MAP 2 SW97

⍟⍟⍟ International Seafood V ☻
01841 532700 | Riverside, PL28 8BY
www.rickstein.com

Still fresh and energetic after all these years

The stone and brick building with its glassed-in terrace on the approach into Padstow is where it all began, it being Rick Stein's stellar career around these parts, but in some sense also Padstow itself, which had been an unassuming north Cornish fishing village, and now looks very much the international tourist destination. Inside, the place still feels fresh and energetic after all these years, with a sense of busy fun pervading most service sessions. People sit around the bar to watch the shellfish platters being assembled, there is a plethora of heterogeneous artwork to catch the eye, and striking thin pendant light fittings to illuminate the evening scene. The experience may well begin with a crisp salt cod fritter to establish the mood, and the simplest things are still done with inspiring confidence, as with the deeply concentrated traditional Provençal fish soup, the portion decanted at the table, with smouldering rouille, croûtons and parmesan on the side. Main might be a straightforward piece of turbot singing with freshness, gently sauced with tarragon-scented béarnaise, but there are also hake baked with onion, garlic, lemon and bay, or perhaps a fiery Goan-style cod curry with cumin pooris. Then calm the palate with a properly fragile pannacotta and pistachio cream.

Chef Stephane Delourme **Seats** 120 **Times** 12–3/6.30–10, Closed 25–26 December, D 24 December **Prices** Set L 3 course menu summer £40, winter £31, Starter £12.50–£26.50, Main £20–£58, Dessert £8.90–£9.50 **Wines** 142 bottles over £30, 22 bottles under £30, 43 by glass **Parking** Pay & display opposite **Notes** Children 3 years +

Cornwall and the Isles of Scilly

Paul Ainsworth at No. 6

MAP 2 SW97

◉◉◉◉ Modern British V 🍷
01841 532093 | 6 Middle Street, PL28 8AP
www.number6inpadstow.co.uk

Defining contemporary cooking in a pint-sized townhouse

Squirrelled away down Padstow's warren of narrow streets just back from
the harbour, Paul Ainsworth's Georgian townhouse restaurant has been a
fixture on the foodie map for over a decade. His restaurant empire may not
extend quite as far as Padstow's most illustrious TV chef, but he has
spread his wings to encompass a second address down the road called
Rojano's in the Square, and if a stopover is on the cards, there are also six
classy suites in a boutique townhouse nearby. Of course, the telly
appearances on the BBC's *The Great British Menu* have done the
Ainsworth brand no harm, spreading the word to armchair gastronomes
across the country that this is the place to head for exciting contemporary
food driven by the superb regional produce that makes Cornwall such a
culinary destination these days.

The restaurant's modest frontage opens to reveal snug-but-light dining
spaces spread over two floors, their intact 18th-century charm overlaid
with a sleek contemporary look, and jazzed up by eye-catching decorative
touches including a stunning piece from sculptor Beth Cullen-Kerridge.
Clued-up staff are at hand to flesh out the details of the tersely worded
menus. John Walton's kitchen delivers impressive renditions of well-
thought-through modern dishes, put together with flashes of

experimentation but with a firm bedrock of finely honed classical technique holding it all together and a strong supporting foundation of premium Cornish ingredients. Given the marine location, Porthilly oysters are hard to ignore, especially here, where they turn up crisp-fried and matched with cured pork, green apple and fennel, or go for another seafood opener that delivers raw scallops with kimchi-style cabbage and the pungent kick of Gentleman's Relish. Next up, local Saddleback pork might star in a Cornish take on Bath chaps, Jerusalem artichokes, black truffle, and tangy Bramley apple gravy – a dish that bursts with full-on flavour. Otherwise, two willing accomplices might tackle a classic rib of beef with Caesar salad, pommes Anna and timur sauce.

Fish is as fresh as you'd hope for in a place where the local day boats land their catch a stone's throw away – perhaps opalescent cod, timed to the second, and ably supported by local crab in mayonnaise, alongside the subtle seafood notes of oyster leaf. Desserts are certainly not to be skipped, perhaps harking back to the nursery comforts of trifle, although here it's a cleverly updated rhubarb and saffron version, and the signature bread-and-butter pudding, as well as offering a richly creamy ewe's milk cheesecake with bitter cocoa sorbet, while cheeses come with the contrasting zing of apple pie.

Chefs Paul Ainsworth, John Walton **Seats** 46, Private dining room 8 **Times** 12–2.30/6–9.30, Closed 24–26 December, 19 January to 12 February, Sunday and Monday (except bank holiday Sundays) **Prices** Set L 2 course £19, Set L 3 course £26, Starter £13–£16, Main £30–£40, Dessert £11–£12 **Wines** 43 bottles over £30, 8 bottles under £30, 14 by glass **Parking** Harbour car park, on street **Notes** Children 4 years +

Cornwall and the Isles of Scilly

Restaurant Nathan Outlaw

MAP 2 SW98

◉◉◉◉ Modern British, Seafood V ⏶
01208 880896 | 6 New Road, PL29 3SB
www.nathan-outlaw.com

Refined multi-course seafood dining from a modern master

Despite all the appearances in armchair foodie slots on the telly, and extending the mini-empire to restaurants in London, Rock, Dubai and a second operation in Port Isaac, Nathan Outlaw has never let the celeb stuff get in the way of cooking fish in a masterful manner. The namesake flagship sits at the top end of the village, with uplifting views out to sea and an understated minimal look involving Cornish art and just enough chunky wooden tables to seat 30 lucky diners, so booking is essential if you're planning to make a pilgrimage to see what the fuss is all about.

Choosing what to eat is easy: seafood is always the star of the show, and it is delivered via lunch and dinner tasting menus. The ethos is to let top-class Cornish materials speak eloquently for themselves, helped along, naturally, with razor-sharp technique and an innate sense of what works with what. Cured monkfish with celery and ginger might kick off proceedings in fine style, before a dish featuring cod's roe, then perhaps smoked mackerel with onion, parsnip and preserved herring. After that, gurnard could appear pointed up with a fathoms-deep Porthilly crab sauce, before progressing to a splendid piece of turbot served with winter vegetables and green dressing.

Next up, a cheese course based, perhaps, around Cornish Jack cheese served with an earthy beetroot and walnut tart. Finally, a brace of desserts, the first delivering a thrilling combination of banana, peanut, espresso and lime, before a clever take on the tried-and-tested theme of red wine pear and chocolate.

Chefs Nathan Outlaw, Chris Simpson **Seats** 30 **Times** 12–2/7–9, Closed Christmas and January, Sunday to Tuesday, L Wednesday to Thursday **Prices** Set lunch 4 course £62, Tasting menu from £125 **Wines** 163 bottles over £30, 1 bottle under £30, 16 by glass **Parking** Adjacent to restaurant **Notes** Children 10 years +

PORTSCATHO

Driftwood

MAP 2 SW83

◉◉◉ Modern European **V**
01872 580644 | Rosevine, TR2 5EW
www.driftwoodhotel.co.uk

Dazzling local cooking above the crashing waves

Those in search of sweetness and light in the far southwest might consider drifting in the direction of Driftwood, a boutique hotel perched like elegant flotsam above Gerrans Bay. A woodland path connects it to its own bit of beach and sheltered cove, while inside, daylight pours in to a dining room done in delicate marine blue and sparkling-spray white, and the sunsets look as though they might have been bought from Heaven's mail-order catalogue.

Chris Eden matches this laid-back mood with cooking of compelling intensity, showing off local materials to dazzling effect. A starter serving of breast and confit legs of roast pheasant in a unifying jus gras comes with a welter of accompaniments, including mushroom duxelles on sourdough toast and apple and barley emulsion, ahead of water-bathed monkfish finished in butter, along with both types of artichoke, dressed in ginger, miso and toasted sunflower seeds, or grilled red mullet and mussels. Otherwise, there may be moorland hogget loin with roast shallots, aubergine, olives, pine nuts and feta, the whole plate powerfully scented with rosemary. The grand finale could be a lemon hommage, with lemon and lemon verbena sorbet, lemon gel tart, crystallised lemon and nutty foam that evokes the rushing waves below.

Chef Christopher Eden **Seats** 34 **Times** 6.30–9.30, Closed early December to early February, L all week **Prices** Set D 3 course from £65, Tasting menu 5/8 course £80–£95 **Wines** 60 bottles over £30, 4 bottles under £30, 6 by glass **Parking** 20 **Notes** Children 6 years +

Cornwall and the Isles of Scilly

ST MAWES
Hotel Tresanton

MAP 2 SW83

@@@ British, Mediterranean

01326 270055 | 27 Lower Castle Road, TR2 5DR

www.tresanton.com

Bright modern cooking in super-stylish seafront hotel

Olga Polizzi reinvented this former yachtie hangout with a dose of cool seaside boutique chic back in 1997, and it's still looking good, with the whiff of the briny in the air, jaunty nautical style, Mediterranean-inspired luminosity, and sweeping views out to sea and towards Falmouth from its sun trap terrace. The restaurant itself is a soul-soothing environment, light and airy with mosaic flooring, oatmeal tongue and groove walls, and shell-like wall lighting; white-clothed tables are simply set, and stylish tableware adds a reassuring touch of class.

Paul Wadham's cooking matches the environment with a pleasing congruity, the simple elegance of the restaurant reflected within the dishes, each reliant on high quality produce for its effect, and many arriving with a warm waft of the Mediterranean – witness a simple starter of exemplary salt cod croquettes, matched with vibrant sauce vierge, and made with the confidence to leave well alone.

The Mediterranean mood continues with a main course starring red mullet with a supporting cast of clams, asparagus and prosciutto, the ingredients all sparkling, its flavours in pleasing balance, or perhaps beef fillet with gnocchi, confit tomato, oyster mushroom and shallots. End on a high note with moist Tunisian orange cake pointed up with gently tart yogurt sorbet.

Chef Paul Wadham **Seats** 60, Private dining room 45 **Times** 12.30–2.30/ 7–9.30, Closed 2 weeks in January **Prices** Set L 2 course from £25, Set L 3 course from £29, Starter £8–£16, Main £18–£42, Dessert £2.50– £12, Sunday lunch from £25 **Wines** 60 bottles over £30, 11 bottles under £30, 11 by glass **Parking** 30 **Notes** Vegetarian available, Children 6 years + at dinner

AMBLESIDE
Lake Road Kitchen

MAP 20 NY30

◎◎◎ Northern European
015394 22012 | Lake Road, LA22 0AD
www.lakeroadkitchen.co.uk

Northern European seasonal food that rings the daily changes

The vogue for Nordic-inspired dining has spawned another real winner here in an unassuming spot just off Ambleside's main street. The setting has the spartan simplicity of a Scandinavian log cabin, all pine plank walls and bare tables – a spot-on look for a self-styled north European bistro. Chef-patron James Cross pursues a dogged determination to work with the seasons and the climate, pickling and bottling for the winter months, foraging for summer berries and autumn mushrooms, as well as bringing in pedigree Lakeland meat, supplemented by northern European seafood.

The five- and eight-course menus change daily, and the hits just keep on coming. A revelatory summer meal might open with a celeriac taco, involving remoulade, pastrami tongue, cured egg yolk and nasturtium, segueing in a carefully-considered progression of tastes and textures to Arctic king crab matched with Sungold tomatoes, fresh cheese and nasturtium. Along the way, there may be Cumbrian milk-fed veal with a hyper-seasonal stew of summer legumes, or a superb piece of monkfish, steamed simply and boosted with chicken dripping and herbs. To finish, excellent pastry work is a hallmark of ideas such as a buckwheat tart of lemon verbena and alpine strawberries. Home-baked breads, served with whey-butter, include an exemplary sourdough with a crunchy dark crust.

Chef James Cross **Seats** 21 **Times** 6–9, Closed Monday and Tuesday, L all week **Prices** Tasting menu 5/8 course £60–£05 **Wines** 29 bottles over £30, 3 bottles under £30, 25 by glass **Parking** On street, car park **Notes** Vegetarian available, Children 12 years +

BRAITHWAITE
The Cottage in the Wood

MAP 20 NY22

◎◎◎ Modern British **V**
017687 78409 | Whinlatter Pass, CA12 5TW
www.thecottageinthewood.co.uk

Stunning views and accomplished cooking

The name may sound like a modest fell walkers' lodge, but this former 17th-century coaching inn trades as a slick boutique restaurant with rooms these days. Lording it in the forest high above Keswick, the views as you snake up Whinlatter Pass show the Lakeland fells in all their rugged glory, and there they are again, unfurled beneath your eyes as you mull over the daily-changing menus in the semi-circular dining room

continued

Cumbria

(a second area lacks the view but has a crackling log fire). The contemporary finish of the interior is matched by the dynamic cooking of Richard Collingwood, whose passion for regional produce is the starting point for one of the area's most memorable culinary experiences. A harmonious opening combo of langoustine, asparagus and almond is held in check by the tang of grapefruit, while veal sweetbreads come with wild garlic and morels. Next up, local Herdwick hogget might be partnered by purple sprouting broccoli and merguez sausage in a technically-accomplished dish, or go for monkfish with burnt celeriac, squid ink and cockles. To finish, perhaps whipped white chocolate with the bold accompaniments of pistachio and Douglas fir. There's a tasting menu with an optional artisan cheese plate, while the canny wine list has options available by the glass.

Chef Richard Collingwood **Seats** 40 **Times** 12–2/6–9, Closed January, Sunday and Monday **Prices** Set D 4 course £55 (groups of 6+), Taste Cumbria 4/6 course £55/£65 **Wines** 40 bottles over £30, 12 bottles under £30, 8 by glass **Parking** 16 **Notes** Children 10 years + at dinner

CARTMEL
L'Enclume
MAP 15 SD37

◎◎◎◎◎ Modern British **V** ♥
See page 56 and advert on page 59

Rogan & Company Restaurant
MAP 15 SD37

◎◎◎ Modern British
015395 35917 | The Square, LA11 6QD
www.roganandcompany.co.uk
Ultra-modern dishes from the Rogan stable

Simon Rogan's other Cartmel place is right next door to L'Enclume, in an old weathered stone building that's been turned inside into an informal contemporary restaurant space, with slender steel columns under the old beams, and a relaxed casual feel. Peter Smit now heads up the kitchen, but maintains the signature style of ultra-modern presentations of Lakeland produce, inspired by culinary traditions from far and wide. A crispy pig's ear makes a satisfying nibble while you consider the main menu business, which might open with smoked sea trout and asparagus in a mustard dressing with crème fraîche, before main courses lead on with fine local meats – lamb flank, pork collar, beef bavette – or a fish such as gurnard with cauliflower, leek and preserved lemon. Vegetarian dishes tend to the robust end of the spectrum, perhaps roasted hispi cabbage with wild mushrooms and wasabi, and are certainly worth a side-order or two, when the offerings may take in potato purée with beef dripping, or confit fennel with fermented celery and almonds.

The breakfast tendency in modern desserts might produce a pear soaked in tea with granola and apple marigold, or else something of the night like dark chocolate torte with honeycomb and walnuts.

Chefs Simon Rogan, Peter Smit **Seats** 40, Private dining room 10 **Times** 12–2/6–9, Closed 1st week January, Tuesday, D Sunday **Prices** Set L 2 course £20-£26, Starter £9–£14, Main £16–£27, Dessert from £8, Sunday lunch **Wines** 26 bottles over £30, 6 bottles under £30, 16 by glass **Parking** On street **Notes** Vegetarian available, Children welcome

GRASMERE
Forest Side

MAP 20 NY30

◉◉◉◉ Modern British **V** 🍷
015394 35250 | Keswick Road, LA22 9RN
www.theforestside.com

Ingeniously conceived dishes from foraged and natural ingredients

The Victorian Gothic house a little outside Grasmere has been creatively reworked into the image of a contemporary eco-friendly hotel. Its large wood-floored dining room has views around three sides, and is furnished with solid plank tables that have been recycled from the previous flooring, between which staff dressed for a rather smart hunting party glide about in serene command, delivering and explaining Kevin Tickle's complex, ingeniously-conceived Lakeland food. Choose either the tasting formula in six or ten stages, or the tripartite format if you want to go à la carte. All routes lead to astonishment and delight, with dishes built from foraged natural ingredients and prime local produce.

The opener might be a bowl of kohlrabi and surf clams, scented with marshland flora, over which a seaweed broth is poured. That salty, sea-fresh start is then counterpointed by earthier, sourer notes in a salad of duck hearts interleaved with ribbons of salt-baked turnip and smashed pickled walnuts. Fish might be Atlantic cod with a scattering of Flookburgh brown shrimps and onion purée, before dry-aged Middlewhite pork arrives with a refined honour-guard of umbellifers, cultured pollen and birch sap. Hedgerow and garden fragrances continue to waft hauntingly over desserts such as sweet cheese parfait with sea buckthorn and coltsfoot, or rhubarb in burnt butter with sweet cicely. Vegetarian dishes might include truffled celeriac with damsons and wood-blewits, and a pairing of artichoke and apple with hen of the woods and scurvy grass. The wine selections are carefully compiled to provide successful matches with these demanding dishes.

Chef Kevin Tickle **Seats** 50, Private dining room 12 **Times** 12–2/7–9.30, Closed L Monday to Tuesday **Prices** Set D 3 course from £60, Tasting menu 6 or 10 course £70–£85 **Wines** 270 bottles over £30, 3 bottles under £30, 18 by glass **Parking** 44 **Notes** Children 8 years +

Cumbria

L'Enclume

MAP 15 SD37

◉◉◉◉◉ Modern British Ⅴ ☙
015395 36362 | Cavendish Street, LA11 6PZ
www.lenclume.co.uk

Cleverly conceived Lakeland cooking from a modern master

If certain chefs have become associated inextricably with certain locations, Cartmel is certainly Simon Rogan's. A mere slip of a Lakeland village, it was modestly geared up for tourist traffic before L'Enclume transformed it into the northern equivalent of Berkshire's Bray or Cornwall's Padstow. A brace of Rogan establishments sits side by side on the river, and it's here at the 'Anvil' – a former blacksmith's forge – where his culinary output reaches its peak. The place itself has resisted all inclination to put on any decorative airs and graces. Roughcast whitewashed stone walls and the low-hanging beams give evidence of the centuries-old venerability of the building, as do the carefully preserved old furnaces, and the plain modern undressed tables and uncovered floor create a neutral surround for the fireworks to come.

Rogan sources primarily from within the Cumbrian locality, his 12-acre smallholding pouring forth organically cultivated vegetables, fruit, herbs and flowers for the lengthy roll call of small but perfectly extraordinary dishes of which the many-coursed menus are formed. The preliminary canapé items alone seemingly go on forever, each a little masterpiece of stunning intensity and constructive ingenuity, including a Maran (French hen's) egg and mushroom in stout vinegar, and the mind-blowingly potent

smoked cod roe with parsley on flatbread. Eventually, after perhaps nine of these little teasers, the individual courses might start with aged veal in coal oil, its miraculous tenderness sharpened with piercingly fragrant wood-sorrel, before native lobster is served in an early summer outfit of broad beans and elderflower. Those edible flowers make a further discreet appearance in the form of nasturtiums to garnish butter-poached turbot and courgettes, while the treatment of the Goosnargh duck that follows seems almost traditional, its cherries underlining the sweetness of the meat, while smoked beetroot emphasises its earthy richness.

All stops are pulled out for the desserts, when pine cones and cornets make texturally entertaining finishing touches after the likes of raspberry and sweet cicely tart, and blackberry mousse with oats and buttermilk. Lunch offers a shorter version of the tasting menu if you're really pressed for time, perhaps taking in a rooty turnip broth garnished with hen-of-the-woods mushrooms and pork fat, with a main course of loin and croquette of Cartmel Valley venison, sweetly underpinned by beetroot and a pear cooked in beeswax. It all adds up to some of Britain's most exciting and cleverly conceived cooking, served by impeccably knowledgeable staff, including a great sommelier who oversees a magisterial wine list.

Chefs Simon Rogan, Tom Barnes, Marcus Noack **Seats** 50, Private dining room 6 **Times** 12–1.30/6.30–9.30, Closed 25–26 December, 2–16 January, Monday **Prices** Set lunch 6 course £49, **Wines** 500 bottles over £30, 30 by glass **Parking** 7, On street **Notes** Tasting menu lunch/dinner 18-20 course, Children 6 years + at lunch, 12 years + at dinner

See advert on page 59

Cumbria

Hipping Hall
MAP 15 SD67

◉◉◉ Modern British V
015242 71187 | Cowan Bridge, LA6 2JJ
www.hippinghall.com

Accomplished modern cooking with national parks on either hand

Standing in glorious mature gardens, Hipping Hall takes its name from the hipping, or stepping stones crossing the little stream that runs past the old wash house. The pocket-sized country house has a timeless appeal, and a real draw is its restaurant, a stylish space with boarded floors, soaring oak beams and a grand fireplace. The setting is in complete contrast to the solidly 21st-century creations of Oli Martin, a sure-footed chef whose cooking is on a roll, creating culinary fireworks from superlative local produce. There are six- and nine-course tasters as well as the carte. Perfectly roasted guinea fowl gets things going, served with confit leg, turnip purée, apple, nut praline and a bitter note of hops. Seafood is a strong suit too: witness a main course showcasing gold-standard Skrei cod matched with puréed and roasted celeriac, plump, gently pickled mussels, with herb oil and judicious use of fresh dill bringing it all to life. If you're in the mood for something meatier, there may be beef with turnip and pine nut. An arsenal of techno bells and whistles are deployed in an inspired dessert involving a chocolate sphere filled with truffle cream and mousse, alongside mandarin sorbet and gel.

Chef Oli Martin **Seats** 32 **Times** 12–2/7–9, Closed L Monday to Friday **Prices** Set lunch 4 course £29.50, Set D 3 course £55, Tasting menu 6/9 course £65–£75, Sunday lunch £29.50–£39.50 **Wines** 60 bottles over £30, 15 bottles under £30, 12 by glass **Parking** 20 **Notes** Children 12 years +

Holbeck Ghyll Country House Hotel
MAP 20 NY30

◉◉◉ Modern British V
See page 60

Hrishi at Gilpin Hotel & Lake House
MAP 20 SD49

◉◉◉ Modern British, Asian influences V
See page 62

The Samling
MAP 20 NY30

◉◉◉ Modern British V ⚑
015394 31922 | Ambleside Road, LA23 1LR
www.thesamlinghotel.co.uk

Dynamic British cooking in a revamped Windermere retreat

It's hard not to go on a bit about the spectacular setting of The Samling, particularly when you've been transfixed by the timeless views from the new restaurant's floor-to-ceiling windows. Culinary matters have moved apace here in recent years, with the arrival of Nick Edgar from Le Manoir aux Quat'Saisons to a brand new kitchen, a development kitchen, and chef's table in the stunning modern stone and glass extension. The charming old country house has had a top-to-toe makeover, too, while its 67 acres include a kitchen garden to ensure a steady supply of first-rate seasonal materials, bolstered by a close-knit community of suppliers proudly namechecked on the menu. The tight-lipped descriptions of the 4-course lunch menu, and 7- and 10-course tasting versions don't give much idea of how spectacular the dishes are, but the proof comes from the off in a first course of buttery veal sweetbreads matched with truffle, wild mushroom risotto, and a creamy mushroom sauce to bind it all together. Next up, pin-sharp technical skills are evident in an immaculately handled piece of cod with leeks, truffle and bacon, or go for venison with chocolate, sprouts, quince and parsley root. A complex dessert involving textures of beetroot with liquorice and olive-oil wild rice seals the deal.

Chef Nick Edgar **Seats** 40, Private dining room 8 **Times** 12–2/6.30–9.30 **Prices** Tasting menu £45–£100, Sunday lunch **Wines** 300 bottles over £30, 26 bottles under £30, 22 by glass **Parking** 40 **Notes** Children welcome

Cumbria

Holbeck Ghyll Country House Hotel

MAP 20 NY30

◉◉◉ Modern British **V**

015394 32375 | Holbeck Lane, LA23 1LU

www.holbeckghyll.com

Creative Lakeland cooking overlooking Windermere

The first thing on most people's tick list when choosing a Lakeland hotel is an uplifting scenic location, and Holbeck Ghyll certainly has that in spades: reached via a long driveway that reinforces the sense of tranquillity, the handsome creeper-festooned mansion looks out over the shimmering expanse of Lake Windermere framed by the soaring peaks of Coniston Old Man, Bowfell and the Langdale Pikes. Inside, the house itself – a former hunting lodge – is a paragon of solid-stone reliability, positioned to make the best of the view and built on a human scale.

Offering the sort of finely-tuned hospitality that visitors are looking for in an upscale retreat, Holbeck is consummately stylish – its bedrooms are as classy as anyone could reasonably wish for, it's art nouveau signature decor is beautifully maintained, and an air of a peaceable retreat reigns supreme – particularly if you have indulged in a spot of pampering in the swish spa. The dining room has an air of refined elegance, all oak panels, opulent swagged drapes and, of course, that to-die-for view. If you're the sort of person that prefers to peek inside the engine room, you can book a seat at the chef's table next to the pass where the final touches are applied to dishes before they are whisked out to diners. Talented young chef Jake Jones took over the culinary helm in January 2017, and he has

a spanking new state-of-the-art kitchen to deliver his own brand of confident country-house cookery discreetly offset with a little well-judged modernity. Whether you go for the seasonal à la carte or the seven-course taster, the menus draw much from the surroundings, whilst taking a broader view when it comes to sourcing top-drawer seafood, as seen in a starter matching Isle of Mull scallops with crispy chicken oysters, charred cauliflower and wild fennel butter. At main course stage, prime materials are reliably excellent, such as the tender fillet and short rib of Belted Galloway beef that arrives with creamy smoked potato, asparagus, ramsons and mushrooms; if you're in the mood for fish, Isle of Gigha halibut might be partnered with Morecambe Bay shrimps, seaweed and broccoli.

Creative desserts maintain the impact, matching the finest garriguette strawberries with white chocolate mousse and elderflower, or you might bow out with an imaginative construction involving chocolate with beets, whipped cheese and stout. The deal is sealed by a pedigree wine list offering interesting bottles from around the globe. If your appetite is up to the challenge, afternoon tea here is something special thanks to that spectacular vista, whether it's by an open fire in one of the Arts and Crafts lounges, or out on the terrace on a balmy day.

Chef Jake Jones **Seats** 50, Private dining room 20 **Times** 12.30–2/7–9.30 **Prices** Set L 2 course £33, Set L 3 course £43, Set D 3 course £68, Tasting menu £88, Sunday lunch **Wines** 270 bottles over £30, 29 bottles under £30, 13 by glass **Parking** 50 **Notes** Children 8 years +

See advert on page 64

Cumbria

Hrishi at Gilpin Hotel & Lake House
MAP 20 SD49

◉◉◉ Modern British, Asian influences V
015394 88818 | Crook Road, LA23 3NE
www.thegilpin.co.uk

Modern European food with Asian influences in Lakeland tranquillity

The Gilpin may take a little finding if you're not from round these parts, but it's worth putting the satnav lady through her paces because the reward is a gorgeously appointed, family-owned Lakeland retreat in which to restore the spirits. The hotel manages to ensure a level of undisturbed tranquillity that may take you from breakfast in bed to champagne in the hot tub before dinner, without so much as a raucous whoop to be heard in the vicinity. Lake Windermere as the backdrop deserves nothing less.

There's gastronomic magic afoot too, in a beautifully appointed dining room, titled with the nickname of its head chef Hrishikesh Desai, a man whose glittering CV has taken him from a distinguished apprenticeship in France to a stage under Thomas Keller at California's French Laundry and a period at Lucknam Park, not to mention a victorious appearance on the BBC's *Chefs on Trial*. In a region where country-house hotels operated to a recognisable template in decades past, Desai has conferred a genuine feeling of individuality and excitement on the menus here (and in Gilpin Spice with 2 AA Rosettes), mingling notes from his own Asian heritage into contemporary European cooking to dynamic and often surprising effect. That's memorably apparent in a signature opener that features poached chilli-glazed lobster garnished with tobiko (flying fish) caviar, served with fritters of the claw meat, avocado mousse, a zesty dressing of grapefruit and lime, and panch phoran (five spices) mango chutney, a dazzling array of contrasting elements. Lochalsh scallops are thinly sliced and ceviched in sherry vinegar and orange, topped with texturally counterpointed blobs of cumined carrot purée and toasted hazelnuts.

Main-course meats are treated with the same mixture of respect and invention, as when a gentle masala sauce accompanies pancetta-wrapped confit lamb shoulder with baby aubergine, asparagus and blowtorched cucumber, while locally-reared Goosnargh duck comes as roast breast and a spring roll of the leg with squash in a chutney-like sauce of apple, sultanas and ginger. There is impressive depth to these dishes, and while there is plenty going on in them, it all hangs together in harmonious balance. Even dishes with a more obviously classical foundation achieve lasting impact, perhaps a serving of Cornish turbot and brown shrimps with hand-rolled macaroni, baby artichokes and wilted lettuce in a truffled emulsion sauce.

Dessert might be almond and citrus cake with textured variations of orange, and bitter almond ice cream, or the decidedly seductive peanut butter semi freddo with salt caramel, candied peanuts, hot fudge and banana ice cream, a bundle of treats that seems to owe more than a little to Desai's time in California. British artisanal cheeses come with properly intense chutney and an assortment of home-made biscuits.

Chef Hrishikesh Desai **Seats** 60, Private dining room 20 **Times** 12–2.30/6–9.30, Closed L Monday to Saturday **Prices** Set dinner 4 course £65 Tasting menu £85, Sunday lunch £35–£40 **Wines** 181 bottles over £30, 6 bottles under £30, 18 by glass **Parking** 40 **Notes** Children 7 years +

HOLBECK GHYLL

MOMENTS TO SAVOUR

Holbeck Ghyll Country House Hotel,
Holbeck Lane, Windermere, Cumbria LA23 1LU
+44 (0)1539 432 375
www.holbeckghyll.com stay@holbeckghyll.com
/holbeck.ghyll @holbeckghyll

THE PEACOCK AT ROWSLEY

The Peacock at Rowsley is a cosy, chic boutique hotel, originally a manor house in the heart of the Peak District National Park and very close to Haddon Hall and Chatsworth House. Perfect for a countryside break with comfortable bedrooms including four posters and one of the best hotel suites in the region. Our award winning restaurant serves a delicious fine dining menu, crafted by Head Chef Dan Smith. Dan worked with notable chefs such as Tom Aikens before joining The Peacock. The atmospheric bar with open fire is a very convivial place to meet for lunch, dinner or just a drink – with its own menu of freshly cooked seasonal food. Treat yourself to a drink from the extensive cocktail menu. Sunday lunch at The Peacock is a local favourite. The hotel is famed for is excellent fly fishing on the Derbyshire Wye and river Derwent.

For further information or to make a booking please call **01629 733518** or email **reception@thepeacockatrowsley.com**. The Peacock at Rowsley, Derbyshire DE4 2EB,

Derbyshire

BASLOW
Fischer's Baslow Hall

MAP 11 SK27

◉◉◉ Modern European V
01246 583259 | Calver Road, DE45 1RR
www.fischers-baslowhall.co.uk
Modern British ideas on a French foundation

Baslow Hall was built at the high-water mark of the art nouveau movement, but there's nothing nouveau about it. Although it may be barely more than a century old, its heart belongs in the Stuart era, as its projecting gabled wings and window mullions and the stone construction attest. In the 1920s, it was owned by the Ferranti electrical family, who installed many of the mod cons on which the place still runs, but has since the late 1980s been in the ownership of Max Fischer, who launched it on its successful career as a modern country-house hotel.

Today there's a fully equipped up-to-the-minute kitchen, complete with that indispensable amenity of today's restaurant scene, ringside counter seating for those who like to see their dinner being constructed. If you're happy not to be on nodding terms with the kitchen brigade, there's an irresistibly elegant dining room to sit in too, with striped pink and gold wallpaper, contrasting upholstery in the seats, and properly dressed tables. It's a restaurant on the human scale, patrolled by staff well-versed in the traditional arts, and also adept at reminding you what's in each dish as it arrives. Rupert Rowley's cooking has an unmistakably French foundation, but overlaid with the exuberant technical flourishes, and unabashedly sourcing from the length and breadth of the country, from

the Scottish islands to Cornwall, with beef from the adjacent estate and honey from beehives within Baslow's own grounds. Classic menus in both standard and vegetarian versions, and an eight-course Taste of Britain cavalcade, structures the whole experience, and there are hits aplenty. A modern classic combination to start manages to feel newly honed: plump, evenly caramelised scallops are paired with the earthy texture of black pudding and softly grainy couscous, with Granny Smith apple and fat little raisins adding tart and sweet notes, the whole dish unified by a smooth cauliflower velouté.

Main course might be crisply seared Creedy Carver duck with a lobe of its sautéed foie gras, alongside a pie of bacon and onion, the textural contrasts achieved by means of stiffly puréed dates and crunchy pumpkin seeds. Fish dishes are carefully composed of elements that add depth and complexity but don't overwhelm the main item, perhaps tempura-battered vegetables with five-spiced cod, or garden kale, caramelised onions and a red wine glaze for sea bass. The signature dessert is the woodland scene fashioned from chocolate, with a tree trunk moulded from intensely rich mousse and aerated chunks, its minty moss thrown into the shade by a piercingly concentrated lime sorbet.

Chef Rupert Rowley **Seats** 65, Private dining room 38 **Times** 12–1.30/7–8.30, Closed D 24 December, 25–26 and 31 December, 1 January **Prices** Set L 2 course £23-£33, Set L 3 course £30-£40, Set D 2 course £62.50, Set D 3 course £78, Tasting menu £85–£135, Sunday lunch £38–£45 Taste of Britain lunch £65/£105, Kitchen bench lunch £70/£110, Dinner £95/£145 **Wines** 110 bottles over £30, 20 bottles under £30, 6 by glass **Parking** 20 **Notes** Children 8 years + (except Sunday lunch)

Derbyshire

The Peacock at Rowsley

MAP 11 SK27

◉◉◉ Modern British V

01629 733518 | Bakewell Road, DE4 2EB

www.thepeacockatrowsley.com

Technically nimble, creative cooking in an aristocratic manor

Deep in the heart of the Peak District, the Peacock does boast a certain social cachet. It's owned by Lord and Lady Manners of nearby Haddon Hall, and also has the Duke of Devonshire for a neighbour, with Chatsworth only a stone's throw. The place itself is a weathered stone-built manor house of the late 17th century that became a hotel at about the time Queen Victoria acceded to the throne, so it has had plenty of practice. The grounds alone are a delight, and certainly worth a wander, while keen fly-fishers might join the in-house club and find the Wye and the Derwent at their disposal. Inside, the place has been maintained with all the conscientious attention to detail you would expect, some of its rooms boasting four-poster beds.

While the bar has the feel of a village inn, with its low ceiling, venerable timber columns and stone walls, the dining room is the last word in contemporary chic, with plum-coloured walls to offset modern fringed light fixtures as well as old oil portraits. This is the setting for Dan Smith's technically nimble, energetically creative British cooking, which sources from nearby estates for organically reared meats, as well as the Peacock's own kitchen gardens, for finely crafted modern dishes. Slow-cooked pork collar is given a finishing crisping to the surface before being

partnered with smoked eel and black pudding for a successful ensemble, with a little celeriac purée and a strong note of Pommery mustard helping things along. Alternatively, there might be a very countrified wild garlic and nettle velouté, adorned with goats' curd, sourdough croûtons, and a floating garnish of croque monsieur.

Main courses turn up the volume, building complex layers of flavour from pedigree prime materials. Brill fillet turns up chaperoned by an oyster for impeccable sea-fresh smartness, alongside leek and hispi cabbage, in a velvety-rich champagne sauce, the detail of hand-rolled macaroni emphasising the labour-intensiveness of the dish, or there may be positively traditional seared cutlet and braised shoulder of local lamb with crushed potatoes, in a vividly green spring array of peas and broad beans and a lamb jus edged with mint vinegar. Neither do desserts stint on intricacy: there's something to be discovered in every corner of a plate that takes in caramelised white chocolate mousse with citrus meringue, cranberry sorbet, jelly and compôte, all sharpened with a little rhubarb. Roasted pineapple with matching sorbet are the accompaniments to golden syrup sponge that comes with spiced caramel for extra richness.

Chef Dan Smith **Seats** 40, Private dining room 20 **Times** 7–9, Closed bank holiday Mondays, D 24–26 December, Sunday **Prices** Starter £7.45–£15, Main £24–£38, Dessert £7.45–£12.35, Sunday lunch £28.50–£38 **Wines** 41 bottles over £30, 9 bottles under £30, 16 by glass **Parking** 25 **Notes** Children 10 years +

See advert on page 65

Devon

Gidleigh Park
MAP 3 SX68

⑨⑨⑨⑨⑨ Modern European V ♟
01647 432367 | TQ13 8HH
www.gidleigh.com

Stunning contemporary cooking in wonderful Dartmoor isolation

As you round the corner on the long, winding drive on the edge of
Dartmoor, the sprawling half-timbered mansion materialises against a lush
backdrop of trees, with the River Teign flowing languidly past the front.
The Aussie shipping magnate who built the property in the Arts and Crafts
style in the late 1920s obviously intended to show his guests that he was
a chap of substance, and it still gets jaws dropping today. It's a charming
and stylish place of impressively high standards, fully in tune with the
needs of 21st-century sybarites, so everything is set up for pure
indulgence and relaxation – there's even a hot tub on the roof – and
something would be amiss if there wasn't an A-list dining option.

In fact, Gidleigh Park has one of the top restaurants in the country. The
place was already in the Premier League of country house destination
dining thanks to the long residency of chef Michael Caines – big boots for
any successor to fill, but Michael Wignall (ex Pennyhill Park in Surrey) is a
chef of the requisite calibre. He took the helm in 2016 and has shown that
there are going to be thrills aplenty under the new regime.

Wignall's cooking is technically precise, clever without ever losing its
way, and everything looks perfect on the plate. A light touch means you
can tackle the seven- or ten-course tasting menus without being
overwhelmed, and meat-free versions of both ensure that veggies are not
sidelined. Otherwise, the carte offers up five choices per course, or lunch
is a good entry point if you want to get a measure of the place for pretty
much half the price.

Opening the show, chicken cooked in umami broth comes with garlic
pannacotta, lovage granita and chicken skin crackers for an array of
fascinating flavours and textures.Producing food this good takes 100%
commitment, focus and perfectionism. Next up, Cornish plaice is as good
as it gets, and it arrives with seaweed, samphire, charred leek and celery
gel, as well as miso potatoes, a stunning seafood casserole and squid ink
gnocchi. Elsewhere, there may be best end and loin of hare with poached
duck liver, parsnip, kohlrabi cannelloni and baked chocolate, an
impressively creative course that balances strong flavours with a sure
hand. Dessert is a highly detailed tour de force combining aerated lemon
verbena parfait, raspberry powder, fresh and crunchy dried lychee and
white chocolate Aero. Canapés and petits fours are as innovative as the
rest, while a refreshingly simple approach is taken with bread, an

appetising sourdough. Ensconced in oak-panelled majesty in one of the three dining rooms, you might as well splash out on some wine. An authoritative list of over 1,000 bins awaits, with a knowledgeable and enthusiastic sommelier to steer the way.

Chef Michael Wignall **Seats** 45, Private dining room 22 **Times** 12–2/ 6.30–9 **Prices** Set L 3 course £60, Tasting menu lunch 7 course £75, Tasting menu dinner 10 course £145 **Wines** 1,000 bottles over £30, 30 bottles under £30, 20 by glass **Parking** 45 **Notes** Children 8 years + at lunch and dinner

DREWSTEIGNTON
The Old Inn
MAP 3 SX79

◉◉◉ International
01647 281276 | EX6 6QR
www.old-inn.co.uk

Well-judged cooking in a Dartmoor village inn

Chef-patron Duncan Walker's charming restaurant with rooms occupies a whitewashed, 17th-century former coaching inn in a picture-perfect village on the fringes of the moor. There's a cosy lounge with squashy sofas by a wood burner, and a pair of smartly inviting dining rooms with bare oak tables, and walls hung with art, but refreshingly free from designer pretentions. Make sure you allow enough time to give the modern European menu and concise, well-chosen wine list a full workout. And with fewer than 20 diners to cater for, you can expect focused cooking of pin-sharp accuracy. Walker is a chef who has the knack of achieving big flavours from harmonious combinations of top-quality ingredients, whether it's a starter of grilled sole with braised endive and citrus juices, or a well-judged marriage of roast quail with artichokes and black trumpet mushrooms. Main courses are intelligently composed too, with vivid flavours to the fore in dishes like spiced pork belly with sautéed scallops and lemongrass, or grilled turbot in a ragout of spring vegetables and Madeira. Puddings push the right buttons with hot prune and Armagnac soufflé with cinnamon ice cream, or a perennial favourite, a classic tarte Tatin.

Chef Duncan Walker **Seats** 16, Private dining room 10 **Times** 12–2/7–9, Closed 3 weeks in January, 2 weeks in June, Sunday to Tuesday, L Wednesday and Thursday **Prices** Set L 3 course from £32, Set D 2 course from £46, Set D 3 course from £52 **Wines** 29 bottles over £30, 16 bottles under £30, 4 by glass **Parking** Village square, village car park
Notes Booking is advisable, Tables 6-10 by prior arrangement, Vegetarian menu on request, Children 12 years +

Devon

Thomas Carr @ The Olive Room

MAP 3 SS54

@@@ Seafood V

01271 867831 | 56 Fore Street, EX34 9DJ

www.thomascarrchef.co.uk

Dishes of resonant depth on the tranquil north Devon coast

One of the most encouraging aspects of the contemporary dining scene is that a cutting-edge kitchen might as easily be found on the tranquil north Devon coast, not far from where the ferries depart for Lundy Island, as in the metropolitan heartlands. So it is with Thomas Carr's thrilling modern repertoire at The Olive Room, which at one glance is just the dining room of a local guest house, but at another is so much more. Cream walls and engaging staff set a relaxing tone, but the cooking will have you sitting up and taking notice. A bowl of fish bisque incorporating stone bass, crab and langoustine also contains fennel, grapefruit and ginger to add layers of depth to a starter full of aromatic appeal. That could be followed by a robust serving of tender venison with an oxtail fritter and a little red onion tart, alongside pickled mushrooms and mash, for a dish that also achieves great resonance. For dessert, carrot cake is reimagined into a luscious cheesecake, served with burnt orange purée and cinnamon ice cream, as well as a garnish of caramelised walnuts. There is a compact list of well-chosen wines to accompany.

Chefs Thomas Carr, John Cairns **Seats** 18 **Times** 12–1.30/6.30–9, Closed Sunday and Monday, L Tuesday to Thursday **Prices** Set D 2 course from £38 , Set D 3 course from £48 , Tasting menu from £75 **Wines** 9 bottles over £30, 14 bottles under £30, 9 by glass **Parking** NCP (Fore Street) **Notes** Children welcome

The Coach House by Michael Caines

MAP 3 SS64

@@@ Modern British V

01271 882295 | Kentisbury Grange, EX31 4NL

www.kentisburygrange.com

Creative modern cooking in a stylish old coach house

The Coach House restaurant at the Grange was once just that – a 17th-century edifice a short scrunch across the gravel from the boutique Kentisbury Grange hotel. Today it is kitted out with rustic-chic oak tables, banquette seating and contemporary artworks. Ingredients are sourced from nearby, including crabs from Lundy and ducks from the farm next door, and with a skilled kitchen team brought on board by the renowned Mr Caines, you can expect plates of technically accomplished food full of contemporary swagger. A first course of langoustine ravioli comes with sauce vierge, lovage and celery salt, or you might start with rabbit ballotine with caramelised carrot purée, pickled vegetables and bitter

Devon

leaves. Main course showcases local game in the shape of roast Exmoor venison partnered with parsnip, pancetta and red wine jus, or if you're in the mood for fish, there may be pan-fried Cornish turbot alongside crab, morels, asparagus, grelot onions and red wine sauce. The cheeseboard flies the flag for Devon, while desserts run to pistachio soufflé, dark chocolate sauce and pistachio ice cream, or classic lemon tart with confit lemon and cassis sorbet. Bargain hunters should make a date for the phenomenal value offered on the lunch menu.

Chef James Mason **Seats** 54, Private dining room 16 **Times** 12–2/7–9.30 **Prices** Set L 2 course £19.95, Set L 3 course £24.95, Set D 2 course £38, Set D 3 course £50, Tasting menu £70, Sunday lunch £19.95–£29.95 **Wines** 34 bottles over £30, 41 bottles under £30, 12 by glass **Parking** 70 **Notes** Children welcome

MORETONHAMPSTEAD
Bovey Castle
MAP 3 SX78
◉◉◉ Classic British V ♟
01647 445000 | Dartmoor National Park, North Bovey, TQ13 8RE
www.boveycastle.com

A taste of contemporary Devon

Built in 1890 by one William Henry Smith (WH Smith to you and me), Bovey Castle was first opened as a 'golfing hotel' by the Great Western Railway company way back in 1930, and both associations are acknowledged in today's dining options: Smith's Brasserie and the big-hitting Great Western restaurant. It's a property with a real sense of drama – big, bold, and glamorous, with a spa and that golf course to help pass the time until dinner. The Great Western is an equally lavishly done out space, suitably romantic with an art deco swagger. The kitchen is headed up by Mark Budd, a local chap who always had his eye on the top job here, and he hasn't wasted any time making his mark. Regional ingredients from land and sea loom large in good-looking contemporary dishes that reveal well-honed technical skills and even a sense of fun. Creative amuse bouche get the ball rolling, along with superb breads (bread gets proper attention here), before a first course such as smoked and cured South Coast sea trout comes multiple ways with beetroot and creamy goats' curd. Next up, perhaps a first-rate bit of fish like Dover sole with a poached oyster, or charred rump of Devon beef with a poshed-up cottage pie, and, among desserts, Black Forest gâteau makes for a stunning finish.

Chef Mark Budd **Seats** 120, Private dining room 32 **Times** 12–2.30/7–9.30, Closed L Monday to Saturday **Prices** Tasting menu £75, Starter £18–£22, Main £28–£35, Dessert £10.50–£15.50, Sunday lunch £35, Afternoon tea £30 per person **Wines** 300 bottles over £30, 11 by glass **Parking** 100 Onsite valet parking only **Notes** Children welcome

Devon

PLYMOUTH
Boringdon Hall Hotel
MAP 3 SX55

◉◉◉ Modern French

01752 344455 | Boringdon Hill, Plympton, PL7 4DP

www.boringdonhall.co.uk

Energetic modern cooking overlooking the Great Hall

Only a few clicks outside Plymouth, Boringdon Hall is a spa hotel with a rich past. Back in the Tudor day, it became crown property during the Dissolution, and was then gifted by Henry VIII to one of his court favourites, Thomas Wriothesley, Earl of Southampton. Today's attractive mix of stone walls and mullioned windows with ultra-mod spa facilities adds up to a powerful enticement, and the deal is surely sealed in the Gallery Restaurant, which, as its name suggests, overlooks the beamed Great Hall with its intricate carved furniture and little crannies. Scott Paton rules this roost, with food that is full of surprises and inventive energy. Proceedings might open with pan-roasted veal sweetbread, served with an assertively sauced teriyaki chicken wing and pickled mooli, and move on to beautifully fresh seared turbot, cleverly balanced with caramelised cauliflower, on a foundation of capers and raisins. The chilly end of the year may produce fallow deer venison with winter-spiced beetroot, scented with juniper and anise, while dessert ends with a flourish – perhaps a brown sugar tart alongside fig purée and spiced apple sorbet.

Chef Scott Paton **Seats Times** 12–3/6.30–9.30 **Prices** Set L 2 course from £22.50, Set L 3 course from £29.50, Set D 3 course from £49.50, Tasting menu from £55, Sunday lunch from £25 **Wines** 39 bottles over £30, 24 bottles under £30, 11 by glass **Notes** Afternoon tea

TORQUAY
The Elephant Restaurant
MAP 3 SX96

◉◉◉ Modern British

01803 200044 | 3-4 Beacon Terrace, TQ1 2BH

www.elephantrestaurant.co.uk

Dynamic cooking of thoroughbred produce next to the harbour

Simon Hulstone is into his second decade at the Elephant, a graceful beast that sits to one side of the harbour. The whole operation, once divided over two floors, now takes place in the split-level ground floor room, an airy, refreshing space, its two wings communicating by giant gilt-framed mirrors, while painted bare wood tabletops enhance the seaside atmosphere. The cooking is dynamic, precisely weighted and inspired, sourced from the Elephant's own farm and thoroughbred Devon producers, and retains the knack of creating an anticipatory thrill from one dish to the next. A seafood route through the menu might be Brixham crab with dashi jelly and crispy chicken skin, the brown crabmeat spread on toast à la croque monsieur, and then Norwegian fjord Skrei cod with smoked leeks and hen of the woods in a glorious broth boosted with allium oil. Otherwise, there could be tip-top local venison loin with variations of celeriac, tartly offset with sauerkraut and apple. At dessert, try a spin on custard tart flavoured with sea-salted caramel and spicy cassia cinnamon ice cream.

Chef Simon Hulstone **Seats** 75 **Times** 12–2/6.30–9, Closed 1st 2 weeks in January, Sunday and Monday **Prices** Set L 2 course £16.50, Set L 3 course £19.50, Starter £8–£14, Main £14–£25, Dessert £8–£12 **Wines** 24 bottles over £30, 30 bottles under £30, 8 by glass **Parking** Opposite restaurant **Notes** Vegetarian available, Children welcome

Dorset

EVERSHOT
Summer Lodge Country House Hotel, Restaurant & Spa

MAP 4 ST50

@@@ Modern British ♥
01935 482000 | Fore Street, DT2 0JR
www.summerlodgehotel.com
Assured modern cooking in peaceful surroundings

Set in peaceful grounds, Summer Lodge is a pretty Georgian dower house with a Victorian extension designed by architect and local literary giant, Thomas Hardy. It has a soft-focus look that has not been affected by passing fashions, its restaurant done out with swagged curtains, floral fabrics and elegantly dressed tables. Steven Titman's cooking is built on impeccable local produce and whatever is grown in the hotel's garden, his style follows British traditions with modern and wide-ranging ideas in the mix. Starters of Jurassic Coast rose veal carpaccio with crispy sweetbreads, local wasabi and Dorset watercress, or grilled Lyme Bay mackerel fillet with celeriac textures and crispy capers show the style. Main course might star Dorset lamb – perfectly-timed roast loin matched with a shepherd's pie of braised shoulder, with Savoy cabbage and rosemary jus. Fish, too, is handled deftly – perhaps John Dory fillets with thyme-flavoured gnocchi, sautéed sprout leaves, chestnuts and white balsamic. The impressive techniques continue in desserts such as hot lemon soufflé with almond praline ice cream, while cheese lovers will swoon over the trolley loaded with over 20 West Country artisan cheeses.

Chef Steven Titman **Seats** 60, Private dining room 20 **Times** 12–2.30/7–9.30, Closed 3–24 January **Prices** Set L 2 course from £24, Set L 3 course £27-£39, Tasting menu 7 course £75–£165, Starter £13–£20, Main £22–£32, Dessert £11–£16, Sunday lunch £39 **Wines** 1,450 bottles over £30, 15 bottles under £30, 25 by glass **Parking** 60 **Notes** Vegetarian available, Children welcome

DARLINGTON
The Orangery   MAP 16 NZ20
◉◉◉◉ Modern British V
01325 729999 | Rockliffe Hall, Rockliffe Park, Hurworth-on-Tees, DL2 2DU
www.rockliffehall.com
Creative contemporary dishes in an ornate dining room

Like many a Georgian country mansion, Rockliffe Hall is big on sport and leisure these days, with its 18-hole golf course, spa pampering and a trio of restaurants. Pick of the bunch is The Orangery, where gilded wrought-iron columns support a soaring glass roof, and views sweep across the gardens and the action on the fairways through the large wall of windows. Richard Allen heads up the team to deliver a contemporary nine-course tasting menu, plus veggie, pescetarian and four-course à la carte options. Local produce and seasonality is key, some of it foraged from Rockliffe's 365-acre estate, and it's all presented in imaginative juxtapositions of flavour, texture and temperature. Pigeon breast with various forms of broccoli, chickpea dhal, and fig and ginger jam is a dish full of creative flair and sound judgement; likewise Staithes Village crab mayonnaise, butter-poached potato and spring beauty sprigs. Next up, saddle of venison sits atop a punchy bolognese-inspired sauce, together with savoury granola, celeriac purée and greens, or richly cooked pork belly, cheek, langoustine, finely chopped white cabbage and apple purée. A seafood option could be a superb pairing of scallops and smoked eel in a picturesque medley with nasturtium, vinegar and rye. At the end comes a refreshing pre-dessert of gin and tonic foam, sea buckthorn gel and sea herbs that leads onto a high-impact dessert of banana and ginger cake with black butter and peanut brittle. The wine list includes some big hitters, and expert advice is at hand to guide the way.

Chef Richard Allen **Seats** 60, Private dining room 20 **Times** 6.30–9.30, Closed Sunday and Monday, L Tuesday to Saturday **Prices** Set D 3 course £55, Tasting menu £65–£95 **Wines** 600 bottles over £30, 3 bottles under £30, 35 by glass **Parking** 300 **Notes** Children welcome

▶ Gloucestershire

BUCKLAND
Buckland Manor   MAP 10 SP03
◉◉◉ British ♟
01386 852626 | WR12 7LY
www.bucklandmanor.co.uk
Classically based cooking with modern flourishes

Nothing screams exclusivity quite like an old rural manor house entered by automated gates, its 10 acres of grounds blending imperceptibly into the surrounding West Country village. The house itself is medieval, full of period detail and elegant modern furnishings, with a white-panelled dining room the centre of attention. With views of the gardens and distant hills as backdrop through three windows, it's a supremely relaxing setting for Will Guthrie's ingeniously balanced modern British menus. Sourcing carefully from regional suppliers, with aromatic lift provided by Buckland's own herb garden, the kitchen manages the impressive trick of presenting classically based cooking with some of today's stylistic flourishes. First up might be breast of smoked wood pigeon, which comes forth in a glass dome filled with its smoke, its potent savouriness offset by preserved orange, crispy feta, radish and pistachios, a bravura composition that might be the prelude to a tender piece of cod topped with a disc of crunchy cracked wheat, a seasoning of ras el hanout competing with subtle saffron sauce, or perhaps veal loin with barbecue-smoked bacon and red onion purée in Madeira jus. A stimulating pre-dessert then announces the main sweet business, which could be a coconut bombe with pineapple salsa, lime curd and passionfruit sorbet.

Chef Will Guthrie **Seats** 40, Private dining room 14 **Times** 12.30–2/7–9 **Prices** Set L 2 course from £24.50, Set L 3 course from £30, Set D 2 course from £50 (3 course from £70), Tasting menu 7 course from £80, Sunday lunch from £32.50 **Wines** 400 bottles over £30, 17 bottles under £30, 15 by glass **Parking** 20 **Notes** Vegetarian available, Children 8 years +

CHELTENHAM
The Beaufort Dining Room
Ellenborough Park

MAP 10 SO92

Modern British **V** ♈
01242 545454 | Southam Road, GL52 3NH
www.ellenboroughpark.com

Modern British cooking in a luxurious Tudor mansion

As we went to press the Rosette award was suspended due to a change of chef – reassessment will take place in due course.

Although the original house had been pottering along unexceptionally since the 1530s, Ellenborough really hit its stride when the first Earl of that ilk, erstwhile governor general of British India, moved himself and his wife into it 300 years later. The place itself is a sumptuous beauty in Cotswold honey, with a high-glitz panelled dining room, the Beaufort, at the centre of operations.

Seats 60, Private dining room 20 **Times** 7–10, Closed Monday, L Tuesday to Saturday, D Sunday **Prices** Set L 2 course from £24, Set L 3 course from £30, Set D 2 course from £45, Set D 3 course from £55 **Wines** 368 bottles over £30, 12 bottles under £30, 26 by glass **Parking** 130 **Notes** Sunday lunch, Children welcome

Le Champignon Sauvage

MAP 5 SO92

◎◎◎◎ Modern French

01242 573449 | 24-28 Suffolk Road, GL50 2AQ

www.lechampignonsauvage.co.uk

Cooking from the heart in a civilised setting

The Champignon turned 30 in 2017, and in those three decades it has never dropped out of the premier league of the UK's culinary big-hitters. And it's all down to the unflagging dedication and sheer staying power of David and Helen Everitt-Matthias, who have never missed a service, Helen presiding over front of house with unflappable calm, and David at the stoves. It's a calm space where decor and ambience are completely free of airs and graces, just soothing neutral shades jazzed up with vibrant modern artworks.

The name is a clear nod to the modern French approach in David's cooking, which retains its cutting edge without chasing ephemeral culinary trends – after all, the Champignon was in the vanguard of restaurants that started to replace luxury ingredients with foraged and more humble ingredients. It takes a particularly confident kind of ingenuity to come up with starters such as scallop and cured jowl, their savoury notes boosted by salsify with milk crumbs, onion dashi and leek purée. At main course stage, wood pigeon with sourdough gnocchi, baby turnips and mountain ham shows an unerring eye for flavour combination, and the same robustness is applied to main fish dishes that might take in sea bream with chicken wings and juices, purple sprouting broccoli and pistachio cream.

Desserts are designed to create sublime counterpoints of flavour and texture too, seen in the likes of blueberry cannelloni with wood sorrel cream and yogurt sorbet, or acorn delice matched with mocha sorbet and beurre noisette purée.

Chef David Everitt-Matthias **Seats** 40 **Times** 12.30–1.15/7.30–8.30, Closed 10 days at Christmas, 3 weeks in June, Sunday and Monday **Prices** Set L 2 course £27-£53, Set L 3 course £34-£67, Set D 2 course £27–£53, Set D 3 course £34–£67, à la carte 2/3 course £53/£67 **Wines** 92 bottles over £30, 30 bottles under £30, 14 by glass **Parking** Public car park (Bath Road) **Notes** Set dinner Tuesday to Friday only, Children welcome

Lumière

MAP 5 SO92

@@@ Modern British V
01242 222200 | Clarence Parade, GL50 3PA
www.lumiere.cc

High-octane cooking from a hands-on chef

In a Regency terrace not far from the town centre, Jon and Helen Howe's restaurant presents an understated face to the world, with its name etched onto the single window and a discreet awning over the door. Inside, it's a gently contemporary affair with mirrors and smart table settings, where Helen runs front of house with charm and confidence, and Jon brings his own highly distinctive stamp to the cooking, delivering a thrilling repertoire brimming with well-judged complexity, confident technique and flashes of genius. Compositions are intelligently thought through, with every flavour and texture making an impact, and the food is very easy on the eye too.

A starter of squab pigeon, for example, arrives in the company of Jerusalem artichoke, black pudding, sauerkraut and fig, while main course brings a sound pairing of Cornish cod (sourced from day boats, naturally) and pork cheek with salsify, celeriac, cockles and red wine sauce. Top-drawer Cotswold meats might be represented by Stokes Marsh Farm beef served up with onion, ceps, a sauce enriched with wheat beer, and the aromatic delights of wild garlic and truffle. Invention extends to desserts such as a brilliant confection involving Valrhona blonde chocolate with pineapple, banana, popcorn, passionfruit and yuzu.

Chef Jon Howe **Seats** 25 **Times** 12–1.30/7–9, Closed 2 weeks in winter, 2 weeks in summer, Sunday and Monday, L Tuesday to Thursday **Prices** Set L 3 course £35, Set D 3 course £65, Tasting menu 7/9 course £65–£80 **Wines** 75 bottles over £30, 14 bottles under £30, 18 by glass **Parking** On street **Notes** Children 8 years +

LOWER SLAUGHTER
The Slaughters Manor House

MAP 5 SP12

@@@ Modern British V
See page 82

Gloucestershire

NETHER WESTCOTE
The Feathered Nest Country Inn

MAP 5 SP21

⚖⚖⚖ Modern British

01993 833030 | OX7 6SD

www.thefeatherednestinn.co.uk

A country inn with a real sense of its past

Tony and Amanda Timmer have undergone what for many would be the reverse journey of their dreams, forsaking a restaurant berth on the sun-washed Algarve for the Evenlode Valley, an Area of Outstanding Natural Beauty in the Cotswolds. 'Beauty' is no hyperbole. The surrounding countryside unrolls about the place in placid acres, crossed by drystone walls, the hills undulating gently against the distant skyline. On fine days, you might settle in one of the wicker chairs outside under the sycamore, and allow the ambient serenity to work its magic.

The Timmers' project, a makeover of an old malthouse turned village inn, has borne fruit in the shape of a modernised country billet with four guest rooms. Inside, solid walls of exposed stone frame a pleasingly old-world set-up with antique furniture and clocks, equestrian prints, landscape paintings and a hulking inglenook fireplace. Naturally enough, the kitchen sources plenty of its prime materials from the environs, and although Kuba Winkowski cooks in the contemporary fashion, his style also displays an undoubted anchorage in various European traditions. Veal sweetbreads with white asparagus and onion is garnished dashingly with scarlet elf cup wild mushrooms, and might be followed by a pairing of

turbot and mussels with all the voguish greenery you can handle – sea kale, monk's beard and parsley roots. When the menu ventures outside Europe for inspiration, the results can be quite as striking, as when a first course of pollock comes with tropical notes of passionfruit, papaya, aji chilli and pisco, while local fallow deer might turn up with beetroot, salsify, radicchio and a sauce incorporating cocoa beans. Desserts try out innovative spins on familiar themes: crème caramel comes with salt-baked pineapple and coconut; passionfruit and banana soufflé is anointed with South Africa's creamy Amarula liqueur. Well-kept Home Counties cheeses are worth a gander too.

The shorter lunch menu, offering a pair of alternatives at each stage, is good value, perhaps turning on a main-course choice of either stone bass with fennel, taramasalata and lemon or hogget with bulgar wheat, peas and wild garlic. Nor does the appeal end with lunch and dinner. If you're passing through at not quite the right time for either, the afternoon teas are the stuff of local legend, supplied as they are with elegant towering cakestands, scones and clotted cream, and trimly turned-out sandwiches. A well-stocked wine list with almost 20 by the glass, and a range of cask-conditioned ales, should keep everyone happy.

Chef Kuba Winkowski **Seats** 60, Private dining room 14
Times 12–2.30/6.30–9.30, Closed 25 December, Monday, D Sunday
Prices Set L 2 course from £29, Set L 3 course from £35, Set D 2 course from £55, Set D 3 course from £68, Sunday lunch £55–£68 **Wines** 260 bottles over £30, 29 bottles under £30, 19 by glass **Parking** 45
Notes Vegetarian available, Children welcome

Gloucestershire

LOWER SLAUGHTER
The Slaughters Manor House
MAP 5 SP12

@@@ Modern British V
01451 820456 | GL54 2HP
www.slaughtersmanor.co.uk
Contemporary cooking in an elegant Cotswolds hotel

This gorgeous, honey-stoned 17th-century mansion in a picture-postcard village got a new look and a new name in 2016. Formerly Lower Slaughter Manor, it epitomises all that the Cotswolds is about: it has olde English charm in spades, gardens with a croquet lawn, and elegant interiors that have been brought fully into the 21st century without jarring with the antiquity of the house. The restaurant extends into part of the original chapel while retaining a large arched fireplace, and neutral colours help create a soothing and unpretentious setting. Nik Chappell delivers modern and creative dishes via table d'hôte and six-and eight-course tasting menus. Begin with a well-tuned dish of fennel-dressed crab with crab custard, melon and chilli, or another where a crisp rabbit croquette is pointed up with sweet raisin jelly, astringent verjus and puffed rice granola. Venison loin stars in a main course rich with the flavours of liquorice, blackberry and a trio of heritage beetroots, or if you're in the mood for fish, try fillet of turbot with barbecued leek, chervil and fregola. There's plenty of technical gloss at dessert stage, too, when burnt butter almond financier comes with raspberry sorbet and rose, or perhaps white chocolate parfait lifted with lemon and mint.

Chef Nik Chappell **Seats** 48, Private dining room 24 **Times** 12.30–2/ 6.30–9.30 **Prices** Set L 3 course £25-£37.50, Set D 2 course from £57.50, Set D 3 course £67.50–£80, Tasting menu £67.50–£80, Sunday lunch £37.50, Afternoon tea £25 **Wines** 180 bottles over £30, 19 bottles under £30, 9 by glass **Parking** 30 **Notes** Children welcome

NETHER WESTCOTE
The Feathered Nest Country Inn
MAP 5 SP21

@@@ Modern British
See page 80

UPPER SLAUGHTER
Lords of the Manor
MAP 5 SP12

Modern British 🍷
01451 820243 | GL54 2JD
www.lordsofthemanor.com
Magical Cotswold hotel offering excellent service all round

As we went to press the Rosette award was suspended due to a change of chef – reassessment will take place in due course. The Manor looks a delightful whatever the time of day, its honeyed stone basking in the

Cotswold sun, lights blazing in the mullioned windows at evening beckoning wanderers in the grounds to come in and join the party. Staff are expertly attuned to enhance the ambience with a wise mix of professionalism and relaxing warmth – the knowledgeable sommelier is a particular asset – and the dining room forgoes vibrant patterning in favour of a soft-focus neutral look with double-clothed tables and a few pictures on plain white walls.

Seats 50, Private dining room 30 **Times** 12–2/6.45–9.30, Closed L Monday to Friday **Prices** Set L 2 course £29.50, Set L 3 course £37.50, Set D 3 course £72.50, Tasting menu £90, Sunday lunch £29.50–£37.50 **Wines** 400 bottles over £30, 95 bottles under £30, 15 by glass **Parking** 40 **Notes** Vegetarian available, Children 7 years +

▶ Greater Manchester

MANCHESTER
Adam Reid at The French
MAP 16 SJ89
◉◉◉ Modern British V ♟
0161 235 4780 | Peter Street, M60 2DS
www.the-french.co.uk

White-hot culinary creativity in a glamorous hotel

Things have moved on a little since the days when the Beatles, a popular music ensemble of the 1960s, were refused entry to the dining room of the Midland Hotel for being inadequately attired. Nowadays, they're much less punctilious, and hooray for that. Not that the French is lacking anything in swellegant glamour, with its spherical jewel-like chandeliers, curved banquette seating and a finishing kitchen for the gawkers.

Adam Reid is a product of Simon Rogan's school of white-hot culinary creativity, and The French trades in tasting menus of six or ten courses, featuring such courses as a pig trotter croquette bound in crisp skin and panko crumb on sharply acidic pickled onion purée. That could precede butter-poached halibut in spice-tinged brown shrimp and caper sauce, or crown of duck aged in a salt cave, brined and stuffed with hay, before being cooked with cherries and honey, and served with beetroot purée and charred cabbage. The signature desserts are built from fruits blown out of gold sugar, possibly a clementine shell filled with white chocolate mousse and sea buckthorn purée, or a golden apple creation mixed with stewed apple, hazelnut crumble and custard.

Chef Adam Reid **Seats** 52 **Times** 12–1.30/6.30–9 (times vary midweek), Closed Christmas, 2 weeks in August, Sunday and Monday, L Tuesday to Thursday **Prices** Tasting menu £65–£85, Starter £7–£10, Main £10–£14, Dessert £4–£15 **Wines** 136 bottles over £30, 6 bottles under £30, 19 by glass **Parking** NCP behind hotel **Notes** Children 8 years +

Greater Manchester

MANCHESTER *continued*
Manchester House Bar & Restaurant
MAP 16 SJ89

Modern British V

0161 835 2557 | Tower 12, 18-22 Bridge Street, M3 3BZ

www.manchesterhouse.uk.com

A modern dining space and modern British dishes

As we went to press the Rosette award was suspended due to a change of chef – reassessment will take place in due course.

Manchester House is a classic modern eatery: you dine amid a riot of hard-edged concrete and steel, beneath ceiling girders and light fittings like metallic lobster pots, the experience beginning with a sense of having come through the tradesperson's entrance as you slip through the kitchen to your table; there's also kitchen counter seating for half-a-dozen.

Seats 78, Private dining room 8 **Times** 12–2.30/7–9.30, Closed 1st 2 weeks in January, 2 weeks in summer, Sunday and Monday **Prices** Set L 2 course £22.50, Set L 3 course £27.50, Tasting menu £70–£95, Starter £15, Main £35–£58, Dessert £8 **Wines** 193 bottles over £30, 26 bottles under £30, 12 by glass **Parking** NCP (King Street West) **Notes** Children welcome

▶ Hampshire

BEAULIEU
The Montagu Arms Hotel
MAP 5 SU30

◉◉◉ Modern European

01590 612324 | Palace Lane, SO42 7ZL

www.montaguarmshotel.co.uk

Direct, purposeful cooking in the heart of the New Forest

Enshrouded by the New Forest, clad in clambering ivy, The Montagu is a brick-built 17th-century hostelry that could charm the birds out of its surrounding trees. Slenderly beamed ceilings within establish the period tone, and an air of unruffled elegance is conveyed by a dining room done in rich mixed fabrics and patrolled by a front-of-house team whose smooth professionalism contributes to the whole experience. Matthew Tomkinson also has a hand in that, getting the best out of the Hampshire bounty that surrounds the place, conjuring direct, purposeful dishes that don't rely on gimmickry for their positive effect. An opening raviolo filled with late season lamb is all about the unctuous, seductive meat, its richness backed up by grilled broccoli and roasted onions in a rosemary-scented broth. That could well be followed by a flawlessly composed fish dish, perhaps slow-poached Cornish monkfish, its firm texture gently emphasised by a rich sauce of smoked bacon and red wine, and by a strongly seasoned accompaniment of crisp potato terrine and a little grilled lettuce, or maybe Alresford roe deer with a croquette of its brisket, glazed beetroot and parsnip purée. At the finish comes a resoundingly successful biscuit-based lemon meringue pie, its tart concentration amply matched by fragrant basil sorbet.

Chef Matthew Tomkinson **Seats** 60, Private dining room 32 **Times** 12–2/ 7–9, Closed Monday, L Tuesday **Prices** Set L 2 course £25-£32.50, Set L 3 course £30-£37.50, Starter £15–£20, Main £30–£35, Dessert £15–£20, Sunday lunch £32.50–£37.50, A la carte dinner 3 course £70, Signature 7 course £90, Tasting Surprise 5 course £80, **Wines** 500 bottles over £30, 10 bottles under £30, 15 by glass **Parking** 50 **Notes** Vegetarian tasting menu, Vegetarian available, Children 12 years + at dinner

BROCKENHURST
Cambium
MAP 5 SU30

◉◉◉ Modern British ♥

01590 623551 | Careys Manor Hotel & SenSpa, Lyndhurst Road, SO42 7RH
www.careysmanor.com/cambium

Refined, contemporary dining in stylish spa hotel

Thoroughly rooted into the New Forest since Victorian times, Careys Manor has grown organically to encompass a luxurious spa to soothe the soul, and three dining options to tickle the palate. The cream of the crop is Cambium (named for the rings that indicate the age of a tree, since you ask), a classy, contemporary restaurant with a serene mood, easy-on-the-eye tones of cream and mossy green, and oak leaf screens and tree motifs inspired by the forest setting. Headed up by executive chef Alistair Craig, the dynamic team in the kitchen let loose their culinary wizardry on the regional larder to create a modern repertoire combining classic flavour combinations with up-to-date techniques. Rabbit terrine sounds a mainstream enough starter, but here it is helped along by grilled pineapple and tarragon granita, before another bright, contemporary idea brings the sweet, natural flavour of crab pointed up with crisp apple, nasturtium root and radish. On the more robust end of the spectrum, perfectly cooked haunch of venison is plated with a meat-packed pithivier, red cabbage and swede. There's refinement all the way through to a dessert showcasing rhubarb (parfait, pressed and gel) creatively partnered by ginger oat crunch and tonka bean ice cream.

Chef Alistair Craig **Seats** 94, Private dining room 40 **Times** 7–9.30, Closed Sunday, L Monday to Saturday **Prices** Set D 2 course £40, Set D 3 course £49, Tasting menu 6 course £65 **Wines** 43 bottles over £30, 13 bottles under £30, 12 by glass **Parking** 83 **Notes** Vegetarian available, Children 8 years +

Hampshire

36 on the Quay

MAP 6 SU70

◉◉◉ Modern British, European

01243 375592 | 47 South Street, PO10 7EG

www.36onthequay.co.uk

High-impact modern cooking on the harbourside

Long-time owners Ramon and Karen Farthing have recently established a new partnership at 36, with Gary and Martina Pearce assuming the running of day-to-day operations at their restaurant-with-rooms on the harbourside of a tranquil Hampshire fishing village. It's a wonderful spot, best enjoyed by starting with a drink in the courtyard, before heading inside to the bright, light-toned dining room.

Gary Pearce's cooking maintains the reputation of the place for carefully crafted modern cuisine that achieves memorable impact. That's certainly the case in an opener of duck pastrami with duck liver parfait, with a little side-serving of truffle-mayonnaised duck sandwich on pumpernickel bread, while main course could be John Dory in a coating of pumpkin seeds and sage, adorned with fresh crab and some pumpkin purée, in light chicken jus, or perhaps seared veal loin and cauliflower cheese made with Hampshire's very own Tunworth, garnished with a crisp-fried veal kidney, turnip tops and pine oil.

The finishing flourish sees spiced figs sweetened with caramelised white chocolate, served with crème fraîche ice cream and richly cinnamoned pain perdu, or will have you reaching for your Larousse to look up the kouign-amann (it's a crusty Breton cake of bread dough) that comes with roasted pear and egg nog parfait.

Chefs Ramon Farthing, Gary Pearce **Seats** 45, Private dining room 12 **Times** 12–2/7–9.30, Closed 25–26 December, 1st 2 or 3 weeks in January, 1 week at end of May, 1 week at end of October, Sunday and Monday **Prices** Set L 2 course £23.95, Set L 3 course £28.95, Set D 2 course £47.95, Set D 3 course £57.95, Tasting menu £29.95–£65 **Wines** 61 bottles over £30, 5 bottles under £30, 8 by glass **Parking** Car park nearby **Notes** Tasting menu (lunch and dinner) for complete tables only, A la carte menu available, Vegetarian available, Children welcome

The Elderflower Restaurant

MAP 5 SZ39

@@@ Modern British, French
01590 676908 | 4A Quay Street, SO41 3AS
www.elderflowerrestaurant.co.uk

Exciting modern dishes near the quayside

A moment's stroll from the quay at Lymington, The Elderflower is a traditional-looking double-fronted restaurant in the old part of town, opened in 2014 by Andrew and Marjolaine Du Bourg, a partnership with its entwined roots in Yorkshire and the Charente. Low-beamed ceilings and smartly linened tables establish a sympathetic ambience within, and Andrew's menus, honed by valuable experience in many of London's premier addresses, are overflowing with intelligence and enthusiasm.

There's something earthy and rootsy about his chunky beef terrine, for all that it comes with the inspired touch of a Brownsea Island oyster and anchovy straws, while main course could be an exciting assemblage of roast Barbary duck with cured duck ham, golden beetroot and a dramatic polenta bedazzled with violet mustard, in an aromatic jus of peach and lavender. In December, a clever menu take on the Twelve Days of Christmas comes into play, with queen scallops standing in for the swimming swans.

Desserts designed like ornamental conversation pieces are all the rage, so expect an intricately textured chocolate creation to arrive in a seashell on a wooden base, while the reinvention of trifle continues apace, when a properly boozy version comes replete with damsons, greengages and orange custard.

Chef Andrew Du Bourg **Seats** 40 **Times** 12–2.30/6.30–9.30, Closed Monday, D Sunday **Prices** Starter £8–£9.50, Main £21–£25.50, Dessert £8.50–£9.50, Market tapas dishes £3.50-£8, Sunday lunch £21–£30.50 **Wines** 65 bottles over £30, 52 bottles under £30, 7 by glass **Parking** Quay car park **Notes** Sunday champagne breakfast, Vegetarian available, Children 8 years +

Hampshire

LYNDHURST

Hartnett Holder & Co

MAP 5 SU30

◎◎◎ Italian **V** ♟

023 8028 7177 | Lime Wood, Beaulieu Road, SO43 7FZ

www.limewood.co.uk

Italian family cooking in a sophisticated New Forest hotel

If you go down to the woods today, the New Forest to be precise, you could hardly do better than to find this beautifully renovated Regency manor house built on the site of a 13th-century hunting lodge, imaginatively reinvented as a modern country bolt hole. As you'd hope for in a distinctly new-wave country hotel, Lime Wood's interiors are replete with luxurious touches created with great panache by in-demand designers David Collins and Martin Brudnizki, the expansive dining room all burgundy leather and parquet, the walls crowded with artworks, with seductive views over the grounds and water features, and any hint of stuffiness or whispered reverence has been kicked into touch in favour of an unbuttoned attitude to service.

With gorgeous bedrooms, cottages in the forest, extensive grounds (with a smokehouse adding its output to the kitchen's arsenal) and a posh spa, guests have little reason to leave the hotel, especially when the restaurant, an eye-catching room with button-back leather seats, is a collaboration between Angela Hartnett, she of Murano and telly celeb fame, and Lime Wood's own head chef, Luke Holder. This productive partnership comes up trumps with some impeccable, thoughtfully composed cooking that spotlights produce from the gardens, forest, local

farmers, and slitheringly fresh south coast seafood. Hartnett's fuss-free Italian signature is stamped all over the food, so it seems only right that you should go about things the Italian way and make room for the full four-course format, starting with splendid antipasti such as barbecued ox tongue with walnut sauce and crispy navaretti, or grilled red mullet with Sicilian-style aubergine and basil. The primi section delivers pasta out of the top drawer – the likes of cavatelli as a base for Dorset cockles, parsley, chilli and lemon, or a full-blooded hare lasagne pointed up with truffle and taleggio cheese. None of this is groundbreaking – it's just top-class materials treated with respect and authentic flair, and the good ideas keep on coming at main-course stage, perhaps partnering Norfolk quail with fennel sausage and spicy nduja ragout beneath a bread crust, or setting monkfish in colourful palate-tingling contrast with romano red peppers, anchovy, basil and mint.

Wrap things up with alluring desserts such as pannacotta with blood orange and Campari, or luscious chocolate and hazelnut tart offset with crème fraîche. Bargain hunters should pop by for the commendable value of the two-course set lunch menu. An antique wooden table in the kitchen seats up to 10 for those who'd like to get up close with the team at work.

Chefs Angela Hartnett, Luke Holder **Seats** 70, Private dining room 16
Times 12–11 **Prices** Set L 2 course £19.50 (3 course £25), Tasting menu £55, Starter £8.50–£14.50, Main £9–£50, Dessert £7–£16, Sunday lunch £37.50, Tavolo Della Cucina 5 course £65 **Wines** 609 bottles over £30, 31 bottles under £30, 14 by glass **Parking** 90 **Notes** Children welcome

See advert on page 90

HARTNETT HOLDER & CO

Book online at www.hhandco.co.uk
T: 023 8028 7177

ALL DAY ITALIAN DINING – MIDDAY TO LATE

Lime Wood, Beaulieu Rd, Lyndhurst, New Forest, Hampshire. SO43 7FZ

PETERSFIELD

JSW

MAP 6 SU72

@@@ Modern British V ♥
01730 262030 | 20 Dragon Street, GU31 4JJ
www.jswrestaurant.com

Dynamic contemporary cooking in a made-over old inn

The chef-proprietor's initials provide the name for this relaxed restaurant in an immaculately whitewashed 17th-century former coaching inn. Jake Saul Watkins is a Hampshire man born and bred who has been cooking up a storm in Petersfield for 18 years. The dining room has heaps of character: venerable oak beams and an understated contemporary decor – neutral hues and generously-sized tables dressed in pristine linen.

This is a chef who cooks with a passion for his craft, starting with the best materials he can lay his hands on, and a belief in keeping things simple, underpinned, naturally, by virtuoso technique and an innate feel for what works together on the plate. Whether you go for the carte, or splurge on the six- or eight-course tasting menus, everything is made in-house with top-level skills. Fish and seafood are a strong suit – perhaps sea-fresh scallops, timed to perfection and partnered with lightly curried mussels and borage. Next up, fallow deer might come with shallot tart, hay-baked parsnip and coffee sauce. Dessert brings a clever reworking of an old favourite, matching baked English custard with rhubarb, ginger beer jelly and gingerbread.

Chef Jake Watkins **Seats** 58, Private dining room 18 **Times** 12–1.30/7–9.30, Closed 2 weeks in January, 2 weeks in May, 2 weeks in summer, Sunday to Tuesday, L Wednesday **Prices** Set L 2 course £35 (3 course £45), Set D 2 course £45 (3 course £55), A la carte 2/3 course £35/£55, Tasting menu 6/8 course £50–£90 **Wines** 385 bottles over £30, 30 bottles under £30, 9 by glass **Parking** 19 **Notes** Children 6 years +

WINCHESTER

Avenue Restaurant at Lainston House Hotel

MAP 5 SU43

Modern British V ♥
01962 776088 | Woodman Lane, Sparsholt, SO21 2LT
www.lainstonhouse.com

Modern cooking in 17th-century country-house hotel

As we went to press the Rosette award was suspended due to a change of chef – reassessment will take place in due course.

The restaurant at this 17th-century former hunting lodge in 63 bucolic acres outside of Winchester gets its name from an impressive mile-long avenue of lime trees in the grounds. The house itself is a delicious red brick affair and its main dining room has plenty of period charm (and a

continued

view of that avenue of lime trees), with rich burgundy leather chairs and tables dressed up in pristine white linen. Four acres of the estate is given over to a kitchen garden to keep the Avenue Restaurant supplied with seasonal goodies.

Seats 60, Private dining room 120 **Times** 12–2/7–9, Closed 25–26 December, L Saturday, Monday and Tuesday, D 24 December **Prices** Set L 2 course £26, Set L 3 course £32.50, Set D 2 course £48, Set D 3 course £58, Starter £6.50–£10, Main £19.50–£28, Dessert £6.50–£10, Afternoon tea £29.50, **Wines** 120 bottles over £30, 30 bottles under £30, 9 by glass **Parking** 100 **Notes** Sunday lunch, Children welcome

▶ Hertfordshire

CHANDLER'S CROSS
Colette's at The Grove   MAP 6 TQ09
◉◉◉ Modern European V ♀
01923 807807 | WD3 4TG
www.thegrove.co.uk
Avante-garde cooking on a grand country estate

Occupying a grand Georgian mansion built for the Earls of Clarendon in 300 acres of prime Hertfordshire countryside, The Grove has all the bases covered for aficionados of the 21st-century luxury country hotel experience. That means a championship golf course, spa pampering and sleek old-meets-new decor – there's even an urban beach in a walled garden. The trio of dining options peaks in Colette's, where Russell Bateman's avante-garde culinary stylings are given free rein. Bateman has served time with some of the big hitters of contemporary Anglo-French gastronomy – Gordon Ramsay, Marc Veyrat and Marcus Wareing – and he's on a mission to dazzle. It all starts with the raw materials of course, many from the estate's organic walled garden. A starter of diver-caught scallops is offset with the flavours of pickled celeriac, toasted hazelnuts and brown butter hollandaise, or the richness of foie gras might be leavened by ginger beer, poached apple and brioche. Main course focuses on the sheer quality of roast brill, which arrives in a picturesque medley with butternut squash purée, rich mushroom duxelle, chicken wings and roasting juices. Dessert brings another expertly worked interplay of texture and flavour, matching tonka bean pannacotta with chestnut foam, chocolate cannelloni, vanilla sorbet and a buckwheat cracker.

Chef Russell Bateman **Seats** 44 **Times** 12–2.30/6.30–9.30, Closed Monday (except bank holidays), L Monday to Saturday **Prices** Set L

3 course £55, Set D 2 course £50, Set D 3 course £65, Tasting menu £85, Sunday lunch £55 **Wines** 8 bottles over £30, 4 bottles under £30, 24 by glass **Parking** 300 **Notes** 7-course vegetarian tasting menu

ST ALBANS
THOMPSON St Albans
MAP 6 TL10

@@@ Modern British **V**

See page 94

▶ Kent

BIDDENDEN
The West House
MAP 7 TQ83

@@@ Modern European **V**

01580 291341 | 28 High Street, TN27 8AH

www.thewesthouserestaurant.co.uk

Vanguard cooking in a charming Kentish village

Graham and Jackie Garrett's low-key restaurant in a beamed and tile-fronted 16th-century Flemish weaver's cottage on the high street looks every inch the old-school Kentish idyll, but is very much a 21st-century operation. Graham has served time in top kitchens, and has done some TV cheffery, but he's happiest at the stoves, relentlessly wringing every molecule of flavour from a larder stocked with impeccable local and seasonal materials. It's the sort of technically savvy cooking that deploys cutting-edge methods to achieve masterful balance of texture and flavour, taking a theme of ham and egg, say, to produce poached egg with Iberico ham dressing, brown butter sabayon and crispy kale, or matching roast, puréed and crisp Jerusalem artichoke with sherry vinegar, chestnut and nitro foie gras. Flavours are sharply judged in main courses too — perhaps roast duck with salt-baked celeriac, braised red cabbage and apple, while fish might appear as monkfish cheek with tandoori cauliflower and mussel masala. Desserts maintain the creative edge – perhaps a fun take on the 'Crunchie' theme comprising white chocolate and honeycomb parfait with dark chocolate sorbet.

Chefs Graham Garrett, Tony Parkin **Seats** 32 **Times** 12–2/7–9.30, Closed 24 to 26 December, 1 January, Monday, L Saturday, D Sunday **Prices** Set L 3 course from £25, Set D 3 course from £45, Tasting menu 6 course from £60 **Wines** 54 bottles over £30, 28 bottles under £30, 22 by glass **Parking** 7 **Notes** Sunday lunch, Children welcome

Hertfordshire

THOMPSON St Albans

MAP 6 TL10

◉◉◉ Modern British **V**

01727 730777 | 2 Hatfield Road, AL1 3RP

www.thompsonstalbans.co.uk

Classy contemporary cooking with interesting combinations

Now in his fifth year with his name above the door of the restaurant, Phil Thompson's cooking has really found its groove. Housed in a row of weatherboarded cottages in the centre of town, the newly made over dining room looks the part in restrained shades of grey, with local artworks hanging on the walls and a stylish contemporary finish. Thompson's output is underpinned by sound classical technique and is all about vivid modern British combinations, with top-notch ingredients sourced diligently from around the UK steadfastly providing a sound foundation, and it's all delivered in storming-value set menus alongside the carte, and the de rigueur tasting menu.

Dishes arrive at the table looking just the ticket, as seen in an inspired starter showcasing red-legged partridge, its breast in a pie of spinach and golden pastry, the leg pointed up with rich gamey jus and partnered with roast and pickled beetroot, sorrel and a punchy ketchup, or a dish involving Cornish mackerel and smoked eel combined with salt-baked beetroot and the clean flavours of crème fraîche, sorrel and horseradish. Next up, roast fillet of sea bass comes with roasted ceps, mushroom purée, onions (crispy rings, pickled and smoked), plus crispy pork and red wine jus to bring it all together. Meat cookery also shows a finely tuned

sense of what works with what – perhaps braised neck and slow-roasted loin of lamb partnered peas, fresh curd and mint, while two might take on a gargantuan Chateaubriand of 40-day-aged Dedham Vale beef served with smoked shallot dauphinoise potato, wild garlic, morels and Caesar salad. Desserts continue to confidently push the right buttons with a well-conceived combo of crème caramel with Calvados-poached apple, apple gel, shortbread and blackberry providing an interesting contrast, or there may be a masterful exercise in textures – gingerbread parfait alongside beurre noisette and thyme roasted pear, toasted pine nut and pear sorbet.

Peripherals all pass muster too, whether it's the light and fluffy onion seed bread, a detailed little amuse of Jerusalem artichoke foam, pickled onion mascarpone, chives, potato puffs and truffle oil, or a palate-sharpening pre-dessert of natural Greek yogurt, mandarin mousse and pomegranate. Veggie versions of the taster and à la carte, plus a children's menu, a Sunday roast special menu and keenly priced mid-week lunch deals broaden the appeal.

Chef Phil Thompson **Seats** 90, Private dining room 50 **Times** 12–2/6–9, Closed Monday, L Tuesday, D Sunday **Prices** Set L 2 course from £18.50 (3 course from £23), Set D 2 course from £21 (3 course from £25), Tasting menu from £59.50, Starter £10.50–£14.50, Main £26–£35, Dessert £8.50–£12, Sunday lunch £25–£29.50, Tuesday to Thursday 4 course with canapes and prosecco £35, Special lunch 3 course with 2 glasses of wine £29.50 **Wines** 36 bottles over £30, 21 bottles under £30, 15 by glass **Parking** 0.25 mile **Notes** Children welcome

See advert on page 96

Mid-Week Dining

THOMPSON
St Albans

Luncheon

2 Course Set Lunch Menu £18.50

3 Course Set Lunch Menu £23.00

Main Course, Side & Beverage £14.50

Ladies That Lunch Package £35.00
Available Wednesday to Saturday

Evening Dining

2 Course Set Evening Menu £21.00

3 Course Set Evening Menu £25.00

Mid-Week Date Night Package £35.00
Available Tuesday to Thursday

Conservatory & Terrace Dining Availability

f *thompsondining*
y *@thompsondining*
o *thompsondining*
www.thompsonstalbans.co.uk

TUNBRIDGE WELLS (ROYAL)

Thackeray's

MAP 7 TQ53

◉◉◉ Modern European **V** ♟
01892 511921 | 85 London Road, TN1 1EA
www.thackerays-restaurant.co.uk

Glossy modern European cooking at the novelist's home

The white-weatherboarded house facing the common dates from around 1660, and this stylish restaurant's name pays due homage to the time when it was home to the eponymous Victorian author of *Vanity Fair*. There's plenty of period charisma in the main dining room, where leafy designer wallpaper dovetails with smartly clothed tables and understated modern looks.

The chefs pride themselves on sourcing top-quality raw materials from local counties and deploy them intelligently and imaginatively, mixing influences in true modern European style. Seriously appealing dishes might start with duck liver parfait and smoked duck breast, matched appropriately with Earl Grey-infused prunes, bergamot and orange-braised chicory. They may sound complex, but sound culinary judgement ensures all elements work together in main courses too, perhaps sea bass with open ravioli of squid ragù, roast and tempura cauliflower, fennel à la Grecque and shellfish bisque. Meat-wise, the big guns might be deployed for a dish of roasted beef fillet and braised ox cheek with potato purée, veal sweetbread, chestnut mushrooms, baby onions and honey-glazed parsnip.

Moving on to the finale, dishes once again make an impact on the eye as well as on the palate, whether it's a reworked Black Forest theme involving Kirsch parfait, pistachio cake, chocolate bark and cherry sorbet, or a perfectly risen apple and cinnamon soufflé.

Chefs Richard Phillips, Shane Hughes, Pat Hill **Seats** 70, Private dining room 16 **Times** 12–2.30/6.30–10.30, Closed Monday, D Sunday **Prices** Set L 2 course from £18, Set L 3 course from £20, Set D 3 course from £55, Tasting menu from £88, Sunday lunch from £35 **Wines** 140 bottles over £30, 17 bottles under £30, 20 by glass **Parking** NCP, On street in evening **Notes** Children welcome

Lancashire

Northcote

MAP 15 SD73

◎◎◎◎ Modern British V ♟
01254 240555 | Northcote Road, BB6 8BE
www.northcote.com

Lancashire manor house with global modernist cooking

The Ribble Valley north of Blackburn is the location of Northcote, an area
that shows rural Lancashire at its most soft-focus, all woodland paths and
centuries-old villages, on the fringe of which stands the Victorian manor
house that is home to Nigel Haworth's flagship. The place has always
aspired to the elevated tone of a classic country house, but successive
decorations and development in recent years have achieved a seductive
blend of traditional and modern. There are deft design touches
everywhere, from a bar that feels a little like a stylish members' club to the
handsome extended dining room, where the natural colour tones of wood
and foliage, near-abstract contemporary landscape paintings and an icicle
chandelier, make for a thoroughly relaxing setting and French windows
look out on to the tree-framed terrace.

Northcote has always been a team effort, and very much remains one
under the triumvirate of Haworth, his general manager and wine man
Craig Bancroft, and executive head chef Lisa Goodwin-Allen. When
Northcote arrived on the scene, few people took seriously the idea that
Lancashire could be a focal point not only for aspirational dining, but in a
style to boot that was founded to a great extent on its own regional food
specialities. Wasn't it the home of black pudding, crumbly cheese and fish

and chips? Well, yes, but who's complaining about those now? If the Lancashire accent has grown fainter with the passing years, that reflects the enormously acquisitive impetus there is in modern British cooking, which might happily source its materials locally, but thinks and invents with a map of the whole world at its disposal. So turn up for Sunday lunch at Northcote, and expect beetroot, shallots and horseradish for sure, followed by roast beef and spuds with Yorkshire pudding, but don't be surprised to see crisp-fried squid and tempura prawns with aïoli and basil oil too, or roast salmon with shiitake mushrooms in soy.

On the carte, imagination is given full flight, with thought-provoking combinations of the recherché and the familiar: white beetroot and coconut textures with white chocolate could almost be a modern dessert until its Daurenki caviar is added, while aged wagyu beef tartare comes with a clump of sticky rice. Venison and kohlrabi might be subjected to a distinctly Mexican note with liquorice mole, and an intense savouriness from winter mushroom ragout and caper jam brings out the best in a wing of skate done in the wood-fired oven. For puddings, the kitchen returns to its roots with ginger sponge and caramel custard, or an unforgettably zesty take on lemon meringue pie, while avant-gardists look to a Valrhona chocolate cylinder with smoked nuts and salted sheep's milk ice cream.

Chefs Lisa Goodwin-Allen, Nigel Haworth **Seats** 70, Private dining room 60 **Times** 12–2/7–9.30, Closed Food and Wine Festival **Prices** Set L 3 course from £33, Tasting menu £90, Starter from £12.50, Main from £26, Dessert from £12.50, Sunday lunch from £45 **Wines** 359 bottles over £30, 31 bottles under £30, 12 by glass **Parking** 60 **Notes** Children welcome

Lancashire

ORMSKIRK
Moor Hall Restaurant with Rooms
MAP 15 SD40

◉◉◉ Modern British
01695 572511 | Prescot Road, Aughton, L39 6RT
www.moorhall.com

Once upon a time, a typical 'restaurant with rooms' consisted of a few simple rooms bolted onto a notable eatery to allow diners to stop over. The approach at Moor Hall is rather more evolved: a megabucks boutique transformation of a 16th-century manor with a chic restaurant and state-of-the-art open kitchen in a modernist barn-style extension. The culinary draw is the showstopping cooking of Mark Birchall, whose time at Simon Rogan's L'Enclume means you can expect virtuoso creations built on prime produce. The drill at dinner is five- and eight-course tasters, opening with home-grown carrots served in multifarious textures boosted with Doddington cheese 'snow', ramsons and sea buckthorn cream, ahead of crab and turnip broth with anise leaves, hyssop and sunflower seed cream. Elsewhere, monkfish is roasted on the bone and matched with garlic and mussel cream, salsify and sea vegetables, while another complex idea showcases Westmorland chicken, the roasted oysters, breast and crispy skin alongside hen of the woods mushrooms, kale in ham fat, and whey cream. Desserts, too, are shot through with creativity: perhaps stem ginger ice cream with candied parsnips and brown sugar tuiles.

Chef Mark Birchall **Times** Closed Monday and Tuesday

WHALLEY
The Freemasons at Wiswell
MAP 15 SD73

◉◉◉ Modern British **V** 🏆
See page 103

▶ Lincolnshire

GRANTHAM
Harry's Place
MAP 11 SK83

◉◉◉ Modern French
01476 561780 | 17 High Street, Great Gonerby, NG31 8JS
Outstanding quality in a restaurant built for ten

The Hallams went for a one-off formula when they opened here about 30 years ago and they have quite rightly stuck to their guns. Things don't get more intimate than the red-walled dining room where 10 guests at three tables are treated to a haven of civilised hospitality, with Caroline seeing that all is well out front and Harry strutting his classically-based stuff in the kitchen. The menu format is as compact as the venue, a daily-changing drill of two choices at each stage, opening with perhaps lightly-seared Orkney scallops with a spiced marinade and julienned orange and red peppers. Harry doesn't faff about with foams, gels and the like, but he's a dab hand with alcohol-fuelled sauces and dressings, as may be seen in mains, when red wine, Armagnac, rosemary, thyme and tarragon might bring to life a dish of Lincoln Red beef fillet with red cabbage, onion, apple, blueberries and horseradish mayonnaise. Finish with the signature cherry brandy jelly with yogurt and black pepper. Booking in advance is a must, especially at weekends.

Chef Harry Hallam **Seats** 10 **Times** 12.30–3/7–9, Closed 2 weeks from 25 December, 2 weeks in August, Sunday and Monday **Prices** Starter £9.50–£22.50, Main £39.50, Dessert £8 **Wines** 19 bottles over £30, 2 bottles under £30, 4 by glass **Parking** 4 **Notes** Vegetarian available, vegetarian meals should be requested when booking, Children 5 years +

WINTERINGHAM
Winteringham Fields
MAP 17 SE92

◉◉◉◉ Modern British, European ☙
01724 733096 | 1 Silver Street, DN15 9ND
www.winteringhamfields.co.uk
Thrilling cooking on the Humber estuary

In an out-of-the-way corner of Lincolnshire near the Humber estuary, chef-patron Colin McGurran's endless pursuit of culinary excellence has established Winteringham Fields as a fixture on any self-respecting foodie's bucket list. Of course, it all starts with the raw materials, and this delectable place has its own farm to ensure that the supply lines are always open to seasonal supplies, and what doesn't come from Winteringham's fertile soil is sourced meticulously from suppliers within a one-mile radius. Done out with an eclectic mix of natural textures, quirky elements and luxurious touches, the restaurant has switched-on staff who keep it all ticking over with professional aplomb. The evening offers up two 'Surprise' menus of seven or nine courses. An opener might be an eye-opening presentation of tomato gazpacho delivered with a bracing wholegrain mustard ice cream to kickstart the tastebuds, then things progress on a fun-packed rollercoaster ride through gastronomic revelation and brilliant technical accomplishment. One idea might see candied beetroot and potato winter salad with gherkins, chorizo and sauce fondue; another could star pan-roasted wild sea bream in a pork crackling crust alongside ratatouille, prawn and red pepper sauce, saffron rouille and ponzu gel. It's all supremely creative stuff, all the way to a knockout finale of unctuous Brillat Savarin cheesecake with Amaretto-marinated pear, pear and grappa sorbet and white chocolate.

Chef Colin McGurran **Seats** 60, Private dining room 12 **Times** 12–1.30/7–9, Closed 2 weeks at Christmas, last 2 weeks in August, Sunday and Monday **Prices** Lunch 4 course £45, Tasting menu £75–£85 **Wines** 316 bottles over £30, 4 bottles under £30, 20 by glass **Parking** 20 **Notes** Vegetarian available, Children welcome

AA Awards

AA Restaurant of the Year for England 2017–18

The Freemasons at Wiswell

MAP 15 SD73

◉◉◉ Modern British V ♈
01254 822218 | 8 Vicarage Fold, Wiswell, BB7 9DF
www.freemasonswiswell.co.uk

Exciting virtuoso cooking in a relaxed village inn

This chocolate-box village in the Ribble Valley is firmly established on the foodie map thanks to the high-flying cooking of chef-patron Steven Smith. Converted from a trio of little cottages, the place successfully pulls off the dual functions of a proper pub and a dining hot spot with a welcoming, convivial atmosphere, and decked out with antiques, rugs on the floor, an open fire and even a stag's head. Steven Smith worked in some of the North's top kitchens before going solo, so he knows exactly how to use Lancashire's finest produce as the basis for inventive, technically-accomplished dishes.

Slow-cooked cheek and crispy belly of suckling pig might be the focus of a starter that delivers real wow factor, particularly when matched with black pudding, baked sweet potato, rhubarb and hoi sin sauce, or you might get things going with a rib-sticking oxtail pie baked in brioche and accompanied by a crispy Colchester oyster and a muscular sauce of dark beer and truffle. Main course could star venison, but not just any old deer: salt-aged and smoked over pine, it comes with loin tartare, parsnips, apple purée, Stilton and a sturdy Grand Huntsman sauce. Fish might appear as roast loin of cod with squid risotto, Jerusalem artichoke, hazelnuts, chorizo and yuzu, or something as uncomplicated as catch of the day simply grilled with lemon and brown butter and served with potted shrimps and chips. Nothing here aims to be revolutionary – it's all about top-class materials treated with care and precision, through to a dessert showcasing Michel Cluizel's unctuous chocolate matched with pineapple poached in Pedro Ximenez caramel, rum, raisin and passionfruit, and coconut ice cream. If you really want to put the kitchen through its paces, there's a six-course tasting menu.

Chefs Steven Smith, Matthew Smith **Seats** 70, Private dining room 14 **Times** 12–2.30/5.30–9, Closed from 2 January for 2 weeks, Monday and Tuesday **Prices** Set L 2 course £20, Set L 3 course £25, Set D 2 course £20, Set D 3 course £25, Tasting menu £70, Starter £9.95–£16.95, Main £19.95–£38, Dessert £9.95–£12.95, Sunday lunch £29.95 **Wines** 108 bottles over £30, 56 bottles under £30, 30 by glass **Parking** In village **Notes** Children welcome

London Plan 1

Restaurants with 3, 4 or 5 Rosettes in the London and the Greater London area are shown by name on London plans 1–6 (pages 104–115) and their full entries are listed in postal district order on pages 116–186. Each

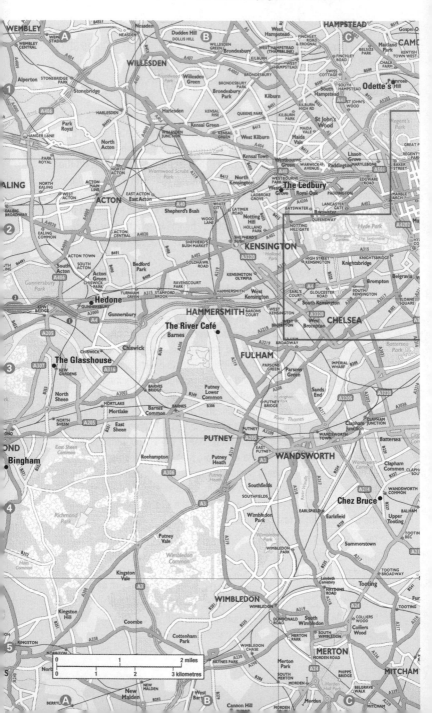

London entry in the guide includes a plan grid reference so you can easily locate the restaurant you need. You can also confirm the location by searching at www.theaa.com/restaurants

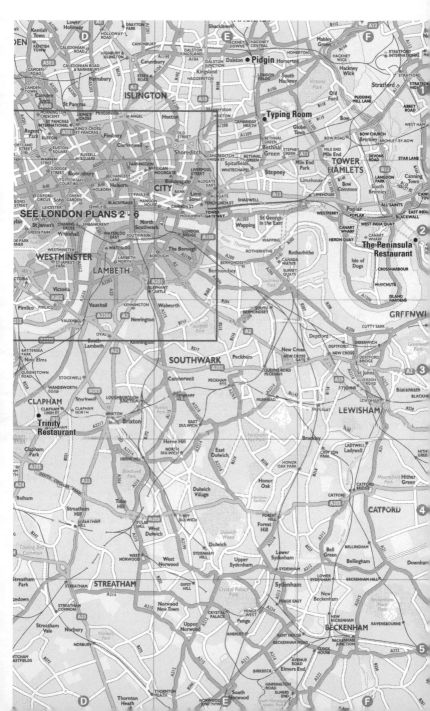

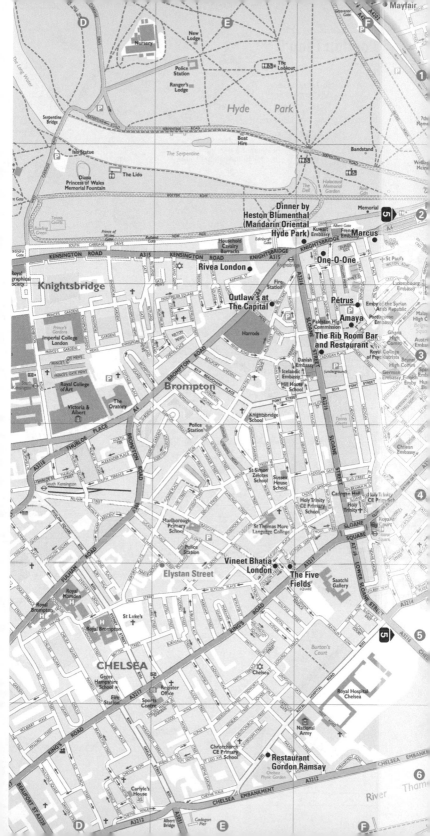

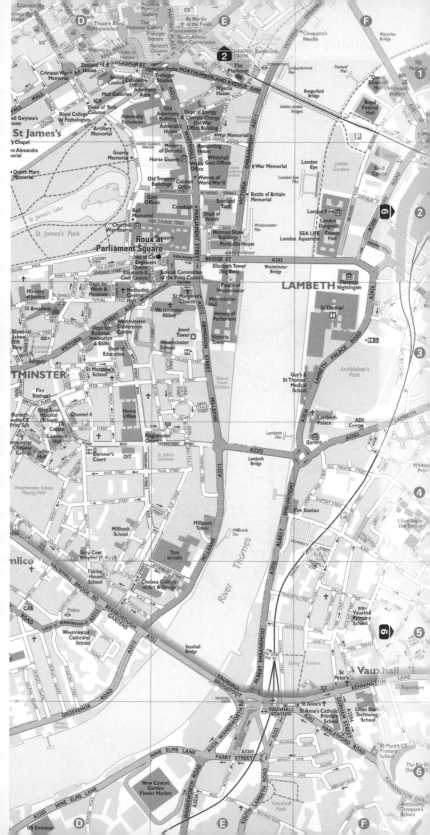

LONDON E1

The Frog Restaurant

PLAN 3 F3

@@@ Modern British, Tapas V

020 3813 9832 | 2 Ely's Yard, Old Truman Brewery, Hanbury Street, E1 6QR

www.thefrogrestaurant.com

Ambition and invention in boho surrounds

In the former Truman Brewery yard in trendy Spitalfields, The Frog's back-to-basics dining room suits its zealous showcasing of young British culinary creativity. The look is industrial and stripped-back, with the de rigueur open kitchen, edgy young artists' work, and a covered area bedecked with foliage. The casual, boho approach is pitch perfect for the hip local crew, and extends to the 'British tapas' menu that entreats diners to 'eat with your hands'. Adam Handling likes his techno kit, and lets rip in exciting cooking fizzing with ambition and creativity, witness finely honed miniature 'snacks' of dinky cannoli filled with smoked cod, crème fraîche and caviar, or punchy little crackers of barbecue beef, chilli and lovage. Another cracking idea sees wafer-thin celeriac encasing egg yolk, with high-impact notes from shredded apple, truffle dust and date, while top-class pork is plated with kimchi, roast and puréed cauliflower and herb oil. Desserts keep the vibrancy and striking flavours on tap, via the likes of a wicked chocolate tart with caramel and cherry dust.

Chef Adam Handling **Seats** 80 **Times** 12–3/5.30–10, Closed 25 December, Sunday and Monday **Prices** Starter £4–£6 Main £10–£15 Dessert £5–£12, Tasting menu £50–£55 **Wines** 35 bottles over £30, 3 bottles under £30, 24 by glass **Notes** Children welcome

Galvin La Chapelle

PLAN 3 F3

@@@ French, European V 🍷

See page 118

LONDON E2

Typing Room

PLAN 1 E1

@@@@ British, Modern European V 🍷

020 7871 0461 | Town Hall Hotel, Patriot Square, E2 9NF

www.typingroom.com

Concentrated creativity amid Edwardian municipal splendour

The old Bethnal Green town hall was built at the end of the Edwardian era, and is uniquely suited to have become a 21st-century hotel. The space where council memos were once hammered out on manual typewriters is now an independent dining room, designed along impeccable modern lines, including an open-to-view theatre kitchen with five evening shows a week and four lunch matinées. Time spent at international reference eateries Noma and Per Se, and productive periods under London maestros

Tom Aikens and Jason Atherton, have refined Lee Westcott's output to a rare pitch of concentrated creativity, and even where dishes look perfectly straightforward, they reveal unexpected depths of intensity from one mouthful to the next. That's certainly the case with an opening salad of Isle of Wight tomatoes, cobnuts and ricotta in chamomile oil and basil, the inspired element being a clutch of raspberries that enhance the tomatoes no end. At main, richly satisfying smoked eel is contrasted with chicken wings and radish in a golden onion consommé, while the game season brings on partridge served with a little sausage of its offals, offset with red cabbage, blackberry relish and sweet cipollini onions in a sturdy game reduction. To finish, there are fragrant desserts such as satin-smooth sheep's yogurt ice cream with apple and dill granita, or cleanly refreshing lemon sorbet with almond cream and salt caramel praline. Canapés are a parade of inventive delights, and bread service is as ingenious as the rest – a sourdough loaf comes with Marmite butter and crunchy barley seeds.

Chef Lee Westcott **Seats** 38 **Times** 12–2.15/6–10, Closed 24 December to 2 January, Sunday and Monday, L Tuesday and Wednesday
Prices Set L 2 course from £27, Set L 3 course from £32, Tasting menu from £65 **Wines** 350 bottles over £30, 24 by glass **Parking** Opposite
Notes Children welcome

LONDON E8
Pidgin
Pl AN 1 F1
◉◉◉ Japanese, Asian
020 7254 8311 | 52 Wilton Way, E8 1BG
www.pidginlondon.com
Thrilling creativity in deepest Hackney

Hidden away on a Hackney backstreet you wouldn't happen on this dinner-only restaurant by chance. The unassuming location – a compact, spartan space of stark white walls decorated with tree branches – seems an unlikely place to find a talented team turning out some radical, pin-sharp food, but there they are, cooking up a storm in a tiny semi-open kitchen like a ship's galley. Led by Dan Graham, the team is inventive with precise techniques and timing in weekly-changing set menus of intricate, Japanese-accented dishes that deliver complex layers of flavour from a sound foundation of high quality materials. An opener of pain perdu with sea urchin custard, corn juice purée and corn powder, smoked sour cream granita and samphire tempura typifies the subtle interplay of textures and flavours, as does lightly blowtorched smoked mackerel and with crisp rice, nettle oil, rice and dashi cream and fresh strawberries. A main of pork loin and belly arrives with roasted yeast, fermented swede, rösti and pomegranate. Close on a high with black sesame and Lapsang Souchong ice cream with charcoal meringue and blood orange textures.

Chef Dan Graham **Seats** 28 **Notes** For more details see Pidgin website

LONDON E1

Galvin La Chapelle

PLAN 3 F3

◉◉◉ French, European **V** ☻

020 7299 0400 | St Botolph's Hall, 35 Spital Square, E1 6DY

www.galvinrestaurants.com

Victorian school chapel with classic meets modern French cooking

Set amid the contemporary glass buildings on Spital Square, La Chapelle is a Spitalfields' top call, the converted red-brick former Victorian chapel of St Botolph's girls' school providing the brothers Galvin a standout destination that fits the bill when a special occasion venue is called for. You really couldn't get much further from the stripped-out industrial warehouse look that is par for the course in many restaurants in this neighbourhood: with its stone archways, marble pillars, arched windows and a roof open to the rafters some 30 metres up, the place is a real jaw-dropper. A shiny steel mezzanine level with glass balustrades strikes a slightly discordant 21st-century pose amid all the 19th-century pomp, but it's worth trying to bag a table up there for the chance to lord it above the dining room below. Throw in well-padded chocolate brown buttoned seats and banquettes at linen-swathed tables, a smart zinc-topped bar and semi-open kitchen, plus an army of attentive, well-drilled staff and you have friendly formality and a definite sense of occasion.

The cooking conforms to the Galvin genre: polished French cuisine underpinned by a classical base and given a light modern gloss. Top-notch produce, uncluttered, sophisticated, fine-tuned cooking is the raison d'être, and it all looks pretty on the plate too. A rich and opulent signature

starter of lasagne of Dorset crab boosts the luxury factor further with its accompanying shellfish bisque and sea herbs – that's if you can pass on the equally indulgent prospect of a pressing of French quail and Landes foie gras partnered by pomegranate and quail's egg. Polished main courses continue to maintain a finely judged balance between modernity and Gallic traditions, perhaps utilising Tokyo turnip and caramelised orange daikon purée as an Asian counterpoint to breast and faggot of Goosnargh duck à l'orange. Technical dexterity also distinguishes fish cookery: a superb slab of wild turbot might be matched with fennel purée, razor clams and a robust sauce Genevoise that's straight out of the Escoffier canon. Sticking with classic mode, you might round things off with a timeless dessert of perfectly caramelised apple tarte Tatin with Normandy crème fraîche, or poire belle Hélène with tonka bean ice cream and chocolate sauce. Nor are vegetarians sidelined: creative meat-free ideas could include textures of golden and ruby beetroot with walnuts, goats' curd and raspberry dressing, followed by a tajine of spring vegetables with couscous, confit lemon and fiery harissa sauce. Prices are deep-wallet, though a prix fixe menu keeps budgets on track. The wine list is a corker, with French big guns leading the way.

Chefs Jeff Galvin, Eric Jolibois **Seats** 110, Private dining room 16 **Times** 12–2.30/6–10.30, Closed 25–26 December and 1 January, D 24 December **Prices** Set L 2 course £29, Set L 3 course £34.50, Set D 2 course £29, Set D 3 course £34.50, Tasting menu 7 course £75, Starter £16.50–£24.50, Main £28.50–£39, Sunday lunch £29–£34.50 **Wines** 317 bottles over £30, 10 bottles under £30, 17 by glass **Parking** On street, NCP **Notes** Set price dinner 6-7 pm, Children welcome

Anglo

PLAN 3 B3

@@@ Modern British V
020 7430 1503 | 30 St Cross Street, EC1N 8UH
www.anglorestaurant.com

Dynamic contemporary cooking in unpretentious setting

The new order of fine dining is to chuck out the chintz and proffer an unpretentious attitude, to focus on the ingredients and to maximise flavour with various whizzy techniques. The guys behind Anglo do just that, in a simple room with a light modern feel, where the small service team are as professional and informed as they are youthfully exuberant. Some plates are brought to the table by the chefs. Owner Mark Jarvis is an experienced hand, having kicked off his career at Le Manoir over a decade ago, and head chef Jack Cashmore has Sat Bains on his impressive CV. They're turning out some eye-catching food, inspired by British produce – hence Anglo – and offered up via a lunchtime à la carte and tasting menus. Everything arrives looking beautiful on attractive crockery, and flavours hit home. Sea trout stars in an opening salvo with tender kombu (seaweed) and a punchy miso foam, followed by a superb Hebridean mutton number, with sweet fermented red cabbage, multiple ways with ceps and a juniper-flavoured yogurt. A sweet course of English apple and caramelised ricotta is no less technically accomplished. Dinner comes with an optional wine and beer pairing for each dish.

Chefs Mark Jarvis, Jack Cashmore **Seats** 32, Private dining room 8
Times 12.30–2.30/6.30–9.30, Closed 24 December to 3 January, bank holidays, Sunday, L Monday **Prices** Tasting menu 5/7 course £39–£45, Starter £9.50–£10.50, Main £18.50–£21.50, Dessert from £8 **Wines** 41 bottles over £30, 4 bottles under £30, 30 by glass **Notes** Vegetarian available

The Clove Club

PLAN 3 F2

@@@ Modern British V
020 7729 6496 | Shoreditch Town Hall, 380 Old Street, EC1V 9LT
www.thecloveclub.com

Magical culinary mystery tour in an old town hall

The grand old Shoreditch Town Hall retired from its local government career in the 1960s, and in step with the neighbourhood's 21st-century reboot as hipster central, the building now houses arts venues and this hyper-cool restaurant. The Clove Club is right at home in this setting with its casual vibe, chunky wooden floors and tables, and open-to-view kitchen pass which positively buzzes with activity. The place raised a few eyebrows when it introduced a pre-paid reservation system (lunch does not require such a commitment), but the cool crew still flock in for the carte, and five- or nine-course tasting menus (with meat-free versions).

What arrives is cutting-edge stuff, with unusual ingredients, off-the-wall combinations and eye-catching presentations that seem custom-designed for posting on social media sites. British ingredients loom large, starting with the devilled Lincolnshire chicken that arrives in little pancakes with crispy skin and mustard leaf, while raw scallop with hazelnuts, clementine and Wiltshire truffle is a compelling mix of flavours. A sublime meat course delivers oh-so-tender roast fallow deer with a dazzling combo of fermented red cabbage purée, beetroot and blackcurrant, while Amalfi lemonade and Kampot pepper ice cream is a thrilling finisher. If you're a lone diner or two-up, eating at the bar counter is on the cards.

Chefs Isaac McHale, Chase Lovecky **Seats** 70 **Times** 12–2.30/6–9.15, Closed 2 weeks at Christmas and New Year, Sunday, L Monday **Prices** Tasting menu 5/9 course £75–£220, Starter £10–£22, Main £18–£29, Dessert £8–£12 **Wines** 400 bottles over £30, 30 by glass **Notes** Children at lunch only

Club Gascon

PLAN 3 C4

@@@ French V ♥

020 7600 6144 | 57 West Smithfields, EC1A 9DS

www.clubgascon.com

Innovation and excitement from southwest France

Pascal Aussignac was in the vanguard of chefs who abandoned the traditional three-course format and embraced the now ubiquitous trend for small-plate dining. Two decades have gone by and his avant-garde take on the cooking of southwest France remains as vibrant and exciting as it ever was. Right by Smithfield Market in what was once the Lyons' teashop, the mothership of the ever-growing Gascon empire is a grand, high-ceilinged space of marble walls, oak floors, and blue banquettes at closely set tables. Aussignac may take his spiritual inspiration from his homeland's southwest, but this is highly-evolved, technical cooking that is a long way from the goose-fat and garlic peasant cuisine of its roots. The two-course set lunch is a snip, or trade up to the carte of tapas-sized dishes in five themed clusters. A selection could include almost mainstream cappuccino of black pudding, lobster and asparagus, to a more radical pairing of hare with cuttlefish and lobster 'sand'. Those in search of meaty delights might find Charolais beef variations with oxtail and caviar, while the duck department supplies the bird flamed with smoked pine and aromatic razor clams. The style continues into puddings such as chocolate crémeux with yogurt pearls, lime and beetroot crisps.

Chef Pascal Aussignac **Seats** 42 **Times** 12–2/6.30–10, Closed Christmas, New Year, bank holidays, Sunday, L Saturday **Prices** Set L 2 course £25, Set D 3 course £45, Tasting menu 5 course £80, Starter £10–£19.50, Main £21–£29, Dessert £9–£10 **Wines** 400 bottles over £30, 30 bottles under £30, 15 by glass **Parking** NCP opposite **Notes** Children welcome

Sosharu
PLAN 3 B3

@@@ Japanese

020 3805 2304 | 64 Turnmill Street, EC1M 5RR

www.sosharulondon.com

Jason Atherton's inspirational foray into Japanese cuisine

The 'social' tag (pronounced here in the Japanese fashion, in case the penny hadn't dropped) neatly links Jason Atherton's unique take on the Japanese izakaya-style restaurant and bar theme with most of his ever-expanding global restaurant portfolio. The traditional Japanese design influence is clear in the glossy, suitably minimalist aesthetic of the whole operation, and includes a cool basement cocktail bar that aims to capture the spirit of Tokyo by night. After a thorough grounding in stellar Japanese establishments, Alex Craciun is adept in Japanese culinary ways, and heads up the team of knife-wielding chefs who deliver exemplary sushi, sashimi and refined, highly-detailed dishes that offer plenty to keep Instagrammers busy. You might set out with blood orange-cured salmon with pungent tosazu jelly and buckwheat, or raw sea bream, rolled and filled with crispy potato shreds and pointed up with orange zest and wild garlic flowers. Next up, every detail makes sense in a sukiyaki hotpot of Wagyu beef that layers flavours of glass noodles, leeks and shiitaki mushrooms. To finish, green tea syrup is poured over shaved ice and matched with green tea ice cream and sweet red adzuki bean purée.

Chefs Alex Craciun, Jason Atherton **Seats** 74, Private dining room 6
Times 12–2.15/5.30–10, Closed Christmas, bank holidays, Sunday
Prices Set L 3 course from £17, Lunch 6 dishes to share £29.50, Tasting menu from £29.50, Starter from £6, Main from £12, Dessert from £4.50
Wines 110 bottles over £30, 11 bottles under £30, 13 by glass **Parking** On street **Notes** Vegetarian available, Children welcome

LONDON EC2

City Social
PLAN 3 E4

@@@ Modern British, European

020 7877 7703 | Tower 42, EC2N 1HQ

www.citysociallondon.com

Atherton's cooking with breathtaking City views

Ascend to the 24th floor of Tower 42 in the heart of the City, and be prepared to take in the heady views of London's new kitchen skyline, where the Gherkin and the Cheesegrater reach into the ether. It's a suitably breathtaking backdrop for one of Jason Atherton's modern urban restaurants. Paul Walsh, who did stints under Anton Edelmann at The Savoy and with Gordon Ramsay, brings authority and innovative impetus to the house style of classically founded cooking. The fashion for sharp contrasting flavours is celebrated in an opener of Brixham crab and

Scottish prawn teamed with pickled kohlrabi, pear, spring onion and sesame seeds, which might be the prelude to an elegant serving of duck in three guises – the breast, confit leg and heart – in a carrot reduction sauce with grilled leeks. Pasta and risotto dishes in two sizes, perhaps prawn and scallop tortellini in coriander-spiked lemongrass velouté, are an appealing feature, and desserts aim to seduce by means of banana parfait with caramelised banana, salt caramel ice cream, honeycomb and passionfruit, or perhaps a baba doused in Havana Club, Cuban golden rum, with pineapple carpaccio, mango and whipped cream.

Chefs Paul Walsh, Jason Atherton **Seats** 90, Private dining room 24 **Times** 12–2.30/6–10.30, Closed 25 December, 1 January and bank holidays, Sunday, L Saturday **Prices** Starter £5–£18, Main £24–£38, Dessert £9.50–£16 **Wines** 209 bottles over £30, 5 bottles under £30, 16 by glass **Parking** NCP (Finsbury Circus) **Notes** Tasting menu (chef's table), Vegetarian available, Children welcome

HKK

PLAN 3 E3

@@@ Modern Chinese V
020 3535 1888 | Broadgate West, 88 Worship Street, EC2A 2BE
www.hkklondon.com

First-class Chinese cooking in revitalised City

Part of the glossy Hakkasan stable, this new-wave Chinese cuts a dash with its minimalist, clean-lined looks – all comfy banquettes, black chairs with slate-blue cushions and a glass-walled kitchen. Chef Tong Chee Hwee's creative take on contemporary Chinese cooking comes up with some striking creations, reinventing old ideas with western twists and liberal use of up-to-date cooking techniques on a range of menus that include a multi-course tasting, with a vegetarian option. As you'd hope, it all relies on produce of outstanding quality, much of it organic and sourced from around the UK, and perhaps predictably, given the city-slicker location, the experience is not for those on a budget. Splash out on a tasting menu dinner, and you will encounter revelatory constructions along the lines of chrysanthemum fish maw soup with dry scallop, coconut, and chicken stock, moving on to steamed wild sea bass with glutinous rice wine, enoki mushrooms and XO sauce, or slow-cooked Dingley Dell pork belly matched with white asparagus, pear and kumquat foam, and white truffle sauce. Desserts pursue the fusion theme with ideas such as coconut cream with lychee granite and tapioca.

Chef Tong Chee Hwee **Seats** 63, Private dining room 14 **Times** 12–2.30/6–10, Closed Christmas and certain bank holidays, Sunday **Prices** Set L 3 course from £35, Tasting menu £58–£93.88, Starter £10.80–£15.80, Main £12–£21.80, Dessert from £8.90, Saturday lunch duck & champagne menu 5 course £49 **Wines** 16 bottles over £30, 4 bottles under £30, 22 by glass **Parking** NCP, On street **Notes** Children welcome

London EC2

Merchants Tavern

PLAN 3 E2

◉◉◉ Modern European
020 7060 5335 | 36 Charlotte Road, EC2A 3PG
www.merchantstavern.co.uk

Shoreditch warehouse with west European comfort food

Located in a converted Victorian warehouse just off Great Eastern Street, Angela Hartnett and Neil Borthwick's 'tavern' is a smartly accoutred modern eatery with bare brick walls, a parquet floor and circular seating bays. The culinary emphasis is a productive amalgamation of everybody's favourite bits of western Europe – essentially France, Spain and Italy – with charcuterie plates and toasted sandwiches to warm the cockles by a log fire in the bar, and a kitchen counter for chef-watchers. The main dining room deals in uncomplicated, but nonetheless imaginative, dishes of robust contemporary comfort food, of the likes of quail with foie gras and remoulade, dressed in hazelnut pesto and Treviso chutney, or a salad of violet artichoke, Swiss chard, pear and pecorino, to start, followed on by hearty main dishes such as braised cuttlefish with grilled polenta and fennel, or Saddleback pork belly on grain-mustardy lentils with pumpkin purée. Finish with profiteroles and pistachio ice cream, or a Seville orange steamed pudding with cream poured over it. Sunday lunches are a draw for lazy weekends, when roast beef with all the trimmings seems too much of a faff at home.

Chef Neil Borthwick **Seats** 104, Private dining room 22 **Times** 12–3/6–11, Closed 25–26 December, 1 January **Prices** Tasting menu £50–£100, Starter £7.50–£12, Main £17–£25, Dessert £6–£12, Sunday lunch £25–£30 **Wines** 61 bottles over £30, 7 bottles under £30, 22 by glass **Parking** NCP (Great Eastern Street) **Notes** Vegetarian available, Children welcome

The Gilbert Scott

PLAN 2 E1

◉◉◉ Modern British 🍷
020 7278 3888 | Renaissance St Pancras Hotel, Euston Road, NW1 2AR
www.thegilbertscott.com

Versatile cooking in Gilbert Scott's majestic St Pancras hotel

Back in 1873, the Midland (now the Renaissance) was arguably Britain's finest railway hotel when it opened as an amenity to St Pancras station. Now meticulously restored, it is once more a London landmark at the heart of the rejuvenated Kings Cross quarter. A masterpiece of Gothic Revival, from its magnificent portico entrance to a sweeping double staircase that is broad enough to allow two crinolined ladies to pass each other without unseemly collision, the place displays the kind of opulence that has to be seen to be believed. A ticket to ride is not required for lunch or dinner at the Marcus Wareing-run restaurant, but the gloriously revamped interior is certainly a trip back in time – breathtakingly ornate and stylish, its glamorous cocktail bar and palatial dining room have soaring ceilings and gilding galore. The British-focused menu takes prime UK produce and a soupçon of French style to steer a course between tradition and modernity. A well-crafted, gently contemporary repertoire might open with torched mackerel with smoked eel, cockles, apple and hispi cabbage, followed by best end and crisp tongue of lamb with lentils, turnip, merguez sausage and salsa verde. Indulgent desserts might run to ricotta and white chocolate cheesecake with fig sorbet and cognac syrup.

Chef Daniel Howes **Seats** 130, Private dining room 18 **Times** 12.15–2.45/ 5.30–10.45 **Prices** Set L 3 course £30, Set D 3 course £30, Starter £7.50– £11, Main £18–£35, Dessert £7–£8, Sunday lunch £35 **Wines** 200 bottles over £30, 2 bottles under £30, 17 by glass **Parking** NCP (St Pancras) **Notes** Vegetarian available, Children welcome

Odette's   PLAN 1 C1

@@@ Modern British V
020 7586 8569 | 130 Regent's Park Road, NW1 8XL
www.odettesprimrosehill.com
Versatile cooking in a north London village

There's always been something of the French auberge about Odette's, ensconced as it is in this most village-like of north London's purlieus, although these days, the interior look is more dressed-down minimal than the flounces and furbelows of yesteryear. Cream-washed brickwork in the front room gives way to flesh-toned walls crowded with idiosyncratic prints and drawings further in, with pendant globe lights hanging on naked wires, and there are tables in the garden too, an alluring prospect indeed when the sun shines and the birds are in full song. A seasonally changing carte, supplemented by a weekly lunch menu, runs the rule over Bryn Williams' versatile repertoire, opening with a winning duo of cured salmon and crab, alongside kohlrabi, apple and cucumber, proceeding to Goosnargh duck breast with turnip, blood orange and endive, or a meaty fish dish such as brill with Jerusalem artichokes and oyster mushrooms in chicken velouté. For dessert, the kitchen is not above reinventing the Jaffa cake, in a version made with orange cream and clementine, or there could be apricot soufflé served with chocolate and tonka bean ice cream. Not the smallest asset of Odette's is a wine list full of interesting and apposite flavours, with a generous spread by the glass.

Chef Bryn Williams, William Gordon **Seats** 70, Private dining room 10 **Times** 12–2.30/6–10, Closed 2 weeks from 24 December, Monday, D Sunday **Prices** Set L 2 course from £16.95, Set L 3 course from £21.95 , Tasting/vegetarian menu 6/10 from £44 , Starter £7–£9, Main £17–£28, Dessert £7–£12.50, Sunday lunch **Wines** 36 bottles over £30, 16 bottles under £30, 16 by glass **Parking** On street **Notes** Children welcome

London SE1

Restaurant Story

PLAN 6 F2

◉◉◉◉◉ Modern British **V** ♟
020 7183 2117 | 199 Tooley Street, SE1 2JX
www.restaurantstory.co.uk

White-hot opening from a global talent

The building is not exactly hard to spot – a Nordic-influenced modern wood-and-glass structure in what is essentially a traffic island at the Tower Bridge end of Tooley Street. It seems an unpromising spot to find one of the most extraordinary talents to emerge on the UK's restaurant scene for many a year, but Restaurant Story is one of London's most personal and compelling dining experiences. Tom Sellers has a CV including stints under Tom Aikens here in London, Thomas Keller in New York and René Redzepi in Copenhagen, so expect a new-wave approach to the whole show, where the waiters and chefs engage with you and generally make you feel more than a mere paying customer, with the meal very much a multi-sensorial experience.

The whole event takes three to four hours, and needs booking way in advance to bag a table. The room has a slick Scandinavian charm, deliberately free of intimidating formality, with floor-to-ceiling windows onto Tooley Street, cool designer chairs, blond wood tables, and an open-to-view kitchen which shows the kitchen team working with zen-like calm. Books line the shelves in meticulous colour co-ordinated order, and Tom invites you to bring a book to add to the collection. The menu arrives in an old book, appropriately enough, and consists of chapter headings from

Childhood to Sea, Land and The End, and offers an eight-course lunch or ten-course dinner, the latter called Full Story, with a shorter mid-week lunch if you don't fancy going the whole hog. Creativity and ingenuity abounds throughout and everything is rooted in something from Tom's own story (or journey if you will). Every dish looks stunning on the plate: sometimes playful, sometimes simple, and always intriguing.

Things get going with the array of 'snacks' that arrive in quick succession, giving a forestaste of the imagination, technical skill, impressive flavours and sheer fun that is to come. The bread and dripping is a signature which should be on the menu for as long as its doors are open — a candle made of beef fat, fabulous sourdough bread, veal tongue and apple jelly, and a powerful beef jelly extract. Onions might star in a dish with lovage, scallops, cucumber and dill ash while pigeon is cooked to perfection, with, say, vanilla and bitter leaves providing a captivating combination. The final chapter might include a knockout pairing of foie gras and clementine, and among sweet courses, 'almond and dill' is an inspired combination of flavours, textures and temperatures. The passion for British ingredients and regionalism extends to fantastic cocktails, British beers, local gins, and there's expert guidance on pairing such eclectic drinks with the unique style of food.

Chef Tom Sellers **Seats** 37 **Times** 12–5/6.30–9.30, Closed 2 weeks Christmas, 2 weeks August, Sunday, L Monday **Prices** Set L 3 course £38, Set lunch 7 course £80, Dinner 10 course £120, Tasting menu £120 **Wines** 147 bottles over £30, 4 bottles under £30, 11 by glass **Parking** On street, NCP **Notes** Children 6 years +

The Peninsula Restaurant

PLAN 1 F2

@@@ Modern European V

020 8463 6868 | InterContinental London - The O2,
1 Waterview Drive, SE10 0TW
www.peninsula-restaurant.com

Creative modern cooking with views over the peninsula

It's all happening on the Greenwich peninsula, which has gradually been transformed into a smart London quarter with its own cultural milieu, and a new InterContinental Hotel to boot. The Peninsula dining room on the second floor has views of the whole district, with Canary Wharf hovering before it, and amid the sleek contemporary design of beige pillars and purple carpeting, a menu of cutting-edge cooking has much to fire the imagination. Chilli-dressed scallop céviche with fennel and apple, dressed in a flurry of lemongrass snow, might open proceedings, before fine lamb with its sweetbreads arrives, alongside confit kumquats and braised chicory. Alternatively, proceedings might open with silky-tender beef tartare with preserved tomatoes, pistachios and whipped fat, and then move on to Dover sole and langoustines with creamed potato in shellfish sauce. Vegetarian dishes have plenty of vigour, perhaps a herbed buckwheat patty with cloud-ear mushrooms, a soy-poached egg yolk and pickled mooli. A dessert of poached cucumber with aerated yogurt and passionfruit sorbet maintains the creative momentum, or there could be perfectly ripe Alphonso mango in lemon verbena soup, garnished with crunchy meringue. Seven-course tasting menus, including appetiser and pre-dessert, run the rule over the kitchen's talents.

Chef Tomas Lidakevicius **Seats** 70, Private dining room 24 **Times** 6–10, Closed Sunday, L all week **Prices** Set D 2 course £28, Set D 3 course £35, Early dinner menu £35, Tasting menu £72, Starter £11–£18, Main £20–£30, Dessert £9–£14 **Wines** 64 bottles over £30, 4 bottles under £30, 16 by glass **Parking** 220 **Notes** Children welcome

Amaya

PLAN 4 F3

@@@ Modern Indian ♥

020 7823 1166 | Halkin Arcade, Motcomb Street, SW1X 8JT
www.realindianfood.com

New-wave Indian cooking with plenty of glamour

In a plum spot just off Knightsbridge, Amaya is one of the new breed of Indian restaurants in London that has brought global glitz to the traditional cooking of the subcontinent. Inside, the mood is full of shimmer and glam, with vividly patterned decor and artworks in unapologetic colours, and the cooking aims for the corresponding gustatory effect. Traditional grilling, in the tandoor, on a flat griddle and over open flame, is the watchword for dishes such as smoked chilli lamb chops, venison seekh kebabs, and tandoori duck tikka with plum chutney. Seafood dishes such as tandoori prawns in an assertive marinade, or a platter of fresh items, are among the most luxurious of the menu offerings, and the vegetarian dishes too – spinach and fig tikki, chargrilled aubergine – are laden with layers of concentrated seasoning. Biryanis made with mature basmati rice will please traditionalists, and meals conclude with a mixture of traditional Indian and more obviously western enticements. A classy wine list that extends into the firmament of premier cru burgundies and classed-growth Bordeaux is supplemented by a list of inventive, fun cocktails.

Chef Karunesh Khanna **Seats** 99, Private dining room 14 **Times** 12.30–2.15/6.30–11.15, Closed D 25 December **Prices** Amaya Platter £25, Set lunch £30/£42 weekends only **Parking** NCP, Knightsbridge car park **Notes** Sunday lunch, Vegetarian available, Children 10 years + at lunch Monday to Friday, No age restriction at dinner, must leave table by 8pm

See advert on page 382

Ametsa with Arzak Instruction

PLAN 5 A2

@@@ Modern Basque 🍷

020 7333 1234 | The Halkin by COMO, Halkin Street, Belgravia, SW1X 7DJ

www.comohotels.com/thehalkin/dining/ametsa

Earthy, modern Basque cooking in wealthy Belgravia

True, the name of the restaurant is not exactly snappy, but the Arzak name carries a lot of weight, with the family restaurant in San Sebastian a global foodie destination for seekers of the molecular fireworks known as 'New Basque cuisine'. Located in the super-cool Halkin, a minimalist mecca with a blue chip Belgravia address, the dining room looks pristine in brilliant white, beneath a conversation-piece of 7,000 dangling golden glass test tubes filled with spices. An à la carte menu supports the tasting menu, while a set lunch option lets budget diners sample the style for a relatively modest outlay; all rely on first-class ingredients, many of which are sourced from these shores. This is a kitchen with focus, creativity, and the confidence to tackle bold ideas, evident from the off in starters such as foie corn cob with cocoa and vinaigrette dressing. Main courses might see the flavour of beef fillet accentuated by green tomato, or venison with longan fruit. To finish, you'll need a spot of help from staff when choosing between desserts with enigmatic titles such as 'chocolate with emeralds and strata' or 'yellow brick road'.

Chefs Sergio Sanz Blanco, Elena Arzack **Seats** 60, Private dining room 24 **Times** 12–2/6.30–10.30, Closed 24–26 December, 1 January, Sunday, L Monday **Prices** Set L 2 course £29, 3 course £36.50, Tasting menu L £52-£68 (D from £110), Starter £18.50–£24, Main £27–£39, Dessert £12.50 **Wines** 156 bottles over £30, 4 bottles under £30, 10 by glass **Parking** On street (after 6pm) **Notes** Vegetarian available, Children welcome

London SW1

A. Wong

PLAN 5 C4

◎◎◎ Chinese

020 7828 8931 | 70 Wilton Road, Victoria, SW1V 1DE

www.awong.co.uk

Exploring China's vast culinary range

In case the 10-course tasting menu isn't enough of a heads-up, Andrew Wong's dynamic eatery is a long way from your average Cantonese takeaway. The setting is pared-back and contemporary, with an open kitchen if you want to get up close and personal with the chefs as they give the repertoire of Chinese regional cuisines a thorough workout. Andrew took over his parents' restaurant, so cooking is in his DNA and he has respect for traditional ways, but this is modern dining too – there are contemporary elements to many of the dishes, which draw influences from a country that has 14 national borders. Dim sum such as the pork and prawn dumpling are fine versions indeed, served on a crisp piece of pork crackling in this case, or go for the inspired clear shrimp version with citrus foam. In the evening, that 10-course tasting menu is hard to resist with its Shaanxi pulled lamb 'burger', or seared beef with mint, chilli and lemongrass, while the regular à la carte offers red braised fermented fish belly, a dish from Anhui province, for the adventurous. Creative desserts are a triumph too, as in tea-smoked banana with nut crumble, slow-cooked pineapple and chocolate sauce.

Chef Andrew Wong **Seats** 65, Private dining room 12 **Times** 12–2.30/ 5.30–10, Closed Christmas, Sunday, L Monday **Prices** Set L 2 course £14.95, Set D 2 course £14.95, 2 course with wine £14.95 until 6.30pm, Tasting menu £60, Starter £5–£12.95, Main £8–£28, Dessert £9 **Wines** 22 bottles over £30, 34 bottles under £30, 16 by glass **Parking** On street **Notes** Vegetarian available, Children welcome

Céleste at The Lanesborough

PLAN 5 A2

◎◎◎ French, British

020 7259 5599 | Hyde Park Corner, SW1X 7TA

www.lanesborough.com/eng/restaurant-bars/celeste

High-flying modern French cooking in ultra-luxe hotel

London is hardly short of gilded relics of empire, but this grand old mansion on Hyde Park Corner is in the premier league. The Lanesborough offers a world-class level of luxury and service, but if your budget's not up for stratospherically-priced rooms – personal butler included – you can sample the hotel's oligarch-friendly glamour by booking a table at Céleste, the opulent dining room. And those tables come glistening with top-class crystal and silverware, beneath a glass-domed ceiling that reflects a trio of shimmering chandeliers, and blue and white friezes resembling delicate Wedgwood china. Modern French cuisine is the kitchen's thing, cooked with top-level skill under the aegis of French super-chef Eric Frechon, although day-to-day delivery of the Frechon style is in the talented hands of head chef Florian Favario. The kitchen and über-professional front-of-house team may be as French as a camembert baguette, but the first-class materials underpinning the menu are resolutely British: a Burford Brown egg comes with pickled and puréed mushrooms, a parmesan sablé biscuit, toasted hazelnuts and a deeply-flavoured chicken jus, while day-boat cod is matched with lemon confit, light butter sauce and butter-laden crushed potatoes. Guanaja chocolate mousse, coffee ice cream and caramelised cashew praline team up to provide a classy finish.

Chefs Florian Favario, Eric Frechon **Seats** 100, Private dining room 12
Times 12–2.30/7–10.30 **Prices** Set L 3 course £38, Tasting/vegetarian menu 5 course £95, Starter £16–£34, Main £36–£44, Dessert £8–£12, Sunday lunch £38 **Wines** 550 bottles over £30, 20 by glass
Parking 25 **Notes** Vegetarian available, Children welcome

Dinner by Heston Blumenthal

PLAN 4 F2

◉◉◉ British ☙
020 7201 3833 | Mandarin Oriental Hyde Park,
66 Knightsbridge, SW1X 7LA
www.dinnerbyheston.co.uk

Researching British culinary history the Blumenthal way

If Bray seems a long way away, the dining room at the Mandarin Oriental, overlooking the broad green swathes of Hyde Park, is the next best bet for a Blumenthal fix. The cooking here, however, isn't in the Fat Duck mould, but represents the interest its presiding figure has always had in researches in the less familiar byways of British culinary history. Tables with kitchen views are the alternative to looking out on Knightsbridge, but either way, the journey back through time is entertaining. The 18th century supplies opening dishes such as salamagundy, a combination of oysters and marrowbone with salsify and horseradish cream, while salmon cured in Earl Grey tea garnished with Gentleman's Relish straddles that century and the next, but the time-travelling doesn't stop there. It's fascinating to know that a principal dish of roast turbot in green sauce might have been eaten in the reign of Henry VI, though it's a fair bet that nobody then would have heard of the hispi cabbage you might pair it with. Chicken cooked with lettuces once graced the Restoration era, as did taffety tart, a thing of caramelised apple all scented up with fennel and rose. British cheeses properly come with fruity accoutrements.

Chef Ashley Palmer-Watts **Seats** 149, Private dining room 12
Times 12–2/6–10.15, Closed 14–27 August **Prices** Set L 3 course £40, Starter £17.50–£23.50, Main £28–£44, Dessert £13–£18.50, Sunday lunch **Wines** 500 bottles over £30, 24 by glass **Parking** Valet parking, NCP
Notes Vegetarian available, Children 4 years +

London SW1

The Goring

PLAN 5 B3

@@@ British V ▼

020 7396 9000 | Beeston Place, SW1W 0JW

www.thegoring.com

A century-old family-run hotel with classical and modern cooking

Run by the Goring family since 1910, this Edwardian treasure holds a royal warrant and remains one of London's most luxurious and impeccably English hotels. The glossy bar is perfect for a glass of bubbly before heading for the dining room; designed by the Queen's nephew David Linley, it's a lavish space with grand proportions, a luminous gold-and-white colour scheme, ornate plasterwork, Swarovski chandeliers and precisely laid tables. It is all kept running as smoothly as a Swiss watch by a skilled service team. Executive chef Shay Cooper strikes a well-poised balance between modernist freshness and respect for tradition that suits a place like The Goring, and the results are impressive. There's plenty to applaud in a starter of pressed game terrine with crispy fried rabbit, pickled vegetables and grape must dressing. Then main course brings a medley of roast Cornish cod partnered luxuriously with lobster dumpling and bisque, young fennel and citrus oils, or two might share a classic fillet of beef Wellington. At the finishing line, a new-fangled spin on the trifle theme delivers decadent layers of black figs, gingerbread, caramel and buttermilk, or you might bow out with a zesty finale involving mascarpone and lime mousse partnered with citrus fruit sorbet and passionfruit.

Chef Shay Cooper **Seats** 70, Private dining room 50 **Times** 12–2.30/6–10, Closed L Saturday **Prices** Set L 3 course from £49, Set D 3 course from £60, Sunday lunch from £50, Pre-theatre 2 course £35 **Wines** 500 bottles over £30, 30 by glass **Parking** 7 **Notes** Children welcome

Marcus

PLAN 4 F2

@@@@@ Modern European, British V ▼

020 7235 1200 | Wilton Place, Knightsbridge, SW1X 7RL

www.marcusrestaurant.com

Impeccable benchmark contemporary cooking

Marcus Wareing has been a major player in the top-end London dining scene for a lot longer than the armchair army who tune in to BBC's *MasterChef: The Professionals* might have realised. He has been involved with The Berkeley for a decade, and since the much-publicised refurb in 2014 kicked the gentleman's club ambience into touch and rebranded the enterprise with the more chilled Marcus moniker, his restaurant continues to rank as one of London's premier league gastronomic experiences. The hotel itself is a sybaritic five-star operation that makes an ideal location for a restaurant that reaches such heady heights of achievement. The dining room has the sort of genteel refinement you might expect at this level (and at these prices), so there's oak panelling for a touch of gravitas, plenty of space between immaculately set tables, and a few striking contemporary artworks to jazz up the discreetly elegant look. The engaging service team work tirelessly (and seemingly without effort) ensure that every element of the experience meets the exacting standards one might hope for in what is essentially a special-occasion venue for many diners.

Wareing has three restaurants under his belt, which is quite restrained by the standards of today's new empire-building breed of chefs, and means he's able to play close attention to his flagship address, while Mark Froydenlund is the man charged with day-to-day interpretation of the house style. At entry level, the three-course lunchtime menu, while not quite a steal, offers very good value for such high-flying cooking, but having gone to the trouble of securing a table, you might as well go for broke via the carte or five- and eight-course seasonal tasting menus. The combination of superb ingredients, measured and creative thinking and precise execution results in compelling stuff such as a starter that deftly matches top-class salmon and langoustine with quince and the citrus freshness of calamansi fruit, or another that serves lobster with pumpkin mousse-filled agnolotti, pumpkin sauce and the gentle glow of Espelette pepper. Everything looks spectacular on the plate, but elegantly so — there's no grandstanding here, for everything is on the plate for a reason. Halibut makes a welcome appearance, topped with razor-thin mushroom scales and matched with clams, razor clams, garlic gnocchi and a deeply-satisfying mushroom sauce, while a meaty option might combine fallow deer with celeriac, blackberry and pine nut in a captivating partnership.

Desserts continue to deliver surprise and excitement with the citrussy aromatics of bergamot used to flavour set cream within master-class pastry, as well as meringue, gel and Earl Grey sorbet. Alternatively, the cheese trolley is as good as you'll find anywhere, while the staggering wine list has all the big guns alongside some more left-field options. There is a private chef's table that seats up to 10 people.

Chefs Marcus Wareing, Mark and Shauna Froydenlund **Seats** 90, Private dining room 16 **Times** 12–2.30/6–10.30, Closed Sunday **Prices** Set L 3 course £55, Set D 3 course £85, Tasting menu £105–£120 **Wines** 950 bottles over £30, 13 by glass **Parking** NCP, on street, valet parking **Notes** Children 8 years +

London SW1

One-O-One

PLAN 4 F2

◉◉◉ French V

020 7235 8050 | The Park Tower Knightsbridge,
101 Knightsbridge, SW1X 7RN
www.oneoonerestaurant.com

Accomplished seafood cookery in landlocked Knightsbridge

Creating a dedicated seafood restaurant, the kind that ought by rights to be sitting on some sun-kissed section of the Côte d'Azur, in landlocked Knightsbridge was a challenge to which Pascal Proyart has risen with triumphant aplomb. Not only is he a brand ambassador for the Seafood Council of Norway, he brings something of his Breton boyhood to proceedings here, against a backdrop of marine blue and driftwood brown, with gentle lighting and discreet music to add a sense of calm.

When Proyart reaches out of his home territory, the results are still stunning, as when yellowfin tuna tartare is matched with soft-shell crab tempura, sushi rice and tobiko, with aromatic notes of lemon, ginger and wasabi (the last a sorbet) lifting a stimulating starter.

Main could be translucent cod with Sicilian red prawns and a 'cassoulet' of Paimpol red beans in a rich bisque sauce, or perhaps sea bass in sauce barigoule with olives, artichokes, capers and basil. There are a couple of meat dishes, while surf-and-turfers can feast on beef fillet and lobster together if they've a mind, and it all concludes with inventive desserts like white chocolate and juniper berry sablé with lemon sorbet, gin and tonic jelly and mint syrup.

Chef Pascal Proyart **Seats** 52, Private dining room 30 **Times** 12–2.30/6.30–10, Closed Sunday and Monday **Prices** Set L 3 course £19.50-£39, Tasting menu 5 course £79, Starter £14–£38, Main £24–£42, Dessert £8–£10 **Wines** 75 bottles over £30, 11 by glass **Parking** UPark **Notes** Children welcome

Pétrus

PLAN 4 F3

@@@ Modern French **V** 🍷

020 7592 1609 | 1 Kinnerton Street, Knightsbridge, SW1X 8EA

www.gordonramsay.com/petrus

Immaculate modern cooking from the Ramsay stable

Restaurant Gordon Ramsay in Royal Hospital Road may well be the flagship of Mr Ramsay's empire, but Pétrus runs it a very close second when it comes to delivering dynamic modern French food. The dining room is a sophisticated space with hues of copper, beige, silver, and splashes of claret red as a nod to the namesake wine, and well-spaced tables dressed up for the business of fine dining around a centrepiece walk-in glass wine room bristling with starry vintages. Larry Jayasekara now heads up the kitchen: a Ramsay protégé (on and off since 2004, with formative stints chez Marcus Wareing and Raymond Blanc, among others), he is well versed in the house style so you can look forward to contemporary dishes that fizz with excitement and technical accomplishment. Luxuries are liberally dispersed throughout, starting with the butter-poached native lobster that arrives with girolles, truffle cannelloni and wood sorrel. Next up, humble Brittany rabbit gets to steal the show in a posh-and-peasant combination comprising a ham-wrapped ballotine filled with a pungent stuffing of its offal, plus a herb-crusted 'rack', a luxurious lobe of foie gras, trompette mushrooms and carrot purée. A reinvented Black Forest gâteau ends the show, pairing chocolate-coated Kirsch mousse with morello cherry sorbet.

Chef Larry Jayasekara **Seats** 55, Private dining room 8 **Times** 12–2.30/6.30–10.30, Closed 22–26 December **Prices** Set L 2 course from £28, Set L 3 course from £37.50, Set D 2 course from £65, Set D 3 course from £75, Tasting menu from £95, Sunday lunch **Wines** 394 bottles over £30, 14 by glass **Parking** On street (free after 6.30pm), NCP (Towers) **Notes** Chef's menu 5 course, Children welcome

The Rib Room Bar and Restaurant

PLAN 4 F3

020 7858 7250 | Jumeirah Carlton Tower, Cadogan Place, SW1X 9PY

As we went to press we learnt that Tom Kerridge, chef and owner of The Hand and Flowers in Marlow (4 AA Rosettes, see page 35), would be opening his own restaurant where The Rib Room was previously situated. Therefore, the Rosette award for this restaurant has been suspended and reassessment will take place in due course under the new chef.

Seats 120, Private dining room 20 **Times** 12–2.45/6.30–10.45 **Wines** 439 bottles over £30, 11 bottles under £30, 29 by glass **Parking** 78

Roux at Parliament Square

PLAN 5 E2

◉◉◉ Modern European V 🏆

020 7334 3737 | Parliament Square, SW1P 3AD

www.rouxatparliamentsquare.co.uk

Modern French gastronomy with a touch of Roux grandeur

Almost within heckling distance of Parliament, this Westminster outpost of Michael Roux Jnr's culinary portfolio serenely purrs with political murmurings and intrigue. The handsome Georgian building itself (also home to the Royal Institute of Chartered Surveyors) lends a certain club-like refinement to its duo of dining rooms. Decorated with modernity and restraint, they offer an appropriate sense of timeless simplicity done-up in their best pastel shades. Crisp white linen, pale grey carpeting, comfy banquettes and chairs, and tempting shelf displays of Cognac and Armagnac add to the gloss.

The cooking – under Steve Groves – unsurprisingly takes its cue from the Roux philosophy, delivering a light modern approach underpinned by a classical French theme, exemplified by smartly-engineered, clean-cut, pretty dishes of skill and professionalism. Witness a perfectly timed pigeon opener, paired with quince, celery and Alsace bacon, while mains might take in Iberico presa (tender, juicy and with distinctive marbling) served with carrot (roasted and puréed) and onions. Lighter dishes might offer sparkling fresh cod simply accompanied by cucumber, dill and seaweed. Dressed-to-thrill desserts aim high too; perhaps a cheesecake of vanilla with citrus creatively set on a hoop-shaped sable base. Staff are expectedly professional and smartly turned out, while wines focus towards the French big guns but without ignoring the rest of the globe. And, why not start, and finish, upstairs at the 'Roux at The Pembury' bar, with its elegant grand hotel opulence.

Chef Steve Groves **Seats** 56, Private dining room 10 **Times** 12–2/6.30–9, Closed Christmas, New Year, bank holidays, Saturday and Sunday
Prices Set L 3 course £42, Set D 3 course £59, Tasting menu £79
Wines 194 bottles over £30, 1 bottle under £30, 16 by glass
Parking NCP (Semley Place) **Notes** Children welcome

Seven Park Place by William Drabble

PLAN 5 C1

◉◉◉◉ Modern French ☻

020 7316 1600 | St James's Hotel and Club, 7-8 Park Place, SW1A 1LP

www.stjameshotelandclub.com

Assured French cooking in a riotously decorated club

Set in the swish St James's Hotel and Club, William Drabble's restaurant is a seductively small-scale operation: with just 34 diners in a pair of intimate dining rooms to cook for, the kitchen can focus on ensuring that timings, textures and flavours are fine-tuned. What the setting lacks in size it more than makes up for in visual impact: mustard-yellow seating meets chocolate-brown walls adorned with expansive art nouveau foliage and eye-catching artworks – it's certainly the polar opposite of the stripped-out minimalism of many a contemporary restaurant.

Drabble's cooking is out of the top drawer, continuing the highly detailed contemporary French style he has honed over his decade-long tenure, and the whole show is backed by assured service that never misses a beat. Menus come liberally sprinkled with high-end ingredients, as in a simple but flavour-packed opener of lobster ravioli with cauliflower purée and lobster butter sauce, or the perfectly harmonious partnership of seared foie gras offset by rhubarb and ginger. The unshouty finesse of main courses is typified in a combination of saddle of venison with parsnip purée, red cabbage, potato fondant and juniper-scented jus. Fish might be beautifully griddled sea bass with celeriac and apple purée, roasted celeriac emulsion and Périgord truffle.

Two willing accomplices could finish with a benchmark tarte Tatin with vanilla ice cream and toffee apple sauce, or you could opt for a tropical number, pina colada bavarois with caramalised pineapple and coconut sorbet. If you go for the set-price lunch menu, you can eat here at an amazingly keen price – as long as you can resist the siren call of the excellent globetrotting wine list.

Chef William Drabble **Seats** 34, Private dining room 40 **Times** 12–2/7–10, Closed Sunday and Monday **Wines** 421 bottles over £30, 3 bottles under £30, 20 by glass **Parking** On street, NCP **Notes** Set 6-course menu gourmand, Vegetarian available, Children welcome

AA Restaurant of the Year for London 2017–18

Elystan Street

PLAN 4 E5

@@@ Modern British

020 7628 5005 | 43 Elystan Street, Chelsea, SW3 3NT

www.elystanstreet.com

Inspired cooking from a consummate chef

When Phil Howard announced the final service at The Square in 2016, the capital's gastronomes awaited his next move with bated breath. With his long-running reputation as an A-list chef, he could have taken the cash and gone the empire-building route, but thankfully Howard just can't stay away from the stoves. And here he is in a discreetly posh Chelsea neighbourhood (in Tom Aikens's former premises, as it happens) at the helm of a more easygoing, yet still stylish gaff, where he seems truly at home, turning out high-flying cooking that doesn't aim for the level of complexity achieved at The Square. The setting has an almost Scandinavian allure – bare tables, pale wood floors and curvy, pastel-hued seats – that chimes well with the more relaxed culinary approach, and the mood is of unbuttoned diners actually enjoying themselves rather than worshipping at a hushed temple of gastronomy.

Howard's technical abilities are beyond question, and now he has shaken off the fussy shackles of high-end fine dining, the results speak for themselves, and the kitchen delivers brilliance at every turn – witness a starter that packs a large raviolo with an ingenious combo of partridge and pear, and serves it with sprouts, butternut squash, bacon and gamey juices, or another partnering deep-fried and poached mussels with a 'salad' of new potatoes, leek hearts, lovage purée and monk's beard Next up, precision-timed John Dory fillet with roasted octopus, scorched onions, cep purée, parsley oil and garlic is a delight in conception and delivery, while meat dishes – perhaps loin of fallow deer with mustard fruits, green peppercorns and a tarte fine of celeriac and quince – show off peerless materials and flawless technique. And then there are the exquisite desserts – a benchmark lemon tart displaying consummate pastry skills, packed with intense lemon curd and served with lemon sorbet.

Chef Philip Howard **Seats** 64, Private dining room 14 **Times** 12.30–2.45/6.30–10, Closed 25–26 December, 1 January **Prices** Set L 2 course from £35, Set L 3 course from £42.50, Starter £15–£32, Main £20–£45, Dessert £12–£14, Sunday lunch from £50 **Wines** 120 bottles over £30, 5 bottles under £30, 13 by glass **Parking** On street **Notes** Vegetarian available, Children welcome

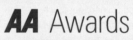

AA Awards

AA Wine Award for England 2017–18

LONDON SW3

The Five Fields

PLAN 4 E5

◉◉◉◉ Modern British **V** 🍷

020 7838 1082 | 8-9 Blacklands Terrace, SW3 2SP

www.fivefieldsrestaurant.com

Light-touch modern English cooking in rural Chelsea

If the name seems to suggest somewhere out in the arable shires rather than just off the King's Road, it was already something of a cartographer's romance when it was coined for this district in the Georgian era. From the outside, Taylor Bonnyman's restaurant could almost be an unassuming bistro, and yet inside is an elegantly styled, expansive space decorated in neutral tones, but with contemporary paintings and smartly clothed tables. So far, so Chelsea, but the restaurant does retain a foot in the shires after all, for much of its fresh produce – fruit and vegetables, herbs and flowers – comes from a smallholding in East Sussex.

Alongside his youthful head chef Marguerite Keogh, Bonnyman offers a light-touch rendition of the modern English style, where dishes are fragrant with hedgerow and seashore gatherings. A bravura opener labelled Sea and Earth is exemplary of the style: scallop and sea buckthorn, langoustine and white asparagus, oyster and pistachio, and – perhaps most revelatory of all – crab and rhubarb. Alternatively, red mullet might be teamed with fennel, but also strawberry and creamy lardo. When main dishes take a more classical path, they are not at all lacking in textural surprises and intensity of flavour. Expect a winning duo of turbot and cuttlefish to star alongside romanesco and lemon, or gamey Herdwick mutton to be gentled with sheep's curd, as well as a bright green spring array of peas and lettuce. The delicacy of touch extends into desserts such as lemon custard with lavender meringue and honeyed almonds, or crème brûlée with poached rhubarb and shortbread.

Wine judging observations: A great list, very neat and tidy in its presentation to the diner. Very good selection at fair prices with plenty of classy wines and producers to choose from, many regarded as bench mark examples which others aspire to. Very accessible with a strong by-the-glass section and halves well represented. Informative, but with subtly too. Wines come from a good cross-section of countries, regions are identified and the varied price points mean all pockets are catered for.

Chefs Taylor Bonnyman, Marguerite Keogh **Seats** 40, Private dining room 10 **Times** 6.30–10, Closed Christmas, 2 weeks January, 2 weeks August, Saturday and Sunday **Prices** Set D 2 course £55–£75, Set D 3 course £65–£85, Tasting menu £85 **Wines** 471 bottles over £30, 11 bottles under £30, 18 by glass **Parking** On street, NCP (150 yards) **Notes** No children's menu, Children 6 years +

Outlaw's at The Capital

PLAN 4 E3

®®® British, Seafood V ⬚

020 7591 1202 | Basil Street, Knightsbridge, SW3 1AT

www.capitalhotel.co.uk

Importing the Cornish formula to Knightsbridge

A grand hotel on a manageable scale, The Capital in Knightsbridge is to be found lurking round the back of Harrods, and has for many years sustained a reputation for classy cooking. Importing Nathan Outlaw's formula from far-flung Cornwall was a very canny move then, and in Tom Brown, the restaurant has a head chef who is fully in tune with what Outlaw is about. Sustainable fish and seafood are the name of the game, here as in Port Isaac, and for all that you're in the big bad city, the atmosphere of bracing coastline and seashore is admirably evoked by the food. A main dish like turbot grilled on the bone, served with charred fennel and sauced with devilled shrimp butter sauce, makes the point eloquently, or there may be lemon sole, its delicacy boosted with an oyster and some tarragon-scented smoked leeks. Before that, there could be a fashionable Scotch egg variation made of crabmeat, set on a lightly curried dressing, or ritzy lobster risotto fragranced with orange and basil. If you're determined on meat, consider duck with pistachios, chicory and pink grapefruit, but don't miss finishers like orange and lemon Pavlova with yogurt sorbet, or the rhubarb ice cream sandwich that comes with golden raisins and ginger beer.

Chefs Nathan Outlaw, Tom Brown **Seats** 35, Private dining room 24 **Times** 12–2/6.30–10, Closed Sunday **Prices** Set L 2 course from £29, Set L 3 course from £33, Tasting menu 5 course from £85 **Wines** 37 by glass **Parking** 8 **Notes** BYO wine on Thursday, Children welcome

Restaurant Gordon Ramsay

PLAN 4 E6

®®®® French V ⬚

020 7352 4441 | 68 Royal Hospital Road, SW3 4HP

www.gordonramsayrestaurants.com

The mothership of the Gordon Ramsay empire

It's hard to keep track, but since The Chelsea flagship first opened its doors in 1998, the Gordon Ramsay brand has spread its wings to 30 or so venues around the globe, taking in 14 addresses in London, a brace apiece for France and Italy, a sprinkling of locations across Asia and the Middle East, and venues across the pond from Las Vegas to Atlantic City. This venue remains the cream of the crop, its clean-lined, art deco-influenced looks and plush, pastel-hued tones giving a sophisticated sheen to the surprisingly intimate dining room. Ramsay's place has long been grounded in French classical ways, and so it continues under the guidance of Matt Abé, who has spent a decade absorbing and perfecting the house style.

The à la carte menu might open with the unmitigated luxury of sautéed foie gras and veal sweetbreads with carrots, almonds and Cabernet Sauvignon vinegar, then follow with poached Isle of Gigha halibut matched with king crab, finger lime, and ras el hanout infused broth. Desserts maintain the truly haute tone via trenchant lemonade parfait with honey, bergamot and sheep's milk yogurt. The fixed-price lunch menu is the entry point for anyone looking to sample the RGR experience on a budget (relatively speaking...), while the Prestige and Seasonal Inspiration menus trade up to the high-rolling end of the spectrum. The service, led by Jean-Claude Breton, has long been a stand-out feature of a visit, while the remarkable wine list is a serious piece of work with the world's best producers vying for your overdraft.

Chef Matt Abé **Seats** 45 **Times** 12–2.15/6.30–10.15, Closed 1 week at Christmas, Saturday and Sunday **Prices** Set L 3 course £65, Tasting menu £145–£175, A la carte menu 3 course £110 **Wines** 1,300 bottles over £30, 5 bottles under £30, 20 by glass **Notes** Children welcome

Vineet Bhatia London   PLAN 4 E5

@@@ Modern Indian **V** ♥
020 7225 1881 | 10 Lincoln Street, SW3 2TS
www.vineetbhatia.london

Ground-breaking Indian cuisine in a Chelsea townhouse

Secreted away down a smart little street just off the King's Road, you endearingly ring the bell at VBL to gain entry to the lovely Georgian townhouse restaurant as though it were still a private home, and, once inside, any preconceptions about Indian cuisine are blown aside. VBL is the reincarnation of Vineet Bhatia's previous Rasoi restaurant, but re-set with a new name, modern makeover and offering just a dinner-only 'experience' tasting menu (plus a vegetarian version). A trailblazer among nouveau Indian chefs for many years, Bhatia is certainly back with a bang. Inspired by his Mumbai heritage and global travels, you can expect evolved, refined, palate-tingling treats that fizz with originality and innovation. Open with unabashed panache via 'smoked prawn chaat and lime soup'. Menu descriptions are brief, like 'duck korma' for instance, with the cheery, knowledgeable, professional service team introducing dishes at the table. Other offerings like 'beet foie gras' might marry silky foie gras (spiced with cardamom, chilli and fennel) with its beetroot element arriving as a featherlight macaroon and accompanying pineapple and saffron chutney. Dessert dishes, like 'chocolate cure' or a palate-cleansing 'clementine kulfi' play their part too.

Chef Vineet Bhatia **Seats** 32, Private dining room 12 **Times** 6.30–10.15, Closed 25–26 December, 1–2 January, Monday, L all week **Prices** Tasting menu £105 **Wines** 120 bottles over £30, 10 by glass **Parking** On street, NCP **Notes** Children welcome

LONDON SW4
Trinity Restaurant
PLAN 1 D3

◉◉◉ British, European ❦
020 7622 1199 | 4 The Polygon, Clapham, SW4 0JG
www.trinityrestaurant.co.uk

Dynamic modern cooking in Clapham

At the heart of Clapham's old town, chef-patron Adam Byatt's Trinity goes from strength to strength. After a dozen years under its belt it's still on a roll. Trinity's open, street-level dining room comes kitted out with contemporary spin – cool pastel tones, an open-plan kitchen and outside terrace, while the wide glass frontage rolls back to give everyone that sunny day alfresco vibe. The place exudes class and confidence without being stuffy; from in-vogue seating to the efficient, cheery, professional service. Byatt's knockout cooking exudes the same poise and ongoing flair, backed by a focus on ingredient quality and flavour rather than being too tricksy. Underpinned by a classical French theme, dishes raise the bar with a light, creative, modern spin. Take a fathoms-deep tasting opener of ravioli of crab, for instance, accompanied by a gobsmacking broth pepped-up by a hint of ginger and added luxury of an oyster beignet. Staying with the seafood theme, a wild sea trout main might be matched with langoustines, seaweed gnocchi and tomato butter sauce. Desserts tempt with salt caramel custard tart or a classic tarte Tatin to share, while the French-led wine list is a corker.

Chef Adam Byatt **Seats** 50 **Times** 12.30–2.30/6.30–10, Closed 24–27 December, 1–2 January **Prices** Set L 2 course from £35, Set L 3 course from £39, Starter £10–£17, Main £28–£34, Dessert £7–£10, Sunday lunch from £39 **Wines** 280 bottles over £30, 22 bottles under £30, 16 by glass **Parking** On street **Notes** Vegetarian available, Children 10 years +

LONDON SW7
Rivea London
PLAN 4 E2

◉◉◉ Modern French, Italian Riviera ❦
020 7151 1025 | Bulgari Hotel, London, 171 Knightsbridge, SW7 1DW
www.rivealondon.com

Franco-Italian cooking in stylish surroundings

French super-chef Alain Ducasse is a master of haute cuisine, whose full-on formal style has made its mark at The Dorchester, but he also has a passion for more simple and humble things, particularly when they involve the sunny flavours of the Riviera. Here at the glitzy Bulgari Hotel is Rivea London, where his protégé Alexandre Nicolas draws on the tastes of Italy and France to create dynamic and classic dishes. A grand staircase sweeps downstairs to a vision of retro-style art deco glamour, cream leather and dark wood, with polished service befitting the postcode, and the menus follow suit with an array of undemanding, but stylishly realised

Mediterranean food. A soft boiled egg sits alluringly atop cod brandade and pumpkin risotto, or you might open with grilled octopus, chickpeas and fennel. This is a kitchen that knows how to buy as well as cook, so the first-class produce continues to shine in a dish of duck breast partnered with textures of beetroot, radish and turnip, or another where halibut fillet arrives in the company of shellfish and Cassis white wine sauce. There's evident technical skill right the way through to a contemporary take on a vacherin of hazelnut, poached pear and caramel.

Chef Alexandre Nicolas **Seats** 82, Private dining room 24 **Times** 12–2.30/ 6.30–10.30 **Prices** Set L 2 course £26, Set L 3 course £32, Starter £8–£14, Main £25–£28, Dessert £6–£7, Sunday lunch £26–£32 **Wines** 420 bottles over £30, 4 bottles under £30, 15 by glass **Parking** NCP (Pavillion Road) **Notes** Vegetarian available, Children welcome

LONDON SW10

Medlar Restaurant

PLAN 4 C6

@@@ Modern European ♥
020 7349 1900 | 438 King's Road, Chelsea, SW10 0LJ
www.medlarrestaurant.co.uk

Highly skilled cooking with a refreshing lack of pretension

Okay, it maybe set at the less glam end of the King's Road, but Medlar is the epitome of a top-flight neighbourhood outfit, and is rightly one of Chelsea's go-to restaurants. Outside, there's a little touch of summer kerb-appeal, with an awning sheltering a few street-side terrace tables and glass doors that open up for that sunny day Med vibe. Inside, the long, narrow room is simple yet smart without being showy; sunshine-green banquettes, cream upholstered chairs, white linen and burnished mirrors. It feels restrained and confident but not over-conceptualised, like Joe Mercer Nairne's cooking that's built around flavour, simplicity and precision. Innovative, colourful, seasonal dishes como underpinned by classical grounding on fixed-price daily-printed menus. Light and fresh with every ingredient justifying its place; witness a sea-shore inspired opener crab raviolo, served with samphire, brown shrimps, a fondue of leeks and a cracking bisque sauce, while to follow, chargrilled pink-perfection veal rump might be partnered by celeriac purée, Savoy cabbage, a passaladière, king oyster mushroom and marjoram. To finish on a light note, perhaps refreshing prosecco and rhubarb jelly served with blood orange sorbet and pistachios.

Chef Joe Mercer Nairne **Seats** 85, Private dining room 28 **Times** 12–3/ 6.30–10.30, Closed Christmas and 1 January **Prices** Set L 2 course from £30, Set L 3 course from £35, Set D 2 course from £41, Set D 3 course from £49, Saturday lunch 2/3 course £25/£30, Sunday lunch £30–£35 **Wines** 384 bottles over £30, 19 bottles under £30, 13 by glass **Parking** On street **Notes** Vegetarian available, Children welcome

London SW17

Chez Bruce

PLAN 1 C4

◉◉◉ Modern British, European ♟

020 8672 0114 | 2 Bellevue Road, Wandsworth Common, SW17 7EG

www.chezbruce.co.uk

Modern European cooking opposite the Common

The aubergine-coloured frontage behind its compact hedge overlooking Wandsworth Common has been a hot-button address since the 1980s. It has spent over 20 years of that under Bruce Poole's aegis, its long service attributable to its dual role as both destination and outstanding neighbourhood restaurant. The decor is relatively muted, pale walls framing a monochrome look, the better to focus attention where it belongs – on the plate. Poole has always favoured an eclectic approach to modern European food, the roots of the menu spreading over that broad arc from France and Spain to Italy. The last produces sterling pasta dishes such as flaked gurnard in tagliatelle with monk's beard in tomato and basil sauce, while southwest France supplies the reference point for a terrine of chicken livers and foie gras, accompanied by cured duck, celeriac remoulade and toasted brioche. At main, the Spanish note sounds with panache in a dish that combines hake and chorizo in sweetcorn velouté with green olive crostini for a fully rounded composition, or there may be crackled pork belly with crushed sweet potato, Toulouse sausage and radish. In among the dessert classics, such as crème brûlée and hot chocolate moelleux with praline parfait, are interspersed more speculative offerings like apple mess tartlet with yogurt sorbet.

Chefs Bruce Poole, Matt Christmas **Seats** 75, Private dining room 16 **Times** 12–2.30/6.30–10, Closed 24–26 December and 1 January **Prices** Set L 3 course from £35, Set D 3 course £55, Weekend/bank holidays set L 3 course £39.50 **Wines** 750 bottles over £30, 30 bottles under £30, 15 by glass **Parking** On street, station car park **Notes** Sunday lunch, Vegetarian available, Children at lunch only

Alain Ducasse at The Dorchester

PLAN 5 A1

◉◉◉◉ Contemporary, Modern French V ♟

020 7629 8866 | The Dorchester, 53 Park Lane, W1K 1QA

www.alainducasse-dorchester.com

Classically based French cuisine à la façon Ducasse

Monsieur Ducasse has a very well-stamped passport, as a result of his having extended his worldwide restaurant empire from New York to Qatar and Hong Kong. The twin centres of the portfolio are undoubtedly Paris and London, where the glitziest and most exclusive venues are to be found, and here in the modernist confines of an elegant dining room in the

Dorchester is the British flagship. Frosted windows offer hazy views of Hyde Park, while the walls are studded with what look like hundreds of little green mushrooms. Jean-Philippe Blondet is in charge of interpreting the master's style, and offers a no-holds-barred rendition of classically based French cuisine with a modernist patina. Certain dishes have made the cut from the previous incumbent, such as the lavishly rich sauté gourmand of lobster, chicken quenelles and hand-turned pasta. Rhubarb adds the all-important note of controlled acidity to an unctuous terrine of guinea fowl and duck foie gras, ahead of principal dishes such as flawlessly timed sea bass with cucumber and juniper, or the incomparable dry-aged beef with artichoke and bone marrow. Accompaniments are designed not to outflank the star of the show – peas and mint with milk-fed lamb, chicory and truffle with veal medallion. At the end come temptations like baked apple with black cardamom ice cream, a vacherin teeming with red berries, or the celebrated baba that is doused to order in your own choice of rum. Wine selections from the gigantic list will help to send the bill soaring.

Chefs Jean-Philippe Blondet, Angelo Ercolano, Alberto Gobbo **Seats** 82, Private dining room 30 **Times** 12–1.30/6.30–9.30, Closed 1st week in January, Easter, 3 weeks in August, 26–30 December, Sunday and Monday, L Saturday, L 31 December **Prices** Set L 3 course £65, Set D 3 course £115, Set D 4 course £120, Tasting menu £140, Seasonal £180, Menu Jardin £115, Black Truffle menu £260 **Wines** 1,015 bottles over £30, 1 bottle under £30, 18 by glass **Parking** 20 **Notes** Children 10 years +

Alyn Williams at The Westbury

PLAN 2 C5

@@@@ French, European V ⬥

020 7183 6426 | 37 Conduit Street, W1S 2YF

www.alynwilliams.com

Innovation, top-flight skills and heaps of glamour

The building itself may not be much of a looker, but The Westbury is firmly entrenched among the A-list pantheon of Mayfair's hotels, so you can expect an interior of glamour and opulence. Alyn Williams's restaurant is understated yet unmistakably glossy with its decor of oatmeal-hued chairs at amply spaced linen-swathed tables, set against darkwood panels, huge mirrors, and romantic, subtly-backlit alcoves. Impeccable, formal service matches the sophisticated mood, and it all makes a confidence-inspiring backdrop for the culinary fireworks to come. Alyn Williams turns out creative and dynamic food, exploring his own territory with a highly personal take on modern European cuisine, using unusual ingredients and techniques. An opening course from the tasting menu might bring beautifully caramelised Orkney scallops of stunning freshness, with ramson custard, dashi and brown butter crumb in supporting roles, while a starter from the carte might deploy mushroom

continued

broth and foraged ingredients – dulse, say – to boost the savoury punch of poached foiegras and smoked eel. A main course dish could showcase Devon Ruby beef and its tartare, together with oyster, confit potato and sherry vinegar, while Cornish turbot gets a Gallic triple whammy from ratatouille, rouille and bouillabaisse. Desserts continue to explore thrilling juxtapositions of flavor and texture via the likes of chocolate tart with crystallised sorrel and lemon sorrel ice cream, or you might bow out with a technically unimpeachable raspberry Pavlova with sweet cicely ice cream. The wine list, naturally enough, lives up to the glitzy surrounds with a feast of starry bottles.

Chef Alyn Williams **Seats** 65, Private dining room 20 **Times** 12–2.30/ 6–10.30, Closed 1–17 January, 13–30 August, Sunday to Monday **Prices** Set L 3 course £30, Set D 2 course £55, Set D 3 course £65, Tasting menu 7 course from £80, Starter £25, Main £35, Dessert £10 **Wines** 450 bottles over £30, 10 bottles under £30, 15 by glass **Parking** 20 **Notes** Children welcome
See advert on inside front cover

L'Autre Pied

PLAN 2 A4

@@@ Modern European **V**
020 7486 9696 | 5-7 Blandford Street, Marylebone, W1U 3DB
www.lautrepied.co.uk
Ingredient-led cooking with bold, assertive flavours

The address in fashionable Marylebone has been a destination dining venue for many years, but it's as the 'Other' branch of Charlotte Street's Pied-à-Terre that it has attained its glitziest reputation. In an ambience of minimal chic, with rosewood tables and white walls, Asimakis Chaniotis produces the signature modern cuisine with which successive chefs have kept the place in the forefront of London dining. It's ingredient-led cooking par excellence, where every component of a dish earns its place on the plate. First up could be breast and leg of smoked quail with Iberico tomatoes and calçot onions, a smartly on-trend lineup of flavours, or there might be a daring tartare of red prawns along with morels and other mushrooms pickled in Sauternes. Cod cheeks in prosciutto with asparagus, peas and mint see in the spring season with stylish panache, or there may be various cuts of suckling pig with leeks and heritage carrots, scented with star anise. Bold, assertive seasonings continue to desserts, which might feature chilli-spiked Guanaja chocolate feuilletine with Manjari chocolate sorbet, or truffled tarte Tatin made with Chantecler apples, served with tonka bean ice cream. Splash out on chef's signature dish, and be regaled with smoked poached sturgeon garnished with imperial oscietra, accompanied by Grey Goose French vodka.

Chef Asimakis Chaniotis **Seats** 53, Private dining room 16 **Times** 12–2.30/ 6–10.30, Closed 4 days at Christmas, 1 January, D Sunday **Prices** Set L 2 course from £24 (3 course from £29), Set D 2 course from £40 (3 course from £49.50), Tasting menu £65–£75, **Wines** 200 bottles over £30, 6 bottles under £30, 10 by glass **Notes** Sunday lunch, Children welcome

Avista

PLAN 2 A6

@@@ Italian

020 7596 3399 | Millennium London Mayfair, Grosvenor Square, W1K 2HP
www.avistarestaurant.com

Luxurious hotel setting for modern Italian dining

Italian cooking in London has come up in the world since the days of the formula trattoria, and these days it's quite as likely to be found within the confines of a luxurious hotel, this one on the south side of Grosvenor Square, with the United States embassy as a near neighbour. The dining room here is a smartly linened beige affair, the central feature of which is a granite-topped counter where dishes can be seen receiving their finishing touches before they wing their way to your table. A youthful Italian chef, Arturo Granato, oversees a menu that brings contemporary flourishes to the best of ancestral regional tradition, producing a first course of seared Orkney scallops with squid in fennel and coral dressing, or adding textured beetroot and hazelnuts to creamy burrata. Opulent primi take in osso buco ravioli scented with saffron, ginger, garlic and truffle, or a risotto encompassing quail, kale and foie gras, before main courses bring on home-smoked pigeon and its confit leg in a chocolate-tinged jus, accompanied by caramelised figs, Swiss chard and celeriac. To round things off opt for Granato's chocolate-crumb take on the boozy classic tiramisù with its coffee wafer, or perhaps the rum baba with matching granita and pear compôte.

Chef Arturo Granato **Seats** 75, Private dining room 12 **Times** 12–2.30/ 6.30–10.30, Closed 1 January, Sunday, L Saturday **Prices** Set L 2 course £26, Set L 3 course £29–£45, Set D 2 course £26, Set D 3 course £29–£49, Tasting menu £49.50–£59.50, Starter £12.50–£16, Main £12.50–£30.50, Dessert £9.50–£13.50 **Wines** 73 bottles over £30, 4 bottles under £30, 14 by glass **Parking** On street, NCP **Notes** Vegetarian available, Children welcome

Corrigan's Mayfair

PLAN 2 A6

@@@ British, Irish **V** ♀

020 7499 9943 | 28 Upper Grosvenor Street, W1K 7EH

www.corrigansmayfair.co.uk

Anglo-Irish cooking with the homely touch

Richard Corrigan's career in London went into the ascendant at a time when the old plutocratic haute cuisine of the late nouvelle era was giving place to more everyday demotic touches, when humble ingredients were brought to the fore, and the culinary reference points were to simple, homely domestic cooking of time-hallowed recipes that everyone recognised. Today's version of such impulses may be seen in the widespread resort to wild and foraged ingredients, many of which haven't informed British food since Shakespeare was a lad, but which have brought new depth and savour to the flashiest of modern technical cooking.

Corrigan has moved with these times, and impressively so. His setting may these days be a very clubbable address in Mayfair, where sky blue awnings beckon us into an environment of glittering marble bars, dedicated tables that allow diners to peer into the kitchen, and a principal dining room where chain-linked chandeliers are suspended above burnished floorboards, deeply upholstered seats and linened tables. The impetus of the menus, though, remains very much readily assimilable dishes that are presented with the requisite artistry, but are still informed

by big-hearted, accessible flavours. A platter of Carlingford oysters speaks neatly both of home and of Mayfair, or go with the unabashed pungency of smoked haddock soup blobbed with wholegrain mustard, or of smoked eel with hashed black pudding and apple. For main courses, there are robustly handled fish, such as John Dory with its wild garlic, peas and asparagus, or a poached monkfish seasoned with garam masala and coconut. Nor do meat dishes beat about the bush, when suckling pig turns up in three different cuts with onion squash, purple kale and granola, or a majestic hunk of bone-in sirloin has been dry-aged for five and a half weeks before making its way to your plate.

Distant Asian notes sound here and there, as for that monkfish, or the squab that is teamed with prawns and seasoned with soy and chilli, but the centre of gravity remains sturdily Anglo-Irish. A classic custard tart is just that, not some deconstructed reboot, but the never-more-popular rhubarb and custard ensemble is allowed a little forgivable foofing in the form of rhubarb crumble soufflé with ginger custard. Staff are knowledgeable and efficient to the nth degree, and there is a list of wines that are admittedly more Mayfair than everyday, but does begin with a set of beauties served in three sizes.

Chefs Richard Corrigan, Ross Bryans **Seats** 85, Private dining room 30 **Times** 12–3/6–10, Closed 25 December, bank holidays, L Saturday, D Sunday **Prices** Set L 2 course £25, Set L 3 course £29, Set D 5 course £55 , Tasting menu 6 course £75, Starter £9.25–£24, Main £15.75–£44, Dessert £6.50–£11, Sunday lunch £29 **Wines** 50+ bottles over £30, 18 by glass **Parking** On street **Notes** Children welcome

London W1

CUT at 45 Park Lane
PLAN 5 A1

◉◉◉ Modern American **V**
020 7493 4554 & 020 7493 4545 | 45 Park Lane, W1K 1BJ
www.dorchestercollection.com/en/london/45-park-lane

High-gloss temple of beef Dorchester-style

Wolfgang Puck may not be a household name in the UK, but this Austrian chef and restaurateur is a big deal Stateside, and his global empire includes several joints under the CUT banner. The Park Lane postcode is a sure sign that you're not going to be eating on a budget – that, plus the location in a swanky hotel in the Dorchester stable. With über-glam decor of striking contemporary chandeliers, swathes of curtain, burnished wooden panels and a cosmopolitan, high-end vibe, this is one posh steakhouse, where top-grade beef sourced from all over the world is treated with due reverence – Australian and Japanese Wagyu, Black Angus New York sirloin, South Devon filet mignon, USDA rib-eye steak with fries – they're all here, expertly aged, sold by weight, and timed to the second on the grill, with eight sauces to choose from. If all that red meat action is too rich for your blood, the menu offers other fare, Dorset crab and lobster cocktail with spicy tomato and horseradish sauce, say, followed by sashimi-grade big-eye tuna steak. The skilled kitchen team comes up trumps with puddings too, perhaps dark Valrhona chocolate soufflé with whipped crème fraîche and toasted hazelnut gianduja ice cream, while cheeses come with nut bread, quince paste, candied walnuts and honeycomb.

Chef David McIntyre **Seats** 70, Private dining room 14 **Times** 12–3.30/ 6–10.30 **Wines** 597 bottles over £30, 22 by glass **Parking** Valet parking **Notes** Brunch, early evening menu, Children welcome

Fera at Claridge's
PLAN 2 B5

Modern British **V**
020 7107 8888 | Brook Street, W1K 4HR
www.feraatclaridges.co.uk

As we were preparing this guide we learnt that Simon Rogan was leaving Fera, therefore the Rosette award for this establishment has been suspended. Reassessment will take place in due course under the new chef. The restaurant's decor elegantly evokes the natural world in the slate-grey and mossy-green palette, burnished walnut tables, and bleached, skeletal branches soaring up to a stained glass ceiling.

Seats 94, Private dining room 12 **Times** 12–2/6.30–10, Closed D 25 December **Parking** On street, NCP **Notes** Children 5 years +

Galvin at Windows Restaurant & Bar

PLAN 5 B1

@@@ Modern French

020 7208 4021 | London Hilton on Park Lane, 22 Park Lane, W1K 1BE

www.galvinatwindows.com

Aspiring modern cooking up in the sky

Restaurants in the sky are common in London's soaring cityscape these days, but the Park Lane Hilton was in the vanguard of wraparound views with its 28th-floor Windows. Naturally, hot-ticket window tables are hard to bag in the sleek art deco-inspired room, but the split-level layout means everyone gets to tick off the landmarks: Canary Wharf, the London Eye, Buckingham Palace, the Houses of Parliament and the green expanse of Hyde Park are all spread below. The Galvin brothers' lustrous modern French bistro-style is the culinary inspiration, with Joo Won at the stoves adding tweaks from further afield – a starter of raw Orkney scallops, say, shifted up a gear with nori emulsion, blood orange, sweet soy and shiso. Top-notch materials are the building blocks of Francophile mains such as Scotch beef fillet made more luxurious with foie gras, mushrooms, braised leek and fragrant truffle, or the roasted fillet of gold-standard Skrei cod that comes timed to perfection and partnered with glazed Suffolk pork belly and a provençale stew of artichoke barigoule. To finish, fantastic seasonal cheeses are delivered at peak ripeness, or you could stick with sweet French tradition and go for a classic apple tarte Tatin with caramel sauce and rosemary ice cream.

Chefs Joo Won, Chris Galvin **Seats** 130 **Times** 12–2.30/5.30–10.30, Closed 26 December, L Saturday, D Sunday **Prices** Set L 2 course from £30, Set L 3 course from £35, Starter £29, Main £40, Dessert £15, Sunday lunch from £55 **Wines** 248 bottles over £30, 36 bottles under £30, 31 by glass **Parking** NCP **Notes** Tasting menu 6 course, Dégustation menu, Vegetarian available, Children welcome

Gauthier Soho

PLAN 2 D5

@@@ Modern French V ♥

020 7494 3111 | 21 Romilly Street, W1D 5AF

www.gauthiersoho.co.uk

Ring the doorbell for creative French cooking

Deep in the heart of Soho, Alexis Gauthier's restaurant occupies an unreconstructed Regency townhouse, and it feels only right that there should be a doorbell that must be rung to gain entry, even if a liveried footman who might announce you isn't on hand. The dining room is upstairs, a pristine white-walled space with windows peering down on the street activity and an elegant old fireplace adding the homely touch. Gauthier favours a subtly creative approach to what is essentially classical

continued

French cooking, and powerfully popular at that. Black truffle tortellini with pancetta to start looks like an Italian job, but is given French polish by means of a deeply concentrated chicken jus, or there may be Dorset crab with cucumber and lamb's lettuce in citrus dressing. Pedigree meats such as Barbary duck, loin and sweetbreads of veal, or Black Angus beef with purple artichoke, glazed turnips and pink garlic compete for main course attention with flawlessly executed fish cookery, such as wild sea bass in a potent fish jus with fondant salsify, butternut crush and cos lettuce. Finish with a high-octane chocolate tart made with Amedei Grand Cru, served with silky caramel ice cream, or perhaps a blood orange trio of sponge, cream and sorbet.

Chefs Gerard Virolle, Alexis Gauthier **Seats** 60, Private dining room 32 **Times** 12–2.30/6.30–10.30, Closed Christmas, bank holidays, Sunday, L Monday **Prices** Set L 2 course £24, Set L 3 course £30, Deluxe L 3 course with wine and champagne £45, Set D 3 course £50, (4 course £60/5 course £70), Tasting menu £65–£75 **Wines** 150 bottles over £30, 30 bottles under £30, 20 by glass **Parking** On street, NCP (Chinatown) **Notes** Children welcome

Le Gavroche Restaurant

PLAN 2 A5

◉◉◉◉ French **V**
020 7408 0881 | 43 Upper Brook Street, W1K 7QR
www.le-gavroche.co.uk

Unwavering commitment to classical French gastronomy

When Le Gavroche opened its doors just short of a half-century ago, French gastronomy was still imperfectly grasped on these shores, even among London cognoscenti, and if that picture was transformed, it is in large measure because Albert Roux and, later, his son Michel, never wavered in their commitment to international cooking's ancien régime. It's true there are a few more new-fangled dishes now, but if there were no solid gold tradition, nobody else would know what they were rebelling against. The setting is a serene basement room, run with the kind of punctilious courtesy that is virtually a dead language in London now, and the bill of fare an extended homage to the most rigorous training in excellence. Start with roast scallops in coral crumb with carrots, sauced with yellow Chartreuse, if you're after new directions, and if you're not, look to the old and flawless standbys – the artichoke stuffed with truffled foie gras mousse, the lobster mousseline and caviar in champagne butter. Extraordinary quality in the prime materials is the hallmark of principal dishes like Pyrenean milk-fed lamb with piquillos in minted jus, and roasted T-bone of turbot in chive butter. A Menu Exceptionnel in this context had better do as it promises, and undoubtedly does, all the way to its little pistachio-chocolate gâteau, garnished with bitter chocolate sorbet and dried fruits doused in rum. French and British artisanal cheeses are the best, served with authoritative knowledge, as is the compendious wine list, which will only make you kick yourself for not buying that EuroMillions ticket.

Chef Michel Roux Jnr **Seats** 60, Private dining room 6 **Times** 12–2/6–10, Closed Christmas, New Year and bank holidays, Sunday and Monday, L Saturday and Tuesday **Prices** Set L 3 course £66, Tasting menu 8 course £150–£245, Starter £21–£74, Main £26–£68, Dessert £18–£46 **Wines** 2,000 bottles over £30, 20 by glass **Parking** On street, NCP (Park Lane) **Notes** Children welcome

The Greenhouse

PLAN 5 B1

◉◉◉◉ Modern French **V** ♛
020 7499 3331 | 27a Hay's Mews, Mayfair, W1J 5NY
www.greenhouserestaurant.co.uk

Avant-garde French cooking by the garden terrace

Not much in Mayfair feels discreet, but along Hay's Mews, despite the obvious opulence of the quarter, it's possible to feel you're somewhere other than the heart of the West End. The little garden terrace that leads up to the entrance of The Greenhouse gives the name of the place its proper resonance, and there's a refreshingly understated feel to the dining room, where leaf-green seating at crisply dressed tables is offset by minimal wall decorations. There has been much changing of the guard in the kitchens over the years, with different culinary styles coming and going, but the present preference, under the restlessly creative Arnaud Bignon, is for highly refined French avant-gardism, with visually striking presentations, from the initial array of appetisers onwards. A menu that credits favoured suppliers the length and breadth of the British Isles, backed by European specialities such as Bellota ham and Greek olive oil, might open with native lobster, rhubarb and puntarelle, given unearthly aromatic impact by green Chartreuse, or match seared foie gras with cocoa nibs and quince. East Asian notes are productively incorporated into main dishes such as John Dory with asparagus and matcha tea, or the Kumamoto oyster and daikon that come with monkfish in squid ink, while Galloway beef is regally enough treated that it comes in two servings, first in yuzu with swede and horseradish, then with mooli, carrot and cucumber in consommé. The aromatic note that distinguishes Bignon's cooking doesn't desert him at dessert stage either, when lemon baba comes scented with sage, or the lychee soufflé is fragrant with hibiscus.

Chef Arnaud Bignon **Seats** 60, Private dining room 12 **Times** 12–2.30/ 6.30–10.30, Closed Christmas and bank holidays, Sunday, L Saturday **Prices** Set L 2 course £35, Set L 3 course £40, Set D 2 course £90, Set D 3 course £100, Tasting menu £125–£145, Starter £35–£45, Main £55–£65, Dessert £18 **Wines** 3,300+ bottles over £30, 20 bottles under £30, 32 by glass **Parking** On street **Notes** Children welcome

London W1

Hakkasan Mayfair

PLAN 2 B6

@@@ Modern Cantonese, Chinese 🍷
020 7907 1888 | 17 Bruton Street, W1J 6QB
www.hakkasan.com

Creatively reworked southern Chinese cuisine

The second London branch of Hakkasan, in well-heeled surroundings just off Berkeley Square, opened in 2010, and has established itself as another destination for innovatively reworked modern Cantonese cuisine. A sense of occasion is one of Hakkasan's big drawing points. The entry along a long dark corridor towards the scent of flowers leads to a subdued, stylish environment of black slate flooring, dark wood tables and mushroom-coloured seating. The most intuitive way of starting is with a dim sum platter, comprised of scallop shumai, har gau, Chinese chive dumpling, and duck in yam bean nest, served with sweet chilli sauce, chilli oil and soy for dipping. A deep understanding of the harmoniously layered flavours in southern Chinese cooking informs main dishes like sanpei chicken cooked in a clay pot with sweet basil, chilli, spring onion and tender garlic cloves, a sticky sauce of the cooking juices coating the chicken. Nor are dishes confined to the overly familiar repertoire, when sweet-and-sour pork with pomegranate, or stir-fried venison with eryngii mushrooms, baby leek and dried chilli, are on offer. The covetable dessert is an apple creation featuring a choux bun filled with poached apple and green tea cream, garnished with fragments of almond feuilletine.

Chefs Tong Chee Hwee, Tan Tee Wei **Seats** 220, Private dining room 16 **Times** 12–5/6–11.15, Closed 24–25 December, L 26 December and 1 January **Prices** Set L 3 course £40-£45, Set D 3 course £68–£128, Taste of Hakkasan £38, Starter £8.50–£29, Main £13.9–£61, Dessert £9.20 **Wines** 400 bottles over £30, 10 bottles under £30, 9 by glass **Parking** NCP **Notes** Vegetarian available, Children welcome

Hélène Darroze at The Connaught

PLAN 2 B6

@@@@@ French V 🍷
020 3147 7200 | Carlos Place, W1K 2AL
www.the-connaught.co.uk

Bold innovative cooking from a star of the French south-west

Much was made of the snazzy makeover that The Connaught underwent last decade, which saw a dramatic silver and green palette thrown against the venerable oak panelling of what was one of central London's most traditional five-star hotel restaurants. In fact, the contemporary look is in total harmony with the shell into which it was coaxed. This is still very much an old-school high-class establishment, and one that works assiduously to make everybody who passes through its portals feel at ease. That is one of the definitions of class after all. A sultrily low-lit ambience pervades the public spaces in the evenings, from the luxe bar where exciting cocktails push whatever envelopes remain to be pushed, to the extensive, and extensively staffed, dining room, over which southwest French chef Hélène Darroze disposes.

Everything about the approach here is designed to subvert expectations, so while you're working out how to order a multi-course menu by means of the solitaire board, its tiny balls each marked with one of the dishes, a trolley with a Bayonne ham hock rolls forth. Why not nibble on a few shavings while you ponder? Darroze's cooking has its roots in the rich gastronomic traditions of the Landes and Gascony, but she also looks further afield, to southern and eastern Asia notably, for dishes that have become classics of her repertoire. The tandoori scallop, dusted in an Indian spice mix, in its lemongrass-sharp citrus sauce, with velvet-soft carrot purée and long carrot curls, is a bravura performance, intense, light and complex all at once. Landais foie gras makes its expected appearance, but offset by shards of lightly cooked rhubarb, and with more exotic notes of Thai basil and long pepper.

Darroze handles fish dishes boldly, giving a fillet of Cornish John Dory a razor clam garnish, visually echoed with white asparagus, the salty and sour notes of samphire and yuzu adding depth, but she wants us to abandon our preconceptions with meats too, so that a very rare presentation of Basque Country lamb is given the North African treatment with a ras el hanout rub, but also has sweet Muscat grapes and piquillo peppers to emphasise the fondant-like quality of the meat. Those discreetly but assertively used spices resurface in desserts, when a tropical fruit baba is black-peppered, or the Venezuelan chocolate sphere of yuzu jelly has a fleeting note of cumin hovering somewhere. Selected wine flights at two price points are worth the extra outlay to do justice to food as good as this.

Chef Hélène Darroze **Seats** 60, Private dining room 20 **Times** 12–2/6.30–10 **Prices** Set L 3 course £52, Sunday lunch £75, A la carte 5/7/9 course £95/£130/£175 **Wines** 735 bottles over £30, 25 by glass **Parking** South Audley car park **Notes** Children welcome

Kitchen Table

PLAN 2 C3

🏵🏵🏵 Modern British V ♥
020 7637 7770 | 70 Charlotte Street, W1T 4QG
www.kitchentablelondon.co.uk

Sitting at the counter, chatting with the chefs

If the up-close-and-personal experience of chef's table dining gets you hot under the collar, Kitchen Table is right up your street. Hidden away at the back of the Bubbledogs gourmet hotdog and champagne joint, it's the kind of place you come not just to concentrate intensely on what you're

continued

eating, but to chat to head chef James Knappett and his team about it while they're getting it ready. Nineteen inquisitive souls perch at the counter for the kitchen theatre as a dozen daily-changing dishes come their way, labelled by main ingredients from trusted suppliers who have told them what's good that day. A menu might go something like this: Oyster; Chicken; Scallop; Monkfish; Sole; Truffle; Asparagus; Duck; Goat; Rhubarb; Orange; Caramel. And that's pretty much all you need to know in advance of the arrival of each explosively creative dish. One or two items are stalwarts of the repertoire, such as the crispy chicken skin with rosemary mascarpone and bacon jam, while others come and go. Roe deer on a bed of shredded onion simmered in yogurt with slivered raw chestnuts and elderberries, burrata with damson purée, the curiously intense pear sponge with svelte liquorice ice cream are all deeply memorable morsels.

Chef James Knappett **Seats** 19 **Times** 6–11, Closed Sunday and Monday, L all week **Prices** Tasting menu £98–£143 (supplements may apply) **Wines** 65 bottles over £30, 8 by glass **Parking** On street

Little Social

PLAN 2 C5

◉◉◉ French, Modern European ♥
020 7870 3730 | 5 Pollen Street, W1S 1NE
www.littlesocial.co.uk
Simple Anglo-French heritage cooking à la Jason Atherton

Across the street on the same little back lane as the Atherton flagship, Pollen Street, the Little Social is a more obviously chattery, clattery venue for London's young at heart, where a cheerful racket of piped pop is fed through ceiling speakers over a dark-panelled bistro-like space. The menu items are of heritage English and French dishes, presented with honest, almost insolent simplicity in portions to assuage the ravenous. There's a take on steak tartare made with Cumbrian bavette, gaufrette potatoes and a yolk of quail egg to begin, as well as a brioche bun slathered with avocado crush and piled to toppling with crab and chive mayonnaise. An enterprising pair might then rock on with 40-day Buccleugh côte de boeuf cooked on the bone, perhaps with sides of horseradish mash and tenderstem broccoli, or go their separate ways for roasted sole meunière, and a cottage pie that comes in a cast-iron pot with a bourguignon bottom layer of stunning richness under a wafer-thin potato coverlet. Finish in style with maple-glazed doughnuts filled with baked Bramley apple, cinnamon and port in crème anglaise sprinkled with cinnamon sugar, or go with the fine Anglo-French artisan cheeses from La Fromagerie.

Chef Cary Docherty **Seats** 55, Private dining room 8 **Times** 12–2.30/6–10.30, Closed 25–26 December, 1–2 January, bank holidays, Sunday **Prices** Set L 2 course £21 (3 course £25), Set D 2 course £21 (3 course £25), Starter £6–£39.50, Main £16–£75, Dessert £5–£16 **Wines** 60 bottles over £30, 6 bottles under £30, 16 by glass **Parking** Cavendish Square **Notes** Vegetarian available, Exclusive hire available, Children welcome

Locanda Locatelli

PLAN 2 A5

@@@ Italian 🍷

020 7935 9088 | 8 Seymour Street, W1H 7JZ

www.locandalocatelli.com

Classically rooted Italian cooking from a famous face

The human dynamo that is Giorgio Locatelli will be familiar to readers from his many TV appearances and cookbooks, but it's here, in an elegant, spacious Marylebone venue, all light wood and cream upholstery, that the intensity of his commitment really makes palpable sense. Locatelli has been at the forefront of the movement to nudge traditional Italian cooking into the 21st century, with a light-touch innovative spark that nonetheless does justice to the regional traditions. So you might start a meal with something as simple as burrata, accompanied by caponata and dressed in aged balsamic vinegar, and yet feel that you are experiencing these familiar tastes for the first time, or you might go straight to the primi, where risottos of snails and nettles, or hand-made pasta such as tagliatelle with kid meat and chilli, await. Main courses respect the elemental simplicity that is the foundation stone of Italian cooking, adding lentils and garlic purée to superbly rich roast squab, or presenting roast brill in a straightforward acqua pazza of wild chicory, green olives and tomato. Tart of the day or tiramisù are the obvious ways to finish, unless you get lured in the direction of vanilla cheesecake with violet jelly and strawberry sorbet.

Chef Giorgio Locatelli **Seats** 85, Private dining room 50 **Times** 12–3/6–11, Closed 24–26 December and 1 January **Prices** Starter £12.50–£24.50, Main £16.50–£33.80, Dessert £7.50–£15.50 **Wines** 576 bottles over £30, 30 bottles under £30, 18 by glass **Parking** NCP adjacent **Notes** Sunday lunch, Vegetarian available, Children welcome

Murano

PLAN 5 B1

◉◉◉◉ Modern European, Italian influences ♥
020 7495 1127 | 20-22 Queen Street, W1J 5PP
www.muranolondon.com

Classy showcase for Italian-led contemporary cooking

One of the UK's foremost chefs, Angela Hartnett now heads up her own mini-constellation of restaurants. Her elegant Mayfair flagship is a fresh, light-filled room whose Mayfair postcode is reflected in the upscale decor, and the namesake Venetian glass stars in arty chandeliers. The lady charged with day-to-day handling of Hartnett's Italian-influenced culinary style is head chef Pip Lacey, and she takes prime ingredients as the starting point for her contemporary Italian ideas. A fresh and simple composition of cured sea bream partnered with kohlrabi, capers, pear and rosemary purée might get things off the mark, or you might set out with a decadent pairing of quail and foie gras with Jerusalem artichoke, red cabbage and almonds. In such a setting, it would be a mistake to pass on the pasta, with the likes of chestnut anolini boosted with mushroom consommé and sprout tops on offer, or black pepper gnocchi with smoked haddock, quail's egg and beurre noisette.

At main course stage, fish is expertly handled – perhaps halibut with baked celeriac, dates, squid and lemon – or there could be a comfort-oriented pairing of crispy pork belly with heritage carrots, roast onion and pickled turnip. Desserts are equally stimulating, with panettone pain perdu with sticky toffee sauce and banana and rum ice cream sitting alongside pistachio soufflé with hot chocolate sauce. The set lunch menu is a top-value entry point, and an impressive wine list naturally features well-chosen Italian growers, and offers some intriguing organic and biodynamic bottles.

Chefs Angela Hartnett, Pip Lacey **Seats** 46, Private dining room 12
Times 12–3/6.30–11, Closed Christmas, Sunday **Prices** Set L 2 course
£28, Set L 3 course £33, Set D 2 course from £55, Set D 3 course from £70,
Tasting menu 3/4/5/6 course £70–£100, Starter £20, Main £35, Dessert
£15 **Wines** 745 bottles over £30, 7 bottles under £30, 21 by
glass **Parking** NCP (Carrington Street) **Notes** Vegetarian available,
Children welcome

The Ninth

PLAN 2 D4

@@@ Modern French, Mediterranean
020 3019 0880 | 22 Charlotte Street, W1T 2NB
www.theninthlondon.com

Cool, chilled-out outfit underpinned by pure pedigree

New York-born chef Jun Tanaka is no stranger to fans of TV cheffery and here he is in his first solo venture, so-called, with irresistible logic, as it's the ninth place he's worked in. After two decades in starry, fine-dining gaffs, Tanaka eschews ostentation here for a relaxed, cool decor that's all exposed brick walls, decorated concrete, floorboards and mirrors, dotted with eye-catching statement pieces like glass pendant lighting or metal wine cages and wine glass racks, while leather banquettes and café-style chairs provide the comforts alongside mahogany or white marble-topped tables. A modern menu of sharing dishes focuses on light Mediterranean ideas underpinned by a classic French influence and bursting with seasonality and flavour. Dividing into nine categories (there's that number again), the roster's focus treats vegetable dishes with the same importance as everything else, serving up the likes of beetroot tarte Tatin with feta and pine nuts. In-vogue snacks like punchy oxtail croquettes or duck Scotch egg get the tastebuds fired up, then osso buco tortellini might come with hazelnut gremolata; big-hitting meat dishes could see salted beef cheeks alongside oxtail consommé and January King cabbage. Desserts are straight-up classics, such as an absolute-perfection tarte Tatin with rosemary ice cream.

Chef Jun Tanaka **Seats** 84, Private dining room 22 **Times** 12–2.30/5.30–10.30, Closed bank holidays, Sunday **Prices** Set L 2 course £19, Set L 3 course £25, Starter £8.50–£12, Main £16–£28, Dessert £6.50–£14 **Wines** 68 bottles over £30, 6 bottles under £30, 29 by glass **Notes** Vegetarian available, Children welcome

Orrery

PLAN 2 A3

@@@ Modern French V
020 7616 8000 | 55-57 Marylebone High Street, W1U 5RB
www.orrery-restaurant.co.uk

Stylish setting for stylish French cooking

Laid on top of the Conran store like a luxurious layer of fondant, Orrery is a long and narrow, but stylishly conceived, space, lit during the day by an end-to-end skylight and arched windows with views over the heart of Marylebone. A roof terrace is not the least of its appeal. Finely crafted French cooking of sensibility and refinement exercises a powerful pull too. Salmon ballotine with fromage blanc, garnished with a quail egg and caviar, is a pleasingly light way in, or there may be truffled potato ravioli

continued

and mushrooms in a buttery emulsion for those who mean to go on as they start. Classic French presentations such as herb-crusted sea bass in chive sabayon, or magret de canard in an orange-tinged jus, served with caramelised fennel and braised cabbage, are among the alluring main dishes. Five- or seven-course menu gourmand deals give a comprehensive tour of the repertoire, concluding with something like lime-poached pineapple and coconut sorbet, or chocolate pannacotta and mango sorbet, but the copiously stocked cheese trolley is worth a detour before you get there. The Coravin system furnishes a fantastic list of wines by the glass, but even the regular glass selections have plenty to entice.

Chef Igor Tymchyshyn **Seats** 110, Private dining room 16 **Times** 12–2.30/6.30–10, Closed 26–27 December, 1 January, Easter Monday, Summer Bank Holiday, D 25 December, L 31 December **Prices** Set L 2 course £24.50, Set L 3 course £28, Set D 2 course £55, Set D 3 course £60, Tasting menu 7/9 course £67–£235, Starter £8–£23.50, Main £15–£39, Dessert £6–£11, Sunday lunch £30 **Wines** 300 bottles over £30, 50 bottles under £30, 16 by glass **Parking** NCP (Marylebone Road) **Notes** Children welcome

Pied à Terre
PLAN 2 D4

@@@ Modern French V ♟

020 7636 1178 & 020 7916 0786 | 34 Charlotte Street, W1T 2NH
www.pied-a-terre.co.uk

Art on a plate in one of Charlotte Street's finest

David Moore's Pied à Terre has been one of London's top dining destinations since the early 1990s, going about its business with an admirable lack of ostentation in a discreet narrow-fronted venue that you might mistake for an art gallery, which is all well and good since the 'artist in restaurant' concept means there's always striking artwork to jazz up the walls of the unshowy dining room. Andy McFadden arrived from sister restaurant L'Autre Pied, in 2015, and continues to deliver inventive modern cooking of finesse and refinement. A first course from the à la carte, for example, matches smoked eel with pork belly, their richness held nicely in check by apple, cucumber and dashi. That may be followed by perfectly timed fallow deer with celeriac, sprouts, watercress and chestnut. Fish could be sea-fresh John Dory, thoughtfully paired with grapefruit, miso, black quinoa and various brassicas. Desserts also bring thrills aplenty, serving coconut rice pudding with sweet cheese, yogurt and a cleansing shot of sake, or you might be tempted by a medley of chocolate, mandarin, honeycomb and stem ginger. For tight budgets, the set lunch offers stonking value, while for high-rollers, the wine list is a class act brimming with weighty classics and new discoveries. Vegetarians and vegans have their own menus.

Chef Andy McFadden **Seats** 40, Private dining room 14 **Times** 12.15–2.30/
6–11, Closed 2 weeks Christmas and New Year, Sunday, L Saturday
Prices Set L 2 course £29.50–£65, Set L 3 course £37.50–£80, Set D 2
course from £65, Set D 3 course from £80, A la carte 2/3 course £65/£80,
Tasting menu £75–£145, Pre-theatre Monday to Friday 6–7.30pm 2 course
£39.50 **Wines** 750 bottles over £30, 16 bottles under £30, 15 by glass
Parking Cleveland Street **Notes** Children welcome

Pollen Street Social

PLAN 2 C5

@@@@@ Modern British **V**
020 7290 7600 | 8-10 Pollen Street, W1S 1NQ
www.pollenstreetsocial.com

Breathtaking panache from Jason Atherton's London flagship

Jason Atherton's platoon of signature restaurants has broken cover from
its expansive London network of operations and been deployed overseas,
with outposts these days in Hong Kong, Shanghai, New York, Sydney, and
Cebu in the Philippines. If he has made something as financially and
logistically challenging as the opening of restaurants look easy, that
deceptive impression has been founded on a distinctive culinary identity,
of which there is no shortage of opportunity back home to get a taste.
Among the portfolio of London venues, Pollen Street Social is leader of the
pack, one of the capital's most beguiling destination eateries, tucked
away on a narrow back-alley off Regent Street, diagonally opposite one of
its junior siblings, Little Social. The interior here is glossy and luxy, with
raw linen napery and chocolate-brown banquettes, the hive-of-activity
atmosphere maintained by a glassed-in pass to the kitchen.

For all that Atherton's venues retain a high-tempo feeling of busy
intensity, his concept is 'relaxed fine dining', the simple notion that there
must be a ready constituency for eating high-end, innovative food in a less
socially conflicted ambience than many top-notch dining rooms are
imbued with. The Pollen Street lieutenant, Dale Bainbridge, interprets the
house style with breathtaking panache, producing dishes that combine
inventiveness with clean, crisp presentations that are complex enough to
be exciting, but still full of direct, full-force impact. Provenance remains
the foundation-stone of these dishes, as witness the starting salad of
superb Colchester crab with apple and coriander, its elemental freshness
and sweetness offset by black garlic, a serving of the brown meat on
toast, with wafer-thin discs of crisp sourdough and the piercing note of
concentrated lemon purée. Equally outstanding is an opener of
Lincolnshire smoked eel with julienne of pickled apple, gnocchi and
buttermilk froth, over which a light beetroot broth is decanted. Succulent
meats such as Cumbrian beef, suckling pig and lamb and Goosnargh duck
are given treatments that emphasise their inherent qualities, that beef rib

continued

for two coming with a whole panoply of macaroni cheese, truffle, roasted carrots, hazelnuts, and green bean and foie gras salad for an unforgettable virtuoso performance, while fish dishes retain all their intrinsic sea savour, perhaps for red mullet and sea scallop in seaweed butter served with bouillabaisse. To finish, there might be a blackcurrant take on Eton Mess, a neat timbale of cream, mousse, compôte and biscuit that's yours to mess, or perhaps intense orange marmalade cake with pain d'épices and sea buckthorn sorbet.

Chefs Jason Atherton, Dale Bainbridge **Seats** 52, Private dining room 12 **Times** 12–2.45/6–10.45, Closed bank holidays, Sunday **Prices** Set L 2 course £32, Set L 3 course £37, Tasting menu £95–£110, Starter £16.50–£50, Main £34–£90, Dessert £11.50–£13 **Wines** 800 bottles over £30, 8 bottles under £30, 20 by glass **Parking** On street **Notes** Children welcome

Portland

PLAN 2 B4

@@@ Modern British 🍷
020 7436 3261 | 113 Great Portland Street, W1W 6QQ
www.portlandrestaurant.co.uk

Compact, seasonal menu of big-hitting flavours

On first impression, Portland feels like the sort of relaxed neighbourhood gaff you'd like to have in your area. Just up the road from the BBC, the place got off the blocks with a flying start in 2015, making headlines of its own with its on-trend take on new-Brit cuisine, scoring high with precision cooking, unstuffy, spot-on service and an intimate, pared-back interior of wooden tables and chairs, plain white walls, retro lighting, and an upbeat vibe. Upfront, the in-vogue counter and high stalls look out streetwise, while at the back, the open kitchen fires up the culinary action. Brimming with innovation and a genuine sense of seasonality, the to-the-point menu offers vibrant small snack plates as a tempting prelude and might include a fun combination of chicken skins, liver parfait, candied walnuts and Muscat grapes or succulent smoked eel paired with kohlrabi and the bracing kick of horseradish. Razor-sharp dishes cleverly balance flavour, texture and colour interest, as in starters such as salsify, pork jowl, confit egg yolk and 18-month-aged Comté cheese. At mains, Denham Estate deer might be counterpointed with alliums and pickled mustard seed, or Cornish cod could appear with oca, a Peruvian root veg, and brown butter sauce.

Chefs Merlin Labron-Johnson, Edoardo Pellicano **Seats** 36, Private dining room 16 **Times** 12–2.30/6–10, Closed 23 December to 3 January, Sunday **Prices** Tasting menu £45–£58, Starter £12–£16, Main £18–£30, Dessert £8–£9 **Wines** 20 bottles over £30, 8 bottles under £30, 22 by glass **Parking** NCP (Portland Place) **Notes** Vegetarian available, Children welcome

The Ritz Restaurant

PLAN 5 C1

@@@ British, French V
020 7300 2370 | 150 Piccadilly, W1J 9BR
www.theritzlondon.com

Arresting dining in sumptuous formal restaurant

The Ritz Restaurant is one of the world's great dining rooms, its extravagant Louis XVI-inspired decor of murals, painted ceilings, statues and glittering chandeliers reflected from mirrored walls akin to stepping into Versailles Palace. When a special occasion meal in stunning surroundings is called for, it's hard to beat, with legions of waiting staff pulling off a correctly polite performance with theatrical classic tableside service involving trolleys and cloches. Auguste Escoffier would find no fault with the whole show, including the classically-inspired menu, although John Williams MBE makes a fine job of tweaking the food for 21st-century diners via his own distinctively contemporary reworkings, such as the mango, gingerbread and tonka bean that accompany goose liver terrine. Elsewhere, ingredients are as good as it gets, with posh beef tournedos served with Jerusalem artichoke, watercress and a powerful red wine sauce appealing to traditionalists, or for those in search of more up-to-date ideas, perhaps sea bass partnered with quinoa, sea vegetables and smoked eel. To finish, a perfectly risen pear Williams soufflé might come with prune and Armagnac ice cream, or you could end the show with a timewarp dessert: crêpes Suzette for two, flambéed theatrically at the table.

Chef John T Williams MBE – AA Chef of the Year 2017–18 *(see page 10)* **Seats** 90, Private dining room 60 **Times** 12.30–2/5.30–9.30 **Prices** Set L 3 course £52-£62, Tasting menu £95, Menu surprise 6 course £95, Live at the Ritz menu £110 Starter £18–£48, Main £40–£52, Dessert £17–£19, Sunday lunch £62 **Wines** 800 bottles over £30, 32 by glass **Parking** 10, NCP **Notes** Children welcome

Roka Charlotte Street

PLAN 2 C4

@@@ Japanese
020 7580 6464 | 37 Charlotte Street, W1T 1RR
www.rokarestaurant.com

Stylish robata cookery full of freshness and umami

This super-cool modern Japanese venue is a magnet for the media crew of Charlotte Street, an area that has long been a barometer of dining trends in the capital. The group has other outposts at Canary Wharf, Mayfair and Aldwych, but this flagship of the Roka brand has been packing them in since 2004, and it's easy to see why: the airy room is flooded with daylight from full-height windows, equipped with chunky hardwood furniture, and

continued

its beating heart is the robata counter, where ringside views of the kitchen action are the hot ticket. The menu's fusion temptations include yellowtail sashimi with truffle yuzu dressing, mizuma and pickled vegetables, or tempura-battered rock shrimp with wasabi pea seasoning and chilli mayonnaise. As for the robata offerings, there may be Korean-spiced lamb cutlets, cedar-roasted baby chicken with chilli and lemon, or scallop skewers with wasabi and miso. Fusion desserts can sometimes be a car crash, but not here: try yogurt and almond cake with mango toffee, and caramel miso ice cream. There's a tasting menu for those that find choosing too much to bear, but rest assured the service team are adept at guiding you through any unfamiliar terminology.

Chef Hamish Brown **Seats** 350, Private dining room 20 **Times** 12–3.30/5.30–11, Closed Christmas **Wines** 200 bottles over £30, 10 bottles under £30, 20 by glass **Notes** Vegetarian available, Children welcome

Roka Mayfair

PLAN 2 A5

◉◉◉ Modern Japanese
020 7305 5644 | 30 North Audley Street, W1K 6ZF
www.rokarestaurant.com
Japanese fusion food with ringside robata seats

The Mayfair outpost of London's Roka quartet is to be found in one of the calmer corners of the West End, its dark awning extending over a few outdoor tables for the intrepid. It's inside, though, that the real action is happening, where under a slatted wood ceiling amid steel columns, a robatayaki counter allows point-blank views of the charcoal-grilling and the lightning-fast ministrations of a talented brigade. A productive hybrid of classical Japanese and the modern fusion approach is the name of the game, and for those with the resources, the opulent tasting menu extends across a broad range, from the initial taste of yellowtail sashimi in truffled yuzu dressing to exquisite dumplings of black cod, crab and crayfish, and wasabi-fired scallops on skewers. Meats get the most regal treatment of all, for smoked duck breast with plum and moromi miso, or Grade 9 Wagyu beef and eringyi mushrooms in ponzu, which somewhat unsurprisingly comes at a substantial supplement. Dessert platters look good enough to eat rather than just photograph, the signature being the cuboid block of chocolate and green tea sponge pudding, garnished with pear ice cream topped with a crisp of Jivara chocolate. You won't want to miss out on the sake selection either.

Chef Luca Spiga **Seats** 113 **Times** 12–11.30, All-day dining, Closed 25 December **Prices** Tasting menu 11/12 course £66–£88, Starter £4.60–£14, Main £9.60–£72, Dessert £7–£56, Sunday lunch **Wines** 100+ bottles over £30, 4 bottles under £30, 32 by glass **Notes** Vegetarian available, Children welcome

Sketch (The Gallery)
PLAN 2 C5

◉◉◉ Modern European ♟

See page 168

Sketch (Lecture Room & Library)
PLAN 2 C5

◉◉◉◉◉ Modern European **V** ♟

See page 170

Social Eating House
PLAN 2 C5

◉◉◉ Modern British **V** ♟

020 7993 3251 | 58-59 Poland Street, W1F 7NS

www.socialeatinghouse.com

Vintage chic and classy cooking with flavours galore

The most casual of Jason Atherton's ever-expanding group of restaurants is helmed by chef-patron Paul Hood, a fruitful partnership that has resulted in an on-trend enterprise that fits nicely into Soho with its stripped-back vintage decor – all bare brickwork, artfully scuffed banquettes and restored furniture. The menu doesn't hold a candle for any particular style of cuisine, but it's a little bit British, a touch French, and more about full-on flavour than anything else. Sharing jars are aimed to accompany a pre-meal sharpener, one being ham hock, piccalilli and chicory. Some lively ideas are given free rein, often bringing unusual combinations. Tartare of Black Angus beef, for instance, might come with beetroot, egg yolk jam and horseradish. Among main courses, slow-cooked venison loin could arrive with roasted morels, dukkah spice, truffled gnocchi, cavolo nero and white onion soubise, and baked Cornish hake is served with hispi cabbage gratin, Salcombe crab, Tokyo turnip and saffron. The kitchen pulls out all the stops for desserts too: consider caramelised milk and brown sugar tart with ginger wine, and fromage frais sorbet, or end with a boozy sundae from the cocktail bar, packing a punch via Kahlua and chocolate brownie, Grand Marnier sorbet, Bailey's ice cream and espresso syrup.

Chef Paul Hood **Seats** 75, Private dining room 8 **Times** 12–2.30/6–10.30, Closed 25–26 December, bank holidays, Sunday **Prices** Set L 2 course £22.50-£29.50, Set L 3 course £26.50-£33.50, Tasting menu £62–£110, Chef's experience £110, Starter £12–£15.50, Main £18–£86, Dessert £8.50–£15.50 **Wines** 183 bottles over £30, 4 bottles under £30, 25 by glass **Parking** Q-Park (Poland Street) **Notes** Children welcome

LONDON W1

Sketch (The Gallery)

PLAN 2 C5

◎◎◎ Modern European 🍷

020 7659 4500 | 9 Conduit Street, W1S 2XG

www.sketch.london

Virtuoso cooking in artist-designed restaurant

The 'modern European gastro-brasserie' option at the super-cool Sketch (where art meets culinary pizzazz) is like no other brasserie you've ever been to. Witty, playful cartoons (courtesy of celebrated Brit artist David Shrigley) fill the walls – 239 of them, to be precise – alongside a touch of designer glam from India Mahdavi. It's a striking open space, with a candy pink hue, low-slung funky barrel chairs and banquettes and clever lighting. The crockery is designed by Shrigley too, so expect a few additional wry messages on the white ceramics to greet last mouthfuls. As always, service remains a highlight, with charming, informed staff positively brimming with enthusiasm like it was the opening night.

To match the glossy, happening vibe, beautiful people and art, über-chef Pierre Gagnaire's food doesn't hold back on creativity either, with vibrancy, sheer skill and a sense of fun evident throughout. The man's a 'flavoursmith'; take an opener that teams twice-baked haddock and scallop soufflé with sauerkraut, Morteau sausage and juniper beurre blanc, all beautifully crafted, executed and presented, or a 'Homage to David Shrigley' that delivers an Asian-accented assemblage of red tuna sashimi partnered with cauliflower and bonito velouté and a cube of soya milk and horseradish, all leavened with the acidity of mango and green

apple. Likewise, splendid main-course fillet of Kentish lamb gets a touch of Mediterranean-meets-Asian fusion sparkle via its accompaniment of aubergine caviar with white miso, and cabbage stuffed with sweetbread and medjool dates, while the same meticulous craftmanship and complex layering of flavours also defines a dish of Iberico pork served with caramelised sweet onion fondue, capers, persimmon, and black pudding and Kirsch ravioli. At the other end of the spectrum, fish cookery can be as classic and unadorned as a fillet of sea-fresh brill served with sauce gribiche and new potatoes.

There's no lack of creativity when it comes to desserts either, so wallow in extravagant creations such as green matcha tea meringues with coconut milk mousseline and dragon fruit syrup. The wine list is a divertingly spectacular thing, too, with lots of good things available – at a price – in fact, the whole experience doesn't come cheap, but the menu does contain a few options that won't have you hauled before the bank manager. Afternoon tea is another treat on offer in The Gallery dining room, with some spectacular cakes and more of Mr Shrigley's tableware to help the conversation flow.

Chef Pierre Gagnaire, Herve Deville **Seats** 126 **Times** 6.30–11 (opening times vary), Closed Christmas, 1 January, L all week **Prices** Starter from £14, Main from £18 , Dessert from £6 Afternoon tea from £58 (daily 12.30–4.30) **Wines** 220 bottles over £30, 2 bottles under £30, 40 by glass **Parking** On street, NCP **Notes** Vegetarian available, Children welcome

LONDON W1
Sketch (Lecture Room & Library)   PLAN 2 C5
◉◉◉◉◉ Modern European Ⅴ ♟
020 7659 4500 | 9 Conduit Street, W1S 2XG
www.sketch.london

Highly conceptualised food from a modern master

When Sketch opened its doors in the last decade, it was with the intention of making a valiant attempt to shift our expectations of what a restaurant ought to do. You were processed at the entrance as though you were arriving at a club for the glitterati, and once admitted, found yourself ascending through a succession of dramatically designed spaces that, other than for the presence of laid-up tables, were doing their best not to look like somewhere you might buy a meal at all. The principal dining space is, after all, still named a Lecture Room and Library, impressing on visitors the need for studiousness and patient attention, perhaps also a quiet reverence, which was the appropriate stance to take towards the highly conceptualised food that would emerge.

If calm reflection was required of the diner, however, the designers had put themselves under no such obligation, and the interiors teem with obstreperous collisions of candy pink, mustard and scarlet, at least in the 'padded cell' of the main dining room. The French modern master Pierre Gagnaire still devises all menus here, aiming to encompass a dizzyingly wide range of ingredients and techniques in a multiplicity of small plates, whose contents are to be consumed in strictly prescribed sequences. Reading the whole lengthy carte has the air of cramming for an essay.

An opening course, Perfume of the Earth, will comprise foie gras and cranberry ravioli flash-smoked in a hay cocotte, an assemblage of pumpkin, pineapple, mango and coconut, pâté en croûte with mustard grains and beetroot and star-anise sorbet, snails à la bordelaise alongside a lettuce leaf stuffed with red onion, and a serving of bone marrow scattered with rye breadcrumbs and paired with puréed nettles. The risk, as Gagnaire well knows, is that the sheer complexity of the approach could result in crossed wires and blurred culinary vision, and yet the minutely detailed three-dimensionality of each element, and the ways the components work in juxtaposition with each other, produces an undeniable alchemy.

Mains might introduce turbot and veal jus-braised endive to each other, or layer Goosnargh duck with all the spices and fruity sweetness it can handle, down to blackcurranted red cabbage and minty courgettes, and it all somehow works. The Grand Dessert brings on a parade of half-a-dozen dishes in two services, the standout being an intensely fragrant coriander lokum in star anise syrup with soy milk and strawberries.

Chefs Pierre Gagnaire, Johannes Nuding **Seats** 50, Private dining room 24
Times 12–1.45/7–10, Closed 19 August to 6 September, 23–30 December, 1 January, bank holidays, Sunday and Monday, L Tuesday to Thursday
Prices Tasting menu 6 course from £120, Starter from £45, Main from £50
Wines 864 bottles over £30, 3 bottles under £30, 73 by glass
Parking NCP, Cavendish Square **Notes** Dinner Saturday from 6.30pm, Children 6 years +

London W1

The Square
PLAN 2 B6

@@@ Modern French **V**

020 7495 7100 | 6-10 Bruton Street, Mayfair, W1J 6PU

www.squarerestaurant.com

Excellent cooking from a long-running Mayfair star

A new era began for The Square in March 2016 when, after a quarter of a century at the helm, former owner and driving culinary force Philip Howard announced its sale to Marlon Abela. Fear not. Abela heads up a high-end transatlantic portfolio and knows a thing or two about the restaurant business, so the formidable reputation built here for refined modern French-oriented cuisine that utilises a wealth of thoroughbred British produce remains intact. The room was never a show stopper, but it is refined and gently contemporary: abstract art on pearlescent walls, polished wooden floors and generously-spaced tables dressed up in pristine linen. This is Mayfair after all. Dishes unashamedly mix high and humble, opening with a sandwich, albeit a dead posh one, involving Scottish langoustine and coral mayonnaise in crisp, wafer-thin rye bread. Delving deep into the French tradition, a whole lobe of Earl Grey-steeped foie gras, coated in pumpkin seeds and sugar, is carved at table, while the sense of flavours firing on all cylinders is strong and true in a main course of Limousin veal chop with cep tart, lemon thyme and parmesan. Exceptional technical ability continues at dessert, when Rwandan coffee soufflé is lifted by intense orange gel and navelina orange sauce.

Chef Yu Sugimoto **Seats** 75, Private dining room 18 **Times** 12–2.30/ 6.30–10.30, Closed 24 to 26 December, 1 January, L Sunday, bank holidays **Prices** Set L 2 course from £35, Set L 3 course from £40, Tasting menu 7 course £125–£195, A la carte 4 course £105 **Wines** 14 by glass **Parking** NCP (London Grosvenor Hill) **Notes** Children welcome

Texture Restaurant
PLAN 2 A5

@@@@ Modern European **V**

020 7224 0028 | 4 Bryanston Street, W1H 7BY

www.texture-restaurant.co.uk

Creative and dynamic cooking with Icelandic soul

A cool, minimal Scandinavian feel with birch twig motifs and bare tables set against elegant Georgian plasterwork ceilings all add up to a backdrop that entirely suits Agnar Sverrisson's pin-sharp Scandi-accented modern European cooking. Creativity and talent at balancing flavours and, yes, textures are Sverrisson's trademark, together with his lightness of touch, avoiding cream or butter among the savoury courses, and using minimal sugar in the sweet stuff. Whether you go for the à la carte or tasting menus (there are versions available at lunch and dinner, as well as fish-only and vegetarian options), or the unmissable value of the set lunch menu, expect sharply executed cooking and flashes of brilliance. Nordic influences are cleverly balanced with more southerly climes in a main course of lightly-salted Icelandic cod plated with brandade, avocado purée, confit tomatoes with basil, and the salty boost of chorizo. High-flying technical skill ensures flavours ring true in ideas such as saddle and haunch of Scottish roe deer with pied de mouton mushrooms, celeriac and redcurrants. For dessert, white chocolate mousse and ice cream are inventively counterpointed by dill and cucumber. The superlative food is backed by a splendid wine list that clearly has a love affair with Burgundies and Rieslings, with expert advice on hand.

Chef Agnar Sverrisson **Seats** 52, Private dining room 16 **Times** 12–2.30/6–10.30, Closed 2 weeks Christmas, 1 week Easter, 2 weeks August, Sunday and Monday, L Tuesday **Prices** Set L 2 course from £29 , Set L 3 course from £33.50, Tasting menus £89–£95, Starter £16.50–£34.50, Main £29.90–£39, Dessert £13.50 **Wines** 600 bottles over £30, 6 bottles under £30, 35 by glass **Parking** NCP (Bryanston Street) **Notes** Children welcome

Umu

PLAN 2 B5

®®® Japanese 🍷

020 7499 8881 | 14-16 Bruton Place, W1J 6LX

www.umurestaurant.com

Creative Kyoto-style menus presented with flair

The blond wood sliding door in Mayfair is easily missed if you haven't been before. Press the buzzer to gain admittance. Inside is a sepulchrally lit space adorned with filigree wood and slatted screens. It manages to convey an atmosphere of intense activity, with busy chefs and sashaying wait-staff giving it some, and yet the ambience is all relaxed civility. The Kyoto-style menu structure allows Yoshinori Ishii much creative leeway, and if the budget permits, the tasting menus are the most impressive and elaborate way to go. Seafood is unimpeachable, from Northern Ireland wild eel which may be charcoal-grilled and dressed in sweet soy, to lightly seared Cornish lobster in a sauce of its coral. Presentations are the last word in labour-intensive elegance, sparse but lovely, pairing a single Icelandic sea-urchin with warm tofu, or offering boomingly rich, gamey woodcock in a sauce of its liver. The savoury dishes end with a bowl of rice, perhaps topped with grey mullet bottarga, and there's imaginative desserts such as blood orange and black rice, served with tofu and white miso ice cream, or warm Manjari chocolate sponge with an ice cream flavoured with genmaicha (green tea mixed with roasted brown rice).

Chef Yoshinori Ishii **Seats** 64, Private dining room 10 **Times** 12–2.30/6–11, Closed Christmas, New Year, bank holidays, Sunday **Prices** Set L 2 course £30-£65, Starter £8–£38, Main £24–£95, Dessert £8–£18, Kaiseki menu £155 **Wines** 860 bottles over £30, 25 by glass **Parking** On street, NCP (Hanover Hill) **Notes** Vegetarian available, Children welcome

London W1–W4

Wild Honey

PLAN 2 B5

@@@ French, International
020 7758 9160 | 12 Saint George Street, W1S 2FB
www.wildhoneyrestaurant.co.uk
Mayfair branch of Demetre's modern European operation

Anthony Demetre's Wild Honey is the Mayfair arm of his modern
European restaurant operation, situated amid luxurious office buildings
and plush hotels. Inside, it has the faint air of an old railway dining car,
the long wood-panelled space extending back past a bar with seating,
under art deco chandeliers, with waiting staff attired in formal black and
white. The menus have departed constructively from their originally
French template, and now incorporate other not-quite-placeable elements
too, distinctively seen in a starter that combines Devon crab with a salad
of white peach, green beans, cobnuts and dill. Main course could be a
carefully constructed bacon-bound roll of rabbit saddle and its offal
forcemeat, served with a cottage pie of its shoulder meat and baked
fennel, dressed with a blob of chilli jam, while fish may be grilled stone
bass with Pink Firs, Cévennes onions, monk's beard tempura and blood
orange. Desserts are simplicity itself, perhaps a plum tart on crisp puff
pastry, or warm chocolate mousse with Amaretto ice cream, but it's as
well to leave room for the Bordeaux-style canelés, custard-filled
caramelised pastries, that come as petits fours.

Chef Anthony Demetre **Seats** 65 **Times** 12–2.30/6–10.30, Closed 25–26
December, 1 January, Sunday **Prices** Set L 3 course £35, Set D 3 course
£35, Starter £8–£16, Main £18–£29, Dessert £8–£9, Early supper menu
3 course £35 **Wines** 45 bottles over £30, 6 bottles under £30, 50 by glass
Parking On street **Notes** Vegetarian available, Children welcome

Hedone

PLAN 1 A3

@@@ Modern European
020 8747 0377 | 301-303 Chiswick High Road, W4 4HH
www.hedonerestaurant.com
Chiswick temple to superb produce cooked with flair

Mikael Jonsson's Hedone is a testament to his untiring, obsessive search
for Europe's finest ingredients. He's chosen an unassuming spot along
Chiswick High Road – far from the bright lights of central London – for
one of the country's most idiosyncratic and thrilling restaurants. There's a
relaxed Scandinavian charm to the room – bare brick, striking artwork,
blond wood and an open kitchen at its beating heart, where produce at
peak freshness and quality turns up daily for transformation into some
incredibly creative dishes. Turn up with an open mind, as the deal is a

brace of tasting menus that can change during service and one table may not get exactly the same as another. An opening salvo of canapés sets the scene, among them an intricate pea cone filled with veal jelly and rare tuna and topped with lemon mayonnaise and dried capers, prefacing an array of easy-on-the-eye plates of sublime flavours and technical virtuosity. Devon crab comes with crisp apple, horseradish and hazelnut emulsion; peerless langoustine is dressed with coral foam, coconut sauce and dashi jelly; superb lamb gets a kick from kale powder, anchovies and cabbage. Among sweet courses, rhubarb ice cream arrives with poached rhubarb, yogurt semifreddo, lemon meringue and sorrel.

Chef Mikael Jonsson **Seats** Private dining room 16 **Times** 12–2/6.30–9.30, Closed Sunday and Monday, L Tuesday to Thursday **Prices** Tasting menu from £95, Carte Blanche lunch and dinner £135 **Notes** Children 6 years +

LONDON W6
The River Café

PLAN 1 B3

@@@ Italian

020 7386 4200 | Thames Wharf Studios, Rainville Road, W6 9HA

www.rivercafe.co.uk

Outstanding Italian cooking from a riverside icon

Culinary fads have come and gone, but not much has changed at The River Café in three decades, and that is because everything was absolutely spot on from day one. The food here is timeless because it has always been driven by fantastic ingredients (which never come cheap, as the prices attest), ruthless seasonality and big flavours. That 'café' tag remains something of a misnomer, although there is a relaxed, unrestauranty mood to the minimalist, light-filled room with its cherry pink wood-burning oven and waterside views, and the whole place is presided over by immensely friendly waiting staff. The daily menus offer an Italophile's tour through the traditional four courses, setting out with antipasti of chargrilled squid with fresh red chilli and rocket, perhaps, followed by primi based on impeccable pasta – the likes of ravioli packed with buffalo ricotta, herbs and lemon zest and pointed up with marjoram butter and pecorino cheese. Fish is always stunning, as in wood-roasted turbot fragrantly dressed with anchovy, capers and flowering oregano, while meat could be a whole Anjou pigeon roasted on bruschetta and served with Allegrini Valpolicella wine and green beans. Puddings toe the classic line with the likes of pannacotta with grappa and raspberries, or benchmark lemon tart.

Chefs Joseph Trivelli, Ruth Rogers, Sian Owen **Seats** 120, Private dining room 18 **Times** 12.30–3/7–11, Closed 24 December to 1 January, D Sunday **Prices** Starter £20–£35, Main £35–£45, Dessert £5–£15 **Wines** 230 bottles over £30, 14 by glass **Parking** 29, Valet parking evening & weekends **Notes** Sunday lunch, Vegetarian available, Children welcome

London W8

Kitchen W8

PLAN 4 A3

◉◉◉ Modern British ♥

020 7937 0120 | 11-13 Abingdon Road, Kensington, W8 6AH

www.kitchenw8.com

Soothing Kensington venue with dynamic cooking

Proprietors Philip Howard and Rebecca Mascarenhas have some London restaurant experience between them, to understate it, and in the refined environs of Kensington, they have created a soothing backdrop for dynamically inspired modern cooking. The room is done in gentle beige, with framed artworks and circular mirrors, and Mark Kempson is achieving great things on the plate, often with a deceptive economy of means.

A starter of barbecue-glazed quail has strong, true flavours, the legs confit, with a little discreet richness added by foie gras and sharpness from rhubarb. Main could be slowly poached Cornish cod in Fowey mussel broth, with a plethora of winter veg and ink-dyed garganelli pasta, or tenderly roasted veal rump with bulgar wheat, charred lettuce, hazelnuts and wild leek.

Desserts may be unexpectedly lighter than their billings, as when pumpkin and bitter chocolate delivers, respectively, an airy vanilla-scented mousse and intensely flavoured sorbet, together with a little caramelised orange to cut through, while the Yorkshire rhubarb makes a return with warm yogurt doughnuts and rhubarb ripple ice cream. The home-made sourdough bread proves to be dangerously moreish. A six-course evening taster and well-stocked wine list offering around 15 by the glass or half-bottle carafe add allure to the whole deal.

Chef Mark Kempson **Seats** 75 **Times** 12–2.30/6–10, Closed 25–26 December, bank holidays **Prices** Set L 2 course £22, Set L 3 course £25, Set D 2 course £25, Set D 3 course £28, Tasting menu £65, Starter £8.95–£16.95, Main £21–£28.50, Dessert £6.75–£8, Sunday lunch £30–£35 **Wines** 110 bottles over £30, 10 bottles under £30, 14 by glass **Parking** On street, NCP (High Street) **Notes** Early-bird menu 6–7pm, Vegetarian available, Children welcome

Min Jiang

PLAN 4 B2

◉◉◉ Chinese

020 7361 1988 | Royal Garden Hotel, 2-24 Kensington High Street, W8 4PT

www.minjiang.co.uk

Exquisitely presented Chinese cooking up in the Kensington air

The Royal Garden Hotel is so named because it looks loftily over Kensington Gardens and its palace, and was designed at a time when the first duty of a modern city hotel was to look like a high-rise office block. If that seems a little more prosaic than you were hoping, banish all thought of spreadsheets as you glide through the lobby and on up to the 10th floor, where Min Jiang waits to beguile the senses in contemporary east Asian style. But first, get a load of those commanding views of Kensington at its leafiest; hardly any type of location succeeds in making quite such an impact as one that's high up in the air. The long smart room itself features shelf displays of ceramics and smartly attired, well-spaced tables, and there's also a private room, Chong Qing, in revolutionary red, hung with photographic images of China old and new.

Min Jiang's first two incarnations were at top-end hotels in Singapore, and the move into London nearly a decade ago began its international expansion. The kitchen deals in a dynamic mixture of traditional and gently modernised Chinese gastronomy, mobilising the multifarious textures and seasonings of one of the world's great cuisines in a productive contemporary synthesis. So crisp-fried salt-and-pepper squid in garlic and dried chilli, or steamed xiao long bao soup dumplings made

with blue swimmer crab, among the appetisers will undoubtedly prove irresistible to traditionalists, but the main dishes bring on exquisitely presented principal proteins, such as stir-fried Alaskan black cod with jade bamboo and cloud ear mushrooms, lobster sautéed in XO sauce, or fine corn-fed chicken stir-fried with broad beans and cashews.

Even something as utterly simple as steamed sea bass in its time-hallowed livery of spring onions and ginger seems to attain whole new depth, the fish delightfully fresh and tender, the dressing full of savoury intensity. Meats are similarly memorable, for stewed pork ribs and chestnuts in best soy, sautéed venison with shimejis in fermented yellow bean sauce, and the less widely seen grilled rack of garlicky lamb. A selection of accompanying leaves, choi sum and gai lan, baby pak choi and spinach, complements the main dishes perfectly, and at dessert stage – not traditionally the most exciting moment on a Chinese menu – the full creative instinct is unleashed for white chocolate and chilli cheesecake with sweet-and-sour strawberries, or lemongrass and lime crème brûlée with coconut shortbread and raspberries. The set menus at both lunch and dinner offer a good way of becoming acquainted with the style, and the dim sum menu covers pretty much all bases.

Chef Weng Han Wong **Seats** 80, Private dining room 20 **Times** 12–3/6–10.30 **Prices** Starter £8.50–£16.50, Main £13.50–£65, Dessert £6.50–£14.50, Dim Sum set menu L £40/£55, D £60/£88 **Wines** 229 bottles over £30, 2 bottles under £30, 11 by glass **Parking** 200 **Notes** Vegetarian available, Children welcome

See advert on page 177

The Ledbury

PLAN 1 C2

◉◉◉◉ Modern British V ♟

020 7792 9090 | 127 Ledbury Road, W11 2AQ

www.theledbury.com

Outstanding modern dining of great creative impetus

Now in its confident second decade, Notting Hill's Ledbury remains one of the reference-points of outstanding modern dining in an area where it still feels like a moment of sweet serendipity to come across it. The frontage done in sober aubergine behind trimly kept shrubbery recalls its erstwhile incarnation as a pub, but inside is a smart monochrome room, where immaculately linened tables on a parquet floor set the tone. The much-garlanded presiding genius Brett Graham was, at 15, a kitchen hand in a simple fish restaurant in Newcastle, Australia. He's come a long way, in every sense, with cooking that lacks nothing in creative impetus and visual delight, or in the unstinting quality of its prime materials.

The four-course dinner format might open with a fashionable pairing of smoked and dried eel with candied beetroot, dotted with caviar, a resonant exercise in counterpointing flavours, and follow on with roast cauliflower and creamed crab, given thermidor-like richness with parmesan and basil. For main, there could be miraculously tender pork cheek with crackling, chanterelles, and a dressing of carrot and gooseberry juices. Depth and complexity are seemingly evoked from even the simplest means, such as the pear braised in brown butter that comes with a caramel of goats' milk, while the signature dessert is the unctuous brown sugar tart with ginger ice cream. An eight-course taster takes in the menu highlights, and there is a sensational wine list, leading off with splendid selections in two glass sizes, before romping off into the broad hectares of the French regions and beyond.

Chef Brett Graham **Seats** 55 **Times** 12–2/6.30–9.45, Closed 25–26 December, Summer Bank Holiday, L Monday to Tuesday **Prices** Tasting menu 8 course from £145, A la carte 4 course £120, Sunday lunch **Wines** 819 bottles over £30, 16 by glass **Parking** Talbot Road **Notes** Children 12 years

L'Atelier de Joël Robuchon

PLAN 2 D5

◉◉◉ Modern French V

020 7010 8600 | 13-15 West Street, WC2H 9NE

www.joelrobuchon.co.uk

Top French cooking with fusion notes

The Atelier is indeed a workshop of sorts, a three-storeyed place of many spaces, from a terrace backed by a screen of foliage to the dark sleek setting of the upper dining room. Stay on ground level if you like chef-watching at open kitchens from amply upholstered counter seats. Jeremy Page and Axel Manes now oversee culinary operations on behalf of the titular presence, and the French cuisine sails serenely on. There is a bistro-like simplicity to some dishes, certainly in a starting composition of morels in vin jaune with asparagus, Comté and Bayonne ham, but Robuchon's imprimatur has never precluded ventures abroad, as witness the undisguised japonaiserie of kombu-wrapped cod fillet, served on yuzu-spiked daikon purée.

The heights of classic haute cuisine are effortlessly scaled too, though, as for quail stuffed with foie gras, served with truffled pomme purée, while desserts go out on a limb again for lemon and limoncello cheesecake with Greek yogurt sorbet, or creamy Manjari chocolate mousse garnished with 'les biscuits Oreo' (no, really). This being the fringe of Covent Garden, pre-theatre menus are an obvious boon, and there is also something called 'L'Unch' for those familiar with the tradition of French unching. It's aimed at busy shoppers and includes a glass of 'choreographed wine'.

Chef Jeremy Page **Seats** 55, Private dining room 12 **Times** 12–3/ 5.30–11.30 **Prices** Set L 3 course £29-£50, Tasting menu 8 course (with wine option) £149 £239, Pre-theatre Monday to Saturday 5.30–6pm 3 course £45, Starter £18–£32, Main £25–£150, Dessert £17 **Wines** 260 bottles over £30, 4 bottles under £30, 16 by glass **Parking** Valet parking service **Notes** Sunday lunch, Children welcome

LONDON WC2
Clos Maggiore
PLAN 2 E5

◉◉◉ Modern French, Mediterranean Ⅴ ♟
020 7379 9696 | 33 King Street, Covent Garden, WC2E 8JD
www.closmaggiore.com

An intimate French oasis in the heart of Covent Garden

Its billing as London's most romantic restaurant may be in the eye of the beholder, but there's no disputing the quality of chef Marcellin Marc's refined modern French cooking. The romance itself revolves around Clos Maggiore's pint-sized conservatory (complete with retractable roof for that starry night experience), which comes bedecked in fake blossom and privet hedging and a faux-flame log fire. Okay, it may not be for everyone, but the staging does seductively transport the romantically inclined from the maddening crowds of Covent Garden to a little courtyard somewhere in sunny Provence. Mirrors help create a larger-than-life illusion, while evening fairy lights add to the charm.

If you can't secure a table in the coveted courtyard, or the roof is closed due to inclement weather, Clos Maggiore still has much to offer, and still feels soothingly romantic: elsewhere, the dining space comes with a cosy clubby air – panelling, burnished floorboards, red banquettes and a narrow bar area. The polished modern French cooking comes underpinned by a classical theme with nods to Provence and passing references to the Italian name of the place and the Med. The à la carte offers a good choice, pre- and post-theatre menus are useful additions given this is Covent Garden and a host of shows are on within a short walk, while there's a set

lunch option for bargain hunters, and a tasting menu if you intend sticking around (including an excellent vegetarian version). Accomplished, smartly engineered dishes deliver pretty plates of standout flavour; a meat-free opener stars creamy burrata fresh from Puglia in a vibrant nest of chargrilled tenderstem broccoli, all revved up by smoked Catalan almonds, pickled vegetables and piquant salsa verde. Otherwise, a top-draw risotto of ebly, chorizo, saffron and basil, topped-off with sautéed squid and langoustines also makes its mark.

Next up, it's hard to argue with a main course that includes oven-roasted and herb-smoked Iberico pork loin, especially when it arrives alongside crisp bone marrow and almond croquettes, and apple and Calvados sauce. If you're in the mood for fish, there may be a picturesque medley of roasted wild halibut, slow-cooked pollock and grilled octopus teamed with carrot and swede in a fathoms-deep shellfish bouillabaisse sauce. Expect some gilding of the lily when it comes to dessert too, with perhaps a dressed-to-thrill Greek yogurt and lemon zest mousse, yuzu curd and honeycomb, a super-light lime and almond sponge, and knockout blackcurrant sorbet.

Chef Marcellin Marc **Seats** 70, Private dining room 23 **Times** 12–2.30/ 5–11, Closed 24–25 December **Prices** Set L 2 course £24.50 (3 course £29.50-£34.50), Set D 2 course £27.50–£32.50 (3 course £32.50–£34.50), Tasting menu £65, Starter £10.80–£22.90, Main £19.50–£47.50, Dessert £8.50 £10.50, Sunday lunch £34.50 **Wines** 1,900 bottles over £30, 10 bottles under £30, 21 by glass **Parking** On street, NCP **Notes** Post-theatre menu Monday to Thursday 10-11pm, Children at lunch only

London, Greater

Chapter One

MAP 6 TQ46

◉◉◉ Modern European **V**

01689 854848 | Farnborough Common, Locksbottom, BR6 8NF

www.chaptersrestaurants.com

Strikingly refined cooking in an out-of-town hotspot

Out in the suburbs, a few miles from the M25, Chapter One proves that culinary excellence is alive and kicking beyond the bright lights of central London. In fact, the accessibility of the place works greatly in its favour, and on a practical note, there's ample parking. The tone within is stylish, refined, with dark floorboards and smartly dressed tables, a feature wall upholstered in red silk and prints of food pictures in abundance. There is a strong classical base to Andrew McLeish's cooking, but he has the confidence to confound expectations with some surprising twists.

Things get off to a flying start when silky smooth velouté of potimarron (or butternut squash to its friends) is poured over a single raviolo stuffed with chestnuts and trompette mushroom duxelles. Seafood cookery is exemplary, if pitched at the richer end of the spectrum, in a main course showcasing poached brill on a bed of crushed new potatoes, with samphire, mussels, tomato and an unctuous butter and chive sauce. The desserts are equally creative and refined: witness red wine-poached pear with pear sponge, vanilla espuma and morello cherry sorbet. One of the stand-out features of Chapter One is its relative value for money, with a three-course lunchtime menu du jour that is a real steal.

Chef Andrew McLeish **Seats** 120, Private dining room 55 **Times** 12–2.30/ 6.30–10.30, Closed 2–4 January **Prices** Set L 3 course £19.95, Starter £6.50–£9.70, Main £17–£22, Dessert £6.45–£8.25, Sunday lunch from £24.95 **Wines** 153 bottles over £30, 65 bottles under £30, 13 by glass **Parking** 90 **Notes** Brasserie menu light lunch Monday to Saturday 12–3, Children welcome

HEATHROW AIRPORT
La Belle Époque
MAP 6 TQ07

◉◉◉ Modern French ♟

020 8757 5029 | Sofitel London Heathrow, Terminal 5, Wentworth Drive, London Heathrow Airport, TW6 2GD

www.la-belle-epoque.co

Airport hotel dining of inventiveness and complexity

Experience may not lead you to expect anything more than bland international cuisine from airport hotels, but the Sofitel group has created something quite special at its Heathrow property, a remarkable piece of modernist styling, reached by a covered walkway from Terminal 5. It seems fitting that this terminal should boast a cutting-edge venue such as La Belle Époque.

There's a change of the guard at the stoves but the menus still deal in contemporary French cooking with distinct Asian accents. Intelligent ideas and sympathetic flavours are there from the off, as when terrine of foie gras and preserved cherries is teamed with smoked duck breast, celery, and pecan crumble, or sesame-crusted tuna loin comes in a lively combination with avocado purée, pink grapefruit, radish and shiso. Mains take in a wealth of choice from roast cod loin with miso, marinated squid and pearl barley, to Scottish venison, the loin roasted in pine, and the haunch served as a faggot, together with parsnip and redcurrant.

There is a lot going on in these dishes, and yet the kitchen keeps its eye firmly on the ball through to dessert – perhaps a straightforward partnership of Granny Smith apple mousse with ginger and lime ice cream. A chef's table, for up to 10 people, will keep you entertained and should take your mind off an impending flight.

Chef Mayur Nagarale **Seats** 88, Private dining room 20 **Times** 12–2.30/6–10, Closed Christmas, bank holidays, Sunday, L Saturday **Prices** Set L 2 course from £24.60, Set L 3 course £29.50, Set D 3 course £45–£60, Tasting menu £59, Starter £9.50–£12.50, Main £21.50–£32, Dessert £9.50 **Wines** 236 bottles over £30, 6 bottles under £30, 16 by glass **Parking** 400 **Notes** Vegetarian available, Children welcome

The Glasshouse

PLAN 1 A3

@@@ Modern International 🍷

020 8940 6777 | 14 Station Parade, TW9 3PZ

www.glasshouserestaurant.co.uk

French-based cooking of exemplary consistency

A hardy perennial that's handy for trips to Kew Gardens, The Glasshouse pays tribute to the nearby horticultural action both in its name and the row of shrubs along its covered flank. In a pale-walled room briskly crowded, though not uncomfortably so, with smartly dressed tables, the place puts on a strong team performance, both out front and in the kitchen, where Berwyn Davies leads the line. The upscale Anglo-French bistro food has remained deservedly popular over the years, and has moved discreetly with the times, now adding sea purslane, truffled potato and preserved lemon to an aromatic soup of red mullet, now pickling rhubarb and puréeing samphire to accompany a starter serving of duck breast. Main courses cast the net far north to the Scottish boats for splendidly fresh fish such as Isle of Gigha halibut, and down to the Cornish catch for Fowey mussels to accompany it, a sauce of blood orange and verjus adding colour and grip, or there may be Suffolk pork with anchovies and salt-baked pear, cavolo nero and Lyonnaise onions. Desserts are full of siren-song indulgence, perhaps tarte Tatin with ginger ice cream, or passionfruit meringue with coconut ice cream and caramelised mango, and the French and English cheeses are properly mature.

Chef Berwyn Davies **Seats** 60 **Times** 12–2.30/6.30–10.30, Closed 24–26 December, 1 January **Prices** Set L 2 course £27.50-£32.50, Set L 3 course £32.50-£37.50, Set D 2 course £45, Set D 3 course £55, Sunday lunch £32.50–£37.50 **Wines** 479 bottles over £30, 20 bottles under £30, 20 by glass **Parking** On street (meter) **Notes** Vegetarian available, Children at lunch only

Bingham

PLAN 1 A4

@@@ Modern British 𝐕 🍷

020 8940 0902 | 61-63 Petersham Road, TW10 6UT

www.thebingham.co.uk

Peerless produce cooked with intelligent simplicity

Wrought from a pair of joined-up Georgian townhouses overlooking the Thames by Richmond Bridge, the Bingham delivers the chic boutique bolt hole experience in spades. An ambience of calm and civility reigns in the mirrored and chandeliered dining room, which has a look taken straight out of a glossy interior design magazine. Thankfully, it's not a case of style over substance when it comes to the culinary output, which relies on top-drawer materials for its effect, handling it all with respect and restraint to deliver well-conceived modern British creations full of sharply-defined flavours and textures. Things start with a fragrant black truffle risotto matched inventively with pickled celery and shimeji mushrooms in white balsamic. Main-course neck and loin of lamb comes in a well-judged and harmonious composition involving wild garlic, Puy lentils and sprouting broccoli, or if you're in the mood for fish, there might be a fresh and vibrant juxtaposition of halibut with tempura oyster, clams and sea vegetables. After that, a zippy lemon tart with pomegranate and white chocolate sorbet illustrates why less is often more. There's excellent value to be had from the Market menu, built around mains such as pork shoulder with black pudding, parsnip and glazed apple.

Chef Andrew Cole **Seats** 40, Private dining room 110 **Times** 12–2.30/ 6.30–10.30, Closed D Sunday **Prices** Set L 2 course £17, Set L 3 course £20, Set D 2 course £17, Set D 3 course £20, Tasting menu £60, Starter £7–£15, Main £19–£30, Dessert £7–£12.50, Sunday lunch £38, Afternoon tea £25, **Wines** 201 bottles over £30, 18 bottles under £30, 14 by glass **Parking** 20 Town centre **Notes** Children welcome

▶ Merseyside

OXTON
Fraiche   MAP 15 SJ38
◉◉◉◉ Modern French, European **V**
0151 652 2914 | 11 Rose Mount, CH43 5SG
www.restaurantfraiche.com

Exquisite destination dining with music and video accompaniment

A journey through the Mersey Tunnel and on to the Wirral peninsula, where the conservation village of Oxton lies not far from Birkenhead, is perhaps the most fitting itinerary for reaching the scintillating culinary adventurism that has put this hitherto neglected area of the northwest on the map. The foundation-stone of Marc Wilkinson's success here has been keeping things on a sensibly restricted rein, with only a small number of covers (great patience will be a virtue when applying for a table), plus the glass-walled kitchen billet, allowing his kitchen to focus to a minute degree on the flawlessly conceived dishes that are the Fraiche stock-in-trade.

Natural colour schemes, discreet musical backing and video projections of landscapes and organic processes all help build the mood. Wilkinson's cooking is informed by that creative fusion of raw nature and advanced technology that is the predominant modern mode, and he has the vision and talent to pull it off. The six-course Signature taster is a cavalcade of

continued

Merseyside

surprises and delights, opening perhaps with a brave pairing of butternut squash and tangerine, before moving on with truffled roasted sweetbreads and textures of apple. Tuna loin presented sashimi-style, an exquisite morsel, then prepares the way for barbecued dry-aged beef with salsify and celeriac. The first and lighter dessert could be an intensely sharp cherry-foamed lemongrass pannacotta, before the final Salt or Sugar option leads you off towards cheeses, each individually garnished, or another finely wrought dessert, perhaps a study in strawberry that incorporates elderflower-stuffed lychees and the technical miracle of shaved meringue.

Chef Marc Wilkinson **Seats** 12, Private dining room 12 **Times** 12–1.30/ 7–close, Closed 25 December, 1 January, 2 weeks in August, Monday and Tuesday, L Wednesday and Thursday **Prices** Tasting menu lunch £45 or dinner £85 **Wines** 260 bottles over £30, 30 bottles under £30, 8 by glass **Parking** On street **Notes** Sunday lunch, Children 8 years +

THORNTON HOUGH
The Lawns Restaurant at Thornton Hall
MAP 15 SJ28

Modern European **V**
0151 336 3938 | Neston Road, CH63 1JF
www.lawnsrestaurant.com
Grand spa hotel with a grand dining setting

As we went to press the Rosette award was suspended due to a change of chef – reassessment will take place in due course.

The grand spa hotel on the Wirral peninsula has an unerring sense for an occasion, whether it be one of the landmark days in the calendar or simply a sumptuous afternoon tea in sweet or savoury versions. Head to the Lawns dining room, though, for the full culinary package, set amid a setting of teardrop chandeliers and ornate wood carvings.

Seats 45, Private dining room 24 **Times** 12–2.30/6–9.30 **Prices** Set L 2 course £20, Set L 3 course £25, Set D 3 course £49, Tasting menu £80 **Wines** 100 bottles over £30, 27 bottles under £30, 18 by glass **Parking** 250 **Notes** Sunday lunch, Children welcome

Morston Hall

MAP 13 TG04

@@@@ Modern British **V** 🍷

01263 741041 | Morston, Holt, NR25 7AA

www.morstonhall.com

Razor-sharp modern cooking on the alluring north Norfolk coast

On the edge of the Blakeney National Nature Reserve in coastal north Norfolk, Morston is a flint-knapped 17th-century country house with commanding views of the briny – a heaven-sent location for sourcing prime produce from land and sea. Inside, it's a supremely civilised set-up, run for a quarter of a century with personable warmth and easy-going charm by chef-patron Galton Blackiston and wife Tracy. The conservatory dining room looks the part in delicate vernal green with fresh flowers abounding, and polished service ensures the evening runs like a well-choreographed routine.

After aperitifs at seven, guests take their seats for the eight o'clock show that is the seven-course tasting menu. A finely-honed appetiser of plump Brancaster mussels in perry sauce with lovage and pommes soufflés sets the tone, and what follows is a succession of pin-sharp contemporary dishes: a miso-glazed chicken wing arrives with a confit egg yolk, cauliflower purée and mushrooms, then salsify ribbons come swathed in a velvety Vacherin Mont d'Or cheese sauce with shaved truffle. There's meticulous attention to detail too in a fish course of monkfish roasted on the bone and matched with raspberry vinegar jus singing with liquorice, lime, mint and dill. As for meat, Middlewhite suckling pig is helped along by burnt apple purée, kohlrabi and rich sauce Robert. A pre-dessert of apple marigold herb sorbet heralds the finale: a beguiling dark chocolate tart with red wine gel, white chocolate ice cream and 25-year-old balsamic. The pre-selected wine flight bears all the hallmarks of thoughtful selection based on testing and tasting, and is well worth the extra layout.

Chefs Galton Blackiston, Greg Anderson **Seats** 50 **Times** 12.15–close/7.15–close, Closed 3 days at Christmas, January, L Monday to Saturday **Prices** Tasting menu from £75, Sunday lunch from £40 **Wines** 140 bottles over £30, 10 bottles under £30, 15 by glass **Parking** 50 **Notes** Afternoon tea (except Sunday), Children welcome

Norfolk

The Neptune Restaurant with Rooms

MAP 12 TF64

🏵🏵🏵 Modern European **V**

01485 532122 | 85 Old Hunstanton Road, Old Hunstanton, PE36 6HZ

www.theneptune.co.uk

Precision-tuned cooking in a smartly converted Norfolk inn

It would take a hard heart not to be seduced by this creeper-clad Georgian coaching inn with its display of local artwork, real fires and a light relaxing colour scheme. Just a short hop from the beach, Kevin and Jacki Mangeolles' small restaurant with rooms has been gently 'boutiqued' into the 21st century, with Kevin's cooking playing a starring role in securing The Neptune's place as a top Norfolk dining destination.

Dishes balance taste, texture and eye-appeal with easy confidence, and it's all built on solid foundations of locally-landed fish and seafood, and regional meat and game that's among the best in England, the latter featuring in main courses such as venison loin teamed with salsify, Jerusalem artichoke purée and wild mushrooms. For the riches of the sea, look to accurately timed brill fillet with baked leek, Brancaster mussels, wild garlic purée, broad beans and Pink Fir apple potato. Bookending these thoughtfully composed ideas, starters might see sake-poached salmon plated with oyster mayonnaise, apple and rocket, and to finish, Columbian white chocolate mousse could be the centrepiece of a delectable dessert that also builds in blueberries and chocolate ice cream, as well as an astringent hit from lime curd.

Chef Kevin Mangeolles **Seats** 24 **Times** 12–1.30/7–9, Closed 26 December, January, 2 weeks in November, Monday, L Tuesday to Saturday (except by arrangement) **Prices** Set D 2 course £45, Set D 3 course £60, Tasting menu £75, Sunday lunch £30–£38 **Wines** 80 bottles over £30, 20 bottles under £30, 18 by glass **Parking** 6, On street **Notes** Children 10 years +

NORWICH

Roger Hickman's Restaurant

MAP 13 TG20

◉◉◉ Modern British ☕

01603 633522 | 79 Upper St Giles Street, NR2 1AB

www.rogerhickmansrestaurant.com

A haven of high-achieving British food with French underpinnings

Tucked away down a quiet cul-de-sac in the fashionable St Giles district, not far from the cathedral, Roger Hickman's place is something of a haven from the city's urban bustle, and it looks like a grown-up restaurant inside, with plain wooden floors, walls hung with colourful original artworks, and tables dressed in their best whites. Staff are a real asset, being attentive and discreet, announcing the composition of each dish as it turns up, and forthcoming with recommendations if needed.

Hickman's refined modern British cooking is first-rate stuff, with the emphasis on intensity of flavour and seasoning, and it's all presented looking as pretty as a picture. The drill is fixed-price menus and tasting options at both lunch and dinner, moving confidently from the likes of foie gras mousse with pistachios and cherries, or cured and smoked mackerel offset with gooseberry, horseradish and dill, to main courses that are a masterclass in composition and skillful technique – roast John Dory, perhaps, partnered with artichoke and the sweet-and-sour counterpoint of pickled shallots and caramelised onion. Stylish finishers might include creamy rice pudding lifted by an exotic array of contrasting sharp flavours in the shape of lime parfait, coconut, mango gel and pineapple.

Chef Roger Hickman **Seats** 40 **Times** 12–2.30/7–10, Closed 2 weeks in January, Sunday and Monday **Prices** Pre-theatre £20 or £25 Tuesday to Thursday, Lunch tasting menu £40 or £70, **Wines** 95 bottles over £30, 14 bottles under £30, 12 by glass **Parking** On street, St Giles multi-storey **Notes** Vegetarian available, Children welcome

Norfolk

TITCHWELL
Titchwell Manor Hotel MAP 13 TF74
◉◉◉ Modern European
01485 210221 | PE31 8BB
www.titchwellmanor.com

Exciting modern cooking at a family-run coastal hotel

The owners certainly had a good eye for a classic Norfolk setting when
they took on the project of converting this Victorian red-brick farmhouse
into a delightful boutique hotel: set beneath north Norfolk's big skies, it's
a perfect bolt hole for twitchers and ramblers, with unbroken views
towards the coast over the RSPB reserve of Titchwell Marsh. Run by the
Snaith family since 1988, the place purrs along with genuinely warm-
hearted efficiency, and its interiors all have a brightness and freshness to
them, with no stinting on bold patterns and vividly coloured fabrics. Dining
goes on across two spaces, the pick of them a light-filled conservatory
restaurant overlooking an abundant walled garden that supplies the
kitchen with vegetables and herbs.

It's a notably laid-back setting for the vibrant contemporary cooking
on offer. The region's produce, particularly excellent seafood, gets star
billing on chef-proprietor Eric Snaith's menus, which take the modern
shopping-list format of principal ingredients, leaving you to discover
what's been done with them when the plate turns up. A knack of
combining unusual flavours and textures produces a first course of
Jerusalem artichoke soup with truffle bread-and-butter pudding and

confit yolk, or there may be a more traditional starter of Brancaster mussels, shallot and white wine. At main course stage, there are first-class locally reared meats and landed fish, the latter perhaps displayed in a precisely cooked plaice on the bone with root vegetables and red wine sauce, or red mullet with bouillabaisse, charred red pepper, monk's beard and fennel. If meat is your thing, loin and belly of venison might make an appearance with roast pumpkin, chocolate and salsify, or there could be another muscular pairing of Aberdeen Angus beef fillet and oxtail with carrot, pine nuts, and a Madeleine given extra savoury depth with beef fat.

Sound technique and intelligent flavour combinations are in consistent evidence right through to a finale of bread pudding with marmalade and currant ice cream or a rich chocolate delice with rum and raisin, or you might bow out with a terrine of Granny Smith apple partnered creatively with caramelised parsnip, cinnamon, toast ice cream and doughnuts. If the occasion calls for a more casual, brasserie sort of vibe, the other dining option is the Eating Rooms, a jaunty space with a sea-view terrace that floods the room with light through full-drop windows, and serves up-to-date small plates that sing with European and British ideas.

Chef Eric Snaith **Seats** 80 **Times** 12–5.30/6.30–9.30 **Prices** Starter £5–£12, Main £13–£29, Dessert £6–£10, Sunday lunch £12–£22 **Wines** 54 bottles over £30, 40 bottles under £30, 9 by glass **Parking** 50 **Notes** Vegetarian available, Children welcome

Northamptonshire

Rushton Hall Hotel and Spa

MAP 11 SP88

◉◉◉ Modern British
01536 713001 | Rushton, NN14 1RR
www.rushtonhall.com

Flavour-driven modern cookery in stately surroundings

Rushton Hall comes with all the stately bells and whistles you would hope for in a grandiose 16-century country house, its stone mullioned windows, monster fireplaces and acreages of oak panelling given historic resonance by its time as the seat of the Tresham family, whose name gained a certain infamy by getting mixed up in the Gunpowder Plot. Seamless, unobtrusive service is part of the deal, starting when dinner guests gather for aperitifs in the Great Hall, before a stately progression to the handsome dining room, where service from silver trays is the norm and classical music plays. Adrian Coulthard's modern British dishes are very much flavour-driven creations of the 21st century, with arty presentation, perfect tuning and clear-as-a-bell flavours all making their impact – a starter of quail, say, where the breast, sticky leg and parfait are partnered with crispy egg and pickled carrots. Multi-layered presentations and thoughtful takes on classic flavour combinations are a hallmark of main courses – loin, belly and barbecued shoulder of lamb, perhaps, matched with ratatouille, tomato and basil oil, while fish might be cod with cured egg yolk, celeriac purée, wild sea herbs and butter sauce. End with a timeless pairing of pistachio soufflé with bitter chocolate ice cream.

Chef Adrian Coulthard **Seats** 40, Private dining room 60 **Times** 12–2/7–9, Closed L Monday to Saturday **Prices** Set D 3 course £55, Sunday lunch £30, Afternoon tea £25 (with champagne £35) **Wines** 57 bottles over £30, 24 bottles under £30, 19 by glass **Parking** 140 **Notes** Vegetarian available, Children 10 years + at dinner

NOTTINGHAM
Restaurant Sat Bains with Rooms

MAP 11 SK53

◉◉◉◉◉ Modern British **V** ♛

0115 986 6566 | Lenton Lane, Trentside, NG7 2SA

www.restaurantsatbains.com

Vanguard British cooking full of excitement and creativity

Here, in the improbable environs of the outskirts of Nottingham, one of Britain's most singular top-drawer restaurant experiences has been created, not as a here-and-gone pop-up, but a long-running fixture that is indisputably worth the journey. Sat Bains makes no claims about tramping the shorelines and woodlands in search of wild ingredients. Instead, there is an on-site urban garden that furnishes the kitchen with almost half its vegetable and salad needs, and the rest is bought from trusted pedigree suppliers and growers. You can sit at a bench in the pastry kitchen, or in a private room with its own view of the kitchen, or if you want to explore ancient restaurant tradition, sit round a table in the dining room. Whichever you choose, a drink in the courtyard is the best way to start.

Sat's food is in the vanguard of current British thinking. It utilises the full panoply of technological wizardry to produce dishes composed of unusual and exciting elements. What sounds like something you recognise turns out to have been subtly modified, like the beef tartare that is fashioned into a kind of burger from meat that has been allowed a long sedate ageing process, or the pasta ribbons that are actually made of kohlrabi, dressed in a pungently aromatic pesto from the produce of the glasshouse, while the utterly unfamiliar is often so instantly appealing that you can't understand why you haven't known it all your life. A scallop is given the porcine treatment by being matched with earthy brawn and served in dashi stock with katsuobushi (dried salted tuna). Meats are reliably sensational for their concentrated flavour and melting texture, with spring lamb a particular draw. Desserts boldly incorporate savoury elements as in chocolate ganache blended with yogurt, olive oil and sea-salt, and produce unexpected matches such as strawberry and tomato.

Presentation is never less than fun, when items arrive in wooden boxes with sliding panels or piled into paper cones, and staff are well-versed in encouraging you to investigate the flavours and textures of each creation. Wine is taken seriously enough to have been subjected to a complex colour-coding system that not only acknowledges the taste categories of the food, but their level of intensity. Once mastered, it really works.

Chef Sat Bains **Seats** 46, Private dining room 8 **Times** 12–1/6–9, Closed 2 weeks December/January, 1 week April, 2 weeks August, Sunday to Tuesday **Prices** Chef's table, Kitchen or Nucleus L 7 course £95, D 10 course £130, Tasting menu 7/10 course £95–£110 **Wines** 200 bottles over £30, 12 bottles under £30, 50 by glass **Parking** 16 **Notes** Children 8 years +

Oxfordshire

The Lamb Inn
MAP 5 SP21

◉◉◉ Modern British V

01993 823155 | Sheep Street, OX18 4LR

www.cotswold-inns-hotels.co.uk/lamb

Intricate contemporary cooking in old weavers' cottages

Appropriately sited on Sheep Street, The Lamb occupies a set of wisteria-festooned former weavers' cottages packed with character and charm. Now a modern country inn, the place has been sensitively converted in a series of stylishly furnished public rooms, warmed by log fires in the cooler months, and with an abundance of original gnarled beams and flagstones to ensure a sense of place. The main dining goes on in the smart restaurant overlooking the garden and courtyard, where the country-chic decor fashions a gently contemporary setting. The skilful team in the kitchen echoes the surroundings, taking ideas that have a classic British foundation, then building some contemporary ideas on top of it. A set-price carte and tasting menu, plus veggie alternatives, deliver complex constructions, starting with the likes of foie gras parfait, its richness offset by rhubarb, apple and gingerbread purée, followed perhaps by a full-bore plate of beef sirloin, ox cheek, bone marrow and snails with sprout flowers and peppercorn sauce. At the meat-free end of the spectrum, mascarpone, chive and spinach pithivier is matched with crispy rocket and balsamic glaze. Among desserts, 'banana' is another good-looking plate with pannacotta the starring element, ably supported by honey and almond cake and citrus gel.

Chef Peter Galeski **Seats** 40, Private dining room 20 **Times** 12–2.30/7–9.30 **Prices** Set L 2 course £25, Set L 3 course £29.50, Set D 2 course £39, Set D 3 course £45, Tasting menu 8 course with dégustation wines £60, Sunday lunch £23.95–£27.95 **Wines** 60 bottles over £30, 40 bottles under £30, 12 by glass **Parking** The Bay Tree Hotel **Notes** Children welcome

Restaurant 56
MAP 5 SU29

◉◉◉ Modern British V ♟

01367 245389 | Sudbury House, 56 London Street, SN7 7AA

www.restaurant56.co.uk

Inventive Cotswold tasting menus in Georgian splendour

Sudbury House was once the classy Georgian residence of a former BBC Controller of Music, Sir William Glock, and now makes an attractive escape hotel for Cotswolds explorers. Alfresco dining on the patio overlooking the smart gardens is a potent lure in summer, and there's an informal brasserie called Magnolia, but the main action goes on in Restaurant 56, where landscape pictures, gilt-framed mirrors and glass treble clefs on the tables make a genteel backdrop for Andrew Scott's energetically inventive cooking. The principal menus, titled Prime and Progressive, are eight-course tasters, though there is a shorter option too. The first of those might begin with a truffled spin on cauliflower cheese, followed by pigeon and goose liver with Madeira jelly. Red mullet in bisque with pineapple then heralds a main course of Creedy Carver duck with squash purée and a coffee-tinged sauce. Another fascinating main dish is Dexter beef with mustard croquettes, salsify and cola gel. A brace of desserts might see apple and blackberry crumble with custard foam succeeded by buttermilk sorbet with fig mousse and gingerbread. Excellent breads and canapés add value to a memorable all-round experience, and there is a superb wine list, with the option of pre-selected glasses to accompany the multi-stage menus.

Chefs Andrew Scott, Nick Bennett **Seats** 24, Private dining room 12 **Times** 6–9, Closed Sunday to Tuesday, L all week (except for private bookings for 8+) **Prices** Set D 2 course £45, Set D 3 course £55, Tasting menu £50–£95, Afternoon tea £28 **Wines** 87 bottles over £30, 14 bottles under £30, 18 by glass **Parking** 70

GREAT MILTON
Belmond Le Manoir aux Quat'Saisons   MAP 5 SP60
◉◉◉◉◉ Modern French V ♜
01844 278881 | Church Road, OX44 7PD
www.belmond.com/lemanoir
Benchmark French cooking of rare excellence

Wherever your path through life may take you, whatever your budget may stretch to, you owe it to yourself to eat – and proferably stop over – one of these days at Le Manoir aux Quat'Saisons, since the place should be on everyone's bucket list. Now part owned by the Belmond group, Le Manoir remains a truly singular place, immaculately beautiful inside and out, and what it offers by way of hospitality is as good as you'll find anywhere in the UK. Looking timeless with its old creeper-garlanded stone walls and the garden primped and manicured to pretty perfection, the manor is an enduring monument to the vision of a young self-taught French chef who set up shop here in 1984.

Make sure to explore the grounds, check out the Japanese tea garden, and take a wander around the organic vegetable garden where much of what you eat is grown. The house itself more than passes muster – the comfort factor is set at eleven – and every room in the place looks elegant and refined, with the conservatory dining room at its best during daylight hours when the garden view can be best appreciated. The service ethos in all departments remains a benchmark by which all others may be judged, while Gary Jones, Benoit Blin and the kitchen team raise the bar skywards in the interpretation of Raymond Blanc's seasonally oriented, thoughtfully

continued

composed dishes, presented on monthly-changing à la carte and five- and seven-course lunch and dinner menus that are noticeably more classical in outlook nowadays than they once were. You might get off the blocks in March with duck liver, seared on the plancha, its richness nicely held in check by Yorkshire rhubarb, ginger and sherry vinegar, while a meat-free idea might see an eye-catching terrine of garden beetroot partnered with a head-clearing hit of horseradish sorbet.

At main course, flavours of remarkable intensity are conjured from often simple ingredients, and without recourse to overt technical complexity – perhaps a generous serving of roasted mallard with braised red cabbage, celeriac and a gloriously powerful roasting jus, or a fish dish that combines spiced monkfish with mussels in an aromatic saffron-scented Gewürztraminer sauce. If you succumb to the temptations of the cheese trolley, you'll be overwhelmed by an array of fine British and European specimens, all ripened to humming perfection. And in case you're thinking the tone is a touch reverential, there's fun at the finishing-line – a take, perhaps, on millionaire's shortbread – soft toffee with bitter chocolate on crumbly shortbread and salted butter ice cream. The wine list continues to offer a stellar array of top-drawer bottles at eye-watering prices.

Chefs Raymond Blanc OBE, Gary Jones, Benoit Blin **Seats** 90, Private dining room 50 **Times** 12–2.30/7–10 **Prices** A la carte lunch £100–£150, dinner £150–£200; Set 5/7 course lunch Monday to Friday £85/£130, dinner £141/£162; Set 6 course lunch weekends £130, **Wines** 650 bottles over £30, 40 by glass **Parking** 60 **Notes** Sunday lunch, Children welcome

HENLEY-ON-THAMES
Orwells   MAP 6 SU77
@@@@ Modern British
0118 940 3673 | Shiplake Row, Binfield Heath, RG9 4DP
www.orwellsrestaurant.co.uk
Creative contemporary dining in a Georgian country pub

Don't be fooled by the unassuming pubby frontage of this whitewashed 18th-century property near the Oxfordshire-Berkshire border: Orwells may look like a rustic old country inn, but the interior is that of a rather splendid contemporary restaurant. The bones of the old pub are still evident in its ancient beams and floorboards, but the decor has moved on a few centuries with mellow duck-egg blue walls, decorously clothed tables and high-backed chairs.

Chef-patrons Ryan Simpson and Liam Trotman have nailed local supply lines and contemporary culinary thinking to deliver a menu fizzing with creative ideas and exciting combinations. Their own smallholding just down the road produces the lion's share of the fruit and veg used in the kitchen, and this fiercely seasonal approach combined with phenomenal technical skill results in beautifully crafted dishes that seldom fail to impress. A starter from the à la carte menu might seek inspiration from Japan in combining scallops with seashore herbs, asparagus, edamame and yuzu. Next up, an on-trend and rather luxurious meat-seafood pairing of Wagyu beef and lobster might be supported by multifarious fungi, wild garlic, potato and carrot, or there could be a splendid piece of turbot with asparagus, clams, cucumber and a trenchant hit of verjus to bring it all to life. Thoughtfully composed desserts might run to lemon tart with fromage blanc and hibiscus. There is a tasting menu, with a wine flight if you fancy going the whole hog, while the set price lunch is a bit of a bargain.

Chefs Ryan Simpson, Liam Trotman **Seats** 40, Private dining room 20 **Times** 12–3/7–9.30, Closed 2 weeks start of January and 2 weeks start of September, Monday and Tuesday, D Sunday **Prices** Set L 2 course from £25 (3 course from £29.95), Set D 2 course from £30 (3 course from £34.95), Tasting menu from £95, Starter £8–£17, Main £23–£40, Dessert £9, Sunday lunch £25–£65 **Wines** 205 bottles over £30, 29 bottles under £30, 37 by glass **Parking** 30 **Notes** Vegetarian available, Children welcome

Shaun Dickens at The Boathouse

MAP 6 SU78

◉◉◉ Modern British V ♀
01491 577937 | Station Road, RG9 1AZ
www.shaundickens.co.uk

Smartly engineered contemporary food and much river business

The Boathouse doesn't just overlook the river from its attractive decked patio, it makes the most of the location with Thames buffet cruises too. If you're up for a weekend breakfast as well, there may be no reason to tear yourself away all day. The place is run with a light touch by experienced, friendly staff, and the kitchen deals in smartly engineered modern food that reinterprets the classics, as well as adding some new ideas of Mr Dickens' own. Juicy Cornish mackerel comes in a smoky consommé with mizuna leaves, toasted oats and a 'spaghetti' of gingery pickled turnip, as a possible prelude to a robust main course of tender ox cheek in a big bold beef jus, served with puréed spiced red cabbage, an espuma of smoked potato, and garnishes of pear, crisp-fried kale and pumpkin seeds. Desserts are as ingenious as everything that precedes them, best seen when a rich blood orange polenta cake appears, accompanied by dehydrated milk crackers and cream cheese ice cream, the dish then copiously dressed at the table with blood orange and sumac tea. Incidentals like breads and the sablé-based pumpkin mousse petit four help to raise the game.

Chefs Shaun Dickens, James Walshaw **Seats** 45 **Times** 12–2.30/7–9.30, Closed Monday and Tuesday **Prices** Set L 2 course from £25.95 , Set L 3 course from £29.95, Tasting menu 6/8 courses £52–£69, Starter £11–£12, Main £20–£26, Dessert £9 **Wines** 51 bottles over £30, 10 bottles under £30, 10 by glass **Notes** Children welcome

Oxfordshire

The Kingham Plough

MAP 5 SP22

◉◉◉ Modern British
01608 658327 | The Green, OX7 6YD
www.thekinghamplough.co.uk

Modernised country food in a family-friendly inn

An idyllic honey-hued stone inn on the green of a pretty Cotswolds village, the Plough presents a quintessentially English picture. Inside, the place has the sort of stylish rustic-chic decor – all venerable beams and exposed stone walls – that you'd hope for in a foodie pub, but kids and Fido are welcome so there's no standing on ceremony. Chef-proprietor Emily Watkins learned to revere fine ingredients during her stint in Heston's team at The Fat Duck, but there's no molecular wizardry going on in this kitchen, instead she offers a modernised take on country food.

The bar menu takes in the likes of crispy pork ears or rabbit parfait with red onion marmalade, while the restaurant sends out more ambitious dishes: a starter of beetroot-cured sea trout, lifted by pickled cucumber and accompanied by horseradish ice cream shows a solid understanding of how flavours work together. Main course could showcase slow-cooked collar of Tamworth pork with buttered swede, cavolo nero and almond pesto, or fish dishes might see poached cod matched with taramasalata, crispy brandade, sea beet, and burnt apple purée.

Dessert is a deeply satisfying trio of chocolate delice, honeycomb, and orange sorbet. Superb local artisan cheeses come with home-made Victoria plum jelly, oatcakes and hazelnut fruit bread.

Chefs Emily Watkins, Tom Waller **Seats** 54, Private dining room 20
Times 12–2/6.30–9, Closed 25 December, D Sunday **Prices** Set L 2 course
£16, Set L 3 course £20, Set D 2 course £16, Set D 3 course £20, Starter
£10–£12, Main £18–£24, Dessert £8, Sunday lunch £20–£24 **Wines** 39
bottles over £30, 7 bottles under £30, 9 by glass **Parking** 30
Notes Set price menu Monday to Thursday and Friday lunch only,
Vegetarian available, Children welcome

The Wild Rabbit

MAP 5 SP22

◎◎◎ Modern British

01608 658389 | Church Street, OX7 6YA

www.thewildrabbit.co.uk

Adventurous British food with no holds barred

A stone-built village inn not far from Chipping Norton in the Cotswolds, The Wild Rabbit is the very model of an updated country hostelry. Its stripped-back interior has been given a light makeover, with pale beams and abstract artworks abounding, and Scandinavian-style woodblock furniture at the outdoor tables. A central feature of the dining room is the framed schedule of charges dating from when the place marked a tollgate, and there's an open kitchen to permit views of Tim Allen's team at their creative business.

What better than to start with a bouquet of spring vegetables from the kitchen garden, served with a buttermilk and pea-juice cocktail, but the home-made black pudding is hard to resist too, when it comes with Agen prunes, curried pickled onion purée, and a slow-cooked pheasant egg. Main dishes might team monkfish with chicken wings in an emulsion of wild garlic and lovage, or offer rump and fricassée of veal with confit onion, truffle curd and baby capers. This is technically and formally adventurous British food with no holds barred, though you can opt for a dry-aged steak cooked over charcoal.

Then a fragrant dessert of lime buttermilk and matching meringues with minted frozen curd and cucumber granita, or perhaps a simple array of uncommonly intense sorbets – passionfruit, blackberry, pear and more.

Chef Tim Allen **Seats** 50, Private dining room 16 **Times** 12–2.30/7–9.30 **Prices** Starter £13–£16.50, Main £20–£32, Dessert £6–£8, Sunday lunch £20–£27 **Wines** 117 bottles over £30, 32 bottles under £30, 13 by glass **Parking** 15 **Notes** Breakfast available, Vegetarian available, Children welcome

Rutland

Hambleton Hall

MAP 11 SK90

◉◉◉◉ British V ♟

01572 756991 | Hambleton, LE15 8TH

www.hambletonhall.com

Simple but powerfully effective country-house cooking

From first sight of the round ornamental pond and properly barbered gardens, you know you're in for more than a touch of class. Built in the 1880s by a brewing magnate for his hunting parties, Hambleton was bequeathed on its first owner's demise to his redoubtable younger sister, Eva Astley Cooper, who oversaw, mostly from a recumbent position on a mattress before the fire, a glittering social set that included Noël Coward, Malcolm Sargent and Charles Scott Moncrieff, translator of Proust.

The British fondness for a stately home with a past has kept the wind in Hambleton's sails, and under its chef of a quarter-century's standing, Aaron Patterson, the old place still exerts a potent pull. A minty-green lounge with period furniture and paintings is the perfect preparation (if it's too chilly for the terrace, that is) for a transit to the interlinked shell-pink dining rooms. Here, you can look out serenely over the gardens and the backdrop of Rutland Water, and staff look after you with impressive attention to detail. Patterson's cooking has simplified in latter years, and the result is dishes that achieve even greater impact than their undoubtedly successful predecessors. The menu was always written in defiantly unflorid prose, its decorative drawings of feathers altogether a delight in themselves, leaving the dishes to speak for themselves.

Caramelised mackerel gets star billing in a starter salad with blood orange and lovage for contrasts, while a serving of white crabmeat is bursting with marine freshness, topped with a tomatoey foam and balanced by a wondrously intense celery sorbet. That might be followed by a piece of thoroughbred Lincolnshire beef fillet that is initially cooked on the bone for full flavour development. Its accompaniments of smoked bone marrow, horseradish mayonnaise and concentrated red wine sauce add the requisite layers, and garnishes of crosnes, sprouting broccoli and nasturtium root are spot on. Then again, there could be superb local lamb in rosemary livery with a serving of vivid piperade creating a sunny Gascon atmosphere.

Fish might be fillet of turbot with chervil roots in a sauce amalgamated from verjus and buttermilk, or red mullet with artichoke on golden saffron risotto, while desserts reimagine modern favourites, such as the tiramisù that comes as Amaretto-soaked flourless sponge with a crisp chocolate coating and airy chocolate mousse, or create new ones, when pear and blackberries are fashioned into a terrine, served with silky caramel ice cream. Cheeses are served with the in-house bakery's bread, which is not to be missed at any cost. Accompanying the whole deal is a wine list of commanding authority, overseen by a courteous sommelier whose recommendations can be followed with confidence.

Chef Aaron Patterson **Seats** 60, Private dining room 20 **Times** 12–1.30/7–9.30 **Prices** Set L 2 course £29, Set L 3 course £37.50, Set D 3 course £69, Tasting menu £92, Sunday lunch £58 **Wines** 200+ bottles over £30, 30 bottles under £30, 10 by glass **Parking** 40 **Notes** Children 5 years +

Shropshire

Fishmore Hall

MAP 10 SO57

◉◉◉ Modern British V
01584 875148 | Fishmore Road, SY8 3DP
www.fishmorehall.co.uk

Renovated country house with high-impact, thoughtful cooking

It's hard to believe that this handsome Georgian country pile just outside
the foodie hub of Ludlow was falling apart until its current owners
restored it in 2007 to the porticoed, pristine white boutique bolt hole (with
a spa tucked away in the garden) that we see today. Housed in an
orangery extension, Forelles restaurant enjoys views of the rolling
Shropshire hills as a backdrop to Andrew Birch's modern take on classic
country-house cuisine. As you'd hope, it's all built on pedigree materials
sourced from within a 30-mile radius (apart from seafood, of course, which
comes from Brixham and the north of Scotland) and delivered via a three-
course carte and six-course tasting menus (including a veggie version) that
deliver thrilling assemblages of flavour and texture. Confit rabbit
cannelloni with black pudding, tarragon, wild leeks and mustard velouté
sets the tone, before the kitchen conjures up well-balanced main courses
of immaculately cooked Shropshire lamb loin, say, supported by ewe's
curd, asparagus and confit potato, the whole thing aromatised with wild
garlic pesto, or Gigha halibut alongside shrimps, sweet potato, sea lettuce
and champagne butter sauce. At dessert stage, the good ideas just keep
coming – perhaps light-as-air orange soufflé with milk chocolate and
aromatic Szechuan pepper ice cream, or salted caramel fondant with
crème fraîche and cider sorbet.

Chef Andrew Birch **Seats** 60, Private dining room 20 **Times** 12.30–2.30/
7–9.30, Closed Monday, L Tuesday, D Sunday **Prices** Set L 2 course from
£24, Set L 3 course from £29.50, Set D 2 course from £40, Set D 3 course
from £50, Tasting menu from £65, Starter from £10, Main from £30,
Dessert from £10, Sunday lunch £24–£29.50 **Wines** 40 bottles over £30,
20 bottles under £30, 10 by glass **Parking** 30 **Notes** Children welcome

Old Downton Lodge

MAP 10 SO47

◉◉◉ Modern British V ♟
01568 771826 | Downton on the Rock, SY8 2HU
www.olddowntonlodge.com

Impressively creative cooking in a fascinating historic setting

A mere six miles from foodie Ludlow, Old Downton Lodge feels lost in a
rural idyll overlooking the hills of the Welsh Marches. The country-chic
restaurant with rooms consists of a fascinating cluster of buildings –
medieval, half-timbered, Georgian – around a courtyard filled with herbs
and flowers. The sitting room occupies the old stables, while the

restaurant, which dates from Norman times, has the feel of a medieval great hall with stone walls, tapestry and chandelier. Dinner takes the form of daily-changing five-, seven- and nine-course menus, all built on local, home-grown and foraged produce of the highest order. Head chef Karl Martin's cooking has an inherent simplicity and intuitive balance, kicking off with an amuse of chicken parfait with chicken, almond and watercress to pave the way for crisp-skinned stone bass matched with caviar, sour cream, cucumber and wild rice. These are highly original compositions where everything is there for a good reason: main course stars rose veal counterpointed with onion, crispy kale, celery, truffle and black garlic, or there may be Wagyu beef with broccoli, sea greens, peanuts and blue cheese. The results are impressive all the way through to a thought-provoking pudding of beetroot sorbet, blackberries, oats, apple and celeriac.

Chef Karl Martin **Seats** 25, Private dining room 45 **Times** 6–9, Closed Christmas and February, Sunday and Monday, L all week **Prices** Tasting menu 5/7/9 course £50–£70 **Wines** 142 bottles over £30, 20 bottles under £30, 26 by glass **Parking** 20

▶ Somerset

BATH

Allium Restaurant at The Abbey Hotel   MAP 4 ST76

Modern British V

01225 461603 | 1 North Parade, BA1 1LF

www.abbeyhotelbath.co.uk

Modern brasserie in a Georgian hotel

As we went to press the Rosette award was suspended due to a change of chef – reassessment will take place in due course.

The Abbey's façade is the epitome of Bath's elegant Georgian style, but beyond the pedimented portico entrance is a contemporary boutique-style interior. At every turn are lots of eye-catching artworks (including one of Warhol's Marilyns in the Artbar) and aesthetic flourishes, not least in the Allium, with its bare dark wood tables, wooden floor, drapes and a relaxed and unbuttoned atmosphere.

Seats 60, Private dining room 16 **Times** 12–3/5.30–9 **Prices** Set L 2 course £17-£25, Set L 3 course £20–£30, Set D 2 course £17–£25, Set D 3 course £20–£30, Starter £5–£16, Main £15–£24.50, Dessert £8.50–£9, Sunday lunch £24–£28 **Wines** 51 bottles over £30, 22 bottles under £30, 15 by glass **Parking** Manvers Street, Southgate Centre (charges apply) **Notes** Set dinner 5.30–7pm, Afternoon tea, Children welcome

The Bath Priory Hotel, Restaurant & Spa

MAP 4 ST76

◉◉◉ Modern European, British **V ▼**
01225 331922 | Weston Road, BA1 2XT
www.thebathpriory.co.uk

Classical treatment of top-notch ingredients

A William IV house in mellow Bath stone, the Priory is smothered in climbing ivy, and located in a quieter part of the city, away from the milling throngs. With views of the lush gardens and outdoor terrace kitted out with parasols, the dining room is an elegant, white-linened sanctuary, where Michael Nizzero uses classical techniques to bring out the best in top-notch ingredients, all presented with a due sense of flourish. Beef tartare bound with an emulsion dressing of oyster topped with raw quail egg, served with crackly pumpernickel, might set things off, or there may be citrus-dressed Cornish crab with avocado for a simple but effective opener. Then comes richly treated roast halibut in a concentrated Madeira jus with wild mushrooms, celeriac and walnuts, or perhaps slow-cooked breasts of pigeon with Pink Firs and cabbage in a lime-tinged sauce. Desserts are ingeniously conceived to be light and refreshing, as well as delivering an array of thrilling flavours, as witness a pistachio cake that comes with spiced poached pineapple and frozen yogurt, or buttermilk mousse with poached rhubarb and mizuna. Spelt bread makes an appetising change to the ubiquitous sourdough, and the appetiser itself might be something like mackerel with pear in a thin avocado soup.

Chef Michael Nizzero **Seats** 50, Private dining room 72 **Times** 12–2.30/6.30–9.30 **Prices** Set L 2 course £25–£80, Set L 3 course £30–£95, Set D 3 course £80–£95, Tasting menu 7 course £95–£115 **Wines** 453 bottles over £30, 20 bottles under £30, 11 by glass **Parking** 40 **Notes** Sunday lunch, Children 12 years +

Dan Moon at The Gainsborough Restaurant

MAP 4 ST76

◉◉◉ British European **V**
01225 358888 | Beau Street, BA1 1QY
www.thegainsboroughbathspa.co.uk

Classy contemporary food in Georgian heritage surroundings

Plumb in the heart of Georgian Bath, and with its own unique private access to the city's thermal springs, The Gainsborough Bath Spa Hotel, formerly a design college and, before that, a hospital, is clearly a place with cachet. Its dining room creates a light, informal impression, with white walls, unclothed tables and a well-stocked wine cabinet. Dan Moon offers impeccably contemporary British food, with the emphasis on bright, fresh combinations and textural contrasts. A first course comprises cured Mendip venison loin with goats' curd mousse, beetroot crisps in two colours and pear gel, before a complex main dish of seared sea bass in lobster bisque with crab risotto and roasted salsify hits every spot available. Another route might be via a sautéed scallop dotted with yuzu-spiked caviar, over which is poured rich smoked haddock chowder containing shards of parmesan crackling, ahead of lamb rump with a stuffed courgette flower, girolles, broad beans and home-made ricotta. Thoughtfully conceived desserts include a light buttermilk pannacotta with strawberry sorbet and baby basil, or else a richer wedge of salt caramel tart served with cocoa-nib ice cream.

Chef Dan Moon **Seats** 70 **Times** 12–2.30/6–10 **Prices** Set L 2 course £24.50, Set L 3 course £32, Tasting menu £60, Pre-theatre menu 3 course £35, Starter £10.50–£13.50, Main £24.50–£28.50, Dessert £9.50–£11.50, Sunday lunch £30 **Wines** 70 bottles over £30, 23 bottles under £30, 10 by glass **Parking** On street, NCP **Notes** Children welcome

The Dower House Restaurant

MAP 4 ST76

◉◉◉ Modern British V ♥

01225 823333 | The Royal Crescent Hotel & Spa, 16 Royal Crescent, BA1 2LS

www.royalcrescent.co.uk

Strong contemporary cooking behind the Royal Cresent

The Royal Crescent is one of the architectural glories of Georgian Bath, so to be located at the heart of it is a powerful incentive indeed. In fact, the Dower House is to be found in a separate building to the rear, reached by traversing a small lawn and summer terrace, with views over the ornamental gardens. Although there are references to classical tradition on the menus, David Campbell's cooking is firmly in the contemporary mould, with unusual combinations and a strong feel for textures evident all through. The show might begin with tea-cured salmon served in a soup of oyster, shiso leaves and yogurt, garnished with daikon radish and wasabi avocado, to be followed by salt marsh lamb with oregano polenta, engagingly served with a warm Greek salad and olive oil jus. Fish dishes are confidently executed, as in lightly spiced brill, Moroccan quinoa and cauliflower, seasoned with orange and coriander, and desserts maintain the creativity by rethinking rhubarb and custard into a creamy set custard base topped with shards of lightly poached rhubarb and cubes of gingerbread. With lovely treacle bread and Iberico ham croquette canapés to have a go at too, this is a classy performance all round.

Chef David Campbell **Seats** 60, Private dining room 20 **Times** 7–9, Closed L all week **Prices** Starter £13.50–£17.50, Main £27.50–£30, Dessert £12.95–£13.50 **Wines** 200 bottles over £30, 18 bottles under £30, 10 by glass **Parking** Charlotte Street car park **Notes** Afternoon tea, Children welcome

Somerset

The Olive Tree at the Queensberry Hotel

MAP 4 ST76

◉◉◉ Modern British **V** ☐

01225 447928 | Russell Street, BA1 2QF

www.olivetreebath.co.uk

Accomplished cooking in chic boutique Georgian townhouse hotel

If you're mooching around Bath to admire its handsome Georgian terraces, then why not go the whole hog and stay in the chic Queensberry Hotel, a picture-perfect piece of local architecture that offers the quintessential 18th-century heritage experience in one of England's prettiest cities. Set in a splendid row of townhouses built by the 8th Marquess of Queensbury in 1771, the place has been lavishly renovated under the ownership of Laurence and Helen Beere, who have worked tirelessly to transform it into a top-ranking boutique hotel and assure its standing as one of the most impressive addresses in the spa city. The owners' passion for hospitality and keen eye for interior aesthetics have created a winning blend of traditional elegance neatly overlaid with a sybaritic contemporary look, resulting in civilised spaces that seem almost timeless.

The Olive Tree restaurant is down in the basement in a series of interconnecting rooms that overcomes any sense of subterranean gloom with a light, minimalist look. Head chef Chris Cleghorn has honed his craft in some top-flight kitchens (stints chez James Sommerin, Michael Caines and Heston Blumenthal to name but three) and his dynamic cooking and sharp technical skills are showcased here via a choice of seasonal tasting menus, including an impressive one for vegetarians, and an admirably

flexible approach allows you to cherry pick a starter, main course and dessert if you're not up to the challenge of the full-on tasting experience. Whichever route you take, the classically inspired modern British dishes are all built on a solid bedrock of the finest West Country produce. Flavour combinations are well considered and intelligently executed – crab lasagne with the pungent kick of basil, for example, or cured mackerel lifted by cucumber, avocado and pink grapefruit.

Main ingredients are often given different stages of treatment, then deepened with layers of aromatic and assertively flavoured accompaniments in thoughtful combinations – duck liver, for example, might be poached and roasted, then matched with orange, chicory and walnuts to keep its richness neatly in check. If you're heading down the meat-free route, lively dishes such as quail's egg, sweetcorn, shiitake mushroom and popcorn are a lesson in texture and well-matched flavours. Scintillating desserts also bring superb displays of tastes, textures and temperatures – a masterly mandarin mousse and granita, say, with 72% Valrhona chocolate and stem ginger, or peanut butter parfait with milk chocolate and salted caramel.

Chef Chris Cleghorn **Seats** 60, Private dining room 30 **Times** 12–2/7–10, Closed 1 week January, last week July/1st week August, 1st week November, Monday, L Tuesday to Thursday **Prices** Set L 2 course from £26 (3 course from £32.50), Tasting menu £67.50–£80, Starter £13.50–£15.50, Main £26.50–£28.50, Dessert £9.50–£10.50 **Wines** 320 bottles over £30, 17 bottles under £30, 18 by glass **Parking** On street (meter) **Notes** Seasonal and Signature tasting menus available, Sunday lunch, Children welcome

Somerset

The Mount Somerset Hotel & Spa

MAP 4 ST22

@@@ British V

01823 442500 | Lower Henlade, TA3 5NB

www.mountsomersethotel.co.uk

Quality cooking in a luxurious hotel

A handsome Regency pile in four acres of hilltop grounds, Mount
Somerset Hotel lords it in the bosom of the Blackdown and Quantock Hills.
Within, it's the very template for classic country-house style, jazzed up
with a modern note here and there, its period features – high ceilings,
ornate plasterwork, polished wooden floors, open fireplaces, and a
sweeping centrepiece staircase for when you feel the need to make a
grand entrance – all remain pristine and play their part in building an air
of luxury and refinement.

New head chef Mark Potts has upped the kitchen's game, steering a
creative, contemporary country house line, and packing its menus with
top-grade produce – the runny A-grade Arlington White egg yolk, for
example, that escapes from perfectly-timed ravioli served with wild
mushrooms, artichoke purée and punchy Lancashire Bomb cheese. West
Country ingredients play a leading role in an intricately constructed dish of
pan-fried Cornish brill and braised chicken wing with hazelnut gnocchi,
salsify and crosnes, all pointed up with a rich parmesan-topped chestnut
purée. Equally deft are desserts, as seen in a superlative well-risen prune
and Armagnac soufflé – a marriage made in heaven with its
accompanying pear sorbet, Earl Grey tea mousse and date purée.

Chef Mark Potts **Seats** 60, Private dining room 50 **Times** 12–2/7–9.30
Prices Set L 2 course from £26.50, Set L 3 course from £35, Set D 2 course
from £26.50, Set D 3 course from £35, Tasting menu from £75 , Starter
£11.50–£14, Main £18–£30, Dessert £8.50–£12, Sunday lunch £26.50–£35
Wines 56 bottles over £30, 30 bottles under £30, 10 by glass **Parking** 100
Notes Children welcome

Little Barwick House

MAP 4 ST51

◉◉◉ Modern British
01935 423902 | Barwick, BA22 9TD
www.littlebarwickhouse.co.uk

Simple but powerful dishes in an atmosphere of perfect hospitality

Tim and Emma Ford have perfected the art of finely detailed hospitality in their enchanting Georgian dower house. This is very much a family concern, with son Olly and his dad making a formidable kitchen double act, and Emma choreographing front of house with pitch-perfect charm. It all happens in a relaxing room looking out on the garden, with clothed tables and seating in windowpane check, a civilized chatter of contented diners, staff who are attentive without pestering, and the focus is firmly on the food.

Rock-solid consistency defines the cooking here – there's no attempt to dazzle with ephemeral trends, just classically-based ideas that are carefully thought through and executed with great technique, as in an opener of pink-roasted quail ballotine, stuffed with wild mushrooms and herbs, and sauced resonantly with Somerset cider and brandy. Fish is handled with exemplary skills: roast fillet of Cornish hake arrives with risotto of Kynance Cove lobster and a well-judged lobster sauce. After that, white chocolate mousse is served atop a wicked dark chocolate brownie, and balanced with vanilla and stem ginger ice cream. The global wine list is clearly a labour of love, offering a selection that has something for everyone from connoisseurs to gluggers.

Chef Timothy Ford **Seats** 40 **Times** 12–2/7–9, Closed New Year, 2 weeks January, Sunday and Monday, L Tuesday **Prices** Set L 2 course £27.95, Set L 3 course £30.95, Set D 2 course £43.95, Set D 3 course £49.95 **Wines** 143 bottles over £30, 23 bottles under £30, 29 by glass **Parking** 25 **Notes** Vegetarian available, Children 5 years +

Swinfen Hall Hotel

MAP 10 SK10

@@@ Modern British **V**
01543 481494 | Swinfen, WS14 9RE
www.swinfenhallhotel.co.uk

Strikingly realised dishes with views of the deer park

It's reassuringly easy to forget you're only a short hop from the A38, so soothing is the prospect over the formal garden and the deer park, where scores of majestic beasts roam as though they owned the place. The kitchen of this palatial Georgian manor house is also served by a walled vegetable garden and beehives, and there may be pigs in the offing soon, we learn.

The impressive Four Seasons dining room with its oak panelling, intricate carvings and ornate ceiling is the fitting scene for Ryan Shilton's striking dishes, which are contemporary in execution, but with a strong underpinning of classical principles. That's easily seen in a serving of new season's asparagus with crumbed smoked haddock and a poached egg yolk, dressed in lemon and marjoram, followed by a serving of pink and succulent cutlets of lamb with chargrilled cauliflower, goats' curd and golden raisins in a richly aromatic rosemary jus.

They may be in landlocked Staffordshire, but a powerful waft of sea breeze enlivens a dish of brill with pickled cockles and sea veg in mussel sauce, while desserts are possessed of great creative impetus, seen in whipped lemon curd scented with wood-sorrel, served with liquorice ice cream and charcoal-black shards of liquorice meringue.

Chef Ryan Shilton **Seats** 45, Private dining room 20 **Times** 12.30–2.30/ 7.30–9.30, Closed 26 December, 1 January, Monday, D Sunday **Prices** Set L 2 course from £25, Set L 3 course from £30, Tasting menu 5 or 9 course £50–£75, Starter £11–£12.50, Main £23–£30, Dessert £11–£14, Sunday lunch £29.50–£38 **Wines** 97 bottles over £30, 38 bottles under £30, 10 by glass **Parking** 80 **Notes** Children welcome

LAVENHAM
Lavenham Great House
'Restaurant with Rooms'

MAP 13 TL94

◉◉◉ Modern French
01787 247431 | Market Place, CO10 9QZ
www.greathouse.co.uk

Modern French cooking in a medieval building

Sitting in pride of place opposite the medieval market town's timber-framed Guildhall, the Georgian façade disguises the Great House's true antiquity, which dates from the 14th and 15th centuries. In the same way that the building is rooted into Lavenham's fabric, the elegant restaurant with rooms is a stalwart of the local dining scene, run by chef-patron Regis Crepy for over 30 years. Period character abounds, but the dining room has a thoroughly modern look combining dark oak floorboards, brick Inglenooks and panelled walls. Despite the quintessentially English setting, the skilled cooking is rooted in the great French repertoire. Creative flair suffuses the menu, starting with duck foie gras terrine, its luxuriant richness cut by blackcurrant gel, fig marmalade, raspberry vinegar and milk bread, while main course partners grilled rack of lamb with baby aubergine and courgette, garlic espuma and delicate lettuce sauce. Fish dishes, too, are characterised by vibrant flavours, perhaps pan-fried wild turbot fillet with crispy caramelised veal sweetbread, cauliflower and truffle oil mousseline, and a chicken broth and porcini oil emulsion. To finish, there's a light-as-air confection of chocolate, peanut cream and mascarpone mousse with chocolate and caramel ice cream.

Chef Regis Crepy **Seats** 40, Private dining room 15 **Times** 12–2.30/7–9.30, Closed January, 2 weeks summer, Monday, L Tuesday, D Sunday **Prices** Set L 2 course £19.95-£31.50 (3 course £25-£36.50), Set D 2 course £31.50 (3 course £36.50), Starter £11.50–£14.95, Main £22.50–£29.95, Dessert £7.95, Sunday lunch £36.50 **Wines** 65 bottles over £30, 75 bottles under £30, 11 by glass **Parking** Market Place **Notes** Vegetarian available, Children welcome

Suffolk

Tuddenham Mill

MAP 13 TL77

◉◉◉ Modern British V ♛
01638 713552 | High Street, Tuddenham St Mary, IP28 6SQ
www.tuddenhammill.co.uk

Inventive regional cooking and a waterwheel taking centre stage

The 18th-century mill, augmented in the Victorian era by a steam engine and towering brick chimney, may have ended its grinding days in the 1950s, but its heritage remains intact at the present-day boutique hotel. For one thing, the fast-flowing stream that turned its waterwheel has been dredged of centuries of silt and is now a thriving wildlife habitat, while the majestic cast iron wheel itself, framed by beams, glass walls and net curtains, forms a diverting centrepiece to the first-floor restaurant. This is what you might call a USP. It's a setting that seems to demand cooking with plenty of personality of its own, and fortunately, in head chef Lee Bye, a country boy with an instinctive feel for the surrounding region, that department is capably taken care of.

The confident style may be seen to striking effect in an opener of seared wood-pigeon with crunchy Roscoff onion, silky girolles and dazzling pumpkin purée, the whole dish unified with a rich chicken jus. An alternative could be a little cauldron of plump mussels in St Edmund's golden ale with crispy kale and garlic, before the main business turns to stone bass in Debenham cider with seaweed butter and lovage, or well-rendered pink lamb rump with a yogurt-laced meatball ragout and pickled courgette. Sticklers for tradition will relish the prospect of a judiciously

timed Angus bavette steak garnished with a walloping great king oyster mushroom, bone marrow, a clump of watercress and chips, while vegetarians set about fenland cauliflower risotto with Bosworth Ash goats' cheese, salsify and raw pear. Texturally varied dessert enticements might take in sea buckthorn curd with Italian meringue, clementine sorbet and blueberries, adorned with crunchy oats, or buttermilk pannacotta with pistachio granola and poached Discovery apple, and for the less sweet of tooth, fine British artisanal cheeses come with Garibaldi biscuits and chutney.

At the outset of proceedings, appetisers run witty variations on cauliflower cheese and pork scratchings, and the barley malt bread is not to be missed either. The five-course tasting menu offers a leisurely-paced tour through Bye's versatile repertoire. Those lucky enough to be staying over can count on fortifying breakfasts into the bargain, built around Dingley Dell pork sausages, locally smoked kippers, and Goosnargh yogurt topped with almond granola. Completing the deal – though not perhaps for breakfast – is an outstanding wine list of resourceful scope, filled with mature vintages of the classics, but with plenty of modern offerings too. A list that can find room for Slovene Malvasia, Chilean Carmenère and Suffolk Pinot Noir among wines by the glass is one that definitely has its heart in the right place.

Chef Lee Bye **Seats** 54, Private dining room 36 **Times** 12–2.15/6.30–9.15 **Prices** Set L 2 course from £17.50, Set L 3 course from £22.50, Starter £7.50–£9.50, Main £19.50–£39, Dessert £8.50–£11, Sunday lunch £22.50–£27.50 **Wines** 138 bottles over £30, 33 bottles under £30, 13 by glass **Parking** 40 **Notes** Children welcome

Matt Worswick at The Latymer

MAP 6 SU96

@@@@ Modern British, European V 🍷

01276 471774 | Pennyhill Park, London Road, GU19 5EU

www.exclusive.co.uk

Stunningly crafted contemporary cooking in a luxurious hotel

Whatever you're looking for, Pennyhill Park has probably got it, from corporate bonding to spa pampering and golf – you might even rub beefy shoulders with the England rugby union team, who use it as a training base. Fortunately, the Victorian estate has room for all in its 120 acres, and a top-drawer gastronomic experience is of course on the cards in a plush setting beneath a wood-beamed ceiling in the original part of the creeper-festooned mansion; the Latymer's kitchen is firing on all cylinders under the talented guidance of Liverpool-born Matt Worswick, who has made his bones in some of our most Rosette-laden kitchens.

His tasting menus certainly deploy bags of technique and promise a thorough culinary workout, the 10-course extravaganza opening with a trio of intricately-wrought 'snacks' – pigs trotter cromesqui with piccalilli gel; truffled parmesan beignet; smoked baba ganoush with cardamom yogurt and Bombay mix, say. That's before the opening salvo of the menu proper, which might deliver sesame-dressed octopus with miso and coriander to fire up the taste buds ahead of smoked eel partnered with pickled turnip, compressed apple and dashi.

Along the way, you may also encounter loin and delicious roasted heart of Sussex venison with chanterelle mushrooms, or braised shoulder of mutton with buttermilk, peas and wild garlic. Ending the show, a flourish of desserts could include chocolate delice with milk crumble and yogurt sorbet, or passionfruit cream with mango gel and coconut ice cream. The five-course lunch deal is a good entry point if you want to sample the wares on a budget.

Chef Matt Worswick **Seats** 40, Private dining room 8 **Times** 12.30–2/7–9, Closed 1st 2 weeks in January, Monday and Tuesday, L Wednesday to Thursday, Sunday **Prices** Set L 5 or 7 course £35 or £49, Set D 5 or 8 course £55 or £75, Tasting menu from £100 **Wines** 300 bottles over £30, 20 by glass **Parking** 500 **Notes** 10-course tasting menu available on Saturday only, Children 12 years +

CHOBHAM
Stovell's

MAP 6 SU96

◉◉◉◉ Modern European ♀
01276 858000 | 125 Windsor Road, GU24 8QS
www.stovells.com

Mexican-tinged modern British cooking in Tudor surrounds

Fernando Stovell has travelled a long way from home to realise his culinary ambition, ensuring in the process that Mexico's loss is Chobham's extravagant gain. The setting could hardly be more photogenically Home Counties, a red-roofed, white-fronted Tudor farmhouse, its interior beams all properly skew-whiff. Stovell gives cookery lessons and produces his own vacuum-distilled organic gin. Talk about going native. For the rest, he is an infectiously confident chef in the modern British school, utilising thoroughbred produce in technically surprising and adventurous ways.

There are touches of his ancestral heritage, to be sure, in a starter that adds barbecued prickly pear hollandaise to caramelised Orkney scallops, while the French veal carpaccio is dressed in a mix of avocado and smoked jalapeño. Elsewhere, main courses bring the much-favoured Asian tang of yuzu to wild sea bass with pickled mushrooms and Jerusalem artichokes, while crisp-edged pressed suckling pig in apple and cauliflower cream attains its irresistible sweet note with prunes braised in manzanilla. The wood-fired grill works wonders for aged Cumbrian beef or chillied-up fish, while aubergine roasted over olive wood is the intuitive accompaniment for lamb cutlets in a startling glaze of rhubarb. Intriguing flavours continue through to desserts such as the reinvention of carrot cake with grilled baby carrots and an icing of smoked sour cream.

Chef Fernando Stovell **Seats** 60, Private dining room 14 **Times** 12–2.30/6–9.30, Closed Sunday and Monday **Prices** Set L 2 course £18 (3 course £22.50), Set D 2 course £37 (3 course £45), Tasting menu £78–£133 **Wines** 87 bottles over £30, 16 bottles under £30, 14 by glass **Parking** 20 **Notes** Vegetarian available, Children welcome

Surrey

EGHAM
The Tudor Room

MAP 6 TQ06

◉◉◉ Modern European **V**

01784 433822 | Great Fosters, Stroude Road, TW20 9UR

www.greatfosters.co.uk

Creative cooking in a grand manor house

It's all about impeccable pedigree at Great Fosters – the magnificent 16th-century mansion really wins hearts with its magnificent gables, soaring chimneys, Saxon moat and glorious landscaped gardens. With 50 acres to explore including a tennis court, croquet lawn and a heated outdoor pool, the place is achingly English and formal, and does a roaring trade on the wedding circuit.

When it comes to dining, the intimate Tudor Room is all you might expect in this setting – richly decorated, plush and stylish, with a 17th-century tapestry taking pride of place. The head chef's first call for fresh fruit, vegetables and herbs is the estate, and what isn't home produced is sourced with quality in mind. His menus demonstrate a deep understanding of how flavours work together, bolstered by respect for the ingredients and a keen instinct for creativity.

A well-conceived starter could see perfectly seared scallops arrive with broccoli purée, crunchy hazelnut and truffle shavings, or the richness of smoked eel offset by grapes and nasturtium. Main courses aim for intense flavours in dishes such as Himalayan salt-aged venison with turnip, chanterelle mushrooms and blackberry, or turbot matched with cauliflower, gnocchi and capers. Well-judged combinations are also the hallmark of desserts such as passionfruit sorbet with mango sorbet.

Chef Douglas Balish **Seats** 24 **Times** 12.30–2/7–9.15, Closed 2 weeks in January, 1 week at Easter, 2 weeks in August, Sunday to Tuesday, L Wednesday and Saturday **Prices** Lunch 4 course £35, Dinner 6 course £70, **Wines** 245 bottles over £30, 15 by glass **Parking** 200 **Notes** Children welcome

RIPLEY

The Clock House

MAP 6 TQ05

◉◉◉ Modern British V

01483 224777 | High Street, GU23 6AQ

www.theclockhouserestaurant.co.uk

Modern cookery in a landmark Georgian house

Formerly known as Drake's, this high-achieving restaurant stands out among the timbered houses in this well-heeled Surrey village thanks to the landmark timepiece (hence the new moniker) on its Georgian red-brick façade. The name wasn't the only change that came along in 2017 – Fred Clapperton has been at the stoves since 2012, and now heads up the kitchen team, ensuring that the eclectic offering continues to be driven first and foremost by considerations of flavour.

Menus are also rejigged to offer a seasonal carte and a seven-course, whole-table taster option, with vegetarians invited to the party via meat-free versions of both. A meal brimming with confident gestures and on-trend gastronomic ideas opens strongly with pitch-perfect gnocchi in an ambrosial onion broth with fresh watercress and crispy leek rings. Next up, a fish course showcases precision-timed cod alongside plump mussels, pumpkin purée, and a vibrant coconut and ginger foam, followed by beef fillet and sweetbreads with brassicas and horn of plenty mushrooms.

An inspired finale unites blackberry textures with hibiscus, apple and shortbread. It all takes place in a light, understated dining room with rustic wood doors and window frames, white tablecloths and modern art on the walls. A heavenly walled garden really comes into its own for aperitifs in summer.

Chef Fred Clapperton **Seats** 40 **Times** 12–2/7–9.30, Closed 1 week at Christmas, 1 week in January, 1 week after Easter, 2 weeks in August, Sunday to Tuesday **Prices** Set L 2 course £26, Set L 3 course £30, Set D 2 course £45, Set D 3 course £55, Tasting menu £49–£120 **Wines** 245 bottles over £30, 9 bottles under £30, 12 by glass **Parking** 2 **Notes** Tasting menu lunch 5 course, dinner 7 course, Children welcome

Sussex, East

The Little Fish Market

MAP 6 TQ20

◉◉◉ Modern Fish

01273 722213 | 10 Upper Market Street, BN3 1AS

www.thelittlefishmarket.co.uk

Simply stunning seafood with a creative edge

Tucked away in a little side street off Hove's Western Road, chef-patron Duncan Ray's modest little operation certainly punches above its weight. After stints at The Fat Duck and Pennyhill Park, Ray knows a thing or two about top-end dining. Here he works alone in the kitchen, and the results speak for themselves: stunning local and sustainable seafood cooked with exemplary attention to detail, accuracy and an intelligent creative edge.

The setting is a light-filled space done out with a bare-bones contemporary look: neutral colours, seafood-themed prints, wooden tables and quarry-tiled floors, and it is comfortable and atmospheric in the evening, with a charming solo server managing front of house for the lucky 20-odd diners.

The tersely-worded fixed-price menu offers five no-choice courses and depends on what's been landed that day, perhaps sea-fresh mackerel with gazpacho, cucumber and basil before the elegant simplicity of slip sole served with seaweed butter. The bright, clean flavours continue in ideas such as a stunning piece of halibut with Jersey Royals, asparagus and St George's mushroom, or a full-on fish and meat pairing of brill with chicken, morels and sherry. To close the show, there may be a clever take on the nougat glacé theme served with passionfruit and chocolate.

Chef Duncan Ray **Seats** 22 **Times** 12–2/7–9, Closed Christmas, 1 week in March, 2 weeks in September, Sunday and Monday, L Tuesday to Friday **Prices** Set L 2 course £20, Set L 3 course £25, Tasting menu £55 **Wines** 14 bottles over £30, 8 bottles under £30, 9 by glass **Parking** On street **Notes** Vegetarian available, Children 12 years +

AMBERLEY
Amberley Castle

MAP 6 TQ01

◉◉◉ Modern European V ▼
01798 831992 | BN18 9LT
www.amberleycastle.co.uk

Refined, contemporary cooking in a historical setting

There are quite a few hotels in the UK with 'castle' in their names, but few can compete with Amberley when it comes to living up to expectations – it's a 900-year-old Norman fortress with twin-towered gatehouse and portcullis, and battlements built to rebuff invaders sweeping over the South Downs. Goodness, it's impressive. Within its hefty stone walls, the public rooms have kept to the spirit of the antiquity of the place, while adding a sense of contemporary luxury.

Its main dining room, the Queen's Room, has a 12th-century barrel-vaulted ceiling, open fireplace, murals, muskets and tapestries, and tables laid for the business of fine dining. The kitchen meets 21st-century expectations, blending modern techniques and European tradition to produce striking, harmonious dishes.

First up could be clam and poached loin of rabbit with langoustine, Alsace bacon and violet artichoke. Then comes either another fish in the shape of pave of halibut, fennel, clams with garganelli pasta, or the more outré Himalayan-style salt-aged lamb with a parcel of the neck meat in wild garlic and anchovy dressing. To finish, a banana parfait, chocolate namelaka and popcorn. The wine list lives up to the setting, with a knowledgeable sommelier on hand to advise.

Chef Conor Tomey **Seats** 56, Private dining room 12 **Times** 12–2/7–9.30 **Prices** Set L 2 course from £25 , Set L 3 course from £34.50, Set D 3 course £67.50, Sunday lunch £34.50 **Wines** 1/1 bottles over £30, 11 bottles under £30, 15 by glass **Parking** 40 **Notes** Children 8 years +

Sussex, West

Langshott Manor

MAP 6 TQ34

@@@ Modern European V
01293 786680 | Langshott Lane, Horley, RH6 9LN
www.langshottmanor.com

Contemporary classic dining in Tudor surroundings

A Tudor manor house in the Surrey countryside may not quite be what you are expecting to come across within striking distance of Gatwick, but Langshott is not a mirage. Indeed, it could barely be better placed to uncrumple you after an arduous air journey, and spa treatments, pretty gardens and suave contemporary design are among its assets. Executive chef Phil Dixon supervises proceedings in the Mulberry dining room, a relaxing modern space with flashes of vibrant colour against a neutral backdrop. Much of the kitchen's produce is grown on site, and so a keen sense of the passing seasons is evident on contemporary classic menus that take in wild duck haggis with foie gras, apple and rhubarb, or spiced crispy squid with red cabbage and pancetta, ahead of seared turbot with mussels, dressed in mustard, orange and dill, or loin of fallow deer with smoked beetroot and horseradish. Fashionable veggie desserts might offer textures of parsnip to go with caramelised banana, or add sweet-sour sherry vinaigrette ice cream to sticky toffee and pear soufflé. Artisan cheeses come with pear and tomato chutney and pickled walnut bread. A generous selection of wines by the glass allows for some productive mixing and matching.

Chef Phil Dixon **Seats** 55, Private dining room 60 **Times** 12–2.30/7–9.30, Closed L Monday to Saturday **Prices** Set D 2 course £42.50, Set D 3 course £49.50, Tasting menu £75–£110, Sunday lunch £32.50 **Wines** 78 bottles over £30, 2 bottles under £30, 11 by glass **Parking** 25 **Notes** Children welcome

Restaurant Tristan

MAP 6 TQ13

@@@ Modern British, French ♥
01403 255688 | 3 Stan's Way, East Street, RH12 1HU
www.restauranttristan.co.uk

Clever, creative cooking in historic surroundings

The 16th-century building in a pedestrianised street in the heart of old Horsham looks pretty historic, but chef-patron Tristan Mason's food is certainly of-the-moment stuff. Within, the setting blends ancient and modern elements with great effect: a striking beamed vaulted ceiling, wall timbers and bare floorboards sit alongside a contemporary decor. As is often the way with this kind of innovative, creative, technically skilful cooking, menus dispense with any description other than listing the

components of each composition, but whether you go for three, four, six or
eight courses, you can be sure that the full gamut of taste categories,
textural contrasts and temperatures will be brought into play. Clever stuff,
then, but this isn't just about techno flim-flam: having trained with Marco
Pierre White, Mason's ideas are solidly grounded in classic French
technique. An impressive, highly-detailed starter might see scallop paired
with beef daube, parsley root and truffle. Fish and meat combinations are
favoured, beautifully cooked and might explore the textures and flavours
of lamb, kid and goat, while partridge could arrive alongside quince and
bacon. Things are brought to a close with tour de force desserts involving,
perhaps, a coconut soufflé with passionfruit, lemongrass and Thai basil.

Chef Tristan Mason **Seats** 40 **Times** 12–2.30/6.30–9.30, Closed Sunday
and Monday **Prices** Lunch 3/4 course £25/£30, Dinner 4 course £45,
Tasting menu 6/8 course £65–£80 **Wines** 105 bottles over £30, 22 bottles
under £30, 15 by glass **Notes** Vegetarian available, Children 10 years +

LICKFOLD
The Lickfold Inn
MAP 6 SU92

◉◉◉ British V
01789 532535 | GU28 9EY
www.thelickfoldinn.co.uk

Smart contemporary cooking at a Tudor inn

The ground floor of The Lickfold is very much what the notion of a Tudor
country inn leads one to expect, with exposed beams and comfortable
seating before the open fire, but upstairs things take a turn for the more
modern, with parquet-designed table tops and grey upholstery against a
backdrop of bared brick. There is more to the menus than just elevated
pub food; these are dishes that wouldn't look out of place in a modern city
restaurant setting. A soft-cooked yolk of duck egg sits in shallot jus,
garnished with artichoke crisps, finely chopped spring onion and wood
sorrel for an attractive starter, or you might opt to open with gin-cured
salmon adorned with seaweed and dill. Fish is handled with care, when
crisp-skinned cod and fat mussels arrive in a welter of samphire and
monk's beard, while meatier appetites are beguiled with confit goose leg,
its richness cut by Yorkshire rhubarb, on braised lentils and sprout leaves.
Layered desserts offer the final flourish, perhaps for chocolate ganache
and blood orange jelly on a base of toasted oats, or crab-apple parfait with
pain d'épices and roast hazelnuts.

Chefs Tom Sellers, Graham Squire **Seats** 40 **Times** 12–3/6–9.30, Closed
25 December, Monday and Tuesday, D Sunday **Prices** Set L 2 course £24,
Set L 3 course £30, Tasting menu £45–£70, Starter £6–£12, Main £26–£32,
Dessert £7–£8, Sunday lunch £26–£35 **Wines** 109 bottles over £30,
11 bottles under £30, 10 by glass **Parking** 20 **Notes** Children welcome

LOWER BEEDING

The Pass Restaurant

MAP 6 TQ22

@@@ Modern British V ♒

01403 891711 | South Lodge Hotel, Brighton Road, RH13 6PS

www.exclusive.co.uk

Ringside seats for a culinary firework display

For the uninitiated, the pass is the part of the kitchen where the head chef gives the final nod to dishes before waiting staff whisk them away, and here at this ultra-modern restaurant in the swanky South Lodge Hotel just 28 or so lucky people at each sitting can grab a pew (or rather a leather banquette or high stool) for a close-up view of the chefs in action and plasma screens to ensure you don't miss a trick. There's a lot more going on in the six, eight and ten-course menus than the terse descriptions imply, but rest assured that it's full of lively invention, built on first-class ingredients that work together and are sent out dressed to thrill. The menus are fun and intruiging to read with names like 'Walk the line', 'Honeymoon in Kyoto' and 'Cut off your nose'.

New head chef Ian Swainson's six-course lunch menu might include potato mousse with confit quail's egg, potato strings and butter foam, followed by red wine-braised snails, watercress and garlic. Striking colours are used to great effect in the likes of confit prawns and leek oil with a black and white lasagne, or red-themed idea involving roasted duck breast, beetroot, red cabbage and liver. There's a cheeseboard, grapes and crackers option before sweet ideas along the lines of poached and puréed rhubarb with rapeseed oil vinaigrette and balsamic meringue, or 'Morning Frost', a tempting concoction of pistachio, chocolate and passionfruit.

Chef Ian Swainson **Seats** 28 **Times** 12–2/7–9, Closed 1st 2 weeks in January, Monday and Tuesday, L Wednesday and Thursday **Prices** Set lunch 6 or 8 course £39.50 or £49.50, Set dinner 6, 8 or 10 course £70, £80 or £90, Sunday lunch £39.50–£49.50 **Wines** 261 bottles over £30, 4 bottles under £30, 16 by glass **Parking** 200

TURNERS HILL

AG's Restaurant at Alexander House Hotel
MAP 6 TQ33

@@@ British, French V

01342 714914 | East Street, RH10 4QD

www.alexanderhouse.co.uk

Inspired modern British cooking in boutique surroundings

In a sprawling 120 acres of Sussex-Surrey borderland, the red-brick manor house is an architectural mash-up comprising a castellated neo-medieval turret and soaring factory-style chimneys. Inside, the designers have been busy funking up the bar and lounge with assertive splashes of psychedelic colour, but sensibly sticking to a more sober palette of royal-blue upholstery and white linen to reinforce the fine dining mood in AG's, the principal dining room (there's also a sleek brasserie called Reflections). Innovative technique and eye-catching presentation are the hallmarks of dishes that have their roots in the classical repertoire.

First off, a slow-cooked Arlington White hen's egg is matched harmoniously with pearl barley risotto, shavings and purée of Jerusalem artichoke and a generous kick of black truffle. Cooking techniques add depth, as when suckling pig is roasted and teamed with gem squash purée, trompette mushrooms, seared onions and rich sage noisette sauce, while a fishy main might see halibut paired with ceps, salsify, kale and Oscietra caviar. French and British cheeses await those whose taste for culinary dynamism hasn't quite yet run to spiced pumpkin ice cream with ginger cake, buttermilk granita and salted butter noisette. Everything including the bread is made with craft and attention to detail, and it's all backed by a compendious wine list.

Chef Darrel Wilde **Seats** 30, Private dining room 12 **Times** 12–2.30/7–9.30, Closed L Monday to Saturday **Prices** Set D 2 course £45, Set D 3 course £60, Tasting menu 8 course (with wine) £85, Sunday lunch £32 **Wines** 70 bottles over £30, 6 bottles under £30, 15 by glass **Parking** 100

Sussex, West

Gravetye Manor Hotel

MAP 6 TQ33

◉◉◉ Modern British **V** ♛
01342 810567 | Vowels Lane, RH19 4LJ
www.gravetyemanor.co.uk

Modernist cooking, an Elizabethan mansion and heritage gardens

As we were preparing this guide we learnt that the restaurant here would be closed from 2nd January to 30 April 2018 in order to build an extension.

When only the full-dress luxury country house experience will do, look no further than Gravetye Manor. The original Elizabethan mansion was built by one Richard Infield as a little something for his new bride — look for their initials above the garden entrance, and if you're lucky enough to be staying over, there's a bedroom that boasts a wood carving of the couple, still united in domestic bliss after four centuries.

Fast forward 300 years, and the great Victorian landscaper William Robinson laid out its 1,000 acres in the quintessentially English style we still see today (the grounds include orchards, glasshouses, a smokehouse and a one-acre kitchen garden supplying freshly plucked seasonal fruit and veg) and gave the interiors a lavish make-over of dark oak panelling, ornate plasterwork ceilings and grandiose fireplaces. George Blogg helms the kitchen, sending out phenomenally dynamic modernist food exploring novel combinations and textural contrasts, and it's all built on produce of the highest quality, the suppliers proudly name-checked at the head of each menu. Choose from a monthly-changing à la carte that follows the seasons with a beady eye, or a seven-course tasting option with an

imaginative vegetarian version – the latter featuring the likes of roasted hen of the wood mushrooms with fermented garlic, watercress emulsion, nasturtium and pickled hop shoots, or a pressing of smoked potato and thyme matched with spring onion, morel mushrooms and wild garlic. Things get off the blocks with a pressing of Rougié foie gras counterpointed by braised chicory, candied walnuts and Kingscote grape verjus, or you might open with Sussex-reared Wagyu beef tartare, its buttery richness offset with black truffle, hop shoots, nasturtium and brassica flowers.

Mains display a confident feel for how flavours work together, pointing up well-timed and rested crown and faggot of local wood pigeon with pickled blackberries, English truffles, Morteaux sausage and Swiss chard; elsewhere, an impeccably seasonal springtime plate of saddle and shoulder of South Downs hogget might be accompanied by a haggis of its offal, alongside green asparagus, mint jellies and hollandaise sauce enriched with lamb fat. Fish cooking, too, is precise and inspired, perhaps locally-landed turbot with confit chicken wings, Jerusalem artichoke, sprouts and gremolata. The thrills continue into a dessert of raspberry crumble soufflé with raspberry and mint sauce and clotted cream ice cream, while caramelised white chocolate mousse could arrive with fennel shoots, treacle gel and fennel seed popcorn.

Chef George Blogg **Seats** 40, Private dining room 20 **Times** 12–2/6.30–9.30 **Prices** Set L 2 course from £30 (3 course from £40), Set dinner 4 course £40, Tasting menu from £85 **Wines** 350 bottles over £30, 18 by glass **Parking** 25 **Notes** All day menu 10am–10pm, Sunday lunch, Afternoon tea, Children 7 years +

Tyne & Wear

House of Tides

MAP 21 NZ26

◎◎◎◎ Modern British **V** ☙
0191 230 3720 | 28-30 The Close, NE1 3RF
www.houseoftides.co.uk

Prime modern British cooking right beside the Tyne Bridge

In today's restaurant world, location counts for a lot. It's often the first
way of conferring distinctiveness on a place, the key to a contented
diner's physical recollection of an occasion. The location here was a
masterstroke of vision on Kenny and Abbie Atkinson's part, their
idiosyncratic northeast venue occupying two floors of a 16th-century
merchant's house on the Tyne quayside, with the famous bridge looming
next to it. Uplighters throw the four-storey brick façade into dignified relief,
and the river itself is but a pebble's toss away.

Have a drink in the flagstoned ground-floor bar with caramel
banquettes to set the ball rolling, and then proceed upstairs to an
atmospherically historic dining space, where solid supporting beams
punctuate the unreconstructed room, there's a majestic fireplace and a
varnished board floor, and the window tables have elevated views of the
river. Kenny Atkinson is one of the country's prime exponents of the
modern British style, his skills and ingenuity spread liberally over
seasonally changing seven-course tasting menus that are full of dynamic
appeal. This is food that doesn't pull any punches, but delivers exactly
where it should, on the palate. The winter journey may begin with a
Lindisfarne oyster intuitively matched with cucumber, ginger and caviar,

with stops along the way for a voguish partnership of sea bass with a chicken wing and artichoke purée, and dry-aged Goosnargh duck with apple and parsnip, to arrive at its final dark chocolate destination, amid garnishes of banana, lime and meringue. Alongside it, the vegetarian version is in itself so full of creative energy and temptation that omnivores might well feel inclined to pitch in. Crown prince squash with sheep's curd, capers and raisins could be followed in the line-up by hen of the woods mushrooms with hazelnuts and pear, and then a truffled spelt and onion dish for main.

Lunch is only one course fewer, the autumn offering taking in onion soup with a scallop, halibut with mussels and sea veg, venison with wild mushrooms and hispi, and a brace of desserts leading with caramelised spiced pear, honeycomb and gingerbread. When springtime comes, it could be Yorkshire rhubarb with white chocolate and violets. Accompanying it all is a strong, user-friendly wine list, grouped by grape variety, showcasing many of today's outstanding growers, with an inspiring and varied selection by the glass. The aromatic signature cocktails are worth a look too. You won't look at a regulation gin and tonic in the same way again once you've tried the version here, made with Hepple's Northumberland gin, Galliano, and dandelion and burdock syrup.

Chef Kenny Atkinson **Seats** 60, Private dining room 14 **Times** 12–2/6–10, Closed 2 weeks at Christmas and New Year, Sunday and Monday, L Tuesday to Thursday **Prices** Tasting menu £55–£75 **Wines** 90 bottles over £30, 15 bottles under £30, 19 by glass **Parking** 70 (£1.20 per hour, free after 6pm) **Notes** Children 9 years +

Jesmond Dene House

MAP 21 NZ26

◉◉◉ Modern British, European

0191 212 3000 & 0191 212 6066 | Jesmond Dene Road, NE2 2EY

www.jesmonddenehouse.co.uk

Imaginative modern cooking in an Arts and Crafts stately home

Part of the allure of Jesmond Dene House is that it has the feel of a grand country house, sitting in a tranquil wooded valley, yet is actually within the city limits of Newcastle. Its original Georgian architect, John Dobson, designed much of the old city centre, but a makeover in the 1870s turned it into an Arts and Crafts gem. Restyled for the 21st century as a boutique bolt hole, it's a welcoming place with two dining rooms and a lovely fair-weather terrace. Head chef Michael Penaluna stocks his larder with the pick of local, seasonal materials and has the confidence to let the flavours speak for themselves. There is refinement, creativity and skill in the execution of dishes: a starter of rabbit terrine comes with rhubarb, carrot gel and morcilla, or there may wood pigeon breast in the forthright company of beetroot and quince. At main course stage, monkfish is handled with aplomb and matched with asparagus, peas and subtly flavoured smoked potato mash. Those in search of more assertive flavours might take loin of Northumberland venison with smoked bacon, parsnips, figs and crispy kale. It all ends with a tricksy dessert of warm apple espuma with vanilla custard, dried apple and apple sorbet

Chef Michael Penaluna **Seats** 80, Private dining room 24 **Times** 12–9, All-day dining, Closed D 25 December **Prices** Set L 2 course £19.50–£22, Set L 3 course £22–£26, Set D 2 course £20.50, Set D 3 course £24.50, Tasting menu 5 course from £55, Starter £7.50–£13.50, Main £15.50–£28, Dessert £6.50–£10.50, Sunday lunch £22–£26 **Wines** 120 bottles over £30, 25 bottles under £30, 18 by glass **Parking** 64 **Notes** Early evening set menu 5-7pm, Vegetarian available, Children welcome

▶ Warwickshire

ROYAL LEAMINGTON SPA

The Dining Room at Mallory Court Hotel

MAP 11 SP36

Modern British V ♕

01926 330214 | Harbury Lane, Bishop's Tachbrook, CV33 9QB

www.mallory.co.uk

Elegant restaurant with countryside views

As we went to press the Rosette award was suspended due to a change of chef – reassessment will take place in due course.

The ivy-clad manor house stands in 10 acres of sumptuous grounds, including its own kitchen garden, a little outside Royal Leamington Spa. Through the arched doorway, you will come across a charming mixture of art deco and Lutyensesque styling indoors, attended by supremely professional staff, the main dining room a restful place with wood panelling and floral drapes framing small windows.

Seats 56, Private dining room 14 **Times** 12–1.45/6.30–8.45, Closed L Saturday **Prices** Set D 2 course from £39.50, Set D 3 course £49.50–£65, Sunday lunch £39.50 **Wines** 200 bottles over £30, 25 bottles under £30, 12 by glass **Parking** 100 **Notes** Tasting menu 7 course, Children welcome

▶ West Midlands

BIRMINGHAM

Adam's

MAP 10 SP08

◉◉◉ Modern British **V** ♟

0121 643 3745 | New Oxford House, 16 Waterloo Street, B2 5UG

www.adamsrestaurant.co.uk

Artfully presented contemporary dishes full of surprise

Adam Stokes' smart modern restaurant in expansive premises near the city Museum and Art Gallery pushes all the right up-to-the-minute buttons. Not only is there a chef's table adjacent to the kitchen, but dishes arrive on patches of grass or in trays of gravel, the successive stages of the multi-course tasters ramping up the surprise quotient as they arrive. Expect foraged ingredients to crop up here and there, when hen of the woods mushrooms appear with a pairing of veal sweetbread and black pudding, as well as combinations of meat and seafood such as octopus and chorizo with avocado and garlic. Some dishes sound almost provocatively classical, such as the corn-fed chicken that comes with morels and truffle, although presentations remain highly innovative, while lamb might turn up in Asian guise with wild rice, seasoned with miso. Desserts retool the populist likes of cheesecake with flavours such as elderflower, apple and ginger, or turn sticky toffee pudding into something unexpected with smoked lemon syrup and vanilla cream, and there are Lincolnshire Poacher butter and smoked pork fat for spreading over the excellent breads. Wine flights with the tasting menus make the most of a resourceful main list of quality bottles that finds room for Devon Bacchus, Portuguese Loureiro and Austrian Blaufränkisch.

Chef Adam Stokes **Seats** 34, Private dining room 16 **Times** 12–2/7–9.30, Closed 3 weeks at Christmas, 2 weeks in summer, Sunday and Monday **Prices** Set L 3 course £35, Set D 3 course £65, A la carte menu 3 course £60, Tasting menu 8 course £85 **Wines** 180 bottles over £30, 10 bottles under £30, 22 by glass **Parking** On street **Notes** Children welcome

West Midlands

BIRMINGHAM *continued*
Purnell's

MAP 10 SP08

◎◎◎ Modern British ♛
0121 212 9799 | 55 Cornwall Street, B3 2DH
www.purnellsrestaurant.com

Superbly accomplished and inventive cooking in a conservation area

Glynn Purnell's eponymous restaurant occupies a corner site in the city's
financial district not far from St Philip's Cathedral. Converted from a red-
brick Victorian warehouse, with no expense spared, its stripy carpets,
boldly patterned wallpapers and bare tables add up to a cool and classy
look. It all makes a soothing setting for the imaginative multi-course
menus (with optional wine flights), or should you eat in the Living Room,
the deal is dinky plates made for sharing – what Glynn calls 'Brummie
tapas'. Wherever you choose, expect adventurous dishes along the lines
of poached duck egg yolk with cauliflower, black pudding, bacon and birch
syrup, or beetroot mousse and salted beetroot with horseradish crumble.
There's a nod to Brum's balti belt culinary heritage in, say, monkfish
masala served with Indian red lentils, carrots, coconut and coriander, but
the compass needle swings back to classical western mode for dishes
such as Balmoral venison served with bordelaise sauce, wild mushrooms
and potato crisp. The tempting three-course lunch deal might take in
barbecued octopus, crispy dried noodles, dried enoki mushrooms, mango,
mooli and miso, and sweet and sour bisque, then Peking duck breast with
almond satay, ponzu and veg noodles, ending with rhubarb and apple tart,
hazelnut crumble and apple sorbet.

Chef Glynn Purnell **Seats** 45, Private dining room 12 **Times** 12–1.30/7–9,
Closed Christmas and New Year, 1 week Easter, 2 weeks late July–early
August, Sunday and Monday, L Saturday **Prices** Set L 3 course £35,
Tasting menu £68–£88, Tapas £55, **Wines** 247 bottles over £30, 12 bottles
under £30, 24 by glass **Parking** On street, Snow Hill car park
Notes Vegetarian available, Children 10 years +

Simpsons

MAP 10 SP08

◎◎◎ Modern British **V** ♛
0121 454 3434 | 20 Highfield Road, Edgbaston, B15 3DU
www.simpsonsrestaurant.co.uk

Aspirational city dining in a Georgian mansion

The large white Georgian house on a corner in Edgbaston may not be
quite what first-timers are expecting to find in Birmingham, but Simpsons
has been quite the beacon for aspirational dining in the city for many
years. Extensive upgrading to the in-house cookery school in 2017 has
been one focus, while in the kitchen, the emphasis remains on cutting-
edge modern British cooking that utilises trending ingredients and

techniques in thrilling profusion. A tasting menu is at the core of operations, and might progress from a duck egg in carrot broth with hen of the woods, pork fat and nasturtiums, through lobster and Evesham tomato in tomato and coriander tea, to a fish offering of wild sea bass and mussels with stem broccoli and sunflowers. Pedigree meat may well be Cornish spring lamb with its sweetbreads, new season's Wye Valley asparagus, hazelnuts and sheep's curd, with a duo of desserts to follow, concluding perhaps with milk sorbet, crispy rice and malted milk cream. The shorter lunch drill is built around lighter main dishes such as gurnard with lovage, yeast flakes and beans.

Chefs Andreas Antona, Luke Tipping, Nathan Eades **Seats** 70, Private dining room 14 **Times** 12–2/7–9, Closed bank holidays, Monday, D Sunday **Prices** Set L 2 course £30-£35 (3 course £35-£45), A la carte 3 course £65, Tasting menu 8 course £85, Sunday lunch £35–£45 **Wines** Over 20 bottles over £30, 5 bottles under £30, 14 by glass **Parking** 12, On street **Notes** Children welcome

Turners at 69
MAP 10 SP08

◉◉◉ Modern British V
0121 426 4440 | 69 High Street, Harborne, B17 9NS
www.turnersat69.co.uk

Classically based modern food in elegant dining room

Richard Turner's place in the Birmingham suburb of Harborne makes quite a statement inside, with mirror-lined walls that emphasise the name reflecting crystal chandeliers and elegantly linened tables, a cheering antidote to the rather humdrum exterior surroundings. Welcoming staff and a buzzy atmosphere help things along too. Turner's preference is for prettily presented plates of sharply etched, classically based food, often garlanded with edible flowers in purples and yellows for that all-important visual appeal. Duck liver parfait with brioche, followed perhaps by lemon sole in herb butter, could whisk you back to the bistro days of the 1960s, except that the interpretations are more up-to-the-minute, that starter dish also adorned with chicken skin and burnt orange. More adventurously, there could be wild sea bass with parsnip purée and barbecued leeks in red wine sauce, or Anjou pigeon Wellington in Madeira jus scented with spruce. Heritage finishers such as rice pudding dobbed with blackberry compôte and scattered with rice crispies will seal the deal.

Chef Richard Turner **Seats** 28 **Times** 12–2.30/6–9.30 **Prices** Set L 2 course from £18.50 (3 course from £25), Starter £8.50–£13.50, Main £21.50–£35, Dessert £7.50–£12.50, Sunday lunch £32.50–£38.50 **Wines** 89 bottles over £30, 3 bottles under £30, 10 by glass **Parking** At rear **Notes** Children welcome

West Midlands

Hampton Manor

MAP 11 SP28

@@@@ Modern British V

01675 446080 | Swadowbrook Lane, Hampton-in-Arden, B92 0EN

www.hamptonmanor.com

Cutting-edge food and interior design dazzle

Half-hidden in the village of Hampton-in-Arden, which is sternly patrolled by a resident peacock, the Manor was built by Sir Robert Peel's son Frederick in the manner of his own Gothic pile at Drayton. Once you pick your way through the trees, it's quite the stately home, with 45 acres of grounds and a half-panelled dining room named after the original owner. A hand-stitched silk wall design of flowers and colourful birds lends an uplifting note to the scene, and it's worth a momentary gander at the gorgeously intricate plasterwork in the ceiling.

With Hampton's own kitchen plots and fine regional produce to conjure with, local lad Rob Palmer does the Manor proud in the way of cutting-edge contemporary culinary dazzle, though that doesn't preclude an absolutely straight serving of new season's asparagus in both colours, garnished with little more than an egg yolk. Then it's off and running with a serving of thinly sliced sea trout with a mousse of the smoked article, dressed with caviar, horseradish cream and compressed cucumber.

The much-prized Wagyu beef is given the full royal treatment, appearing first as an outrider of shredded cheek meat fried in a crumb coating with truffled mayonnaise, and then slices of the glorious fillet, the vegetable accompaniments of shredded white cabbage and red cabbage purée playing second fiddle, perhaps to the truffled cauliflower cheese. Nitrogen-crisped chocolate mousse might be the texturally fascinating finale, served with hazelnut crémeux and fragments of sweet nutty meringue.

Chef Rob Palmer **Seats** 26, Private dining room 14 **Times** 6.30–9, Closed Sunday and Monday, Lunch all week **Prices** Set D 2 course £40, Set D 3 course £55, Tasting menu £60–£80, Afternoon tea £25–£35 **Wines** 91 bottles over £30, 12 bottles under £30, 13 by glass **Parking** 30 **Notes** Children 12 years +

CASTLE COMBE
The Bybrook at The Manor House

MAP 4 ST87

◉◉◉ Modern British **V** ♟

01249 782206 | SN14 7HR

www.exclusive.co.uk

Confident cooking in a pretty medieval village

The Manor House at the heart the unspoilt medieval village of Castle
Combe has been around since the 14th century, and remains the centre of
the action to this day with a golf course in its 365 acres of parkland, and
high-flying contemporary country-house cooking. The Bybrook restaurant
also exudes heritage and class with its mullioned windows, sober colours
and pristine white linen, but there's nothing old-fashioned about the food.

The man heading up the kitchen is Rob Potter, whose cooking is defined
by well-thought-out and enterprising ideas, clear flavours and razor-sharp
accuracy, based, of course, on top-drawer ingredients, some supplied by
the hotel's kitchen garden and estate – the slow-cooked duck eggs, for
example, that appear in a starter with an entertaining medley of duck
ham, pickled shimeji mushrooms, Wiltshire truffle and parmesan salad.

Next up, braised Gigha halibut could be teamed with lettuce, mussels,
cockles, and a classic chive beurre blanc sauce, while loin and faggot of
Salisbury Plain fallow deer come with parsnip purée, sprouts, salsify and
bacon, all brought together by a fruity sloe gin sauce. The impressive
technique and creativity continues with prettily presented desserts such
as Brillat Savarin cheesecake, its decadent creaminess offset by a
trenchant trio of confit lemon, and blackberry sorbet and jelly.

Chef Robert Potter **Seats** 60, Private dining room 100 **Times** 12.30–2/
7–9.30, Closed L Monday to Saturday **Prices** Set D 3 course £66, Tasting
menu 7 course £89, Sunday lunch £35 **Wines** 300 bottles over £30,
25 bottles under £30, 20 by glass **Parking** 100 **Notes** Children 11 years +

COLERNE
Restaurant Hywel Jones by Lucknam Park

MAP 4 ST87

◉◉◉ Modern British **V** ♟

See page 238

Wiltshire

The Harrow at Little Bedwyn

MAP 5 SU26

◉◉◉ Modern British **V** 🍷
01672 870871 | SN8 3JP
www.theharrowatlittlebedwyn.com

Cooking of stunning intensity in tranquil surroundings

The Harrow may look like many another attractive country pub, a foursquare redbrick edifice in a pretty village on the cusp of Wiltshire and Berkshire, and yet nothing about it is in the least ordinary. It's been the labour of love of Roger and Sue Jones for nigh on 20 years, and has benefited from assiduous polishing in every aspect, from the warmth of the welcome to the undisputed quality of what Roger Jones' kitchen puts out. On sunny days, the tables on the terrace are a treat, with the gardens laid out before you and a contented sense of English tranquillity in the air, while the dining rooms themselves are stylishly appointed, with crisply clothed tables and muted colour schemes.

The menu drill is multi-course tasters, with five stages at lunch, and a choice of six or eight later on. It's all intensely market-driven and therefore impeccably seasonal, with the day's fresh fish and wild foragings often driving the more remarkable aspects of the production. What is most impressive is the sheer energy there is to the food. Even the most everyday ingredients and their preparations have resonant depth of impact brought out of them, and yet without the extensive denaturing to which many kitchens are given. Take a canapé-sized starter serving of tuna, soft as Turkish Delight and topped with diced Niçoise. It's simplicity itself, and yet

so sharply etched in three dimensions. Even better is the truffled mushroom risotto that follows. Seasoned eaters-out are hardly new to a portion of finely timed arborio filled with sliced wild mushrooms, scented with Périgord black truffle, and yet – again – the magisterial intensity of it is stunning. Cod too is worth its journey from Orkney when it's this tender and fresh, its light grilling supported by gently spiced chorizo, red pepper and diced black pudding, as well as spring greens and a vivid pea purée. The lengthier dinner menus might hinge on main course meats such as Northumberland roe deer, the properly developed gamey flavour matched by a bonbon of confit duck and parsnip purée, or fillet, cheek and tail of Highland Shorthorn beef.

The signature pre-dessert is the 'boiled egg and soldier', mango mousse set in Italian meringue with a tuile representing the finger of toast, while dessert itself could be a chocoholic's dream vision of cappuccino-frothy mousse in dark and white, a mini-bombe of chocolate and orange, and chocolate-filled coffee sponge. Otherwise, there could be a red berry soufflé, or a tangy composition of lemon, yuzu and passionfruit. Quite as imaginative is the vegetarian version of the main menu, on which, at the heart of proceedings, textural variations of cauliflower precede an Indian-inspired take on tarka dhal with a bhaji.

Chefs Roger Jones, John Brown **Seats** 34 **Times** 12–3/7–11, Closed Christmas and New Year, Sunday to Tuesday **Prices** Set lunch 5 course £40, Set dinner 6 or 8 course £50 or £75, Gourmet menu 8 course £75 **Wines** 750 bottles over £30, 250 bottles under £30, 20 by glass **Parking** On street **Notes** Children welcome

Wiltshire

COLERNE

Restaurant Hywel Jones by Lucknam Park
MAP 4 ST87

◉◉◉ Modern British V ⏳

01225 742777 | Lucknam Park Hotel & Spa, SN14 8AZ

www.lucknampark.co.uk

Sharply focused cooking in a magnificent country-house hotel

The long undulating drive between an honour-guard of mature trees prepares you for an entrance to what could well be one of Sir Noel Coward's stately homes of England, though in rather better repair. The magnificence of Lucknam's interiors is properly jaw-dropping, from a lounge watched over by oil portraits of the notability to a temple-like dining room with a ceiling fresco of cloud wisps in an azure sky. Hywel Jones has loyally manned the kitchens here long enough to have this room now named after him, which is only fitting, as this has been one of the most productive residencies in the West Country. The years have sharpened his focus, and the food retains a competitive edge in the modern British era. An opener of flaked Cornish crab is garnished with Exmoor caviar and violet artichoke, its balanced flavours strongly punctuated with the citrus blast of yuzu, or there may be truffle-fragrant poached rose veal with its sweetbreads in pancetta. At main, the signature dishes are done with dazzling panache, when slow-roasted rolled pork belly with apple and foie gras has its richness underpinned by gloriously creamy mash, and on-trend desserts feature a glossy chocolate bar with salt caramel ice cream, honey-roast peanuts and glazed banana. Excellent and varied breads are not to be missed.

Chef Hywel Jones **Seats** 70, Private dining room 28 **Times** 12.30–2.30/7–10, Closed Monday and Tuesday, L Wednesday to Saturday **Prices** A la carte menu 3 course £87, Tasting menu from £110, Sunday lunch from £42 **Wines** 270 bottles over £30, 30 bottles under £30, 12 by glass **Parking** 80 **Notes** Children 5 years +

MALMESBURY

Whatley Manor Hotel and Spa
MAP 5 ST98

Modern British V ⏳

01666 822888 | Easton Grey, SN16 0RB

www.whatleymanor.com

Luxury-hotel cooking

As we went to press the Rosette award was suspended due to a change of chef – reassessment will take place in due course.

Niall Keating is now at the stoves here and his blend of modern British with Asian influence has created a new dining experience. The manor house is late Victorian and was originally part of the farmland estate of a rear admiral and his family. Its winning good looks made it perfect for transformation into a magnificent country-house hotel. There's a strong sense of stepping back in time as you pass through the huge doors, although the principal dining room is an understated modern place, with cream walls, bare floors and a good measure of space around each table.

Chef Niall Keating **Seats** 46, Private dining room 30 **Times** 7–10, Closed Monday and Tuesday, Lunch all week **Wines** 16 by glass **Parking** 120

PEWSEY
Red Lion Freehouse

MAP 5 SU15

◉◉◉ Modern British

01980 671124 | East Chisenbury, SN9 6AQ

www.redlionfreehouse.com

Top-class produce handled with great skill

England's best country inns often take a bit of effort to find, and the thatched Red Lion, tucked away among the sinuous B-roads and high hedges around Salisbury Plain is no exception. The Mannings have created an immensely appealing gastronomic oasis, all beams and bare bricks, charming staff, and every effort is made to maintain the pub feel of the place, with comforting pub grub and sandwiches up for grabs. Even when the chef pulls out all the stops, it's still the sort of flavour-driven, down-to-earth stuff that people actually want to eat, as seen in a starter of tortellini packed with scallops and black pudding. Menus are built of the pick of local materials, bolstered by their home-reared pigs, eggs from rescue hens and a productive kitchen garden, with pretty well everything made in house. If you want soul-soothing mains, look no further than herb-roasted guinea fowl breast with girolles and bean cassoulet, or there might be an immaculately executed portion of halibut with caramelised smoked pork jowl and the Mediterranean glow of black olive crumb and pistou. At the end comes raspberry parfait and sorbet with pistachio purée and a sablé biscuit, or Valrhona chocolate crémeux with cocoa crumbs and sea salt.

Chefs Guy and Brittany Manning, Dave Watts **Seats** 45, Private dining room 20 **Times** 12–2.30/6–9, Closed D 24–25 December **Prices** Set L 2 course from £20, Set L 3 course from £25, Set D 2 course from £20, Set D 3 course from £25, Tasting menu from £85, Starter £7.50–£9, Main £20–£30, Dessert £7.50–£10, Sunday lunch from £24 **Wines** 17 bottles over £30, 10 bottles under £30, 23 by glass **Parking** 14, On street **Notes** Prix fixe menu Monday to Thursday lunch and dinner, Friday lunch only, Vegetarian available, Children welcome

Worcestershire

CHADDESLEY CORBETT
Brockencote Hall Country House Hotel
MAP 10 SO87

◉◉◉ Modern British **V**

01562 777876 | DY10 4PY

www.brockencotehall.com

Authoritative modern cookery in a grand Victorian manor house

Ensconced in 70 acres of landscaped gardens and parkland, the impressive Victorian manor presents a striking sight when reflected in the waters of its ornamental lake. The sweeping pastoral views are best appreciated from either a seat in the Colonial lounge-bar or a table in the suitably elegant setting of the Chaddesley dining room, or if you are going about things in the right spirit, one after the other. Expect bright, beautifully-presented food with a clever contemporary edge courtesy of Tim Jenkins. His cooking steps up to the mark with a precise and skilful interpretation of modern thinking in dishes that balance a certain robustness with unusual and unexpected flavours, as witnessed in an opening partnership of pan-fried scallops and belly pork served with passionfruit cream. A punchy main course partnering pan-fried venison loin with a croquette of shoulder meat and Oxford Blue cheese, baked Jerusalem artichoke skins, sprouts and hazelnut jus shows a sound grasp of what works with what. Another idea might see pan-roasted monkfish matched with spiced cauliflower, various forms of brassicas, mussel velouté and almonds. Technically impressive interplays of flavour and texture shine once again at dessert, when iced coconut parfait is delivered with lime sorbet and pineapple.

Chef Tim Jenkins **Seats** 40, Private dining room 16 **Times** 12–2/6.45–9.45 **Prices** Set L 2 course £27, Set L 3 course £35, Set D 2 course £36.50–£44.95, Set D 3 course £47.50–£59.95, Tasting menu from £75, Sunday lunch £35 **Wines** 120 bottles over £30, 16 bottles under £30, 12 by glass **Parking** 50 **Notes** Afternoon tea £25, Children welcome

▶ North Yorkshire

BAINBRIDGE
Yorebridge House
MAP 21 SD99

◉◉◉ Modern British **V** ♛

See page 242

BOLTON ABBEY

The Burlington Restaurant

MAP 16 SE05

Modern British ♜

01756 710441 | The Devonshire Arms Hotel, BD23 6AJ

www.thedevonshirearms.co.uk

Seasonal menus in a lovely setting

As we went to press the Rosette award was suspended due to a change of chef – reassessment will take place in due course.

The Duke of Devonshire's estate unrolls over an extensive stretch of North Yorkshire, on the edge of the Dales National Park, not far from Skipton. The name of the hotel may sound self-deprecatingly pubby, The Devonshire Arms, but best set your faces to 'stunned' for the indisputable grandeur of the place.

Seats 70, Private dining room 90 **Times** 7–9.30, Closed Christmas and New Year, Monday, L all week **Prices** A la carte dinner menu £69.95, Tasting menu £79.50 **Wines** 2,000 bottles over £30, 20 bottles under £30, 30 by glass **Parking** 100 **Notes** Vegetarian available, Children welcome

HARROGATE

Horto Restaurant

MAP 16 SE35

◉◉◉ Contemporary British

01423 871350 | Rudding Park Hotel, Spa & Golf, Follifoot, HG3 1JH

www.ruddingpark.co.uk

Creative cooking driven by garden produce

Set in the sleek spa area of the posh Rudding Park Hotel, the casual daytime café cranks things up a notch or two and puts on its Horto badge to serve up six-course tasters in the evening. If your Latin's a bit rusty, the name means 'garden' and that's where much of the seasonal ingredients come from, bolstered by the best materials the area can offer. Chef Murray Wilson's modern cooking is driven by an acutely seasonal eye, delivering big flavours from simple combinations with minimum posturing. You know you're on to a good thing when the bread is a superb tangy sourdough paired with showstopping chicken and thyme butter. Mozzarella mousse with tomato water and a crisp tomato tuile opens the show, then that splendid garden produce is showcased in a pretty plate of spring salad boosted with herb pannacotta, chicken skin and millet. Elsewhere, there's a wonderful interplay of tastes and textures in a dish of super-fresh crab partnered with peas, yuzu and peanut, while perfectly timed hogget loin comes with broad beans and a vibrant mix of yogurt and verbena. Desserts are clever and creative too, as seen in a deconstructed cheesecake, macerated strawberries, elderflower and sweet cicely.

Chef Murray Wilson **Notes** For more details see the restaurant's website

Yorkshire, North

BAINBRIDGE
Yorebridge House

MAP 21 SD99

◉◉◉ Modern British Ⓥ ⌘
01969 652060 | DL8 3EE
www.yorebridgehouse.co.uk

High-impact modern dining in the former headmaster's residence

The old Yorebridge grammar school was established here in the 17th century, although the present schoolhouse and headmaster's residence date from around 1850. What a pleasant spot it must have been in which to cram your Latin grammar, the luxuriant Yorkshire Dales unfolding all around you, the rivers Bain and Ure flowing peaceably by on either hand. Following the First World War, it went daringly co-ed, and after its last ever pupils had bid the place a fond farewell, it had a career as head office of the Dales National Park.

Today, the trim greystone buildings make a fine country hotel, and while it may be hard to imagine the last headmaster neck-deep in a hot tub in the great outdoors, that was surely only for want of the technology. The main building and guest rooms have indeed been boutiqued to perfection, with an understated palette of charcoal-grey against louvred doors deployed to stylish effect in the dining room. Dan Shotton and his brigade favour a straightforward, unpretentious approach to the modern British repertoire, founded on ingredients of unimpeachable quality – suppliers are proudly listed on the menus – and presented in ways that don't render them unrecognisable, but work with the grain of their natural flavours for maximum impact. The menus give little away as to what delights the

kitchen has created – for example '62°C duck egg, butternut squash and Iberico'. Dishes certainly look attractively intricate, but in an enlightening rather than obfuscating way, and combinations that have passed into the modern classic pantheon are given new point and impetus, as when salmon ballotine is equipped with the earthy notes of heritage beetroot and horseradish, or when a scallop starter is teamed with meaty smoked eel and the concentrated tartness of Granny Smith apple. Sound northern meats such as Gressingham duck and beef fillet from nearby Wensleydale are accorded intuitive, satisfying treatments, the former with red cabbage, parsnip purée and boulangère potatoes, the latter with salsify and kale and a portion of glutinously braised ox cheek. The first duty of chicken these days is often to support a fish dish, and here a nice sticky wing plays supporting role to a perfectly timed fillet of stone bass, along with pied bleu mushrooms and leeks.

The finale could be an impressive array of British cheeses, including some fine local specimens, with chutney and lavoche crispbread, or there may be mandarin cheesecake with honeycomb and ginger. If it's pedigree rhubarb you're after, you've come to the right region, and could well find it starring in a 'Caramac' dessert with white chocolate. An admirably clear wine list with helpful notes helps matters no end.

Chef Daniel Shotton **Seats** 35, Private dining room 18 **Times** 12–3/7–9 **Prices** Set L 2 course £17.50, Set L 3 course £22.50, Starter £20, Main £30, Dessert £10, Sunday lunch £17.50–£22.50 **Wines** 90 bottles over £30, 10 bottles under £30, 8 by glass **Parking** 30 **Notes** Children welcome

HELMSLEY
Black Swan Hotel

MAP 16 SE68

◉◉◉ Modern British **V**

01439 770466 | Market Place, YO62 5BJ

www.blackswan-helmsley.co.uk

Art on a plate in a gallery restaurant

Sprawling through a trio of houses spanning the ages from Elizabethan to Georgian to Victorian, the Black Swan still possesses much of its old character, albeit with a distinctly 21st-century boutique look to go with its antiques and open fires these days. The Gallery restaurant (so named because it doubles as a daytime gallery showcasing original artworks for sale) is where Alan O'Kane gets to show off his confident grasp of modern flavours and combinations, sourcing the finest Yorkshire ingredients and turning them into dishes that wow with their technical flair and beautiful presentation. Bright ideas are there from the off in the home-made sourdough bread with to-die-for beef butter, then an opener of cured mackerel offset by the clean flavours of apple, lemon, cucumber and a knockout oyster ice cream. Next up, superb Texel lamb rump comes with the rich accompaniments of fiery Merguez sausage ragout, dukkah spices, sweet red pepper salsa, and gnocchi enriched with lamb fat, or there may be sea bream with black garlic, dashi, purple sprouting broccoli and Anna potatoes. A lively thread of imagination runs all the way through to a delightful finale of strawberries with compressed watermelon, green almond, mascarpone and a lime 'cigar'.

Chef Alan O'Kane **Seats** 65, Private dining room 50 **Times** 12.30–2/6.30–9.30, Closed L Monday to Saturday **Prices** Tasting menu from £65, Starter £8.50–£13.95, Main £18–£28, Dessert £10–£12.50 **Wines** 166 bottles over £30, 39 bottles under £30, 19 by glass **Parking** 40 **Notes** Sunday lunch, Children welcome

MASHAM

Samuel's at Swinton Park

MAP 16 SE27

Modern British

01765 680900 | Swinton, HG4 4JH

www.swintonpark.com

Modern cooking in a glorious country estate

As we went to press the Rosette award was suspended due to a change of chef – reassessment will take place in due course.

Swinton Park makes quite an impression, with its solid-looking tower and castellated walls hung with creeper. The interior boasts antiques and family portraits (the Cunliffe-Listers have owned the property since the 1880s), that enhance the feeling of being in a stately home. The dining room is particularly grand, with its high carved ceilings, gilt-framed mirrors and plush drapes at the windows.

Seats 60, Private dining room 20 **Times** 12.30–2/7–9.30, Closed 2 days January, L Monday to Friday **Prices** Set L 3 course from £28, Set D 3 course from £50, Tasting menu from £70 **Wines** 111 bottles over £30, 33 bottles under £30, 13 by glass **Parking** 80 **Notes** Sunday lunch, Vegetarian available, Children 8 years + at dinner

MIDDLETON TYAS

The Coach House

MAP 16 NZ20

@@@ Modern British **V**

01325 377977 | Middleton Lodge, DL10 6NJ

www.middletonlodge.co.uk

Yorkshire menu at the heart of a Georgian country estate

At the heart of Middleton Lodge, an expansive Georgian country estate not far from Richmond, The Coach House is a restaurant with rooms in the modern style. Its continuing development extends to the current planning of a 2.5-acre kitchen garden, due to come on stream in 2018.

Inside, well-spaced chunky wood tables and shelves displaying ornamental glassware beneath a beamed ceiling are the setting for a Yorkshire menu influenced by the bounty of the local countryside. Dishes are pleasingly based in British culinary tradition, with modern flourishes in the form of wild ingredients and eye-catching presentation.

Chargrilled meats are a feature, including 32-day Galloway rib-eye and Cheviot lamb, served with skinny fries and salad, while the rest of the menu deals in cured sea trout with oyster mayonnaise, horseradish and apple, and mains such as grilled hake in wild garlic butter with sea spinach, brown shrimps and toasted almonds, or locally reared chicken with hen of the woods and gnocchi. At the end, there are fashionable tweaks to old favourites, adding rhubarb sorbet to custard tart made with duck egg, or tropicalising the rice pudding with coconut and a mango sorbet. A top-value market menu offers the likes of slow-cooked brisket with pancetta, onions and wild leeks for mains.

Chef Gareth Rayner **Seats** 80, Private dining room 24 **Times** 12–2/ 6–9 **Prices** Set L 2 course from £15, Set L 3 course from £20, Starter £6–£12, Main £10–£24, Dessert £4–£12, Sunday lunch £15–£28 **Wines** 47 bottles over £30, 43 bottles under £30, 20 by glass **Parking** 100 **Notes** Children welcome

OLDSTEAD

The Black Swan at Oldstead

MAP 16 SE57

@@@@ Modern British V ⚆
01347 868387 | YO61 4BL
www.blackswanoldstead.co.uk

Exceptional cooking rooted in the surrounding earth

The old farmstead is very much a family affair, scions of the Banks clan
having the place capably in hand. James runs the front of house in the
dining room, while his brother Tommy is in charge at the stoves. It sits on
the edge of the North York Moors, north of York itself, and is at the hub of
an industrious farming and foraging operation, supported by terraced
kitchen gardens out back, where oca and romanesco grow – take a look.
Once installed at your table in the understated dining room, you can
expect a tour of vanguard cooking, presented with visual dash and
utilising much modern technique.

The tasting menu is the way to go. From appetiser pairings of smoked
eel and apple, or langoustine and caramelised whey, there are interesting
tastes all the way. Crapaudine beetroot slowly cooked in beef fat is a
tantalising marriage of elements, while beer-fed Dexter beef is scented
with some of last year's garlic. Fish dishes maintain the pace too, perhaps
teaming monkfish with hen of the woods mushrooms and broccoli, and for
afters, it's a matter of dressing sheep's milk yogurt in Douglas fir oil, and
filling any remaining gas with a vegetable cake made from artichoke,
chicory root and thyme.

This cooking springs naturally from the earth in which it is grown.
The wine list is innovatively furnished with a kind of cartographic chart
orienting the user to the different styles on offer, but the menu has helpful
individual suggestions under most dishes too.

Chefs Tommy Banks, Will Lockwood **Seats** 50, Private dining room 12
Times 12–2/6–9, Closed L Sunday to Friday **Prices** Saturday lunch £50
Tasting menu £95 **Wines** 90 bottles over £30, 2 bottles under £30, 81 by
glass **Parking** 20 **Notes** Children 10 years +

Yorkshire, North

SCAWTON
The Hare Inn

MAP 16 SE58

◉◉◉ Modern British V
01845 597769 | YO7 2HG
www.thehare-inn.com

Dramatic moorland cooking at a medieval inn

There isn't much to the unassuming little village of Scawton, near
Helmsley, at the southern fringe of the North York Moors National Park,
but it does boast The Hare Inn, and that's reason enough for tracking it
down. It's a modest-looking medieval inn dating back to the 13th century,
red-roofed and whitewashed, its window frames done in pale khaki. There
are a couple of wrought-iron tables outdoors if you fancy taking the
country air before dining, and the surrounding tranquillity is certainly
sufficient to inspire such a thought on balmy days and early evenings, but
then the place has such an air of unmolested venerability that you'll soon
be hastening into the stone-walled indoors, with its iron wood-burner,
deeply upholstered clubby armchairs, cask-conditioned, hand-pump ales
and pervasive air of relaxing bonhomie.

Paul Jackson likes to share his culinary panache, and can often be seen
demonstrating at regional fairs, from the Scarborough Seafest to the
Harrogate Flower Show. Back at The Hare, Liz Jackson makes a capable
and effective front-of-house advocate for the kitchen, though nothing
quite prepares you for the gastronomic dramatics to come. In the best
present-day fashion, Paul sources locally, drawing on the produce of
moorland farmers and growers for menus that combine great creative

energy with concentration and intensity on the palate. Every dish is imaginatively conceived, with a mixture of textural and colour variations in one intricate construction after another. The core menu is a multi-course affair, with a longer taster to supplement it, and there is the option of what are discreetly called 'beverage pairings' (for which, read thoughtfully chosen wines) to go with the successive dishes.

After a selection of ingenious appetisers, the principal dishes might open with a serving of sea bass and a bunch of its seafood friends, a king oyster, mussel and cockle, before a serving of marinated Dexter beef with bone marrow, radishes and macadamias. The voguish technique of offering one of the central dishes in two servings is observed here, but often for fish rather than meat surprisingly, so that the ever-versatile mackerel might appear first in Japanese guise with cucumber in shiso, ponzu and soy, before a follow-up take presents it with anchovies in lemon verbena and garlic. The main meat might be tenderly rare pigeon, accompanied by asparagus, ramsons and spelt, and a refreshing granita primes the palate for the brace of desserts to follow. Expect perhaps a chocolate and cherry pairing charged with Kirsch, and then strawberries with sheep's curd and fennel. A list of discerningly chosen wines is on hand, although opting for the pre-selected beverages is well advised as they could range from Drouhin Chablis to a South African Red Muscadel.

Chef Paul Jackson **Seats** 22 **Times** 12 2.30/6–9, Closed Sunday to Tuesday, L Wednesday to Friday. Annual holiday closures vary (see The Hare Inn website for details) **Prices** Tasting menu £55–£70 **Wines** 20 bottles over £30, 8 bottles under £30, 12 by glass **Parking** 12 **Notes** L Thursday to Saturday must be booked in advance

YORK
The Grand Hotel & Spa, York

MAP 16 SE55

@@@ Modern British ♥
01904 380038 | Station Rise, YO1 6HT
www.thegrandyork.co.uk
Grand railway hotel with contemporary dining

The UK's grand old Edwardian edifices are often ideal candidates for
reinvention as upmarket hotels, and such is the case with the former HQ
of the North Eastern Railway. Hard by the city's ancient walls, today's
luxurious establishment seamlessly blends opulent original features with
swish 21st-century facilities – an elegant cocktail bar sets the mood for
up-to-date dining in Hudson's, a brasserie-style venue with a
sophisticated sheen and professional service to match. Head chef Craig
Atchinson and his team turn out contemporary, well-crafted dishes with a
local flavour, and present-day cooking techniques deployed to full effect.
Torched mackerel might be partnered with pork belly, apple, kohlrabi and
mackerel broth in a well-judged starter, or go for a classic chicken liver
parfait with red port, pickled onion, pear and spiced bread. At main course
stage, loin and shoulder of salt-aged lamb could arrive alongside parsnip,
brassica and pickled capers, while a fishy alternative could see stone bass
served with langoustine, fennel, buckwheat and langoustine bisque.
Finish on a local note with poached Yorkshire rhubarb with buttermilk
custard, elderflower and toasted oats.

Chef Craig Atchinson **Seats** 60, Private dining room 32 **Times** 6.30–10,
Closed 25 December, Lunch all week **Prices** Tasting menu from £65
Wines 137 bottles over £30, 25 bottles under £30, 5 by glass **Parking** NCP
(Tanner Row) **Notes** Vegetarian available

The Park Restaurant

MAP 16 SE55

@@@ Modern, Traditional British V
01904 540903 | Marmadukes Town House Hotel, 4-5 St Peters Grove,
Bootham, YO30 6AQ
www.marmadukestownhousehotelyork.com
Contemporary dining in a townhouse hotel

Adam Jackson may have been here for less than two years but this
smartly refurbished conservatory-style restaurant, part of a Victorian
townhouse hotel not far from the city centre, has already made a name for
itself as somewhere to find sharp contemporary cooking. An intimate
space, it is only open for dinner, allowing everyone involved to concentrate
on delivering the ambitious menu exactly as the chef intends. It's a
friendly and informal setting, while still having an air of switched-on
professionalism. The eight-course tasting menu changes regularly and
Jackson, a Yorkshireman born and bred, makes the very best use of the
wonderful produce available in this neck of the woods. You can take the

menu either with or without the suggested wine pairings, and there is no flowery verbiage on the menu – descriptions, in fact, are quite terse – 'mushrooms, sorrel, gnocchi', for example, is followed by 'beetroot, salmon, apple', and then a main course of 'duck, foie gras, artichoke and hazelnut'. Never fear, however – you're in safe hands with a thoughtful, imaginative chef who knows exactly what he's doing as he guides you on a journey of taste, texture and aroma.

Chef Adam Jackson **Seats** 28, Private dining room 25 **Times** 7–10, Closed 25–29 October, Sunday and Monday, L all week **Prices** Tasting menu 8 course £48–£52 **Wines** 20 bottles over £30, 9 bottles under £30, 13 by glass **Parking** 12

▶ West Yorkshire

ILKLEY
Box Tree
MAP 16 SE14

◉◉◉ Modern & Traditional French ♥
01943 608484 | 35-37 Church Street, LS29 9DR
www.theboxtree.co.uk

Yorkshire culinary excellence since the early 1960s

In a property dating from 1720, the Box Tree has been a beacon on the local restaurant scene since the early 1960s. The timewarp look of the elegant interior – all deep sofas, pictures in gold frames and antiques dotted around – wouldn't look out of place in that era, but the food tells a different story. Simon Gueller handles his top-quality ingredients sensitively and intelligently, his modern French style underscored by the classical repertoire and techniques. An amuse-bouche – perhaps onion and lemongrass foam with coriander oil – announces that we're firmly in 21st-century territory, before starters such as hand-dived scallops with celeriac purée, fresh truffle and Granny Smith apple, or Yorkshire deer tartare with oyster emulsion, egg yolk, and beer-pickled onions. Mains such as stone bass fillet with razor clam and mussel chowder, lemon oil and caviar, or French squab pigeon with roast foie gras, beetroot, and a sharp orange purée also make their point via uncluttered mixtures of flavours and textures. Sound culinary judgment is applied to puddings, too: a textbook passionfruit soufflé with coconut ice cream, for instance.

Chef Simon Gueller **Seats** 50, Private dining room 20 **Times** 12–2/7–9.30, Closed 27–31 December, 1–7 January, Monday and Tuesday, L Wednesday to Thursday, D Sunday **Prices** Set L 3 course £37.50 (Friday to Saturday), Set D 3 course £47.50–£65, Tasting menu £80, Sunday lunch £37.50 **Wines** 11 bottles over £30, 12 bottles under £30, 7 by glass **Parking** NCP **Notes** Children 5 years + at lunch, 10 years + at dinner

Yorkshire, West

The Man Behind The Curtain
MAP 16 SE33

◉◉◉ Modern European **V**

0113 243 2376 | 68-78 Vicar Lane, Top Floor Flannels, LS1 7JH

www.themanbehindthecurtain.co.uk

Thrilling modern dining with bags of style

The whimsical name comes from a quote from *The Wizard of Oz*, and makes it clear from the off that this establishment above Flannels clothes store is as idiosyncratic as they come. The place is the brainchild of Michael O'Hare, and it goes for a minimalist, sharply contemporary look that suits the avant garde style of cooking. A 10-course tasting menu is the deal (a shorter Menu Rapide is available at lunch), and dishes all come on arty, tailor-made vessels – an opener of fabulous 'hand massaged' octopus with caper lemon butter and paprika emulsion, say, which arrives on a tentacle-shaped silver spoon.

O'Hare gives full rein to his creativity in a menu full of bold ideas that unleash every techno trick in the book to explore textures, flavours and ingredients. Be prepared for a display of culinary fireworks through dishes such as veal sweetbread slider in a siracha steamed bun with Chinese XO sauce and pickled shiitake mushrooms, or ox cheek with foie gras, puffed wild rice, black truffle and spinach.

The excitement continues through to inspirational and revelatory sweet courses – an impressive, highly detailed combination of milk chocolate mousse with lavender and honey, violet ice cream and warm potato custard, perhaps, or a confection exploring the possibilities of praline and passionfruit.

Chef Michael O'Hare **Seats** 42 **Times** 12.30–2/6.30–8.30, Closed 21 December to 13 January, Sunday and Monday, L Tuesday and Wednesday **Prices** Lunch menu £60, Tasting menu £60–£90 **Wines** 18 bottles over £30, 18 by glass

CHANNEL ISLANDS

▶ Jersey

ST BRELADE

Ocean Restaurant at The Atlantic Hotel

MAP 3 inset map

Modern British **V ♀**

01534 744101 | Le Mont de la Pulente, JE3 8HF

www.theatlantichotel.com

A light, bright dining space in a top hotel

As we went to press the Rosette award was suspended due to a change of chef – reassessment will take place in due course.

With exotic palm trees, white louvred shutters, a deep blue pool straight out of a Hockney painting and a whiff of art deco in its low-slung white façade, The Atlantic Hotel could be in 1930s Miami. The Ocean Restaurant has views over the gardens towards the sea, a New England palette of blues, whites and beiges, and modern artwork on the walls – it's a wonderfully light and airy setting. Service is pitch perfect, and the sommelier will guide the way through a list of thoroughbred wines that teems with quality.

Seats 60, Private dining room 60 **Times** 12.30–2.30/7–10, Closed January **Prices** Set L 2 course £22.50, Set L 3 course £27.50, Set D 3 course £55, A la carte 2 or 3 course £55 or £65, Tasting menu 7 course £85, Sunday lunch £32.50 **Wines** 498 bottles over £30, 32 bottles under £30, 30 by glass **Parking** 60 **Notes** Children welcome

Jersey

Bohemia Restaurant

MAP 3 inset map

◎◎◎◎◎ Modern French, British **V**

01534 880588 | The Club Hotel & Spa, Green Street, JE2 4UH

www.bohemiajersey.com

Exploratory cooking led by quality ingredients

The Club Hotel and Spa is as city-slick an operation as you'll find on a holiday island, in an operation that maintains the boutique element but with unexpected design touches too. If the cool cocktail bar with its fabric patterns of stripes and tessellating triangles, and its vivid abstract washes, feels like quite the ocular jolt, consider a dining room that looks decidedly sober by contrast, with modern dark wood panelling and a single pendant light-fixture poised above each table, an understated space that does nothing to prepare you for Steve Smith's vivaciously creative cooking. Smith did a stint at the leading edge of global gastronomy in Melbourne, and has imbibed the full-frontal style of modern cuisine.

Dishes are very much ingredient-led rather than recipe-oriented, which allows room for an exploratory approach that produces complex, but always carefully considered dishes. Start with a savoury custard tart, its filling made with rich brown crabmeat, while to one side a separate pastry disc is piled with the shredded white, decorated with glops of mango gel and wasabi mayonnaise. Holding the seafood line, you might continue with spangling-fresh turbot, served with plump mussels, carrot purée and roasted whole carrots in a sauce of tangy sea buckthorn. Fashionable meat pairings might take in glazed breast and confit leg of duck in rhubarb with kohlrabi and pistachios, while lamb appears as loin and braised neck, with accompaniments of Jerusalem artichoke and goats' cheese. At the top end of the kitchen's output, all the stops are pulled out for the tasting menus, one of which is a fish-lover's special encompassing an oyster dressed in cucumber and dill, sea bass in Madeira with butternut squash purée and chanterelles, and the signature scallop with truffled celeriac, smoked eel and apple in truffle vinaigrette, before that majestic turbot surfaces.

Dessert could be multi-layered in every sense, as is the case with the chocolate sponge that supports bands of Jivara mousse, then yuzu mousse, then a richer ganache, alongside yuzu and lactose ice cream on a rubble of biscuit crumbs. All the expected frills and furbelows are present around the principal dishes, from ingeniously complex savoury canapés to a pre-dessert that incorporates just about every possible texture of apple and blackberry, and labour-intensive chocolates with coffee, their fillings ranging from pink grapefruit and chai tea to pecan butterscotch. Those who like to get up close and personal can opt for the table in the kitchen, and there is an elegant private room for celebrations.

Chef Steve Smith **Seats** 60, Private dining room 24 **Times** 12–2.30/ 6.30–10, Closed 24–30 December, Sunday (except Mothers Day and Fathers Day), bank holiday Mondays **Prices** Set L 2 course from £19 (3 course from £24.95), Set D 2 course from £50 (3 course from £59), A la carte 3 course £59, Surprise lunch/dinner menu 6 course £45 or £49, Tasting menu £75–£85 **Wines** 275 bottles over £30, 19 bottles under £30, 30 by glass **Parking** Opposite **Notes** Children welcome

Ormer
MAP 3 inset map

◉◉◉ Modern European **V** ♏
01534 725100 | 7-11 Don Street, JE2 4TQ
www.ormerjersey.com

Shaun Rankin's sophisticated St Helier venture delivers the goods

On a balmy summer's night, the lush roof garden and roof terrace of Shaun Rankin's high street operation is hard to beat, but there's some superlative dining to be done before you round off an evening beneath the Jersey skies. There's a lively ground-floor bar, a pavement terrace for people watching, and the ground-floor restaurant is done out with sleek art deco-style glamour reminiscent of a 1920s ocean liner, all wooden floors, chandeliers, plush royal blue velvet buttoned sofas and mustard yellow leather seats at dark wood tables simply decorated with small lamps. After almost two decades on the island, Rankin is a firm believer in Jersey's fine produce, and his menus showcase the best the island has to offer in modern dishes that astonish with their depth of natural flavour and beautiful presentation. A thrilling starter could bring together red mullet and scallop, pointed up with the vivid notes of fresh blood orange, Fourme d'Ambert cheese and white chocolate. Next up, perhaps Dover sole with 'fish pie flavours', roast leeks, sea vegetables and parsley oil, or if you're not taken by the maritime mood, how about trying venison with parsnip purée, medjool date, ginger and smoked chocolate tortellini? To finish, try treacle tart with macerated raspberries and clotted cream ice cream.

Chef Shaun Rankin **Seats** 70, Private dining room 14 **Times** 12–2.30/ 6.30–10, Closed 25 December, Sunday **Prices** Set L 2 course £22 (3 course £35), Tasting menu £75, Starter £14–£18, Main £28–£35, Dessert £9.50– £10 **Wines** 196 bottles over £30, 48 bottles under £30, 15 by glass **Parking** On street, Sand Street car park **Notes** Children welcome

Jersey

Restaurant Sirocco@The Royal Yacht

MAP 3 inset map

◉◉◉ Modern British

01534 720511 | The Weighbridge, JE2 3NF

www.theroyalyacht.com

Bright Jersey cooking with harbour view

This Royal Yacht is most definitely not an actual seagoing vessel, but its curvaceous, wave-shaped balconies do lend a maritime air to the glossy harbourside hotel. It's a distinctly upmarket affair, with acres of plate glass facing the harbour, a glitzy spa centre to pamper you into submission, and a host of dining and drinking opportunities, including a grill restaurant, the casual all-day Zephyr eatery, and the pick of the bunch being the snazzy Restaurant Sirocco with its huge terrace affording views over the harbour through floor-to-ceiling windows. The stylish space brings a cosmopolitan ambience and designer chic to proceedings, with its coffee-hued napery, tones of magenta and eye-catching light fittings conjuring a slick setting.

The team in the kitchen is dedicated to delivering local ingredients, and the imaginative menus – à la carte, set price and tasting versions – showcase their ambition. These are pin-sharp modern dishes, with successful flavour combinations, plenty of technical ability on display, and put together with an acute eye on the seasons. Dishes arrive looking pretty as a picture, a starter of succulent butter-poached lobster, say, with cocoa butter, parsnip and caviar, while another opener sees a fashionable surf 'n' turf pairing of seared scallops and oxtail alongside cauliflower and

cheddar cheese. As you would hope in the island setting, fish gets a good outing among main courses – perhaps a classic treatment of Dover sole, simply grilled and matched with caper butter sauce and Jersey Royals, or a more contemporary combination of pan-fried sea bass with black garlic, crab and gnocchi. On the meatier side of things, the island's beef could be showcased as succulent fillet and tender cheek, served with morels and asparagus, while those who have a soft spot for theatrical service might sign up for a timeless steak Diane, flambéed at the table and partnered with Lyonnaise potatoes and green beans.

Desserts are equally focused on maximizing flavour and textures, and arrive looking easy on the eye, whether you go for a perfectly risen apple crumble soufflé with its accompanying apple sorbet, or a chocolate sphere with salted caramel and honeycomb. If you just can't make your mind up, a pair of willing accomplices might go for a sharing assiette and have a bit of everything, or bow out on a savoury note with a cosmopolitan plate of expertly ripened local, British and continental cheeses. The pedigree wine list starts close to home in France then spreads its wings to take in carefully chosen bottles from all over the world.

Chef Steve Walker **Seats** 65, Private dining room 20 **Times** 12–4/7–9.30, Closed L Monday to Saturday **Prices** Set D 3 course from £32.50, Tasting menu £70–£99, Starter £9.50–£12.75, Main £17.50–£34.50, Dessert £9–£12, Sunday lunch £23.50–£26.50 **Wines** 108 bottles over £30, 49 bottles under £30, 20 by glass **Parking** Car park **Notes** Vegetarian available, Children welcome

See advert on page 258

ST HELIER *continued*

Tassili

MAP 3 inset map

@@@ British, French **V**

01534 722301 | Grand Jersey, The Esplanade, JE2 3QA

www.handpickedhotels.co.uk/grandjersey

Refined Anglo-French cooking in a historic bayfront hotel

Full of elegance and swagger since it opened in 1890, the majestic Grand Jersey hotel still holds an undeniable allure with its glitzy spa and slew of eating options. Soaking up the view over the sparkling waters of St Aubin's Bay, champagne in hand, on the terrace is a prime attraction. Likewise in the main restaurant, Tassili, an elegantly understated contemporary space with a high-gloss finish that has the good sense not to try to compete with that wonderful view.

Nicolas Valmagna heads up the kitchen team, lending class to culinary matters with his well-honed French technique, keen eye for local materials, and talent for mixing global ideas: crab, say, might appear in a starter with passionfruit gel, Combava lime, bisque dressing and coconut espuma, or pan-fried goose liver could be paired with rhubarb, pistachio, pain d'épices purée and lychee espuma.

Carefully structured mains leave an overall impression of lightness and grace, whether it's skillfully handled turbot with subtly flavoured saffron risotto, mussels, sea veg and caviar, or a more visceral combo of grass-fed lamb, the best end and sweetbreads lifted with samphire, spring onion, tempura anchovies and wild garlic pesto. Creative ideas and contemporary technique follow through into desserts such as a trio of chestnut purée, quince mousse and buttermilk sorbet.

Chef Nicolas Valmagna **Seats** 24 **Times** 7–10, Closed 25 December, 1–30 January, Sunday and Monday, Lunch all week **Prices** Set D 3 course £45, Tasting menu £67–£75, Vegetarian Menu £62 **Wines** 70 bottles over £30, 14 bottles under £30, 12 by glass **Parking** 32, NCP

Jersey

Longueville Manor Hotel

MAP 3 inset map

@@@ Modern Anglo-French V ♀

01534 725501 | JE2 7WF

www.longuevillemanor.com

Compelling cooking from a long resident chef

A family-owned hotel since just after WWII, Longueville has sailed serenely through the generations. Parts of the building date back to the late medieval era, but the whole package these days is of a boutique spa hotel on the grand scale, complete with ornamental fountain before the entrance, acres of ancient woodland and a Victorian kitchen garden.

The latter comes under the watchful eye of Andrew Baird, whose continued incumbency in the kitchens here has been one of the reasons for Longueville's success. Dining extends from the austerely panelled Oak Room to a lighter space overlooking the grounds, and nobody will bat an eyelid if you find a lunchtime salad arriving while you bask on the sundrenched pool terrace.

Baird's touch is light, but dishes are compelling nonetheless, as when vivid beetroot-cured salmon comes with figs, orange and crème fraîche for an appetising opener. Mains might take in a pioneering partnership of lamb (loin and shoulder) with lightly curried deep water crab, with butternut purée in a high-gloss garlicky jus, or more classical poached lemon sole with assorted shellfish in lobster sauce. The long-running passionfruit soufflé with raspberry sorbet is a masterpiece of acute timing, or there could be baked apple terrine with black butter bavarois and Calvados ice cream.

Chef Andrew Baird **Seats** 65, Private dining room 40 **Times** 12.30–2/7–10 **Prices** Set L 3 course £25-£36, Set D 2 course £52.50–£58.50, Set D 3 course £60–£66, Sunday lunch £45–£61, Discovery menu £80 –£110, A la carte 2/3 course £52.50/£60 **Wines** 300 bottles over £30, 69 bottles under £30, 25 by glass **Parking** 45 **Notes** Children welcome

SCOTLAND

Aberdeenshire – Angus

TARLAND
Douneside House

MAP 25 NJ40

◉◉◉ Modern Eurpoean
013398 81230 | AB34 4UL
www.dounesidehouse.co.uk

Spectacular contemporary cooking in a grand holiday retreat

Douneside was built by the MacRobert family in 1888 as a holiday home, and a rather sumptuous one at that, complete with a central battlemented tower. For many years, the house served as a vacation retreat for members of the armed forces, but has now been relaunched more comprehensively as a destination hotel. The Royal Deeside surroundings provide plenty of pastoral tranquillity, while David Butters' kitchen aims to hit the heights, with a five-course tasting menu and three-stage carte of spectacular, seasonally based contemporary dishes. An opening morsel of beetroot sorbet on creamy lardo with candied pecans and apple julienne has plenty to say for itself, and may be succeeded by smoked pigeon and foie gras, anointed with crystal-clear consommé at the table. Then comes very lightly smoked salmon done in a bain-marie with keta and beluga caviars, before a majestic principal dish showcases Highland venison in a deep chocolate-infused jus with spring cabbage and salsify. Dessert could be rich chocolate delice with magically perfumed pear sorbet, cherry purée and chocolate tuiles.

Chef David Butters **Times** Closed Christmas, mid July to end August.
Notes Bookings required for non-residents

▶ Angus

INVERKEILOR
Gordon's

MAP 25 NO64

◉◉◉ Modern Scottish
01241 830364 | Main Street, DD11 5RN
www.gordonsrestaurant.co.uk

Striking modern Scottish cookery in a coastal hamlet

Thanks to the Watsons family's efforts over 30-odd years, the sleepy coastal hamlet of Inverkeilor is firmly established on the map of culinary destinations. The place is hard to miss on the quiet high street, and once inside, the contemporary look in the intimate beamed and stone-walled dining room makes a strong first impression. These days, Gordon's son Garry Watson takes care of the kitchen side of things, keeping the local fan base happy with his high-definition modern Scottish cooking. The drill is a set-price menu of four courses at dinner, opening with sea bream céviche, say, with mango, coconut and a bracing dressing of pomegranate to bring it all together. An intermediate soup course offers the silky charms of artichoke, cauliflower and Isle of Skye scallop velouté, then mains might showcase loin of wild Scottish venison partnered by purple cabbage, shallot Tatin, beetroot and carrot pureé, and juniper sauce. Fishy compositions could bring North Sea turbot with a well-balanced array of chargrilled sweetcorn, crispy chicken wings, mushroom pureé and burnt cabbage. At the end, Valrhona's finest provides for a lush chocolate moelleux, the feel good factor boosted further by salted caramel ice cream and balanced by the fruitiness of pear poached in red wine syrup.

Chef Garry Watson **Seats** 24, Private dining room 8 **Times** 12.30–1.45/7–9, Closed January, Monday, L Tuesday to Saturday, D Sunday (winter) **Prices** Set L 3 course from £35, Set D 5 course £60, Tasting menu from £60 **Wines** 11 bottles over £30, 33 bottles under £30, 5 by glass **Parking** 6 **Notes** Booking essential, Vegetarian available, Children 12 years +

▶ Argyll & Bute

PORT APPIN

Airds Hotel and Restaurant
®®® Modern Scottish V ♟
01631 730236 | PA38 4DF
www.airds-hotel.com

MAP 23 NM94

Fine Scottish produce on the Linnhe shore

If a watery view is restorative to the spirits, the white-fronted former ferry inn on the shore of Loch Linnhe, not far from Oban, is ideally sited. Sunsets over the distant hills are a particular draw in the summer months, and the dining room is a delight whatever the weather, with deeply upholstered chairs, smart linen-draped tables and sprays of flowers adding to the welcoming tone. The cooking has taken on a modern sheen in recent years, but without abandoning its commitment to the clear, resonant flavours of unimpeachable Scottish produce. Smoked salmon from Inverawe is the focal point of a starter plate that also includes pickled and beetroot-cured incarnations, matched with some mild goats' cheese, or there could be old-school crab ravioli in shellfish sauce scented with wild garlic and lemon gel. Main courses mobilise gentle Asian hints, as in the Indian-spiced mussel and clam vinaigrette that comes with monkfish and sea veg, while meat might be a trio of lamb cuts with baby vegetables and fondant potato. Desserts such as honey cheesecake with poached pear and yogurt sorbet are very much a lure.

Chef Chris Stanley **Seats** 30 **Times** 12–5/7.15–9.15 **Prices** Set L 2 course from £18.95, Set L 3 course from £23.50, Set D 5 course £56, Tasting menu 7 course £74, Starter £5–£9, Main £10.95–£23.95, Dessert £4–£8 **Wines** 300 bottles over £30, 15 bottles under £30, 12 by glass **Notes** Sunday lunch, Children 8 years +

Argyll & Bute

Inver Restaurant

MAP 23 NS09

◉◉◉ Modern Scottish V

01369 860537 | Strathlachlan, PA27 8BU

www.inverrestaurant.co.uk

Creative ideas and heavenly views

Pam Brunton and Rob Latimer have made quite a metaphorical splash on the shores of Loch Fyne. Their low-slung whitewashed cottage sits in splendid isolation by the water's edge, and a well-designed interior spec provides contemporary simplicity tempered by a couple of real fires. A stack of vinyl records provides a cool backing track. If the interior brings to mind the purity of Scandinavian design, well, that is perhaps no coincidence, for Pam's time spent at Noma in Copenhagen has helped inspire her culinary approach too (check out the cookbooks on show to find further clues).

The menu reflects the seasons and the local terroir, and modern cooking techniques enhance the ingredients to maximum affect. Lunch can be Loch Fyne langoustines with sourdough bread, while the evening four-course menu might get going with a heavenly bowl of girolles and potato dumplings, enriched with an egg yolk. Roe deer stars with fresh walnuts and walnut milk, the tender meat concealed under wafer-thin slices of celeriac, with a glorious sweet-sharp hit from some local brambles, or go for cured halibut with lard and cauliflower. To finish, almond cake with greengages and bitter almond custard is a bang on bit of baking. Children have their own wee menu, and the wine list, like everything else here, lifts the spirits.

Chef Pamela Brunton **Seats** 40, Private dining room 20 **Times** 12–2.30/ 6.30–9, Closed September to December, Christmas, January to February, Monday and Tuesday (except bank holidays), D Wednesday, Sunday March to June **Prices** Tasting menu from £46, Starter £5.50–£9, Main £11.50–£23, Dessert £5.50–£8, Sunday lunch **Wines** 7 bottles over £30, 9 bottles under £30, 4 by glass **Parking** 20 **Notes** Dinner & Disco/Music & Meal Friday monthly, Steak night monthly, Children welcome

BALLANTRAE
Glenapp Castle

MAP 19 NX08

@@@ Modern British V
01465 831212 | KA26 0NZ
www.glenappcastle.com

Dining experience to remember in Scottish baronial style

A lengthy tree-lined drive is always a good start, and when a Victorian castle façade in the Scots baronial manner looms before you at the end of it, you know you're in good hands. Glenapp looks the regal part throughout, with swagged curtains and deep floral upholstery as standard, and a reigning sense of calm civility. The place maintains reassuring professionalism, as well as a reputation for dependable French-influenced cooking under the aegis of executive chef David Alexander. Much of the produce is grown within the grounds, and arrives in the context of a six-course menu at dinner, including a pre-dessert, that might kick off with a bowl of satiny pea and mint velouté, before proceeding to a classic terrine of smoked ham hock and foie gras with brioche and apricot chutney. Seared scallops in sauce vierge provides the sea interlude, and then main course delivers a fish or meat choice, either sea bass on ratatouille couscous in red pepper sauce, or full-flavoured breast of chicken with a black pudding bonbon and mash in tarragon-laced Madeira jus. If the Scottish cheeses don't lure you away from dessert, expect something like Calvados parfait with green apple sorbet.

Chefs Tyron Ellul, David Alexander **Seats** 34, Private dining room 20 **Times** 12.30–2/6.30–9.30 **Prices** Set L 3 course £39.50, Set D 3 course £45, Tasting menu 6 course £65 (dinner), Sunday lunch £39.50 **Wines** 115 bottles over £30, 9 by glass **Parking** 20 **Notes** Children 5 years +

TROON
Lochgreen House Hotel

MAP 19 NS32

@@@ Modern French
01292 313343 | Monktonhill Road, Southwood, KA10 7EN
www.lochgreenhouse.com

Modern cooking in a stunningly restored manor house

Standing proud amid 30 acres of woodland and immaculately tended gardens, Lochgreen House overlooks the fairways of Royal Troon and the glorious Ayrshire coastline. Built in 1905 for a wealthy lace mill owner, the handsome white-painted mansion is as well turned out as its grounds, and sympathetically extended to provide oceans of space in the formal Tapestry restaurant, where crystal chandeliers hanging from a lofty beamed roof, well-spaced tables dressed in their best whites, and plush tapestry-upholstered seats (spot the clue in the name) set a smart tone.

continued

Dumfries & Galloway

The French-accented cooking aims for sophistication and impact, using prime Scottish materials in thoughtful dishes starting with duck and foie gras terrine, served alongside foie gras croustillant, apple purée, chestnut crumb, brioche and duck skin butter. Top-drawer Scottish produce leads the charge again in a main course of wild halibut with hazelnut butter, charred salsify, poached grapes and squid ink hollandaise, while fans of local game might go for Culzean Estate venison with spiced red cabbage purée, celeriac remoulade, chanterelle mushrooms and fondant potato. Desserts are perfectly conceived and impeccably balanced confections: classic custard tart is served with fig compôte, liquorice and clotted cream, or pear tarte Tatin with vanilla ice cream and crème anglaise.

Chefs Andrew Costley, Iain Conway, George Sharpe **Seats** 80, Private dining room 40 **Times** 12–2/7–10 **Prices** Set L 2 course from £19.95, Set L 3 course from £24.95, Set D 4 course £45, Tasting menu from £60, Starter from £9.50, Main from £17, Dessert from £7, Sunday lunch from £25 Afternoon tea £18.95 (with champagne £24.95) **Wines** 70 bottles over £30, 40 bottles under £30, 11 by glass **Parking** 90 **Notes** Vegetarian available, Children welcome

▶ Dumfries & Galloway

PORTPATRICK
Knockinaam Lodge   MAP 18 NX05
◉◉◉ Modern Scottish Ⅴ ♞
01776 810471 | DG9 9AD
www.knockinaamlodge.com
Scottish country-house cooking in historic setting

Not too far to drive from Stranraer, Knockinaam is nonetheless ensconced in such joyous isolation that you'll need to negotiate a single-track road to get here. Churchill and Eisenhower once met here to plot a course towards the postwar world, and doubtless enjoyed the 30 luxuriant acres and private shingle beach to which the former hunting lodge lays claim. The kitchen, meanwhile, lays claim to the hugely experienced talent of Tony Pierce, whose carefully considered, finely crafted Scottish country-house cooking continues to win converts. The dinner format is a set menu that changes every day. A spring evening might open with grilled salted monkfish in a rich béarnaise, before proceeding to the intermediate soup course, perhaps creamed celeriac garnished with crisp pancetta. Lochmaben roe deer is much favoured for main, and rightly so, its majestic roast loin crusted in brioche and thyme, and served with potato gaufrette and salt-baked celeriac in a juniper-scented reduction of port. At the end comes the only moment of choice: will it be mature British and French cheeses with walnut and sultana bread, or a dessert such as poached plums with cardamom pannacotta and honeycomb?

Chef Tony Pierce **Seats** 32, Private dining room 18 **Times** 12–1.15/7–9 **Prices** Set L 4 course £40, Set D 5 course £67.50, Sunday lunch from £32.50, **Wines** 350 bottles over £30, 30 bottles under £30, 8 by glass **Parking** 20

▶ West Dunbartonshire

BALLOCH

Martin Wishart at Loch Lomond
MAP 23 NS38

◉◉◉◉ Modern European V ♟

01389 722504 | Cameron House on Loch Lomond, G83 8QZ

www.martinwishartlochlomond.co.uk

Natural produce with head-turning visual display

These days, just about every name chef has a place in the city and somewhere in the countryside, and Edinburgh star Martin Wishart has a gorgeously sited venue on Loch Lomond, probably literally a stone's skim from the front door to the water's edge. Naturally, views from the dining room are over the gently ruffled waters of the loch, and a little creative ruffling has been brought to the latest Ian Smith designs. Chairs are upholstered in tangy lime or Everton mint stripes of black and white, and an illuminated glass store divides the main space from the service doors.

Graeme Cheevers brings his own productive energies to the Wishart style, which matches a strong commitment to natural produce with head-turning visual display. A marriage of heavenly foie gras mousse and quince purée on oloroso sherry jelly with brilliant brioche is all classical authority, or you might opt for something much more 'now', in the shape of bergamot-marinated sea bream of surpassing freshness, with an array of bracing accompaniments – ponzu, radish, sea herbs and dill. A pair of conjoined fillets of lemon sole topped with parsnip brunoise is a bright main course idea, the creamed Brussels sprouts and vermouth-laced velouté adding richness, while barbecued Angus onglet is a fine steak cut, its positive flavour deepened with a lightly set custard of bone marrow. Desserts to beat the band include chestnut parfait with Cox's apple mousse and featherlight cinnamon ice cream. Incidentals, from canapés to petits fours, show exemplary attention to detail.

Chef Graeme Cheevers **Seats** 40 **Times** 12–2.30/6.30–10, Closed 25–26 December and 1 January, Monday and Tuesday, L Wednesday to Friday **Prices** Set L 3 course £32, A la carte menu £75, Tasting menu 6/8 course £80–£95, **Wines** 240 bottles over £30, 12 bottles under £30, 12 by glass **Parking** 150 **Notes** Sunday lunch, Children welcome

Edinburgh

Castle Terrace Restaurant

EDINBURGH PLAN C1

◉◉◉ Scottish, French V 🍷

0131 229 1222 | 33-35 Castle Terrace, EH1 2EL

www.castleterracerestaurant.com

Classic French-oriented cooking in the castle environs

The castle environs in Edinburgh are a desirable address by any stretch, and Dominic Jack's place on the opposite side of the Mound to Princes Street, on the ground floor of a four-storey Georgian terrace, fits its location to a tee. Designed in modern minimal style inside, with a striking outline image of the castle itself in royal blue on the wall, the place is sibling to The Kitchin in Leith, which is ample indication of the level of quality to expect. With a bundle of gold-standard French training under his belt, Jack cooks in recognisably classic style.

Start with pané veal kidney, turnip purée and rosemary, or lightly curried Orkney scallops, as possible preludes to flawlessly timed monkfish tail parcelled in Ayrshire ham with peas à la française, while the sought-after Gartmorn Farm duck comes, for a small supplement, with seared foie gras, rhubarb and ginger.

Desserts to tempt even the sternest abstainer include mascarpone-based apple cheesecake with caramelised sesame seeds and apple sorbet, or caramel soufflé with chocolate ganache and caramel ice cream. A trolley laden with French and British cheeses in prime condition is an exemplar of the genre. The surprise tasting menus offer a comprehensive insight into Dominic Jack's abilities.

Chef Dominic Jack **Seats** 75, Private dining room 16 **Times** 12–2.15/6.30–10, Closed 11–17 April, 18–24 July, 17–23 October, 23 December to 15 January, Sunday and Monday **Prices** Set L 3 course from £33, Set D 3 course from £70, Tasting menu from £80 **Wines** 445 bottles over £30, 2 bottles under £30, 30 by glass **Parking** NCP (Castle Terrace) **Notes** Children 5 years +

EDINBURGH

0   200 m

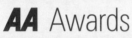

AA Awards

AA Restaurant of the Year for Scotland 2017–18

EDINBURGH

The Dining Room
EDINBURGH PLAN C3

®® Modern French, Scottish **V**

0131 220 2044 & 07496 146652 | 28 Queen Street, EH2 1JX

www.thediningroomedinburgh.co.uk

French classicism at Scotch Malt Whisky Society

Climb the spiral staircase to the restaurant of the Scotch Malt Whisky Society in the heart of the city centre, to where a light, smart, bare-floored room is furnished with linened tables, primrose-hued walls and colourful food and drink-themed pictures. The business of matching food and drink, indeed, has been honed to a fine art here, and given the tutelary spirit of the place, it shouldn't come as any surprise to learn that it isn't necessarily wine with which the dishes are paired, but fine single malt Scotch too. The cooking has more than a hint of French classicism to it, but it is very much overlaid with modern combining, so expect to start perhaps with a rich ballotine of pheasant and foie gras with pickled vegetables and trompettes, or a roasted scallop teamed with salt cod, fennel and blood orange, for starters that make bold opening statements.

Following those, main dishes aim to showcase their principal ingredients at their best advantage, with thought-provoking but intuitive supporting elements. A serving of firm-textured halibut with spätzle and Jerusalem artichoke in crisp and purée guises pulls out all the stops, or the game season brings on roast partridge with parsnips, Brussels sprouts, and a quince simmered in sherry. Traditionalists will doubtless make a beeline for Scotch beef with cavolo nero in sauce diable. Featherlight mandarin cheesecake with cranberry sorbet is a refreshing finish, while the crème brulee arrives glammed up with poached rhubarb, white chocolate and rhubarb sorbet. Thoroughbred cheeses with oatcakes, red onion chutney and quince jelly are the real deal. For the full pairing experience, go with the tasting menu, five courses gleaned from the main menu, perhaps hinging on venison loin with beetroot, purple carrots and orange in fir needle oil. Vegetarian dishes are up to the mark too.

Chef James Freeman **Seats** 66, Private dining room 20 **Times** 12–2.30/5–10, Closed Sunday and Monday **Prices** Set L 2 course from £18.50 (3 course from £21.95), Set D 2 course from £18.50 (3 course from £21.95), Tasting menu from £75, Pre-theatre menu (5–6.30pm) £18.50–£21.95 **Wines** 44 bottles over £30, 13 bottles under £30, 18 by glass **Parking** On street **Notes** Children 14 years +

Edinburgh

The Kitchin

MAP 24 NT27

◉◉◉◉◉ Scottish, French **V** 🍷
0131 555 1755 | 78 Commercial Quay, Leith, EH6 6LX
www.thekitchin.com

Ambitious modern Scottish cooking with French roots

The rejuvenated waterfront district of Leith has been one of the success stories of development in the Scottish capital in recent years. There is something to see all over the show, including a phalanx of high-quality restaurants, at the forefront of which is Tom Kitchin's destination venue, now embarked on its second decade. Sited in an old bonded whisky warehouse, it's an atmospheric space, with something of the subterranean feel of old wine cellars. A deep grey is the prevailing tone, and the separate zones of the dining room are divided by columns of brick and little stone walls that seem to suggest farming country. An illuminated glass shelf display of single malts reminds us of the original purpose of the building.

Kitchin's cooking, deeply rooted in his French training with modern masters Pierre Koffmann, Guy Savoy and Alain Ducasse, but Scottish to its finger-ends in its commitment to thoroughbred Highland and Lowland produce, has grown in ambition over the past decade. The publication of his first book, *From Nature to Plate* (2009), helped bring the philosophy of the restaurant into focus, and put it in the vanguard of the natural foods movement. Television appearances have been a regular gig, but the principal emphasis remains here. The full panoply of menu options is put into practice, from the shorter lunch deal – perhaps red mullet escabeche with fennel, peppers and orange, and roe deer pithivier with quince purée, carrot and apple, finishing with apple crumble soufflé and vanilla ice cream – to a dinner carte, the seasonal taster and a six-stage menu surprise for the intrepid. The dishes are full of cleverly worked layers of flavour, coaxed from first-class materials brought together in productive and ingenious compositions, their visual complexity on the plate matched by the three-dimensional impact on the palate. A long-standing opener has been the boned and rolled pig's head, served for bracing contrast with a roasted Tobermory langoustine and a salad of crispy pig's ear, dressed in the pungent richness of creamy gribiche.

Principal fish dishes might be simpler in conception, perhaps turbot roasted on the bone and served with squid and garlic confit and garlicky potatoes, a dish that could hardly be more purely French in orientation, but lack for nothing in resonance, while meats favour an all-singing, all-dancing approach, a preliminary dish bringing together Inverurie veal sweetbreads, crispy ox tongue and bone marrow marmalade with roasted parsley roots, while the main might be an array of Scottish beef cuts with marrowed potato and roast parsnip. At the end might come silky yogurt pannacotta, cut with razor-sharp Granny Smith sorbet in a consommé of sea buckthorn, or perhaps choose a little something or two from the laden cheese trolley.

Chef Tom Kitchin **Seats** 75, Private dining room 20 **Times** 12.15–2.30/ 6.30–10, Closed Christmas, New Year, 1st 2 weeks January, 4–8 April, 25–29 July, 10–14 October, Sunday and Monday **Prices** Set L 3 course £33, Set D 3 course £75, Tasting menu 6 course £85 **Wines** 363 bottles over £30, 36 by glass **Parking** 300 (site parking evening only, all day Saturday) **Notes** Children 5 years +

Number One, The Balmoral

EDINBURGH PLAN D2

@@@@ Modern Scottish **V** ☻
0131 557 6727 | 1 Princes Street, EH2 2EQ
www.roccofortehotels.com
Opulent cooking in a grand station hotel

City travellers arriving by train once expected rather more of a railway hotel than another high-rise branch of one of the budget chains. And when they did, The Balmoral is pretty much what they got. It sits in state at one end of Princes Street, a short stumble from Waverley Station, sentinelled by kilted doormen, and secreting within a series of glamorous public spaces that have been impressively maintained, culminating in the Number One dining room, where crimson walls crowded with small prints are offset by seating in primrose and grey. Executive chef Jeff Bland and head chef Brian Grigor oversee a menu of unashamedly opulent grand-hotel cooking, but with regional roots and more than a splash of modern panache too. A hand-dived Dingwall scallop in cock-a-leekie with prune ketchup might set the ball rolling, or it may be a bowl of satiny wild garlic velouté with morels, adorned with crisped ox tongue and chicken tortollini. What follows might be a classy combination of lemon sole and Peelham ham with white asparagus in beurre blanc, or perhaps a more loin-girding meat dish, such as fillet of Scotch beef with its hay-cooked short rib, aubergine, and bone marrow fondant. Gentle dessert textures favour mousses and pannacottas, perhaps a combination of Amedei chocolate and buttermilk, respectively, in a productive partnership with mango and mint, or there may be vanilla soufflé with poached rhubarb and almond ice cream. A glance at the protean cheese trolley seems only polite, as does a little exploration of the authoritative wine list.

Chefs Jeff Bland, Brian Grigor **Seats** 60 **Times** 6.30–10, Closed 2 weeks in January, Lunch all week **Prices** Set D 3 course from £80 (4 course £85), Tasting menu 7/10 course £89–£120 **Wines** 350 bottles over £30, 30 by glass **Parking** On street, NCP **Notes** Children welcome

EDINBURGH

Restaurant Mark Greenaway

EDINBURGH PLAN C3

◉◉◉ Modern British ♟

0131 226 1155 | 69 North Castle Street, EH2 3LJ

www.markgreenaway.com

Astonishing modern cooking at a handsome Georgian address

The entrance is on a corner in handsome Georgian Edinburgh, a few steps leading up between large planters to a navy blue door. If it feels a little like you're here to talk to your financial advisor, let all such thought perish as you step into the serenely enveloping slate-blue dining room, where a Cézannesque mountain landscape overlooks the smartly laid-up tables, and a light-fixture like a cluster of golden grapes casts a soft glow over the evening scene. Earlier on, daylight floods through the retracted shutters, and whatever the time, the place is run with the kind of quiet command that inspires confidence.

Mark Greenaway has established a presence for himself outside the confines of his self-named restaurant, using today's circuit of television appearances and cookbook publishing to help establish his identity, and ensure that those in search of fine dining in a well-provisioned city will be sure to include him on the itinerary. Greenaway's food is complex in the modern way, technologically driven, but full of natural colour and uplifting flavours too, so that no one element overshadows any other. Whether you choose to go à la carte, or with the eight-course taster, there is astonishment and excellence at every turn. A roast breast and leg of Perthshire quail is accompanied by a structurally perfect Scotched quail egg with accoutrements of beetroot, pistachios and golden raisins, or you

might begin with a brace of corpulent scallops in dashi stock, their sweetness counterpointed by salty pork crackling and re-emphasised by soy caramel, the taste categories exhaustively completed by the sharpness of a jelly of rice wine vinegar. Fish and seafood are reliably on point, never more so than in a main of hake fillet with shellfish cannelloni, its clams and cockles bringing a bracing blast of the shoreline, with fennel and dill purée for force 10 aromatic impact. Duck is from Alloa's Gartmorn Farm and comes as the confit leg with duck fat chips of unearthly succulence, accompanied by red cabbage and salsify, the traditional fruity note with duck coming from puréed figs, all underpinned by a robust tarragon jus. If you're all about savoury finishes, note that the tip-top artisanal cheeses come with brittle home-made oatcakes, celery and frozen grapes, while for the rest, there may be baked brown sugar cheesecake with tomato caramel, candied ginger and cinnamon ice cream, or perhaps white chocolate sponge laden with yuzu variations – ice cream, curd and gel.

Scottish gins and a Shetland vodka are among the temptations of a drinks list built on authoritatively selected wines, opening with a good spread by the standard glass, with smaller measures of finer wines poured by the Coravin system, a handy device that permits the dispensing of wine without pulling the cork.

Chef Mark Greenaway **Seats** 60, Private dining room 16 **Times** 12–2.30/5.30–10, Closed 25–26 December, 1–2 January, Sunday and Monday **Prices** Set L 2 course £21-£35 (3 course £26-£45), Set D 2 course £21–£35 (3 course £26–£45), Tasting menu from £69.50 **Wines** 148 bottles over £30, 16 bottles under £30, 30 by glass **Notes** Market menu lunch and early evening (pre-theatre) menu, Vegetarian available, Children 5 years +

Edinburgh

EDINBURGH *continued*

Pompadour by Galvin

EDINBURGH PLAN B2

@@@ Modern French V ℉

0131 222 8975 | Waldorf Astoria Edinburgh, The Caledonian,
Princes Street, EH1 2AB

www.galvinrestaurants.com

Hotel dining in genteel Galvin style

The Galvin brothers' Edinburgh bolt hole might have been conceived as
the very antithesis of industrial brutalism dining, situated as it is within
the comforting confines of a Victorian railway hotel on Princes Street. Wall
panelling with hand-painted foliage, crisply dressed tables, ice buckets,
and views of the Castle Mound through semi-circular windows establish a
tone of inspiring gentility, and in head chef Daniel Ashmore, the venue
has somebody to bring a due sense of culinary occasion to proceedings
too. Seasonal and à la carte menus run the rule over pedigree raw
materials in a repertoire that displays the Galvin combination of French
classicism and modern British styling.

Start with pastis-cured sea bream and pickled vegetables, its potent,
finely etched flavours underlined by beurre noisette and carrot purée, or
maybe a pearl barley kedgeree with smoked eel, apple and an egg yolk,
before moving on to haunch and faggot of Highland venison with pumpkin
agnolotti, chestnuts and pomegranate, or perhaps a marine array of lemon
sole, North Berwick crab and cockles in sea herbs with pommes
boulangère. Completing the allure are seductive finishers such as banana
soufflé with chocolate sorbet, or tarte Tatin for two with silky vanilla ice
cream, with artisan cheeses as savoury backup.

Chefs Fraser Allan, Daniel Ashmore **Seats** 60, Private dining room 20
Times 12–2.30/6–10, Closed 2 weeks in January, Monday and Tuesday,
L Wednesday to Friday and Sunday **Prices** Set D 2 course from £29, Set D
3 course from £35, Tasting menu 5/7 course £55–£75, Starter £12.50–
£21.50, Main £28.50–£37.50, Dessert £8–£10.50 **Wines** 135 bottles over
£30, 3 bottles under £30, 10 by glass **Parking** 42 **Notes** Children welcome

Restaurant Mark Greenaway

EDINBURGH PLAN C3

@@@ Modern British ℉

See page 274

Restaurant Martin Wishart

MAP 24 NT27

◎◎◎◎ Modern French V ♀
0131 553 3557 | 54 The Shore, Leith, EH6 6RA
www.restaurantmartinwishart.co.uk

Outstanding cooking from a national mover and shaker

One of the movers and shakers of the present-day Scottish dining scene, Martin Wishart is these days as at home by the edge of Loch Lomond as he always has been in the big city. The Edinburgh address, on the approach to the rejuvenated Leith quarter, is anything but extrovertly glitzy. It's a smart, faintly anonymous room in mellow coffee tones, with wood blinds and white table linen, but no over-assertive modern artworks to trouble the eye. Instead, the focus is very much where it ought to be, on plates of finely crafted contemporary food that showcase some of Scotland's outstanding regional produce.

Smoked salmon served gently warm with accompaniments of parsnip, verjus and smoked butter offers a neat assemblage of rich, sharp and salty notes, or there could be an in-vogue pairing of langoustine and foie gras on potato croustillant with braised fennel, whose aniseedy savour cleverly balances both the sweet shellfish and the rich liver. An intermediate course might offer pasta in the shape of snail ravioli with mussels in garlic velouté, before the main business brings on turbot with spring cabbage, white asparagus and morels in truffle cream, or glazed black beef onglet steak crusted in bone-marrow and Comté, alongside its braised short rib and green beans Lyonnaise in classic red wine sauce.

Lightness is the watchword of desserts that take in yuzu fromage blanc bavarois with nectarine, honeycomb and lime sorbet, or a partnering of poached apricot florentine and orange olive oil cake garnished with almonds.

Chefs Martin Wishart, Joe Taggart **Seats** 50, Private dining room 10 **Times** 12–2/6.30–9.30, Closed 25–26 December, 1 January, 2 weeks in January, Sunday and Monday **Prices** Set L 3 course from £32, Set D 3 course from £75, A la carte D 4 course £85, Tasting menu 6 course from £85, Starter from £25, Main from £35, Dessert from £15 **Wines** 250 bottles over £30, 9 bottles under £30, 24 by glass **Parking** On street **Notes** Children 7 years +

Edinburgh

EDINBURGH
Timberyard
EDINBURGH PLAN C1

◉◉◉ Modern British **V** ♆
0131 221 1222 | 10 Lady Lawson Street, EH3 9DS
www.timberyard.co

On-trend regional cooking in an old warehouse

It's just possible that future generations will look back on the present era of restaurant design and surrender to frank puzzlement. The backlash against soft furnishings, floral decorations, virtually any sort of fabric covering on tables, windows or floors, has resulted in a generation of hard-edged, rough-and-ready, take-it-as-you-find-it dining spaces, often fashioned out of buildings that once had industrial purposes or traded in heavier basic commodities than lunch and dinner.

The Timberyard is a case in point: entry through garage doors painted fire station red, interior brick walls slapped with whitewash, old bare floorboards, stark white columns, bare halogen bulbs, and chairs that could furnish the annual general meeting of the parish council. Wine is stacked in racks next to the bar, the upper levels reached by ladder. Prior to its incarnation in the wood trade, it was a Victorian theatrical warehouse, where costumes and props were stored. Today, it incorporates an in-house smokery and butcher, as well as finding little nooks for growing herbs and edible flowers. There are a couple of tables outside under the saplings in the yard. Dishes arrive on chunky unglazed pottery, the bread on a slab of varnished wood. Ingredients are sourced in the contemporary way from Lothian growers and breeders, as well as foragers,

and the wines are the kind that would once have been considered faulty, full of unleashed oxidation, unexpected spritz and fermentation hazes. Eating is naturally to a multi-course taster template, in four, six or eight courses, with fish and veggie versions to supplement the omnivore's offering, and the cooking, under Ben Radford, is an unalloyed delight. A heap of white crabmeat is daisy-fresh and appetising, offset with daikon and robust artichoke purée, in crystal-clear crab broth. That's followed by crisp-topped salmon in buttermilk with anise top notes of fennel seeds and dill, and then breast of mallard cooked pink, accompanied by crunchy cereal grains, beetroot and chard, plus heart and liver for added richness.

The finisher might be simplicity itself, perhaps a serving of poached rhubarb with sheep's milk yogurt and a milk sorbet. The longer menus might yield squid broth with fennel, spinach and garlic to set the ball rolling, before a raw scallop and oyster with kohlrabi and apple, the two principal dishes offering halibut and clams with sea-beets, celery, salsify and artichoke in various textural manifestations, and lamb in a welter of green things – flower sprouts, broccoli, kale. Small-bite versions of the dishes are available for those heading to the theatre, or wanting only the lightest lunch. Not the least asset of the Timberyard is a bevy of staff who obviously all love the place, and are consummate advocates for it.

Chef Ben Radford **Seats** 65, Private dining room 10 **Times** 12–2/5.30–9.30, Closed 24–26 December, 1st week January, 1 week April, October, Sunday and Monday **Prices** Set L 4 or 6 course £30–£65, Set D 4/6/8 course £30–£75, Starter £5, Main £10, Dessert £5 **Wines** 380 bottles over £30, 22 bottles under £30, 12 by glass **Parking** NCP, On street **Notes** Children 12 years + at dinner

Edinburgh

21212

EDINBURGH PLAN E3

◉◉◉◉ Modern French ♟

0131 523 1030 & 0345 222 1212 | 3 Royal Terrace, EH7 5AB

www.21212restaurant.co.uk

Intense flavours and fun from a true culinary genius

Paul Kitching and Katie O'Brien's luxurious restaurant with rooms is a real one-off. Occupying a sandstone Georgian townhouse, there is true personality on the inside, with contemporary design and classic elegance combining to create somewhere rather special. The four bedrooms have a classy finish, and the high-ceilinged restaurant features ornate plasterwork, curvaceous banquettes, some quirky design touches – yes, those are giant moths on the carpet – and a glass partition separating diners from the open-to-view kitchen.

Paul is one of the UK's most idiosyncratic chefs, and with Katie leading the line front of house with charm and efficiency, they form a potent partnership. If you're wondering what the name is all about, the answer lies in the five-course menu format: a choice of two starters, two mains and two desserts, with one soup course and a cheese course in-between, with the line-up jumping to 31313 at dinner.

There's a sense of fun in the menu descriptions, which will need some elucidation from Katie, but rest assured, this is creative and dynamic modern food, where peerless ingredients are cleverly worked into dishes that inspire and amaze. Dinner might open with prawn and haddock curry, the accompaniments of apricot, asparagus, coconut and mushroom adding bursts of earthy and sweet flavours. 'Beef fillet nut muesli' might appear as a main course, the top-class fillet matched with swede, turnip, Chardonnay and mayonnaise. Next up is cheese, before the finale, perhaps the playfully described 'Boss's glazed lemon meringue marzipan, apple nut crumble thingy', or a reworked 'trifle meets compôte' featuring pears, plums and nuts.

Chef Paul Kitching **Seats** 36, Private dining room 10 **Times** 12–1.45/ 6.45–9.30, Closed 2 weeks in January, 2 weeks in summer, Sunday and Monday **Prices** Set L 2 course from £24, (3 course from £32, 4 course £42, 5 course £55), Set D 3 course from £65 (4 course £72, 5 course £79) **Wines** 245 bottles over £30, 7 by glass **Parking** On street **Notes** Saturday D 5 course only, Vegetarian available, Children 5 years +

ANSTRUTHER

The Cellar

MAP 25 NO50

@@@ Modern British
01333 310378 | 24 East Green, KY10 3AA
www.thecellaranstruther.co.uk

A new modernist lease of life for an old stager

The old stager was relaunched in 2014 under the aegis of local chef Billy Boyter and family, and long may it reign anew. It may once have been a cooperage, a smokehouse and a store for fishing tackle, but for the past four decades it's been a destination restaurant. The ambience could hardly be more rustic, with beamed ceilings, massive stone walls and friendly staff contributing substantially to its appeal, while Boyter's unabashed modernist food has given the old place a new lease of life.

Seven-course tasting menus are very much what today's diners expect to see, and the seasonally changing format has plenty to ponder. A winter parade begins with smoked haddock and cured egg yolk, before offering a slow-cooked truffled beef cheek in local Anster cheese. Crab in buttermilk and sweetly pickled onion is a canny balance of flavours, and a scallop in smoked bacon dashi stock and sesame brings the east Asian note. Main meat might be Black Isle hogget with cabbage, pickled apple and yogurt, and the finale arrives in the form of a triumphant assemblage of chocolate cream with Jerusalem artichoke purée, hazelnuts and calamansi. The Cellar has always been good at wine, and the imaginative pairings to go with each course are well worth signing up for.

Chef Billy Boyter **Seats** 28 **Times** 12.30–1.30/6.30–9, Closed 25–26 December, 1 January, 3 weeks in January, 1 week in May, 10 days in September, Monday and Tuesday, L Wednesday **Prices** Set L 5 course £35, Set D 7 course £60, Sunday lunch £35 **Wines** 54 bottles over £30, 12 bottles under £30, 14 by glass **Parking** On street **Notes** Vegetarian available, Children 10 years + at lunch and 12 years + at dinner

Fife

Road Hole Restaurant

MAP 25 NO51

◉◉◉ Modern Scottish, Seafood

01334 474371 | The Old Course Hotel, Golf Resort & Spa, KY16 9SP

www.oldcoursehotel.co.uk

Steaks, seafood and modern dishes with views of the golf course

If it sometimes seems as though you can't have an upmarket hotel in
Scotland without some golf going on in the vicinity, the other way of
looking at it is that you wouldn't want to come to a course as illustrious as
the one at St Andrews, the largest public golf complex in the whole of
Europe in fact, without expecting to be fed and watered in grand style too.
The Old Course Hotel has it all, grandly surveying as it does both the links
themselves and the West Sands beach and a majestic stretch of coastline.

As any seasoned putter will tell you, the most fiendish part of the
St Andrews course is the Road Hole, the par 4 17th, and it seems only
right that the main dining room here has been named after it. Enjoying all
the aforesaid views, so that you won't miss a single thwap of the ball in
the infernal sand trap, should the urge so fanatically possess you, it's a
civilised spot for a mix of traditional and modern Scottish cooking. Martin
Hollis's menus now include some classic local seafood and steak options,
so you might choose to open with some thoroughbred shellfish, perhaps
oysters in shallot vinegar and lemon, West Coast langoustines in garlic
mayonnaise, or – for the determined splashers-out – laden platters of
lobster, cockles, scallops, dressed crab, and much more. Otherwise, a

more modernist route might lead from ballotine of foie gras with chilli, peppered pineapple and brioche, or tartare of charred mackerel with horseradish and cucumber, to show stopping main dishes such as herb-crusted loin and braised shoulder of excellent lamb, with aubergine purée and courgettes, or perhaps a fillet of grey sole with crab in sauce Grenoble served with seasonal crushed Jersey Royals. Steak aficionados can expect prime cuts of pedigree Black Isle rib-eye or fillet, or a surf and turf pairing of rib-eye chops and lobster.

A welter of thrilling flavours adds allure to a dessert list that takes in tonka bean parfait with cherry blossom crémeux and pressed apricot, as well as Venezuelan Araguani chocolate mousse in basil oil with olive oil sponge and raspberry sorbet. Artisanal cheeses come with truffle honey and black grapes. Sunday lunch might revolve around ever-popular roast beef rib and Yorkshire puddings, or perhaps Loch Awe sea trout with cockle risotto and samphire. It's all served forth by highly professional, genuinely engaged staff who know what they're about. Champagnes and magnums lead off a deeply classical wine list, which offers a handful of small glasses before getting on with the serious business of crus classés and gran reservas.

Chefs Martin Hollis, Savich Phannoi **Seats** 70, Private dining room 16 **Times** 12.30–2/6–10, Closed L Thursday to Sunday (April to September), Friday to Sunday (October to March) **Prices** Set L 3 course £24.50, Starter £6.50–£12.50, Main £14.50–£60, Dessert £8.50–£9.50, Sunday lunch from £19.50 **Wines** 100 bottles over £30, 15 bottles under £30, 11 by glass **Parking** 100 **Notes** Vegetarian available, Children welcome

Fife

The Peat Inn

MAP 25 NO40

◎◎◎ Modern British
01334 840206 | KY15 5LH
www.thepeatinn.co.uk

Regional cooking on the shores of Loch Ness

The inn, six miles southwest of St Andrews, has been in the hospitality
game one way or the other since the middle of the 18th century, from the
era of horse-drawn coaches to the age of unleaded petrol. It's run with
appealing bonhomie and informality by Geoffrey and Katherine Smeddle,
who have created a comforting environment in the three interlinked dining
rooms that showcase Geoffrey's impressively assured modern British and
Scottish country cooking.

A firm classical underpinning bolsters starters such as poached quail
eggs with mushroom duxelles in hollandaise, or potato-crusted cured
salmon with cucumber in oyster cream sauce. The balance of upstanding
flavours and gentle richness is sustained into main courses like honey-
glazed breast of duck from Alloa's Gartmorn Farm, which comes with a
sweet-and-sour slew of Jerusalem artichokes and salsify, as well as the
fruity elements of gingered plum purée and a bitter orange sauce. Fish
could be a mix of red mullet and langoustines in seaweed butter with
poached white beans and scarlet elf cap mushrooms.

Finish on an airily risen high with mango and passionfruit soufflé,
served with salted banana ice cream and rum and raisin madeleines, or
with a plate of pedigree Scottish cheeses in impeccable condition from
the trolley. A six-course tasting menu is on hand in the evening for those
who find themselves indisposed to choose.

Chef Geoffrey Smeddle **Seats** 50, Private dining room 14 **Times** 12.30–2/
6.30–9, Closed 25–26 December, 1–14 January, Sunday and Monday
Prices Set L 3 course £22-£45, Set D 3 course from £50, Tasting menu
6 course (dinner) £70, Starter £8–£19, Main £15–£30, Dessert £8–£9.50
Wines 350 bottles over £30, 10 bottles under £30, 16 by glass
Parking 24 **Notes** Chef's menu 4-course lunch, Vegetarian available,
Children welcome

Road Hole Restaurant

MAP 25 NO51

◎◎◎ Modern Scottish, Seafood
See page 282

Rocca Restaurant

MAP 25 NO51

◉◉◉ Modern British **V**

01334 472549 & 01334 474321 | Macdonald Rusacks Hotel,
Pilmour Links, KY16 9JQ

www.roccarestaurant.com

Fine Scottish dining next to the 18th hole

The Macdonald Rusacks Hotel seems to have a little of everything going for it, from its proximity to the West Sands beach seen in *Chariots of Fire* to its adjacency to the Old Course at the Royal and Ancient. Your whistle wetted in the R Bar overlooking the clubhouse, you'll be ready to proceed to the Rocca dining room, where, naturally enough, there are panoramic views of the putting, with the all-important 18th hole just below the windows. Tony Borthwick cooks to a classical template, with less emphasis on the Italian these days, though saffron risotto and truffled tagliatelle still adorn the menus. A satisfyingly rich fish soup might open proceedings, perfectly timed salmon, sole and scallops generously crammed into a gingery broth, to be followed by prime Angus beef, the roast sirloin and Burgundy-braised cheek accompanied by smoked carrots and shallots. Classy fish dishes may include Gigha halibut served with brown shrimps, spring leeks and beach herbs. It all ends with a flawlessly risen soufflé flavoured with the ingredients of cranachan, principally incomparable Scottish raspberries, or perhaps something from further afield in the shape of pineapple baked in rum and spices with brown sugar custard and sweet tapioca. The five-course tasting menu offers a comprehensive tour.

Chef Tony Borthwick **Seats** 70, Private dining room 35 **Times** 12.30–2.30/ 6.30–9.30, Closed Sunday and Monday (November to March), D all week (October to April) **Prices** Tasting menu £40–£65, Starter £8–£20, Main £20–£35, Dessert £6–£12, Sunday lunch £10–£50 **Wines** 100 bottles over £30, 7 bottles under £30, 16 by glass **Parking** 23 **Notes** Pre-theatre menu, Children welcome

Glasgow

Cail Bruich

MAP 24 NS56

◉◉◉ Modern Scottish ⑲
0141 334 6265 | 752 Great Western Road, G12 8QX
www.cailbruich.co.uk

Popular West End venue for modern Scottish cooking

The Charalambous brothers' smart eatery in Glasgow's West End may be a city venue to its fingertips, but it looks to the Scottish natural larder for its culinary inspiration. A positive, laid-back tone pervades the place, with wine-red banquette seating at unclothed tables beneath copper-shaded lamps, and the menus deal in the kind of food that informed modern diners like to see. A double act of scallop and squid garnished with smoked roe and celeriac purée offers a mixture of sea-fresh and earthy flavours, or there could be a more obviously French-inflected opener of sautéed veal sweetbreads with morels, wild garlic and foie gras. Fish main dishes are full of pronounced intensity, perhaps teaming skate wing and smoked haddock with wild leeks and peppered dulse, while pedigree meats might include fine Scots venison with black pudding and mixed grains, or look south of the border for Goosnargh duck with puréed squash in clementine-tinged jus. Finish with the house take on Highland crowdie, turned out with rhubarb, sorrel and yogurt, or go for a cheese selection from Glasgow specialist George Mewes. The flexibility of approach brings in a shorter Market Menu, as well as the tasting format of six or eight courses, which comes in pescatarian and veggie versions too.

Chef Chris Charalambous **Seats** 48 **Times** 12–2/6–9.30, Closed 25–26 December, 1 January, 1 week in January, L Monday and Tuesday **Prices** Set L 2 course £20–£26, Set L 3 course £25–£34, Set D 2 course £30–£37, Set D 3 course £40–£50, Tasting menu £45–£55, Sunday lunch £25–£28 Early evening menu 6–7pm 3 course £25 **Wines** 31 bottles over £30, 4 bottles under £30, 20 by glass **Parking** On street **Notes** Children 5 years +

The Gannet

MAP 24 NS56

◉◉◉ Modern Scottish
0141 204 2081 | 1155 Argyle Street, G3 8TB
www.thegannetgla.com

Hebridean-influenced cooking at a family-run venue

A venue named after the famously greedy seabird surely has the diner's interest at heart, but the Reid family enterprise has more of a backstory than that. Conceived after a journey of gastronomic exploration undertaken in the summer of 2012 to the Hebridean coastlines of western Scotland, The Gannet makes a conscientious attempt to bring some of the bracing air of the wild islands to Finnieston. The culinary results are resonant and striking, and the presentations as modern as can be. That's seen to perfection in an opening course of poached and scorched leeks with burnt leek purée, salt-baked celeriac and pearl barley in hazelnut dressing, its assertive flavours and contrasting textures making a bold intro to mains such as sea bass with Barra cockles, purple sprouting broccoli, salsify, monk's beard and parsley root, or a regally presented serving of red deer with sweet-sour beetroot purée and whole heritage beets in a richly gamey jus. Glasgow food hero George Mewes supplies the thoroughbred farmhouse cheeses, if you're not intending to head in the direction of a dessert such as milk chocolate feuilletine with malted barley ice cream, or the tastebud-challenging parsnip mousse with candied parsnip, white chocolate and cloveroot ice cream.

Chefs Peter McKenna, Ivan Stein **Seats** 45, Private dining room 14 **Times** 12–2.30/5–9.45, Closed 25–26 December, 1–2 January, Monday, L Tuesday to Wednesday **Prices** Set L 2 course £19.50, Set L 3 course £23.50, Set D 2 course from £19.50, Set D 3 course from £23.50, Starter £7–£12, Main £16–£23, Dessert £6–£9, Sunday lunch £30–£39, Champagne Sunday menu 3 course with glass of champagne £35 **Wines** 33 bottles over £30, 14 bottles under £30, 9 by glass **Parking** On street **Notes** Set early evening menu 5–6.30pm, Vegetarian available, Children welcome

Hotel du Vin at One Devonshire Gardens   MAP 24 NS56

@@@ French, European
0141 339 2001 | 1 Devonshire Gardens, G12 0UX
www.hotelduvin.com

Smart, creative cooking in an elegant townhouse hotel

The jewel in the crown of the HdV group occupies a supremely elegant Victorian terrace in the West End that has been a foodie address for many a year. The Bistro – as the restaurant is named, in keeping with the rest of the group – is a rather grander room than its title suggests, with glitzy new chandeliers to light up uncovered floors and upholstery that matches the building's stone façade. Barry Duff heads up the kitchen and has put his own contemporary stamp on the output, which aims to soar above the HdV's core repertoire of straightforward French bistro cooking. Things start strongly with an opener of Jerusalem artichoke velouté with hand-dived scallops and crispy Serrano ham, or there could be roast wood pigeon breast with game bird boudin, braised endive and crunchy hazelnut. Main courses, too, display a clear French accent but loyalty to prime Scottish produce: Gigha halibut, say, partnered with pumpkin risotto, salsify beignet, crispy kale and jus de roti, while well-timed duck breast appears with a crisp bonbon of leg meat, pommes Anna, creamed cabbage, carrot

continued

Glasgow

and star anise. A complex dessert of gingerbread, frosted rosemary and blueberries, parsnip and white chocolate purée, and maple and rosemary ice cream ends the show.

Chef Barry Duff **Seats** 78, Private dining room 80 **Times** 12–2/5.30–10, Closed D 25 December, L 31 December **Prices** Set L 2 course from £21.95, Set L 3 course from £26.95, Tasting menu 7 course from £59, Starter £10.50–£17.95, Main £17.50–£32, Dessert £8–£14.50, Sunday lunch £29, Pre-theatre (before 7pm) 2/3 course £21.95/£26.95 **Wines** 200+ bottles over £30, 10 bottles under £30, 18 by glass **Parking** On street **Notes** Vegetarian available, Children welcome

▶ Highland

FORT AUGUSTUS
Station Road
MAP 23 NH30

◉◉◉ Modern British **V**
01456 459250 | The Lovat, Loch Ness, PH32 4DU
www.thelovat.com

Dynamic, stimulating cooking with loch views

A hotel since 1869, The Lovat has been run by the Gregory family for the past 12 years and it remains a landmark hotel in the Highlands. Located a brisk uphill walk from the southern end of Loch Ness, it offers stylish accommodation but it has retained much of the building's Victorian appeal. Whether you choose the brasserie or Station Road Restaurant, you can be sure of some gastronomic fireworks along the way. Chef Sean Kelly is a master of ambitious and innovative cooking, but it's all executed with a degree of playfulness.

The hotel's environmentally friendly ethos extends to the kitchen, where food miles and provenance are taken very seriously. With views over the loch, the oak-panelled dining room provides a refined setting for dynamic food delivered via a five-course tasting menu (including a vegetarian version). The menu descriptions are terse and often cryptic but the presentation of each dish is designed to excite and surprise. An amuse-bouche of duck liver, beetroot and muesli might kick things off before a starter of seafood carbonara. A main course of Highland beef might make way for a spirited dessert of garden rhubarb, lemon and toast. A closing 'Kinder Surprise' displays solid technical skills.

Chef Sean Kelly **Seats** 24, Private dining room 50 **Times** 7–9, Closed Sunday to Tuesday (November to March), Lunch all week **Prices** Tasting menu £50–£65 **Wines** 25 bottles over £30, 35 bottles under £30, 13 by glass **Parking** 30 **Notes** Children 8 years +

FORT WILLIAM
Inverlochy Castle Hotel

MAP 23 NN17

@@@ Modern French V ☻

01397 702177 | Torlundy, PH33 6SN

www.inverlochycastlehotel.com

Dining chez Roux in a grand castle

Inverlochy is the quintessential Victorian baronial castle, all castellated stone walls and turrets surrounded by 500 green acres overlooking its own loch. Pretty impressive then, and inside it's no less luxuriant, with its paintings, crystal chandeliers and open fires all adding to an ambience of grandeur and opulence. Queen Victoria was particularly taken with the place, and some of the furniture in the three dining rooms was a gift from the King of Norway. You feel the need to put on the glad rags for dinner, and in any case, dining here without a jacket, gentlemen, is not permitted.

Now under the auspices of a couple of culinary legends, father and son Albert and Michel Roux Jr, the cooking is surprisingly modern, based on the finest native produce, and liberally sprinkled with luxurious touches. The six-course dinner menu might kick off with pickled Shetland mussels, kelp jelly, dill oil and sea vegetables, then progress through mushroom tarte fine to halibut cauliflower purée, truffle and sunflower seed pesto and pickled muscat grapes, a masterly contrast of flavours and textures. Meat courses show the same technical expertise and unerring confidence, perhaps duck breast with honey-roast parsnip, curried parsnip purée, blood orange, and pomegranate salsa. Bow out with ginger cake served with bee pollen ice cream

Chef Andrew Turnbull **Seats** 40, Private dining room 20
Times 6–10, Closed Lunch all week **Prices** Tasting menu from £67
Wines 240 bottles over £30, 4 bottles under £30, 11 by glass
Parking 20 **Notes** Children 8 years +

KINGUSSIE
The Cross

MAP 24 NH70

@@@ Modern Scottish V ☻

01540 661166 | Tweed Mill Brae, Ardbroilach Road, PH21 1LB

www.thecross.co.uk

Modern Scottish cooking in an old mill

Originally a 19th-century tweed mill alongside the Gynack Burn, The Cross is surrounded by four acres of woodland and garden. It's a soul-soothing and uplifting spot; on a balmy day there's a terrace beside the river where you can bask in the serenity of the setting — and, if you're lucky, spot a red squirrel or roe deer. Expect stylish public rooms, eight pretty bedrooms and a smart, traditional restaurant with dark wood ceilings, whitewashed stone walls, and a snazzy yellow and black carpet. The owners Derek and

continued

Celia Kitchingman take a hands-on approach front of house, while at the stoves, David Skiggs delivers creative modern food via a three-course set-price menu or a tasting version with optional matching wines, all driven by seasonal and local ingredients. Proceedings might start with a pairing of seared John Dory and crisp pork belly with spinach, baby onions and sauce épice, followed by a muscular teaming of venison loin and braised oxtail with creamed cabbage, pickled beets, celeriac, and red wine jus. A fish option might be roast halibut with parmesan gnocchi, cauliflower, wild mushrooms, samphire and fish velouté. For dessert, perhaps an invigorating duo of raspberry soufflé and lemon sorbet.

Chef David Skiggs **Seats** 26 **Times** 12–1.30/7–8.30, Closed Christmas and January (except New Year) **Prices** Set L 3 course £30, Set D 3 course £55, Tasting menu 6 course £65, Sunday lunch £30, Afternoon tea £17 **Wines** 95 bottles over £30, 29 bottles under £30, 6 by glass **Parking** 12 **Notes** Children welcome

NAIRN
Boath House
MAP 28 NH95

◉◉◉◉ Modern British **V**
01667 454896 | Auldearn, IV12 5TE
www.boath-house.com

Polished Highland cooking from a long-serving chef

Don and Wendy Matheson call their place on the Moray Firth coast a restaurant with rooms, which slightly undersells its innate grandeur. It's an A-grade Georgian mansion with portico entrance, rescued assiduously from a state of ruination, and sitting in beautifully maintained expansive gardens. Both house and grounds are adorned with contemporary works by Highlands and Islands artists in a constantly updated rolling exhibition, and the crockery and furniture for the attractive dining room with its full-length windows are also the bespoke productions of Highland craftspeople. It comes as no surprise then to find that regional food heroes feature strongly on menus that incorporate wild foragings, together with gleanings from Boath's kitchen gardens and beehives, in a modern Scottish style that scores many a hit. Charlie Lockley has been here for nigh on 20 years, a record that shows up eloquently in the highly polished cooking. The drill for dinner is either three or six courses, the former perhaps offering mackerel and cucumber in verjus, followed by beef fillet with beetroot and nasturtiums, and a dessert that mobilises a Caribbean array of coconut, pineapple and rum. The latter adding introductory courses like potato, wild garlic and buttermilk, and chicken liver with rhubarb and yeast, to the mix, as well as a cheese course that might be truffled Connage Brie, a soft cow's milk cheese from near Inverness, with sourdough bread. A stunning wine list only adds to the appeal.

Chef Charles Lockley **Seats** 28, Private dining room 10 **Times** 12–1.30/7–close **Prices** Set L 2 course from £24, Set L 3 course from £30, Set D 3 course from £45, Tasting menu from £70, Sunday lunch £24–£30 **Wines** 120 bottles over £30, 20 bottles under £30, 15 by glass **Parking** 25 **Notes** Afternoon tea, Children welcome

TORRIDON
The Torridon
MAP 27 NG85

British, French V ♀
01445 791242 | By Achnasheen, Wester Ross, IV22 2EY
www.thetorridon.com

A piece of lochside Highland luxury

As we went to press the Rosette award was suspended due to a change of chef – reassessment will take place in due course.

The Earl of Lovelace did well when he chose the site of his 1887 shooting lodge (some lodge: it's actually a substantial property with a clock tower and turret) at the end of Loch Torridon within 58 acres surrounded by magnificent mountain scenery. Highland cattle roam the fields beside the hotel, chickens and Tamworth pigs are raised on the estate, and fruit and vegetables flourish in the two-acre kitchen garden. Within, there's an unusual zodiac ceiling in the drawing room, more than 350 whiskies in the bar, and the restaurant has those Highland views.

Seats 38, Private dining room 16 **Times** 12–2/6.45–9, Closed 5 weeks from 2 January **Prices** Set D 3 course £50 (4 course £60), Tasting menu £75 **Wines** 8 by glass **Parking** 20 **Notes** Children 10 years +

▶ South Lanarkshire

BLANTYRE
Crossbasket Castle
MAP 24 NS65

❀❀❀ French, Scottish
01698 829461 | Crossbasket Estate, Stoneymeadow Road, G72 9UE
www.crossbasketcastle.com

Luxurious dining chez Roux

Crossbasket is a castellated beauty and following a multi-million pound refurbishment it surely can't have looked this good in all its 500-year history. The luxurious, traditional decor is entirely in keeping with the building. The restaurant follows suit with its lavish colour scheme of red

continued

and gold, and with the names Albert and Michel Roux Jnr looming large, well, you just know the culinary bar is set very high too. The service is formal, professional and spot on, while head chef Alex Thain is the man charged with delivering on the promise of the Roux association. There's evidence of classical thinking on the menu, alongside a light modern touch and contemporary ideas, so you might start with torched duck liver perfectly pointed up with peach purée (and the fruit au naturel), or Scottish Blue Tail lobster-filled tortellini in a light shellfish bisque. Scottish ingredients create a sense of place – wild sea trout, say, with earthy girolles and a consommé flavoured with sea herbs, or the variations of strawberry with floating islands that make for an impressive finale. Attention to detail runs from the impressive breads to the petits fours, and the wine list covers the globe while remaining true to the auld alliance.

Chefs Albert Roux and Michel Roux Jnr, Alex Thain **Times** 12–2/7–9.30, Closed Monday and Tuesday **Prices** Set L 3 course £35, Tasting menu £67–£97, Starter £11–£14.50, Main £19–£25, Dessert £8–£14.50, Sunday lunch from £35, Afternoon tea from £25 **Notes** Children welcome

▶ Perth & Kinross

AUCHTERARDER
Andrew Fairlie at Gleneagles
MAP 24 NN91
@@@@ Modern French V ♟
See page 295

PITLOCHRY
Fonab Castle Hotel & Spa
MAP 24 NN95
Modern Scottish V
01796 470140 | Foss Road, PH16 5ND
www.fonabcastlehotel.com
Modern Scottish cooking in a magical setting

As we went to press the Rosette award was suspended due to a change of chef – reassessment will take place in due course.

With its conical corner turret and handsome gables, this magical, castellated pile of reddish stone wouldn't look out of place in a film adaptation of a Sir Walter Scott novel. Built around a core of sweeping staircases and panelled interiors, Fonab's refurbishment has conjured a contemporary country-house hotel and spa from the place, with glassed-in views over Loch Faskally from both the Brasserie and the upmarket restaurant Sandemans, named in honour of the port-shipping family who once lived here.

Seats 60, Private dining room 40 **Times** 12–2.30/5–9.30 **Wines** 114 bottles over £30, 36 bottles under £30, 15 by glass **Parking** 50 **Notes** Sunday lunch, Tasting menu 6 course, Pre-theatre menu, Children welcome

▶ Skye, Isle of

COLBOST

The Three Chimneys & The House Over-By

MAP 26 NG24

◉◉◉ Modern Scottish ♥
See page 297

ISLEORNSAY

Kinloch Lodge

MAP 26 NG71

◉◉◉ French, Scottish Ⅴ ♥
01471 833214 | Sleat, IV43 8QY
www.kinloch-lodge.co.uk

Stimulating cooking in the wilds of Skye

The ancestral home of the Clan Donald high chief is a fittingly grand white building, standing in brooding isolation at the head of Loch na Dal. Unlike many such an old house, the present scions of the family still live in it, and see to it that it provides a warm island welcome to guests from far and wide. Lady Claire Macdonald has long been a cookery author in her own right, and with the extravagantly gifted Marcello Tully in the kitchens, it's clear that fine food is guaranteed to be front and centre. The set-price dinner menu doesn't just linger in country-house hotel territory, but mobilises exciting flavours and excellent ingredients to stimulating effect. After an opener of gently Indian-spiced butternut squash soup, it could be seared West Coast scallops bundled up in Parma ham with peanut sauce, and then sublime Angus beef fillet with a mousse of Strathdon Blue, celeriac and confit shallots, sauced in brandy. Reverse the fish and meat order, and it may be a pairing of pigeon breast and Stornoway black pudding with beetroot in citrus jus, followed by Shetland cod and Drumfearn mussels and caper pesto. Vanilla pannacotta made with crème fraîche comes with orange and mint sorbet.

Chef Marcello Tully **Seats** 55, Private dining room 12 **Times** 12–2.30/6.30–9 **Prices** Set L 3 course £40 (4 course £45), Set D 5 course £80, Tasting menu £90–£150, Sunday lunch £32.99–£37.99 **Wines** 165 bottles over £30, 5 bottles under £30, 19 by glass **Parking** 50 **Notes** Children welcome

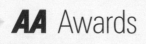

AA Wine Award for Scotland 2017–18

AUCHTERARDER
Andrew Fairlie at Gleneagles
MAP 24 NN91

◉◉◉◉ Modern French V ♛
01764 694267 | The Gleneagles Hotel, PH3 1NF
www.andrewfairlie.co.uk

Dazzling technical skills not confined to the golf course

Not everybody who pitches up at Gleneagles has come for the golf, although if you have, its setting scarcely gets any more opulent than this majestic estate. Inside the palatial surroundings of the hotel, however, there are discreet signs towards the autonomously run restaurant under Andrew Fairlie's aegis, one of Scotland's premier addresses for highly glossed contemporary cooking. The room itself is large and deliberately underlit, with nary a window from which to see the greens.

What you're here for is food that combines impeccable prime materials with dazzling technical skill and polish. Certain dishes have become hardy perennials, but are no less impressive for that: the home-smoked lobster in lime and herb butter is an unforgettable lesson in matching sweet, rich and sharp flavours in one concise package. The same could be said of the ballotine of foie gras and peach with almond milk, another harmoniously realised dish, which acts as the perfect curtain-raiser on the dégustation menu to a plump roast scallop matched with crab and salsify.

Meat cooking is nervelessly assured too, as when tenderly roasted Highland roe deer comes with a bonbon of game, truffled celeriac and kale in a stickily reduced game jus. It's hard to miss the classical French underpinnings of these dishes, and yet the depths that are evoked from them are something else. A cheese interlude – deliquescent Brillat-Savarin served in a cornet water – precedes a frozen dessert of ringing intensity, perhaps coconut parfait with lychee sorbet and carpaccio-sliced pineapple.

Wine judging observations: For such a classic restaurant, Andrew Fairlie has a surprisingly accessible list, which is really clearly laid out, making it user-friendly and easy to navigate. A well-balanced selection with plenty of quality at a variety of price points. There are some serious, top class wines to choose from with a prominent sommelier's selection, which grabs the attention.

Chefs Andrew Fairlie, Stephen McLaughlin **Seats** 54 **Times** 6.30–10, Closed 25–26 December, 3 weeks in January, Sunday, L all week **Prices** Starter £31–£41, Main £41, Dessert £18, A la carte 3 course £95, 8 course degustation £125 **Wines** 246 bottles over £30, 16 by glass **Parking** 300

AA Awards

AA Food Service Award Winner
for 2017–18

COLBOST
The Three Chimneys & The House Over-By   MAP 26 NG24
◉◉◉ Modern Scottish ♟
01470 511258 | IV55 8ZT
www.threechimneys.co.uk
Exceptional dining experience in a wild, romantic setting

Jaw-dropping landscapes bring many visitors to Skye, but so does Eddie and Shirley Spear's restaurant. The strength of its attraction is even more remarkable given the effort it takes to get there – this truly is destination dining. The unassuming, whitewashed cottage is framed by timeless views of loch and land, but this is not a place that stand on its laurels.

Head chef Scott Davies continues to maintain respect for the island's identity with his inventive approach, which draws from the Scottish and Nordic heritage of the Highlands and Islands and allows superlative raw materials (many grown within walking distance of the kitchen) the opportunity to speak for themselves, truly living up to the ethos of 'the best of Skye, Land and Sea'. Many traditional techniques are employed including salt curing, smoking, and cooking in a salt and ash crust. It is all delivered via concise menus and things get going with a sparkling medley of local seafood – smoked and seaweed-poached monkfish, Dunvegan crab and cured scallops, all enlivened with sour plum, or you might take a meaty route in via woodland pigeon with crispy pork, turnip, and sherry vinegar sauce.

Next up, Skye red deer with a crust of seaweed and ash, is plated imaginatively with haunch hot pot, bramble, cauliflower in various guises, and a deeply flavoured beetroot sauce – a flawless main course of perfect balance. Fish dishes might showcase cod loin with seared scallop, salsify and shellfish dashi. For dessert, it's hard to pass by the legendary hot marmalade sponge pudding with Drambuie custard. The wine list is a fine piece of work, and clearly a source of great pride for the charming sommelier Petri Pentikainen as he helps diners home in on the right bottle.

Chef Scott Davies **Seats** 40 **Times** 12.15–1.30/6.30–9.15, Closed 10 December to 19 January, L 12 November to 9 December, 20 January to 31 March **Prices** Set L £38, A la carte D 3 course £65, Tasting menu from £90, Sunday lunch £38 **Wines** 162 bottles over £30, 8 bottles under £30, 13 by glass **Parking** 12 **Notes** Vegetarian available, Children 5 years + at lunch and 8 years + at dinner

See also page 13

Skye, Isle of

Ullinish Country Lodge

MAP 26 NG33

◉◉◉ Modern Scottish V
01470 572214 | IV56 8FD
www.theisleofskye.co.uk

Inventive Scottish cooking on the wild west coast

Marooned on the wild west coast of Skye, with the hulking rock formations of Black Cuillin and MacLeod's Tables looming behind you for company, and little skerries popping up out of the water, Ullinish lacks for neither dramatic scenery nor soul-deep tranquillity. Messrs Johnson and Boswell liked it anyway when they stayed in 1773, and were gratified to see a garden. Inside the old lodge, dark wood, plum-coloured walls and tartans predominate, as does a sense of genuinely warm hospitality. David Smith's inventive modern Scottish dishes hit the mark too, as witness a satisfying combination of seared scallop, white crabmeat rolled in a slice of Granny Smith, and celeriac purée in herbed velouté. Fine prime materials are allowed the starring roles in main dishes such as breast and confit leg of Barbary duck with parsley roots in red wine jus, or crisp-skinned roasted stone bass with gnocchi and asparagus in sauce Normande, and then the final flourish brings on thick-based passionfruit cheesecake with mango gel and coconut sorbet. Sneaked in between the main and a pre-dessert comes a single showcased cheese, such as Isle of Arran Cheddar with pineapple chutney. Incidentals adorn the menu all the way through, from well-made canapés to irresistible petits fours, including (if you're lucky) a cardamom-laced chocolate truffle.

Chef David Smith **Seats** 22 **Times** 7.30–8.30, Closed 24 December to 31 January, Lunch all week **Prices** Set D 5 course £59.95 **Wines** 36 bottles over £30, 40 bottles under £30, 16 by glass **Parking** 10

▶ Stirling

Roman Camp Country House Hotel

MAP 24 NN60

◉◉◉ Modern French V
01877 330003 | FK17 8BG
www.romancamphotel.co.uk

Jacobean country house with modern cooking

Built in 1625 for the grand old Dukes of Perth, the pale pink country house by the River Teith stands in 20 acres of gardens in the sumptuous national park that incorporates Loch Lomond and the Trossachs. The building's lack of height may make it look modest enough from outside, but step within, and be prepared to gasp in wonderment. The magnificent period interiors progress from a panelled library with a small concealed chapel to a pair of supremely elegant dining rooms, where silver service, spotless linens and gleaming glassware create an elevated tone. A short carte offers three courses at each stage for modern country-house cooking that keeps an eye on the seasons. Start with marinated turbot, served with the up-to-date accoutrements of cucumber gel and cauliflower purée in a red wine jus, as a prelude to roast rabbit loin with a braised ballotine of the shoulder in grain mustard and maple jus, or perhaps sea trout matched with chorizo, peas and baby gem. Finishing treats include a covetable chocolate and orange gâteau with blood-orange sorbet, or farmhouse cheeses served with toasted fig and walnut bread and membrillo.

Chef Ian McNaught **Seats** 120, Private dining room 36 **Times** 12.30–2/7–8.30 **Prices** Set L 3 course from £28.50, Tasting menu from £55 Starter £12.80–£21.90, Main £28.50–£32.90, Dessert £11.50–£13.80, Sunday lunch £28.50 **Wines** 180 bottles over £30, 15 bottles under £30, 16 by glass **Parking** 80 **Notes** Children welcome

DUNBLANE
Cromlix and Chez Roux
MAP 24 NN70

◉◉◉ French, Scottish
01786 822125 | Kinbuck, FK15 9JT
www.cromlix.com
Lively modern cooking at Andy's place

Cromlix has had a lively history. It was built to more or less its present specifications in 1874, and promptly burned to nothing four years later. Little daunted, its architectural mirror-image rose again, and it's been a hotel since the 1980s. In 2013, the year he first won Wimbledon, Andy Murray, who grew up three miles away in Dunblane, acquired it, and the place has benefited from a sensational modern makeover. A contemporary dining room in light primary colours has views of the gardens or of the kitchen, depending on your priorities, and is supplied with lively modern cooking by Darin Campbell, under the aegis of Albert Roux. First up might be a brace of seared Mull scallops with rose veal sweetbreads, smoked red pepper purée and aubergine caviar, an attractively balanced array of flavours, before main course brings on Gartmorn duck, the breast cooked pink, the leg meat stuffed into hispi cabbage, alongside a chicory tartlet and baby turnips in raspberry vinegar jus, or perhaps seared stone bass with artichoke and a crab and lemon thyme croquette. Finish with Perthshire strawberry soufflé with matching ice cream, or with formidably rich Valrhona chocolate millionaire tart and Baileys ice cream.

Chefs Albert Roux, Darin Campbell **Seats** 60, Private dining room 50 **Times** 12–2/6.30–9.30 **Prices** Set L 3 course £32.50, Set D 3 course £35, Starter £7–£12, Main £12–£60, Dessert £7–£12 **Wines** 100+ bottles over £30, 3 bottles under £30, 17 by glass **Parking** 30 **Notes** Vegetarian available, Children welcome

WALES

MENAI BRIDGE

Sosban & The Old Butcher's Restaurant
MAP 14 SH57

◉◉◉◉ Modern V

01248 208131 | Trinity House, 1 High Street, LL59 5EE

www.sosbanandtheoldbutchers.com

Fixed-time tasting menu of sensational dishes

The former butcher's shop at the top of the high street looks plain and unprepossessing enough from the outside, and indeed things remain pretty simple inside, with stripped wood tables and feature walls displaying some of the original slate. That's where the ordinary ends, however, as the menus take a giant leap out of it. Stephen Stevens offers a refined and accomplished rendition of market-driven modern cooking, with scientific principles applied for the fun element.

It's a fixed taster served at a fixed time (allow four hours) on three evenings a week, and the food is reliably sensational. A lamb's cheek on a block of wood is for picking up in the fingers, its satisfying crunch derived from a counter-intuitive coating of pork crackling, alongside the gentling element of laverbread mayonnaise. That could be followed by an eggshell filled with salted leeks and mushroom velouté, topped with threads of crisped yolk. Pink duck breast comes with desserty accompaniments of liquorice sponge and gel, and the next item, served on an old butcher's tea-towel, is a piece of crisp cod skin, as a prelude to the fish itself, a glorious meaty fillet served with pommes Anna, onion rings and a portion of ground heart.

No modern restaurant worth its sea salt is lacking a spin on rhubarb and custard, and Stevens obliges, prior to a cylindrical construction of lemon ice cream encased in dark chocolate, garnished with freeze-dried olives. With fantastic soda bread and a simple but confidently chosen batch of wines to accompany, this is the fully rounded modern dining experience.

Chef Stephen Stevens **Seats** 16 **Times** 12.30–1.30/7–11, Closed Christmas, New Year, January, Sunday to Wednesday, L Thursday to Friday **Prices** Tasting menu £65 **Wines** 10 bottles over £30, 16 bottles under £30, 26 by glass **Parking** On street, car park

AA Wine Award for Wales and the Overall Winner 2017–18

EGLWYS FACH

Ynyshir

MAP 9 SN69

@@@@@ Modern British **V** 🍷
01654 781209 | SY20 8TA
www.ynyshir.co.uk

Daring contemporary cooking amid birdsong and ancient trees

Hidden away in splendid gardens within a 1,000-acre RSPB reserve, Ynyshir was once owned by Queen Victoria. The place has long been known as one of the gastronomic destinations of Wales, with a contemporary dining room that's easy on the eye, and chef-patron Gareth Ward's culinary magic playing the lead role. After a stint at Sat Bains in Nottingham, he brings with him that inventive and forward-looking chef's ethos of weaving intricate combinations of flavours, texture and temperature. Ingredients of the highest order, including produce from the hall's gardens and foraged wild ingredients, form the basis of tersely-worded nine- and 17-course tasting menus.

Opening the show, 'Not French onion soup' is made from Japanese dashi stock flavoured with onion oil, diced tofu, pickled shallots, sea vegetables, onion and miso purée and brown butter croûtons, while mackerel comes in a vibrant sea-fresh partnership with bramble and sorrel. Elsewhere, duck liver comes with Cox's apple and smoked eel, while salted plums and shiso are used to enhance wild duck. Melt-in-the-mouth Welsh Wagyu beef stars in a complex three-part presentation: in a 'burger' with shallots and sesame seeds, glazed with soy sauce and Marmite and matched with pickled shiitake mushrooms, and in a deeply-flavoured beef 'fudge'. After that there's desserts such as miso treacle tart, rhubarb with marjoram and rice, or a thoroughly deconstructed take on tiramisù.

Wine judging observations: A considered, highly individual and quirky wine list, clearly put together with a lot of hard work and thought. Its presentation is punchy, modern and easy to follow. There's excellent producers across the list, and it's clear that there has been no messing about when it comes to sourcing quality. It is very well-priced, meaning you won't have to break the bank for something truly special. It's not the largest of lists, but has sufficient depth to stand out, and it's nice to see some space made for a few sakes. *See also pages 16–7.*

Chef Gareth Ward **Seats** 16, Private dining room 6 **Times** 12–1/6.30–9.30, Closed 6 weeks each year, Sunday and Monday, L Tuesday **Prices** Tasting menu £39.50–£110, **Wines** 65 bottles over £30, 22 by glass **Parking** 15 **Notes** Sunday lunch, Chef's table 20+ courses £130, Children welcome

Conwy

Bodysgallen Hall and Spa

MAP 14 SH57

◉◉◉ Modern & Traditional V ♟
01492 584466 | The Royal Welsh Way, LL30 1RS
www.bodysgallen.com

Grand National Trust property with suitably elegant cooking

Surrounded by 200 acres of parkland and glorious rose gardens, and with views sweeping across the skyline to Snowdonia, Conwy Castle and the Isle of Anglesey, National Trust-owned Bodysgallen Hall is in the premier league of Welsh country piles. If the grounds and exterior make a fine first impression, the same goes for the interiors of the hotel, which form a genteel world of antiques, oil paintings, dark oak panelling and stone mullioned windows, yet this is no stuffy country house, thanks to the efforts of charming, on-the-ball staff.

Located in the Main Hall, the dining room is rich with grand period character, and John Williams's cooking is a nice balance of old-school country house grandeur and finely judged modernity, producing starters of crispy hen's egg with marinated chard, beetroot and turnip from the Bodysgallen Estate, or perhaps grilled mackerel fillet with crab fritter and wasabi. The main event matches slow-cooked loin of lamb with braised lentils, roasted shallots and parsnip purée, while fish dishes could deliver hake in a brioche and herb crust with haricot beans, chorizo, and tomato cream. Dynamic desserts such as a deconstructed lemon and goats' cheese cheesecake with lemon curd ice cream end the show. The blue-blooded wine list does justice to John's tremendous cooking.

Chef John Williams **Seats** 60, Private dining room 40 **Times** 12.30–1.45/ 7–9.30, Closed 24–26 December, L Monday **Prices** Set L 2 course from £18.50, Set L 3 course from £25, Set D 2 course from £43, Set D 3 course from £55, Sunday lunch from £28.50 **Wines** 123 bottles over £30, 37 bottles under £30, 8 by glass **Parking** 40 **Notes** Pre-theatre dinner, Tasting menu available on request, Children 6 years +

BALA
Palé Hall Hotel & Restaurant
MAP 14 SH93

@@@ British, European V

01678 530285 | Llandderfel, LL23 7PS

www.palehall.co.uk

Grand Victorian mansion hotel with a highly gifted chef

Palé is still very much a grand monument to its original builder, the industrialist Henry Robertson, whose don't-spare-the-horses project this was in 1871. The original hydro-electric system, with power to the house supplied by the River Dee, is still in place, and has in its time warmed the cockles of both Queen Victoria and Sir Winston Churchill.

Its restaurant menus, served in a sunflower-yellow room named after the first owner and hung with appetising pictures of bowls of fruit, has benefited from the consultancy of the tireless Michael Caines, and in Gareth Stevenson, the Hall has its own highly gifted resident practitioner.

A labour-intensive opener of ox cheek rolled into spinach cannelloni garnished with onion purée, deep-fried flat parsley, shallot rings and pickled mustard seeds, with a side-serving of roast onion consommé, is a flavour-drenched triumph. Main courses embrace a wholesomely simple braised turbot with a butter-poached scallop and baby leeks in chive beurre blanc, or fabulous Welsh roe deer loin with braised red cabbage and pancetta, accompanied by a brace of complementing purées, one fig, the other chestnut. Finish with an assembly of lemon elements – shards of meringue, drizzle cake and creamy mousse – finished with fragrantly intense basil sorbet.

Chef Gareth Stevenson **Seats** 40, Private dining room 40 **Times** 12–2.30/6.30–9 **Prices** Set L 2 course from £28, Set L 3 course from £37, Set D 2 course from £60, Set D 3 course from £85, Sunday lunch £28–£37 **Wines** 28 bottles under £30, 15 by glass **Parking** 40 **Notes** Children welcome

Monmouthshire

The Walnut Tree Inn

MAP 4 SO31

◉◉◉ Modern British ♇
01873 852797 | Llanddewi Skirrid, NP7 8AW
www.thewalnuttreeinn.com

Blissfully unfussy and focused cooking by a culinary mastermind

Considering its status as a foodie pilgrimage destination for a couple of generations, the whitewashed, slate-roofed old inn in the foothills of the Black Mountains is an unassuming-looking property, and there's nothing fancy-pants about the interior either, with its wooden tables, plain walls hung with artwork (for sale, if something takes your fancy) and flower arrangements adding splashes of colour.

The Walnut Tree first became a culinary beacon under Franco Taruschio and now its position as one of the UK's great epicurean institutions is assured under the aegis of Shaun Hill. He cut his teeth at Robert Carrier's Islington restaurant, and during the decade spent putting Ludlow on the culinary map at his much-lauded Merchant House, Hill often popped over the Marches border to eat at the Walnut Tree in its glory days with Mr Taruschio at the helm, so it's entirely fitting that he picked up the mantle. Never one for chasing ephemeral culinary fads and trends, Shaun Hill prefers to keep it real, sourcing the best ingredients he can lay his hands on and unleashing his formidable, seemingly effortless technical skills on making it all look deceptively simple. From the daily-changing menus, starters cover plenty of ground, ranging from the Mediterranean glow of red mullet and scallop bourride, perhaps, to a masterful omelette filled with the made-in-heaven combo of Brillat-Savarin cheese and black truffle; vegetarians are assuaged with an option like twice-baked Lancashire cheese soufflé with beetroot and leeks. Hill's cooking follows no particular culinary path other than one of good sense and integrity, with the produce centre stage, and full-bore flavours making their impact without pointless embellishment — as typified by main courses that deliver the full-blooded meaty hits of loin and haunch of venison partnered with goats' cheese gnocchi, or rib-eye of beef with pommes sarladaises and truffle butter. Fish makes an impact too: perhaps cod fillet in a herb and hazelnut crust, or sea bass with tempura prawns and red pepper sauce.

Desserts are no less well crafted and irresistible: warm rice pudding with prune and Armagnac ice cream, maybe; milk chocolate and peanut parfait with caramel bananas, or even somloi, a Hungarian trifle made with rum, apricots and walnuts. Make sure you fully explore the excellent wine list's cornucopia of bottles from small artisan producers. If you've only time for a flying visit, the set lunch deal offers barnstorming value.

Chef Shaun Hill **Seats** 70, Private dining room 26 **Times** 12–2.30/7–10, Closed 1 week at Christmas, Sunday and Monday **Wines** 50 bottles over £30, 40 bottles under £30, 8 by glass **Parking** 30 **Notes** Vegetarian available, Children welcome

See advert on page 308

The Walnut Tree

offers proper dining and good wine for not too frightening amounts of money. The setting is informal with the emphasis shared between the produce, its handling and cooking, and of course south Wales's fine countryside. There are no chandeliers, bells or whistles and no dress codes or similar pomposities to contend with. Come if this appeals and keep on going if it doesn't.

The Whitebrook

MAP 4 SO50

◉◉◉◉ Modern British, French V ▽
01600 860254 | NP25 4TX
www.thewhitebrook.co.uk

Flavourful foraging in the Wye Valley forests

Deep in the Wye Valley, in the village of Gwenffrwd (or Whitebrook, if your Welsh isn't up to snuff), near Monmouth, Chris and Kirsty Harrod run an elegant restaurant with rooms. Its outdoor terrace fits snugly into the surrounding greenery, and there's a pleasingly natural quality to the interiors too, where stripped oak floors, cream leather seats and high-quality table linen offer a stylish backdrop for the ultra-modern cooking.

Tasting menus are the format, and the woodland environment provides the productive foraging that supplies much of the detail. Don't be alarmed at the 'forest findings' that might turn up with an appetiser of roast Jerusalem artichokes; just enjoy their earthy aromatics. Charlock may be a new one on you, adding an appealing mustard tone to a serving of brown and flaked white crab with horseradish and chicken skin, while an intermediate course of partridge comes with parsnips roasted in woodruff. Fish might be firm-fleshed brill with smoked bacon, served with caraway-scented cabbage, while Ryeland lamb appears as a quartet of pinkly roasted loin, braised shoulder, crisp belly and wondrously tender liver, punctuated by salt-baked turnip, leeks and ramsons in a lightly viscous jus. On another night, it could Rhug Estate venison with smoked beets and celeriac, the wild note emphasised by mugwort and bitter leaves.

The finale could be Ashmead's Kernel apple and cinnamon sorbet, with chocolate crisp and a melty-textured jelly made with Ty Gwyn cider, or perhaps poached pear in buttermilk, scented with pine and served with ingenious yogurt crumble.

Chef Chris Harrod **Seats** 32 **Times** 12–2/7–9, Closed 1st 2 weeks in January, Monday, L Tuesday **Prices** Set L 3 course £35, Set D 3 course £59, Tasting menu £74, Sunday lunch £35–£74 **Wines** 98 bottles over £30, 32 bottles under £30, 15 by glass **Parking** 20

Epicure by Richard Davies

MAP 4 ST39

◉◉◉ Modern British

01633 413000 | The Celtic Manor Resort, Coldra Woods, NP18 1HQ

www.celtic-manor.com

Elevated modern cooking at a huge resort

Situated within Newport's stupendously sprawling Celtic Manor resort, where there are three golf courses to choose from, not to mention around 2,000 acres of rolling parkland, Richard Davies's Epicure restaurant could be forgiven for feeling a little lost, were it not for the fact that the venue has carved out a reputation for itself as a regional hotspot. An exposed walnut floor and dripping chandeliers hanging from circular ceiling recesses set an elevated tone for the finely chiselled modern British cooking in which Davies specialises.

There's an appealing blend of classical foundation and modern combining in dishes such as the potently rich foie gras torchon with orange, rhubarb and gingerbread, or torched mackerel with celeriac, apple and walnuts. Textural contrasts and forthright seasonings lend point to main dishes like the sea bass that turns up in its provençale gear, with confit peppers, courgette and aubergine, or perhaps Asian-spiced belly and cheek of pork, alight with Sichuan peppercorns and gentled with a little carrot purée. Explore a wealth of counterpointing flavours in desserts that take in pineapple and coconut soufflé with rum and raisin ice cream, or strawberries and cream parfait. If you can't resist trying a few more dishes while the going's good, there's a six-course tasting menu.

Chef Richard Davies **Seats** 50, Private dining room 12 **Times** 12–2.30/
7–9.30, Closed 1–14 January, Sunday and Monday, L Tuesday to Thursday
Prices Set L 3 course from £29, A la carte 3 course £39–£59, Tasting menu
£49–£69 **Wines** 195 bottles over £30, 40 bottles under £30, 12 by glass
Parking 1,000 **Notes** Vegetarian available

Pembrokeshire

NARBERTH
Grove
MAP 8 SN01

@@@ Modern British V ♚
See page 312

Powys

LLYSWEN
Llangoed Hall
MAP 9 SO14

@@@ Modern British V ♚
01874 754525 | LD3 0YP
www.llangoedhall.co.uk

Refined contemporary dining in a grand country house

Llangoed Hall is enviably situated in its own 17 acres of the Wye Valley, including pristine lawns, manicured gardens, a kitchen garden and maze, while glorious views over rolling countryside and the Black Mountains add to the sense of tranquillity. The original Jacobean mansion was rebuilt in the early 20th century by Clough Williams-Ellis (of Portmeirion fame), so it's all about old-fashioned elegance inside, with luxurious lounges full of original features, fine furniture, and original artworks by Whistler and Augustus John creating a sophisticated old-school atmosphere.

The restaurant is done out in delicate Wedgwood blue and white, and head chef Nick Brodie and his team in the kitchen make good use of the hotel's organic kitchen garden in four-course à la carte or multi-course tasting menus (including an inventive veggie version) of polished modern British cooking. Minimally worded menus move from steak tartare with capers, shallots, brioche and mushrooms through foie gras with smoked eel and apple sauce, to a main event of venison with red cabbage and crisp lichen. The presentation of each plate is a visual treat, and there's no lack of invention among desserts either; a pumpkin-themed workout involving mousse, burnt cream and purée is lifted with lemon verbena and nitro yogurt.

Chef Nick Brodie **Seats** 40, Private dining room 80 **Times** 12–2/7–9 **Prices** Set L 3 course £19.50-£25, Set D 4 course £75, Tasting menu £75–£95, Sunday lunch £15–£25 **Parking** 150 **Notes** Prestige and Vegetarian 9-course menus, Children welcome

Pembrokeshire

NARBERTH

Grove

MAP 8 SN01

🏵🏵🏵 Modern British V 🍷
01834 860915 | Molleston, SA67 8BX
www.thegrove-narberth.co.uk

Tireless attention to detail in a beautifully restored country house

Resurrected from a sorry state by its current owners, this boutique bolt
hole has secured its place over the last decade in the premier league of
Pembrokeshire's destination dining getaways. And what's not to like? Its
idyllic grounds are watched over by venerable old oaks and beeches, there
are uplifting views of the Preseli Hills, and the beaches and walking paths
of the Pembrokeshire Coastal National Park are a short drive away. What's
more, the place itself is an architectural historian's paradise, consisting of
the original Plantagenet longhouse, where family and livestock once
rubbed along together side by side, the main 17th-century manor, and the
inevitable extensions by a Victorian owner. Smartly attired with botanical
wallpapers, elegant furniture and a mellow decorative tone in the dining
room, it aims to soothe at every turn.

Staff contribute to the restful demeanour of the place, and Allister
Barsby's arrival as executive chef in early 2016 (after a three year stint at
Gidleigh Park with Michael Caines) guarantees that culinary imagination
remains the principal driver. Whether you go for the à la carte or the eight-
course tasting extravaganza, what emerges is intelligently constructed
food of impeccable modernity, all built from impressive local materials,
including fine seasonal pickings from the hotel's own kitchen garden.

Starters open with an impressive intensity — perhaps quail partnered with wild garlic, gnocchi, confit egg yolk and parmesan, or a full-on combination of sweetbread-packed ravioli boosted by caramelised celeriac, pickled pear and coffee-scented jus. Main courses step up a gear and keep the good ideas and pin-sharp technique flowing in dishes such as the Aylesbury duck that arrives in a captivating medley with caramelised chicory, turnips, roast garlic, and five spice jus adding a touch of eastern exoticism, while local Preseli lamb receives its due celebration in an impressive, highly detailed dish involving kohlrabi, charred leeks, mint, capers and raisins. Flavours and textures are judged to perfection in fish dishes too — perhaps stone bass with caramelised cauliflower, cumin, lemon thyme and langoustine.

Desserts continue to hit the high notes, whether it's something as unabashedly classical as an apple strudel soufflé with vanilla ice cream, or more obviously contemporary trends in the shape of roasted pineapple with caramelised brioche, pineapple sage, pistachio, and black pepper ice cream. Welsh cheeses are from the top drawer, and so is the magnificent 300-bin wine list, which offers a world of exploration.

Chefs Allister Barsby, Peter Whaley **Seats** 54, Private dining room 25 **Times** 12–2.30/6–9.30 **Prices** Set L 3 course £29, Set D 2 course £46, Set D 3 course £64, Tasting menu 8 course £94, Sunday lunch £29 **Wines** 300 bottles over £30, 2 bottles under £30, 18 by glass **Parking** 42 **Notes** No children under 12 years after 8pm

See advert on page 316

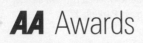

AA Restaurant of the Year
for Wales 2017–18

Beach House Restaurant at Oxwich Beach   MAP 8 SS58
@@ Modern British V
01792 390965 | SA3 1LS
www.beachhouseoxwich.co.uk
Fresh contemporary cooking and fresh sea air

Occupying a fabulous seaside spot on the Gower peninsula, overlooking the sandy beach of Oxwich Bay, here's a place to blow the cobwebs away, if ever there was. Its spacious, light-filled interior is done in New England style, with marine blues and pale wood furniture creating a supremely relaxing feel, and there are tables outdoors to soak up the glorious coastal sunshine.

Hywel Griffith honed his craft at some of Britain's most prestigious hotels, on a trajectory from London's Lanesborough to the Chester Grosvenor to Ynyshir at Machynlleth, and brings a fresh contemporary sensibility to the menus here, which are firmly founded on tip-top Glamorgan produce. Fish and seafood are a particularly strong suit, with opening dishes setting the tone. A scorched mackerel fillet is enterprisingly served with avocado, cucumber, apple and passionfruit, or there could be roast salmon partnered with Bristol Channel crab, as well as pickled daikon, nettles and a blistering note of wasabi. Asian notes resurface in main courses, perhaps for tandoori-roasted hake with crisp-cooked pork shoulder, tomato fondue, confit onion and natural yogurt, but if it's a thoroughgoing meat dish you're after, look to charred sirloin and treacled rib of Ammanford beef with spring onions and hen of the woods.

Innovative takes on classic desserts produce a bara brith soufflé with lapsang souchong ice cream, or egg custard tart with poached rhubarb and ginger ice cream. Five-course and eight-course tasters are virtually menu surprise options, the one-word descriptions vouchsafing none of their detail. Sign up for 'Asparagus, Hake, Salmon, Pork Belly, Hazelnut' and hold on to your hat.

Chef Hywel Griffith **Seats** 46 **Times** 12–2.15/6–9.15, Closed 2nd and 3rd week in January, Monday to Tuesday (except bank holidays) **Prices** Set L 3 course £28, Tasting menu 5/8 course £55–£75, Starter £10–£17, Main £19–£29, Dessert £8.50–£12 **Wines** 80 bottles over £30, 30 bottles under £30, 14 by glass **Parking** Beach car park **Notes** Children welcome

GROVE

Restaurant James Sommerin

MAP 9 ST17

◉◉◉◉ Modern British V

029 2070 6559 | The Esplanade, CF64 3AU

www.jamessommerinrestaurant.co.uk

Dazzling displays of contemporary cuisine

James Sommerin's sleek restaurant with rooms may be in pole position by the pier on Penarth's seafront and come with cracking views of the Severn Estuary, but the diners' attention is riveted by what's on their plates. The space is a snazzy picture of understated contemporary style with white linen tablecloths, curvaceous grey velour seats, sky blue banquettes and a long narrow window onto the cheffy action in the kitchen. Sommerin's refined and precisely-engineered cooking takes the finest, locally-sourced materials as its starting point and deploys pin-sharp technique in some entertaining ideas.

The tersely worded menu gives no detail on the brilliant interplay of flavour and texture that arrives in openers such as belly pork and slow-cooked octopus with peanut and soy sauce, or wood pigeon with black pudding, raspberry and beetroot. At main course, classical foundations are clear in the likes of a slab of 32-day aged sirloin, partnered with oxtail, shallots and red wine jus; quail, asparagus, tarragon and truffle; or there may be brill with Jersey Royal potatoes, salsify and kale.

The virtuoso display of creative ideas continues into desserts, when an infallible eye for how flavours work together produces, strawberries and cream, say, with vanilla and white chocolate, or a thoroughly reworked riff on the apple tarte Tatin theme. For the ultimate dining experience here, be tempted to try his tasting menus – either six or nine courses.

Chef James Sommerin **Seats** 65, Private dining room 12
Times 12–2.30/ 7–9.30, Closed 1 week in January, Monday
Prices Tasting menu 6/9 course £70–£150, Starter £8–£14, Main £17–£28, Dessert £9–£12 **Wines** 100+ bottles over £30, 15 bottles under £30, 14 by glass **Parking** On street **Notes** Chef's table (maximum 4 people) £150, A la carte Tuesday to Thursday, Children welcome

NORTHERN IRELAND &
REPUBLIC OF IRELAND

BALLYMENA
Galgorm Resort & Spa
MAP 1 C5

◉◉◉ Modern Irish V ♟

028 2588 1001 | 136 Fenaghy Road, Galgorm, BT42 1EA

www.galgorm.com

Ambitious contemporary cooking and river views

Surrounded by 163 acres of parkland with the River Maine flowing through, Galgorm is a pretty desirable prospect. There's no excuse for boredom or failing to come to table with a hearty appetite here – unless, of course, you over-indulge in a lavish afternoon tea in the gorgeous conservatory lounge: lavish spa and treatment areas, including a Thermal Village, extensive meetings, conference and wedding facilities, a champagne and gin bar, a pub and live entertainment, it all adds up to a package that ticks most people's boxes.

There's a trio of dining options too, the pick of the bunch being the aptly named River Room Restaurant, where the fast-flowing river is floodlit at night to create a magical atmosphere and its floor-to-ceiling windows ensure that everyone gets the watery views. The kitchen sources its ingredients diligently from a network of local suppliers (and as you'd hope with all those acres out there, there's room for a kitchen garden to produce a haul of freshly-plucked bounty) and, under the direction of Jonnie Boyd, transforms it all into vibrant contemporary dishes with a clear seasonal focus, delivered via a five-course taster or a well-composed à la carte. Things get off to a flyer with a well-crafted starter of succulent suckling pig, its richly flavoured belly and crunchy crackling boosted with

the sweetness of heritage carrots, white raisins and an intense black pudding, or you might take a lighter route in with a luxurious duo of Dover sole and lobster with shellfish bisque, celeriac and celery. Next up, a main course of halibut and lobster arrives in a pretty-as-a-picture medley with silky hazelnut purée adding an earthy note to counterpoint lightly pickled parsnip, white cabbage and sea herbs – a masterclass of real flair and sensitivity towards the balance of components and their impact on the palate. Meat courses, too, show real skill and confidence – perhaps beef fillet and oxtail matched with oyster mushrooms, Roscoff onion, cavolo nero and foie gras.

Desserts are a high point, especially when buttermilk pannacotta comes with the tart contrast of rhubarb, plus honey and the early summer perfume of elderflower, or you might find the cheese trolley laden with Irish cheeses in prime condition a hard prospect to ignore. Everything, from the excellent home-made bread and inventive canapés to the superb petits fours is crafted with impressive attention to detail. Supporting it all is a wine list put together with authority and knowledge.

Chefs Israel Robb, Jonnie Boyd **Seats** 50 **Times** 1–4/6.30–9.30, Closed Monday and Tuesday, L Wednesday to Saturday **Prices** Tasting menu from £55, Starter £12–£14, Main £28–£29, Dessert £7.50–£8.50, Sunday lunch £30.95–£34.95 **Wines** 220 bottles over £30, 40 bottles under £30, 14 by glass **Parking** 200 **Notes** Children 12 years +

See advert on page 318

Belfast

Deanes EIPIC

MAP 1 C5

◉◉◉ Modern European **V**

028 9033 1134 | 36-40 Howard Street, BT1 6PF

www.deaneseipic.com

Classy and confident cooking chez Michael Deane

Michael Deane is a pillar of Belfast's quality dining scene, with a little empire around the city providing something that fits the bill for any occasion. The Howard Street flagship is a high-flying sort of set-up, with a sober, predominantly grey decor, upholstered dining chairs at clothed tables, heavy drapes at the windows, and the overall demeanour of a place that means business. Danni Barry heads up the stoves and she's the driving force behind some exciting, progressive cooking, built on the very finest fresh local produce, and delivered via set-price, multi-course menus (including a veggie version). An opening combo of beef fillet tartare with oyster emulsion and pickled turnip is typically forthright, while flawless fish cookery brings roast halibut with celeriac fondant and purée, sea purslane and a rich bisque-like sauce. When it comes to meat, loin and shoulder of heather-fed lamb is partnered with Jerusalem artichoke purée and black garlic – another idea that is simply focused on flavour and executed with a high degree of skill. At the end, blackberry and meadowsweet crumble comes with meadowsweet ice cream and custard.

Chefs Michael Deane, Danni Barry **Seats** 30, Private dining room 50 **Times** 12–2.30/5.30–9.30, Closed 20–27 December, 12–15 April, 12–22 July, Sunday to Tuesday, L Wednesday to Thursday, Saturday **Prices** Tasting menu £40–£60 **Wines** 76 bottles over £30, 25 bottles under £30, 8 by glass **Parking** On street (after 6pm), car park (Clarence Street) **Notes** Children welcome

OX

MAP 1 C5

◉◉◉ Modern Irish

028 9031 4121 | 1 Oxford Street, BT1 3LA

www.oxbelfast.com

Exciting modern cooking in a defiantly basic room

The pared-back venue on the waterfront with the Spirit of Belfast sculpture right outside looks a little like a modern urban loft space, with its whitewashed brickwork, stipped floor, blue tiling and little mezzanine space for extra seating, and yet the level of culinary excitement going on here quite belies the defiantly basic surrounds. Stephen Toman's menus are full of modern takes and touches, with foraged ingredients and fastidious seasonality to the fore on the daily-changing tasters. An opener of thin-sliced smoked rose veal, black garlic purée, fermented kohlrabi and spring herbs takes possession of the tastebuds straight away. Fish is a strong suit, perhaps tender brill with sprouting broccoli and gnocchi in lemongrass-scented coral butter, while meat could be lamb from the mountains of Mourne with cauliflower, miso and – counter-intuitively – sea herbs. An almost savoury approach to desserts produces coarse-grained polenta cake dressed in olive oil with sherry jelly and segments of blood orange, although sweeter natures may be assuaged with a composition of chocolate, passionfruit, jasmine and rosemary. Nowhere is anywhere without a selection of speciality gins nowadays, and OX obliges, with an expertly compiled wine list to back them up.

Chef Stephen Toman **Seats** 40 **Times** 12–2/6–9, Closed Christmas, 1 week April, 2 weeks July, Sunday and Monday **Prices** Set L 2 course £20, Set L 3 course £25, Tasting menu £50–£80 **Wines** 53 bottles over £30, 2 bottles under £30, 15 by glass **Parking** Car park **Notes** Vegetarian available, Children welcome

▶ County Fermanagh

ENNISKILLEN
Lough Erne Resort   MAP 1 B4
◉◉◉ Modern & Traditional Irish **V**
028 6632 3230 | Belleek Road, BT93 7ED
www.lougherneresort.com
Dynamic modern Irish cooking at a luxury resort hotel

With a luxurious Thai spa and a golf course, this glossy resort hotel on its own 60-acre lough peninsula deserves every one of its accolades. When it comes to fine dining, head for the expansive, vaulted Catalina restaurant with its views across the water and golf course. Noel McMeel's kitchen team is firing on all cylinders, producing thoughtful, exuberant modern Irish cuisine. Vegetarians have their own menu, and the standard carte is just as considered, offering remarkably well-constructed dishes such as a starter of Kilkeel crab that arrives with pickled fennel and chervil, quince water ice, tangerine and black pepper dust. Mains display the same lively imagination and technical flourishes – perhaps roast duck breast matched with roasted and puréed artichoke, black garlic, blackberry and buckthorn gel, fermented blackberry, toasted hazelnuts and thyme jus, or if you're up for fish, pan-fried hake fillet with a hake bonbon, butternut squash fondant and purée, shimeji mushrooms and samphire, all brought to life with a glossy chive emulsion. Round things off with a lush bitter chocolate delice with salted caramel gel, caramel ice cream and glazed pecans.

Chef Noel McMeel **Seats** 75, Private dining room 30 **Times** 1–2.30/6.30–10, Closed L Monday to Saturday **Prices** Set D 2 course £40, Sunday lunch **Wines** 70 bottles over £30, 36 bottles under £30, 13 by glass **Parking** 200 **Notes** Children welcome

County Clare

BALLYVAUGHAN
Gregans Castle
MAP 1 B3
◉◉◉ Modern Irish, European
065 7077005
www.gregans.ie
Modern, classy cooking in the beautiful Burren

The 18th-century manor house stands in the photogenic southwestern wilderness that is The Burren, with sweeping distant views towards Galway Bay. If it's more country retreat than castle as such, nobody's counting, as the family-run hospitality is warm and welcoming, and the surrounding country has been an inspiration to many celebrated writers. In an elegantly understated dining room, David Hurley's modern European cooking suits the occasion to a tee. There could be an inventive start in the shape of lamb tartare with celeriac and sheep's milk yogurt, spiced with dukkah and dressed in lovage oil, before the main stage brings on a duo of glazed halibut and smoked eel, supported by purple sprouting broccoli, turnips and peanuts, or maybe loin and shin of venison with roasted onion, confit potato and date purée. The finishing line is reached with such richnesses as dark chocolate truffle cake adorned with passionfruit and coconut, or with a selection from the present generation of pedigree Irish farmhouse cheeses. With the likes of eggs Benedict and organic porridge at breakfast, a stop at Gregans will set you up well for a stout day's walking hereabouts.

Chef David Hurley **Seats** 50, Private dining room 30 **Times** 6–9, Closed November to mid February, Sunday (except bank holiday Sundays), Wednesday, L all week **Prices** Set D 3 course €72 **Wines** 58 bottles over €30, 14 bottles under €30, 11 by glass **Parking** 20 **Notes** Vegetarian available, Children 7 years +

Dublin

DUBLIN
One Pico Restaurant
MAP 1 C4
Modern French and Irish
01 6760300 & 6760411 | Molesworth Court, Schoolhouse Lane
www.onepico.com

Modern cooking in an old coach house

As we went to press the Rosette award was suspended due to a change of chef – reassessment will take place in due course. Down a narrow lane, a revamped 18th-century coach house is the setting for some of the most contemporary cooking in Dublin. The dining room is a soothingly refined space with a mellow colour scheme, velour seats, modern art and closely-packed tables dressed up to the nines.

Seats 70, Private dining room 43 **Times** 12–2.45/5.30–10, Closed 25 December, 1 January, bank holidays **Prices** Set L 2 course from €25 (3 course €49–€68), Starter €12.50–€14.50, Main €29–€32, Dessert €8.50–€12, Sunday lunch €27–€49 **Wines** 137 bottles over €30, 10 bottles under €30, 25 by glass **Parking** Dawson car park **Notes**, Vegetarian available, Children welcome

Restaurant Patrick Guilbaud   MAP 1 C4
◎◎◎◎ Modern French V
See page 326

▶ County Kilkenny

THOMASTOWN
The Lady Helen Restaurant   MAP 1 C3
◎◎◎ Modern Irish V
056 7773000 | Mount Juliet Hotel
www.mountjuliet.com

Cooking of artistry and impact in a manor-house hotel

If you want to play at being aristocracy for a day, a visit to Mount Juliet should do the trick. The imposing Georgian manor house stands on a sprawling estate where boredom is kept at bay by river and lake fishing, woodland strolls and a golf course. The focus for gastronomes is The Lady Helen dining room, an opulent space with views over the grounds. Wild game from the estate and named local producers get full credit, whether you order from the carte or take on the tasting menus, whose simple descriptions don't tell the full story of what's going on in the intricate dishes. Seared scallops and smoked eel are offset by charred, pickled and puréed carrot and charred orange in a well-balanced starter. Main course brings rose veal of exemplary quality and depth of flavour, with girolles, peas and roast potato foam. There's attention to detail in fish dishes too – perhaps cod with parsley, salted lemon, mussels, and a chicken jus to give the tastebuds a thorough workout. The multi-faceted approach continues into a dessert that plays with textures on a citrus theme, together with avocado and champagne foam.

Chefs Ken Harker, John Kelly **Seats** 60, Private dining room 80 **Times** 6.30–9.45, Closed Sunday and Tuesday, L all week **Prices** Set D 3 course €65, Tasting menu €85–€99 **Wines** 10 by glass **Parking** 200 **Notes** Children welcome

Dublin

Restaurant Patrick Guilbaud

MAP 1 C4

◉◉◉◉ Modern French **V**

01 6764192 | Merrion Hotel, 21 Upper Merrion Street

www.restaurantpatrickguilbaud.ie

Outstanding French cooking at the pre-eminent Dublin address

Paris-born Monsieur Guilbaud's mission to serve up haute cuisine in the city began back in 1981 at a different address, but the luxe Merrion Hotel – an elegant Georgian townhouse – has been home to this bastion of the Dublin fine dining scene since the late 1990s. Now that's what you call staying power, and more remarkable still is that the winning team of Patrick and his head chef, Guillaume Lebrun, have been at the helm since day one. Restaurant manager Stéphane Robin has been here since 1986.

This dedication and consistency is reflected in every element of this business, from the supply lines bringing the country's best produce to the doorstep, the professionalism and charm of the service, and the pin-sharp contemporary French cooking on offer. There's nothing stuffy about the place, with a bright, contemporary finish that combines colourful artworks with soothingly neutral tones, a vibrant carpet which is a work of art itself, and it's all kept ticking over smoothly by a switched-on service team who know their onions. French culinary traditions lie at the heart of the menu, but this is modern stuff, too, with creativity running through from top to bottom, and Irish produce getting a good turnout. The technical skill in the kitchen is evident from the off, with dishes delivering interesting

combinations, compelling flavours, and visual impact. Take a first-course dish of suckling pig croquettes, for example, which comes with fried quail's egg, foie gras and red pepper mostarda, or another where blue lobster ravioli arrives in a coconut-scented lobster cream with toasted almonds and a split curry dressing.

The thrills, technical virtuosity and pretty-looking plates continue into main courses, with the likes of lacquered Challand duck brought into focus with a supporting cast of orange miso, iodised pink onions and toasted buckwheat, or the solidly classical inspiration that serves fillet of Irish beef and roast foie gras with Madeira and truffle jus. The kitchen brings the same thoughtful approach and pin-sharp skills to fish dishes – perhaps Atlantic turbot served meunière style alongside spelt, sunflower seeds, and celeriac, all pointed up with an astringent sauce of Arbois vin jaune. Ingredients are impeccable every step of the way through to dessert, which might be a suitably Gallic Grand Marnier soufflé, or an indulgent plate of Guanaja chocolate and peanut parfait with popcorn ice cream and salted caramel. The wine list covers the whole world while ensuring that France stays centre stage.

Chef Guillaume Lebrun **Seats** 80, Private dining room 25
Times 12.30–2.15/7.30–10.15, Closed 25 December, 1st week in January, Sunday and Monday **Prices** Set L 2 course €50, Set L 3 course €60, A la carte menu 2, 3 or 4 course €90, €120 or €140, Tasting menu €120–€185
Wines 1,200 bottles over €30, 20 by glass **Parking** Merrion Square
Notes Children welcome

County Waterford

MAP 1 B2

ARDMORE
The House Restaurant
@@@@ Modern Irish **V**
024 87800 | Cliff House Hotel
www.cliffhousehotel.ie
Tirelessly innovative Irish cooking overlooking the ocean

Clinging to the cliffs in a wild and windswept spot, Cliff House has been around since the 1930s, but began a new chapter a decade ago when a top-to-toe revamp transformed it into the boutique bolt hole of today. Panoramic views of the ocean and headland are pretty much guaranteed to soothe the soul, while spa treatments sort out the stress, and the restaurant offers the kind of cooking that reaches endlessly for innovation and aims to produce gasps of pleasure.

The kitchen is led by Martijn Kajuiter, a Dutchman with an evident passion for Irish ingredients and who has fully embraced contemporary cooking techniques. Expect excellent presentation and results that are often sensational. Pigeon opens the show, the breast and leg appearing with foie gras pâté in an array of black rice, chervil root, grapefruit and tapioca cracker. A palate-stimulating hit of carrot sorbet with matcha green tea foam intervenes, then sea bass fillet arrives atop salty brandade, together with girolle mushrooms, fennel herb coulis and edible flowers, or there may be fillet and sausage of Black Angus beef with spinach, potato, Kilbeggan whiskey, beef tea and garden herbs.

Even at dessert stage, the same determination to attain impact through complex multi-layering focuses on pear, softly poached, partnered by air-light mousse and sponge, and surrounded by pear pearls poached in various syrups, all afloat in glossy, buttery caramel. There's a tasting menu as you might expect, with wines matched to every dish if you want to go the whole nine yards.

Chefs Martijn Kajuiter, Stephen Hayes **Seats** 64, Private dining room 20 **Times** 6.30–10, Closed 24–26 December, Sunday and Monday (occasionally on Tuesday), L all week **Prices** Set D 2 course €65, Set D 3 course €80, Tasting menu €95 **Wines** 100 bottles over €30, 7 bottles under €30, 20 by glass **Parking** 30 **Notes** Afternoon tea €35, Children welcome

1 & 2 ROSETTE RESTAURANTS

1 and 2 Rosette Restaurants

Restaurants are listed in country and county order, then by town and then alphabetically within the town.

1. County name
2. Location name
3. Name of establishment
4. Number of AA rosettes
   (see pages 8–9)
5. Style of cuisine
6. Vegetarian menu
7. Notable wine list
   (see pages 16–17)
8. Phone number and address

ENGLAND

Bedfordshire

BOLNHURST
The Plough at Bolnhurst
Modern British
01234 376274 | Kimbolton Road, MK44 2EX

FLITWICK
Hallmark Hotel Flitwick Manor
British, Modern European
01525 712242 | Church Road, MK45 1AE

HENLOW
The Crown
Modern British
01462 812433 | 2 High Street, SG16 6BS

LUTON
Adam's Brasserie at Luton Hoo
Modern British
01582 734437 | Luton Hoo Hotel, Golf & Spa, The Mansion House, LU1 3TQ

Wernher Restaurant at Luton Hoo Hotel, Golf & Spa
Modern European
01582 734437 | The Mansion House, LU1 3TQ

WOBURN
The Woburn Hotel
Modern British, French
01525 290441 & 01525 292292
George Street, MK17 9PX

WYBOSTON
The Waterfront Restaurant at Wyboston Lakes
Traditional British, European
0333 700 7667 | Great North Road, MK44 3BA

Berkshire

ASCOT
The Barn at Coworth
British
01344 756784 | Blacknest Road, SL5 7SE

Bluebells Restaurant & Garden Bar
◉◉ Modern British
01344 622722 | Shrubbs Hill,
London Road, Sunningdale, SL5 0LE

BRAY
Caldesi in Campagna
◉◉ Traditional Italian
01628 788500 | Old Mill Lane, SL6 2BG

The Crown
◉◉ Traditional British
01628 621936 | High Street, SL6 2AH

The Riverside Brasserie
◉ Modern European
01628 780553 | Bray Marina,
Monkey Island Lane, SL6 2EB

CHIEVELEY
Crab & Boar
◉◉ Modern British
01635 247550 | Wantage Road,
RG20 8UE

COOKHAM
The White Oak
◉◉ Modern British
01628 523 043 | The Pound, SL6 9QE

FRILSHAM
The Pot Kiln
◉◉ British, European
01635 201366 | RG18 0XX

HUNGERFORD
Littlecote House Hotel
◉◉ Modern European
01488 682509 | Chilton Foliat,
RG17 0SU

HURLEY
Hurley House
◉◉ Modern British
01628 568500 | Henley Road, SL6 5LH

The Olde Bell Inn
◉◉ Modern British
01628 825881 | High Street, SL6 5LX

MAIDENHEAD
Boulters Riverside Brasserie
◉◉ Modern European
01628 621291 | Boulters Lock Island,
SL6 8PE

Fredrick's Hotel and Spa
◉◉ Modern British, French
01628 581000 | Shoppenhangers Road,
SL6 2PZ

NEWBURY
The Brasserie –
Mercure Newbury Elcot Park
◉ British
0844 815 9060 *(calls cost 7p per minute*
plus your phone company's access charge)
Mercure Newbury Elcot Park, Elcot,
RG20 8NJ

Donnington Valley Hotel & Spa
◉◉ Modern British V ♔
01635 551199 | Old Oxford Road,
Donnington, RG14 3AG

The Woodspeen – Restaurant
and Cookery School
◉◉ Modern British
01635 265070 | Lambourn Road,
RG20 8BN

READING
Caprice Restaurant
◉◉ Modern British, Indian
0118 944 0444 | Holiday Inn Reading
M4 Jct 10, Wharfedale Road, RG41 5TS
See advert on page 332

Forbury's Restaurant
◉ French, Mediterranean ♔
0118 957 4044 | RG1 3BB

The French Horn
◉◉ Traditional French, British V
0118 969 2204 | Sonning, RG4 6TN

Malmaison Reading
◉ Modern European, International
0118 956 2300 | Great Western House,
18-20 Station Road, RG1 1JX

Millennium Madejski Hotel Reading
◉◉ British, International V
0118 925 3500 | Madejski Stadium,
RG2 0FL

Mya Lacarte
◉ Modern British
0118 946 3400 | 5 Prospect Street,
Caversham, RG4 8JB

THATCHAM
The Bunk Inn
◉◉ Modern British, French
01635 200400 | Curridge, RG18 9DS

Caprice Restaurant
Holiday Inn Reading M4 Jct10

Enjoy relaxed dining in the 2 AA Rosette Caprice Restaurant & Terrace at this exceptional AA 4 Silver Star hotel, serving superb modern British cuisine. The hotel is transformed at night, with music from the talented resident pianist.

For something more informal, try the stunning Monty's Lounge Bar, serving authentic Indian specialties.

The Afternoon High Teas are also highly recommended.

The Hotel offers a range of great features including the Esprit Spa & Wellness with 19m Pool, Sauna, Steam Room and large Gym, and the 'Academy', the ideal venue for hosting Meetings & Conferences, Weddings and Christmas Parties.

To make a reservation, please contact: T: 0118 944 0444

E: fb@hireadinghotel.com

W: www.hireadinghotel.com

Wharfedale Road, Reading, RG41 5TS

WHITE WALTHAM
The Beehive
◉◉ British
01628 822877 | Waltham Road,
SL6 3SH

WINDSOR
The Brasserie at
Sir Christopher Wren
◉ Modern European
01753 442400 | Thames Street,
SL4 1PX

The Dining Room Restaurant
◉◉ Modern British V
01753 609988 | The Oakley Court,
Windsor Road, Water Oakley, SL4 5UR

The Greene Oak
◉ Modern British
01753 864294 | Oakley Green, SL4 5UW

Scottish Steakhouse@Caleys
◉ Scottish, Modern British
01753 483100 | Macdonald Windsor
Hotel, 23 High Street, SL4 1LH

WOKINGHAM
Miltons Restaurant
◉◉ European, International V
0118 989 5100 | Cantley House Hotel,
Milton Road, RG40 1JY

▶ Bristol

BRISTOL
Adelina Yard
◉◉ Modern British
0117 911 2112 | Queen Quay,
Welsh Back, BS1 4SL

Berwick Lodge
◉◉ Modern British
0117 958 1590 | Berwick Drive,
Henbury, BS10 7TD

The Bird in Hand
◉ Modern British
01275 395222 | Weston Road,
Long Ashton, BS41 9LA

Bordeaux Quay
◉ Modern European
0117 943 1200 | V-Shed, Canons Way,
BS1 5UH

The Brasserie – Mercure Bristol
North The Grange
◉ British, International
01454 777333 | Northwoods,
Winterbourne, BS36 1RP

Glass Boat Restaurant
◉◉ Modern French
0117 929 0704 & 332 3971
Welsh Back, BS1 4SB

Hotel du Vin Bristol
◉ French, British
0117 925 5577 | The Sugar House,
Narrow Lewins Mead, BS1 2NU

The Ox
◉ Modern British
0117 922 1001 | The Basement,
43 Corn Street, BS1 1HT

Paco Tapas
◉◉ Andalusian tapas
0117 925 7021
3A Lower Guinea Street, BS1 6SY

The Pump House
◉◉ Modern British
0117 927 2229 | Merchants Road,
Hotwells, BS8 4PZ

riverstation
◉ Modern European
0117 914 4434 | The Grove, BS1 4RB

Second Floor Restaurant
◉◉ Modern European ♟
0117 961 8898 | Harvey Nichols,
27 Philadelphia Street, Quakers Friars,
BS1 3BZ

The Spiny Lobster
◉ Mediterranean, Seafood
0117 973 7384 | 128 Whiteladies Road,
Clifton, BS8 2RS

The White Horse
◉ European
0117 329 4900 | 24 High Street,
Westbury on Trym, BS9 3DZ

▶ Buckinghamshire

AMERSHAM
Gilbey's Restaurant
◉◉ Modern British
01494 727242 | 1 Market Square,
HP7 0DF

AYLESBURY
The Chequers Inn
◉ Modern British
01296 613298 | 35 Church Lane,
Weston Turville, HP22 5SJ

Buckinghamshire

AYLESBURY *continued*
Hartwell House Hotel,
Restaurant & Spa
❀❀ Modern British ♟
01296 747444 | Lower Hartwell,
HP17 8NR

BEACONSFIELD
Crazy Bear Beaconsfield
❀ British, International
01494 673086 | 75 Wycombe End,
Old Town, HP9 1LX

The Jolly Cricketers
❀ Modern British
01494 676308 | 24 Chalfont Road,
Seer Green, HP9 2YG

BUCKINGHAM
Buckingham Villiers Hotel
❀ Modern British
01280 822444 | 3 Castle Street,
MK18 1BS

BURNHAM
Burnham Beeches Hotel
❀❀ Modern British, European
01628 429955 | Grove Road, SL1 8DP

CUBLINGTON
The Unicorn
❀ Modern, Traditional British
01296 681261 | 12 High Street,
LU7 0LQ

GERRARDS CROSS
The Bull Hotel
❀ Modern British
01753 885995 | Oxford Road, SL9 7PA

GREAT MISSENDEN
Nags Head Inn & Restaurant
❀ British, French
01494 862200 | London Road,
HP16 0DG

LONG CRENDON
The Angel Restaurant
❀ Modern European, Mediterranean **V**
01844 208268 | 47 Bicester Road,
HP18 9EE

MARLOW
Danesfield House Hotel & Spa
❀❀ Modern British
01628 891010 | Henley Road, SL7 2EY

Glaze Restaurant
❀ Modern British, Indian
01628 496800 | Crowne Plaza Marlow,
Field House Lane, SL7 1GJ
See advert on opposite page

The Riverside Restaurant
❀❀ Modern British
01628 484444 | Macdonald Compleat
Angler, Marlow Bridge, SL7 1RG

Sindhu by Atul Kochhar
❀❀ Modern Indian **V**
01628 405405 | Macdonald Compleat
Angler, Marlow Bridge, SL7 1RG

The Vanilla Pod
❀❀ British, French **V** ♟
01628 898101 | 31 West Street,
SL7 2LS

MEDMENHAM
The Dog and Badger
❀ Modern British
01491 579944 | SL7 2HE

MILTON KEYNES
Mercure Milton Keynes
Parkside Hotel
❀ Modern British
01908 661919 | Newport Road,
Woughton on the Green, MK6 3LR

TAPLOW
Berry's Restaurant and Terrace
❀ Classic British
01628 670056 | Taplow House Hotel,
Berry Hill, SL6 0DA

WADDESDON
The Five Arrows
❀❀ Modern British
01296 651727 | High Street,
HP18 0JE

WOOBURN
Chequers Inn
❀❀ British, French
01628 529575 | Kiln Lane,
HP10 0JQ

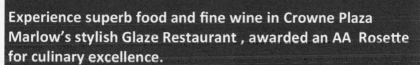

Glaze Restaurant
Crowne Plaza Marlow

CROWNE PLAZA
MARLOW

Experience superb food and fine wine in Crowne Plaza Marlow's stylish Glaze Restaurant , awarded an AA Rosette for culinary excellence.

Glaze Restaurant offers contemporary, eclectic cuisine in a great atmosphere,with floor-to-ceiling windows providing stunning and uninterrupted views over the terrace and lake.

Choose from the new modern British A-la-carte menu or the new authentic Indian menu, all created in house by our new team of international chefs.

Whether you wish to enjoy an intimate meal for two whilst enjoying live music by our resident pianist Richard Snow, or simply meet a few friends for drinks, we've got the perfect environment for you!

To make a reservation, please contact: Glaze Restaurant
T: 01628 496 800 | E: enquiries@cpmarlow.co.uk
W: www.cpmarlow.co.uk/dine
Crowne Plaza Marlow, Fieldhouse Lane, Marlow, SL7 1GJ

Cambridgeshire

▶ Cambridgeshire

BALSHAM
The Black Bull Inn
◉ Modern British
01223 893844 | 27 High Street,
CB21 4DJ

CAMBRIDGE
The Carpenters Arms
◉ Modern British
01223 367050 | 182-186 Victoria Road,
CB4 3DZ

Hotel du Vin Cambridge
◉ French Bistro
01223 227330 | 15-19 Trumpington
Street, CB2 1QA

Hotel Felix
◉◉ Modern British, Mediterranean
01223 277977 | Whitehouse Lane,
Huntingdon Road, CB3 0LX

Quy Mill Hotel & Spa, Cambridge
◉◉ Modern European, British, French
01223 293383 | Church Road,
Stow-Cum-Quy, CB25 9AF

Restaurant 22
◉ Modern European
01223 351880 | 22 Chesterton Road,
CB4 3AX

ELLINGTON
The Mermaid
◉ Fusion, European, Asian V
01480 891106 | High Street, PE28 0AB

ELY
The Anchor Inn
◉ Modern British V
01353 778537 | Bury Lane,
Sutton Gault, Sutton, CB6 2BD

The Dining Room
◉ Modern British
01353 887777 | Poets House,
40-44 St Mary's Street, CB7 4EY

FORDHAM
The White Pheasant
◉◉ British, European
01638 720414 | 21 Market Street,
CB7 5LQ

HINXTON
The Red Lion Inn
◉ Modern British
01799 530601 | 32 High Street,
CB10 1QY

HUNTINGDON
The Abbot's Elm
◉ Modern European
01487 773773 | Abbots Ripton,
PE28 2PA

The Old Bridge Hotel
◉ Modern British ☻
01480 424300 | 1 High Street,
PE29 3TQ

KEYSTON
Pheasant Inn
◉◉ Modern British, European ☻
01832 710241 | Loop Road, PE28 0RE

MELBOURN
Sheene Mill
◉◉ Modern, Traditional British
01763 261393 | 39 Station Road,
SG8 6DX

PETERBOROUGH
Best Western Plus
Orton Hall Hotel & Spa
◉ Modern British
01733 391111 | The Village,
Orton Longueville, PE2 7DN

Bull Hotel
◉ Modern European, British
01733 561364 | Westgate, PE1 1RB

ST NEOTS
The George Hotel & Brasserie
◉◉ Modern British
01480 812300 | High Street,
Buckden, PE19 5XA

STILTON
Bell Inn Hotel
◉◉ Modern British V
01733 241066 | Great North Road,
PE7 3RA

WANSFORD
The Haycock Hotel
◉ Modern British
01780 782223 | London Road,
PE8 6JA

WHITTLESFORD
The Red Lion at Whittlesford Bridge
◉ Modern, Traditional British
01223 832047 & 832115
Station Road, CB22 4NL

WISBECH
Crown Lodge Hotel
🌸 Modern, Traditional
01945 773391 | Downham Road,
Outwell, PE14 8SE

▶ Cheshire

BROXTON
Carden Park Hotel,
Golf Resort & Spa
🌸 Modern British
01829 731000 | Carden Park, CH3 9DQ

BUNBURY
The Yew Tree Inn
🌸 British
01829 260274 | Long Lane, Spurstow,
CW6 9RD

BURWARDSLEY
The Pheasant Inn
🌸 British, European
01829 770434 | Higher Burwardsley,
CH3 9PF

CHESTER
ABode Chester
🌸🌸 Modern British **V**
01244 405820 | Grosvenor Road,
CH1 2DJ

La Brasserie at The Chester
Grosvenor & Spa
🌸🌸 Modern European
01244 324024 | Eastgate, CH1 1LT

The Chef's Table
🌸🌸 Modern British
01244 403040 | Music Hall Passage,
CH1 2EU

Grosvenor Pulford Hotel & Spa
🌸 Mediterranean, European
01244 570560 | Wrexham Road,
Pulford, CH4 9DG

Hallmark Hotel Chester The Queen
🌸🌸 British
01244 305000 | City Road, CH1 3AH

Restaurant 1539
🌸 Modern British
01244 304611 | Chester Race Company
Limited, The Racecourse, CH1 2LY

The Sticky Walnut
🌸🌸 Modern European
01244 400400 | 11 Charles Street,
CH2 3AZ

CONGLETON
Pecks
🌸 British
01260 275161 | Newcastle Road,
Moreton, CW12 4SB

CREWE
Crewe Hall
🌸 Modern European
01270 253333 | Weston Road,
CW1 6UZ

KNUTSFORD
Belle Epoque
🌸🌸 Modern French
01565 633060 | 60 King Street,
WA16 6DT

Cottons Hotel & Spa
🌸 Italian, Mediterranean
01565 650333 | Manchester Road,
WA16 0SU

Mere Court Hotel
& Conference Centre
🌸 Modern Mediterranean
01565 831000 | Warrington Road,
Mere, WA16 0RW

The Mere Golf Resort & Spa
🌸🌸 International
01565 830155 | Chester Road, Mere,
WA16 6LJ

LYMM
The Church Green British Grill
🌸🌸 Modern British
01925 752068 | Higher Lane,
WA13 0AP

MACCLESFIELD
The Shrigley Hall Hotel,
Golf & Country Club
🌸 Modern British **V**
01625 575757 | Shrigley Park,
Pott Shrigley, SK10 5SB

MOTTRAM ST ANDREW
Mottram Hall
🌸 Modern British
01625 828135 | Wilmslow Road,
SK10 4QT

NANTWICH
Rookery Hall Hotel & Spa
🌸🌸 Modern British
01270 610016 | Main Road, Worleston,
CW5 6DQ

Cheshire

PUDDINGTON
Macdonald Craxton Wood Hotel
◉ Modern British **V**
0151 347 4000 | Parkgate Road,
Ledsham, CH66 9PB

SANDIWAY
Nunsmere Hall Hotel
◉◉ British, European
01606 889100 | Tarporley Road,
Oakmere, CW8 2ES

TARPORLEY
Macdonald Portal Hotel Golf & Spa
◉ Modern British
01829 734100 | Cobblers Cross Lane,
CW6 0DJ

WARMINGHAM
The Bear's Paw
◉ Modern European, British
01270 526317 | School Lane,
CW11 3QN

WARRINGTON
Hallmark Hotel Warrington Fir Grove
◉ Modern British
01925 267471 | Knutsford Old Road,
WA4 2LD

The Park Royal
◉ Modern British
01925 730706 | Stretton Road,
Stretton, WA4 4NS

WILMSLOW
**Best Western Plus
Pinewood on Wilmslow**
◉ Modern, Traditional
01625 529211 | 180 Wilmslow Road,
SK9 3LF

The Stanneylands
◉◉ British
01625 525225 | Stanneylands Road,
SK9 4EY

▶ Cornwall and the Isles of Scilly

BODMIN
Trehellas House Hotel & Restaurant
◉ Traditional
01208 72700 | Washaway, PL30 3AD

BOSCASTLE
The Wellington Hotel
◉◉ Modern British, French
01840 250202 | The Harbour, PL35 0AQ

BUDE
The Beach Restaurant
◉◉ Modern British
01288 389800 | The Beach Hotel,
Summerleaze Crescent, EX23 8HJ

CALLINGTON
Langmans Restaurant
◉◉ Modern British
01579 384933 | 3 Church Street,
PL17 7RE

FALMOUTH
Falmouth Hotel
◉ British **V**
01326 312671 | Castle Beach,
TR11 4NZ

The Greenbank Hotel
◉◉ Modern British
01326 312440 | Harbourside, TR11 2SR

Merchants Manor
◉◉ Modern British
01326 312734 | 1 Weston Manor,
TR11 4AJ

Oliver's Eatery
◉◉ Modern, Traditional British
01326 218138 | 33 High Street,
TR11 2AD

Penmorvah Manor
◉ Modern British
01326 250277 | Budock Water,
TR11 5ED

The Royal Duchy Hotel
◉◉ Modern British
01326 313042 | Cliff Road, TR11 4NX

St Michael's Hotel and Spa
◉◉ Modern Mediterranean, British
01326 312707 | Gyllyngvase Beach,
Seafront, TR11 4NB

FOWEY
Fowey Hall
◉◉ British
01726 833866 | Hanson Drive,
PL23 1ET

The Fowey Hotel
◉◉ Modern European **V**
01726 832551 | The Esplanade,
PL23 1HX

GOLANT
Cormorant Hotel & Restaurant
◉◉ Modern European
01726 833426 | PL23 1LL

Cornwall and the Isles of Scilly

HAYLE
Rosewarne Manor
@@ Modern British
01209 610414 | 20 Gwinear Road,
TR27 5JQ

HELSTON
New Yard Restaurant
@@ British, Italian
01326 221595 | Trelowarren Estate,
Mawgan, TR12 6AF

LIZARD
Housel Bay Hotel
@ Modern British, French **V**
01326 290417 | Housel Cove,
TR12 7PG

LOOE
Trelaske Hotel & Restaurant
@@ Modern British
01503 262159 | Polperro Road,
PL13 2JS

LOSTWITHIEL
Asquiths Restaurant
@@ Modern British
01208 871714 | 19 North Street,
PL22 0EF

MAWGAN PORTH
The Scarlet Hotel
@@ Modern European 🍷
01637 861800 | Tredragon Road,
TR8 4DQ

MAWNAN SMITH
Budock Vean Hotel
@ Modern British **V**
01326 250288 & 252100
TR11 5LG

Meudon Hotel
@ Modern Classic **V**
01326 250541 | TR11 5HT

MEVAGISSEY
Trevalsa Court Hotel
@@ Modern British
01726 842460 | School Hill,
Polstreth, PL26 6TH

MULLION
Mullion Cove Hotel
@@ Modern British
01326 240328 | TR12 7EP

The Restaurant at the
Polurrian Bay Hotel
@@ Modern British
01326 240421 | TR12 7EN

NEWQUAY
Samphire
@@ Modern British
01637 872211 | Fistral Beach,
TR7 1EW

Silks Bistro and Champagne Bar
@ Modern British
01637 839048 | Atlantic Hotel,
Dane Road, TR7 1EN

PADSTOW
The Metropole
@@ Modern British
01841 532486 | Station Road,
PL28 8DB

Rojano's in the Square
@ Italian, Mediterranean
01841 532796 | 9 Mill Square,
PL28 8AE

St Petroc's Bistro
@ Mediterranean, French
01841 532700 | 4 New Street,
PL28 8EA

Treglos Hotel
@@ Traditional English **V**
01841 520727 | Constantine Bay,
PL28 8JH

PENZANCE
The Bay@Hotel Penzance
@@ French
01736 366890 | Britons Hill, TR18 3AE

Ben's Cornish Kitchen
@@ Modern British
01736 719200 | West End, Marazion,
TR17 0EL

Harris's Restaurant
@ British, French
01736 364408 | 46 New Street,
TR18 2LZ

The Tolcarne Inn
@ Seafood
01736 363074 | Newlyn, TR18 5PR

POLPERRO
Talland Bay Hotel
@@ International
01503 272667 | Porthallow, PL13 2JB

Cornwall and the Isles of Scilly

PORT GAVERNE
Port Gaverne
◉◉ Modern British **V**
01208 880244 | PL29 3SQ

PORTHLEVEN
Kota Restaurant with Rooms
◉◉ British, Pacific Rim, Seafood
01326 562407 | Harbour Head,
TR13 9JA

PORT ISAAC
Outlaw's Fish Kitchen
◉◉ Modern British, Seafood
01208 881183 | 1 Middle Street,
PL29 3RH

PORTLOE
The Lugger
◉◉ European
01872 501322 | TR2 5RD

REDRUTH
Penventon Park Restaurant
◉◉ Modern British
01209 203000 | TR15 1TE

ST AGNES
Rose-in-Vale Country House Hotel
◉◉ Modern British
01872 552202 | Mithian, TR5 0QD

ST AUSTELL
Austell's
◉◉ Modern British
01726 813888 | 10 Beach Road,
PL25 3PH

Boscundle Manor
◉◉ Modern British **V**
01726 813557 | Boscundle, PL25 3RL

Carlyon Bay Hotel
◉ Modern & Traditional British
01726 812304 | Sea Road,
Carlyon Bay, PL25 3RD

The Cornwall Hotel, Spa & Estate
◉ Modern British **V**
01726 874050 | Pentewan Road,
Tregorrick, PL26 7AB

ST IVES
Carbis Bay Hotel
◉◉ International
01736 795311 | Carbis Bay, TR26 2NP

The Garrack
◉ Modern
01736 796199 | Burthallan Lane,
TR26 3AA

Porthminster Beach Restaurant
◉◉ Modern Mediterranean,
Pacific Rim **V**
01736 795352 | TR26 2EB

Porthminster Kitchen
◉ British, Seafood
01736 798874 | Wharf Road, TR26 1LG

ST MELLION
St Mellion International Resort
◉◉ Modern International
01579 351351 | PL12 6SD

TRESCO (THE ISLES OF SCILLY)
New Inn
◉ Modern & Traditional
01720 422849 | TR24 0QQ

TRURO
The Alverton Hotel
◉◉ Modern British, European
01872 276633 | Tregolls Road,
TR1 1ZQ

Hooked Restaurant & Bar
◉ Modern British, Seafood
01872 274700 | Tabernacle Street,
TR1 2EJ

Mannings Hotel
◉◉ Modern, Pacific Rim
01872 270345 & 247900
Lemon Street, TR1 2QB

Tabb's Restaurant
◉◉ Modern British
01872 262110 | 85 Kenwyn Street,
TR1 3BZ

VERYAN
The Quarterdeck at The Nare
◉◉ Traditional British ♟
01872 500000 & 500111
Carne Beach, TR2 5PF

WATERGATE BAY
Fifteen Cornwall
◉ Italian
01637 861000 | On The Beach,
TR8 4AA

▶ Cumbria

AMBLESIDE
The Old Stamp House Restaurant
@@ Modern British **V**
015394 32775 | Church Street,
LA22 0BU

Rothay Manor Hotel & Fine Dining
@@ Modern British
01539 433605 | Rothay Bridge,
LA22 0EH

Waterhead Hotel
@ Modern British
015394 32566 | Lake Road, LA22 0ER

APPLEBY-IN-WESTMORLAND
Appleby Manor Hotel & Garden Spa
@ Modern British **V**
017683 51571 | Roman Road,
CA16 6JB

ASKHAM
Askham Hall
@@ Modern British
01931 712350 & 07887 724857
CA10 2PF

BARROW-IN-FURNESS
Abbey House Hotel & Gardens
@ Traditional British, French
01229 838282 | Abbey Road,
LA13 0PA

BASSENTHWAITE
Armathwaite Hall Hotel and Spa
@@ British, French **V**
017687 76551 | CA12 4RE

The Pheasant
@@ Modern British
017687 76234 | CA13 9YE

**Ravenstone Lodge
Country House Hotel**
@ British
01768 776629 | CA12 4QG

BORROWDALE
Borrowdale Gates Hotel
@ British, French **V**
017687 77204 | CA12 5UQ

Hazel Bank Country House
@ British
017687 77248 | Rosthwaite,
CA12 5XB

Leathes Head Hotel
@@ British
017687 77247 | CA12 5UY

Lodore Falls Hotel
@ Modern British **V**
017687 77285 | CA12 5UX

BOWNESS-ON-WINDERMERE
Belsfield Restaurant
@ Modern British
015394 42448
Laura Ashley The Belsfield,
Kendal Road, LA23 3EL

The Ryebeck
@@ Modern British
015394 88195 | Lyth Valley Road,
LA23 3JP

CARLISLE
Crown Hotel
@ Modern British
01228 561888 | Station Road,
Wetheral, CA4 8ES

CARTMEL
Aynsome Manor Hotel
@ Modern, Traditional British
015395 36653 | LA11 6HH

COCKERMOUTH
The Trout Hotel
@ International, Classic **V**
01900 823591 | Crown Street,
CA13 0EJ

CROSTHWAITE
**The Punchbowl Inn
at Crosthwaite**
@@ Modern British **V**
015395 68237 | Lyth Valley,
LA8 8HR

ELTERWATER
Stove at Langdale Hotel & Spa
@ Modern British
015394 37302 & 38080
The Langdale Estate, LA22 9JD

GLENRIDDING
Inn on the Lake
@@ Modern European **V**
017684 82444 | Lake Ullswater,
CA11 0PE

Cumbria

GRANGE-OVER-SANDS
Clare House
@ Modern British
015395 33026 | Park Road,
LA11 7HQ

GRASMERE
The Daffodil Hotel & Spa
@ Modern British
015394 63550 | Keswick Road,
LA22 9PR

The Dining Room
@@ Modern British
015394 35217 | Oak Bank Hotel,
Broadgate, LA22 9TA

Rothay Garden Hotel
@@ Modern British V
01539 435334 | Broadgate, LA22 9RJ

The Wordsworth Hotel & Spa
@ Modern British
015394 35592 | Stock Lane,
LA22 9SW

HAWKSHEAD
The Queen's Head Inn & Restaurant
@ British
01539 436271 | Main Street,
LA22 0NS

The Sun Inn
@ Traditional British
015394 36236 | Main Street,
LA22 0NT

IRTHINGTON
The Golden Fleece
@ Modern British
01228 573686 | Rule Holme, CA6 4NF

KENDAL
Castle Green Hotel in Kendal
@@ Modern British
01539 734000 | Castle Green Lane,
LA9 6RG

KESWICK
Brossen Steakhouse
@ Modern British
01768 773333 | Inn on the Square,
Main Street, CA12 5JF

KIRKBY LONSDALE
Carters at the Sun Inn
@@ Modern British V
015242 71965 | 6 Market Street,
LA6 2AU

Pheasant Inn
@ Modern British
015242 71230 | Casterton, LA6 2RX

KIRKBY STEPHEN
The Inn at Brough
@ Modern British
01768 341252 | Main Street, Brough,
CA17 4AY

LEVENS
The Villa Levens
@ Modern & Traditional V
01539 980980 | Brettargh Holt,
LA8 8EA

LUPTON
Plough Inn
@ Modern British
015395 67700 | Cow Brow, LA6 1PJ

NEAR SAWREY
Ees Wyke Country House
@ Modern & Traditional British,
French, Mediterranean
015394 36393 | LA22 0JZ

NEWBY BRIDGE
Lakeside Hotel Lake Windermere
@@ Modern British V
015395 30001 | Lakeside, LA12 8AT

PENRITH
Stoneybeck Inn
@ Traditional British V
01768 862369 | Bowscar, CA11 8RP

RAVENGLASS
The Pennington Hotel
@ British
0845 450 6445 | CA18 1SD

ROSTHWAITE
Scafell Hotel
@ Modern British
017687 77208 | CA12 5XB

TEMPLE SOWERBY
**Temple Sowerby House Hotel
& Restaurant**
@@ Modern British
017683 61578 | CA10 1RZ

ULVERSTON
Virginia House
◉◉ Modern British
01229 584844 | 24 Queen Street,
LA12 7AF

WATERMILLOCK
Macdonald Leeming House
◉ Modern British
01768 486674 | CA11 0JJ

WINDERMERE
Beech Hill Hotel & Spa
◉ Modern British V
015394 42137 | Newby Bridge Road,
LA23 3LR

Briery Wood Country House Hotel
◉ Modern British V
015394 33316 | Ambleside Road,
Ecclerigg, LA23 1ES

Cedar Manor Hotel & Restaurant
◉ Modern British
015394 43192 | Ambleside Road,
LA23 1AX

Cragwood Country House Hotel
◉ British, French
015394 88177 | Ambleside Road,
LA23 1LQ

Gilpin Spice
◉◉ Pan Asian
015394 88818 | Gilpin Hotel & Lake
House, Crook Road, LA23 3NF

**Lindeth Howe Country House Hotel
& Restaurant**
◉◉ Classic French V
015394 45759 | Lindeth Drive,
Longtail Hill, LA23 3JF

**Macdonald Old England
Hotel & Spa**
◉ Traditional British, European
015394 87890 | 23 Church Street,
Bowness, LA23 3DF

Merewood Country House Hotel
◉◉ Modern British
015394 46484 | Ambleside Road,
Ecclerigg, LA23 1LH

Miller Howe Hotel
◉◉ Modern British V ♆
015394 42536 | Rayrigg Road,
LA23 1EY

Porto
◉◉ Modern British
015394 48242 | 3 Ash Street,
Bowness, LA23 3EB
See advert on page 344

Storrs Hall Hotel
◉◉ Modern British V
015394 47111 | Storrs Park, LA23 3LG

**The Wild Boar Inn,
Grill & Smokehouse**
◉ Traditional British
015394 45225 & 48050
Crook, LA23 3NF

▶ Derbyshire
BAKEWELL
Piedaniel's
◉ Traditional French, European
01629 812687 | Bath Street,
DE45 1RX

BASLOW
Cavendish Hotel
◉◉ Modern British V
01246 582311 | Church Lane,
DE45 1SP

BEELEY
The Devonshire Arms at Beeley
◉ Modern British ♆
01629 733259 | Devonshire Square,
DE4 2NR

BRADWELL
The Samuel Fox Country Inn
◉◉ Modern British
01433 621562 | Stretfield Road,
S33 9JT

BUXTON
Best Western Lee Wood Hotel
◉ British, European
01298 23002 | The Park, SK17 6TQ

CHESTERFIELD
Casa Hotel
◉◉ Modern British, Mediterranean
01246 245990 | Lockoford Lane,
S41 7JB

Peak Edge Hotel at the Red Lion
◉◉ Modern British V
01246 566142 | Darley Road,
Stone Edge, S45 0LW

PORTO

RESTAURANT

Porto provides award winning dining just a short stroll from England's largest lake. We deliver freshly-prepared food, created by Head Chef David Bewick and his team, making the most of the local larder and Cumbrian traditions.

After many years refining his trade working with the likes of Gordon Ramsey and Nigel Haworth, David took on the role of Head Chef at Porto in 2011. His use of hand-butchering and lovingly preparing local ingredients has earned him 2 AA Rosettes.

Enjoy our food alfresco, on the heated roof terrace, or in either of our 2 newly refurbished, relaxed & modern dining rooms and complement it with a comprehensive wine list, cocktails or local ales.

COME & JOIN US

OPEN 7 DAYS A WEEK.

LUNCH: 12PM - 2PM

DINNER: FROM 6.00PM (5.30PM ON SATURDAYS)

3 ASH STREET, BOWNESS-ON-WINDERMERE LA23 3EB **T:015394 48242**

VISIT OUR WEBSITE FOR OUR SPECIAL OFFERS

WWW.PORTO-RESTAURANT.CO.UK

CLOWNE
Hotel Van Dyk
@ Modern British
01246 387386 | Worksop Road,
S43 4TD

DARLEY ABBEY
Darleys Restaurant
@@ Modern British V
01332 364987 | Haslams Lane,
DE22 1DZ

DERBY
Masa Restaurant
@ Modern European V
01332 203345 | The Old Chapel,
Brook Street, DE1 3PF

FROGGATT
The Chequers Inn
@@ Modern British
01433 630231 | S32 3ZJ

GRINDLEFORD
The Maynard
@@ Modern British
01433 630321 | Main Road, S32 2HE

See advert on page 347

HATHERSAGE
The Plough Inn
@ Modern
01433 650319 & 650180
Leadmill Bridge, S32 1BA

HIGHAM
Santo's Higham Farm Hotel
@ Modern International
01773 833812 | Main Road, DE55 6EH

HOPE
Losehill House Hotel & Spa
@@ Modern British V
01433 621219 | Lose Hill Lane,
Edale Road, S33 6AF

MATLOCK
Stones Restaurant
@@ Modern British V
01629 56061 | 1 Dale Road, DE4 3LT

MELBOURNE
Amalfi White
@@ Modern British
01332 694890 | 50 Derby Road,
DE73 8FE

The Bay Tree
@ Modern British, New World V
01332 863358 | 4 Potter Street,
DE73 8HW

Harpur's of Melbourne
@@ Modern French
01332 862134 | 2 Derby Road,
DE73 8FE

MORLEY
The Morley Hayes Hotel
@@ Modern British
01332 780480 | Main Road,
DE7 6DG

REPTON
The Boot Inn
@ Modern British
01283 346047 | 12 Boot Hill,
DE65 6FT

SANDIACRE
La Rock
@@ Modern British
0115 9399 833 | 4 Bridge Street,
NG10 5QT

THORPE
The Izaak Walton Hotel
@@ Modern & Traditional
01335 350981 | Dovedale, DE6 2AY

▶ **Devon**

AXMINSTER
Fairwater Head Hotel
@ Modern British
01297 678349 | Hawkchurch,
EX13 5TX

BAMPTON
The Swan
@@ Modern British
01398 332248 | Station Road,
EX16 9NG

BEESANDS
The Cricket Inn
@ Modern British
01548 580215 | TQ7 2EN

BIGBURY-ON-SEA
The Oyster Shack
@ Seafood
01548 810876 | Stakes Hill,
TQ7 4BE

Devon

BRIXHAM
Quayside Hotel
@ Modern British
01803 855751 | 41-49 King Street,
TQ5 9TJ

BURRINGTON
Northcote Manor
@@ Modern British **V**
01769 560501 | EX37 9LZ

CHAGFORD
Mill End Hotel
@@ British
01647 432282 | Dartmoor National Park,
TQ13 8JN

CHITTLEHAMHOLT
Highbullen Hotel,
Golf & Country Club
@@ Modern British
01769 540561 | EX37 9HD

DARTMOUTH
The Dart Marina Hotel
@ Modern British **V**
01803 832580 | Sandquay Road,
TQ6 9PH

The Grill Room
@ British, Seafood
01803 833033 | Royal Castle Hotel,
11 The Quay, TQ6 9PS

The Seahorse
@@ Mediterranean, Seafood **V**
01803 835147 | 5 South Embankment,
TQ6 9BH

DODDISCOMBSLEIGH
The Nobody Inn
@ Modern British
01647 252394 | EX6 7PS

DOLTON
The Rams Head Inn
@@ Modern Classic
01805 804255 | South Street,
EX19 8QS

ERMINGTON
Plantation House
@@ Modern British **V**
01548 831100 | Totnes Road,
PL21 9NS

EXETER
The Olive Tree
@ Modern
01392 272709 | Queens Court Hotel,
6-8 Bystock Terrance, EX4 4HY

EXMOUTH
Les Saveurs
@@ Modern French, International
01395 269459 | 9 Tower Street,
EX8 1NT

HAYTOR VALE
Rock Inn
@@ Modern British, European
01364 661305 & 661556
TQ13 9XP

HONITON
The Deer Park Country House Hotel
@@ Modern British
01404 41266 | Weston, EX14 3PG

The Holt Bar & Restaurant
@@ Modern British
01404 47707 | 178 High Street,
EX14 1LA

ILFRACOMBE
The Quay Restaurant
@ British, European
01271 868090 | 11 The Quay, EX34 9EQ

Sandy Cove Hotel
@@ Modern British
01271 882243 | Old Coast Road, Combe
Martin Bay, Berrynarbor, EX34 9SR

ILSINGTON
Ilsington Country House Hotel
@@ Modern European
01364 661452 | Ilsington Village,
TQ13 9RR

KINGSBRIDGE
Buckland-Tout-Saints
@@ Modern British **V**
01548 853055 | Goveton, TQ7 2DS

KNOWSTONE
The Masons Arms
@@ Modern British
01398 341231 | EX36 4RY

LIFTON
Arundell Arms
@@ Modern British **V**
01566 784666 | Fore Street, PL16 0AA

The Maynard

themaynard.co.uk

The Maynard boasts a privileged and peaceful location, set within the Peak District National Park.

Our 2 AA rosette awarded restaurant serves seasonal, locally sourced food which is prepared by our Head Chef and his team of experienced chefs. Guests can enjoy lunch served from 12.00pm until 3.00pm or dinner served from 6.30pm until 9.00pm whilst overlooking the stunning gardens and valley beyond. During the summer months the garden offers a perfect retreat for al fresco dining or afternoon tea.

Our 10 en-suite bedrooms offer luxury and comfort to guests with a full choice of hot or cold breakfast served in the restaurant each morning.

Main Road, Grindleford, S32 2HE

Tel: 01433 630321

Email: info@themaynard.co.uk

the maynard

Devon

LYNMOUTH
Rising Sun
🏵🏵 British, French
01598 753223 | Harbourside, EX35 6EG

PLYMOUTH
Artillery Tower Restaurant
🏵 Modern British
01752 257610 | Firestone Bay,
Durnford Street, PL1 3QR

Barbican Kitchen
🏵 Modern International
01752 604448 | Plymouth Gin Distillery,
60 Southside Street, PL1 2LQ

Best Western Duke of Cornwall Hotel
🏵 Modern British, European
01752 275850 | Millbay Road, PL1 3LG

The Greedy Goose
🏵🏵 Modern British
01752 252001 | Prysten House,
Finewell Street, PL1 2AE

Langdon Court Hotel & Restaurant
🏵🏵 Traditional British, French V
01752 862358 | Adams Lane,
Down Thomas, PL9 0DY

Rock Salt Café and Brasserie
🏵🏵 Modern British V
01752 225522 | 31 Stonehouse Street,
PL1 3PE

The Wildflower Restaurant
🏵 Classic British
01822 852245 | Moorland Garden Hotel,
Yelverton, PL20 6DA

PLYMPTON
Treby Arms
🏵🏵 Modern European
01752 837363 | Sparkwell, PL7 5DD

ROCKBEARE
The Jack In The Green Inn
🏵🏵 Modern British V
01404 822240 | EX5 2EE

SALCOMBE
The Jetty
🏵 Modern, International V
01548 844444 | Salcombe Harbour
Hotel, Cliff Road, TQ8 8JH

Soar Mill Cove Hotel
🏵🏵 Modern British
01548 561566 | Soar Mill Cove,
Marlborough, TQ7 3DS

South Sands Hotel
🏵🏵 Modern British
01548 845900 | Bolt Head, TQ8 8LL

SAUNTON
Saunton Sands Hotel
🏵 Traditional & Modern British V
01271 890212 | EX33 1LQ

SHALDON
ODE dining
🏵🏵 Modern British V
01626 873977 | 21 Fore Street,
TQ14 0DE

SIDMOUTH
Hotel Riviera
🏵🏵 Modern British
01395 515201 | The Esplanade,
EX10 8AY

The Salty Monk
🏵🏵 Modern British 🍷
01395 513174 | Church Street,
Sidford, EX10 9QP

The Victoria Hotel
🏵 Traditional
01395 512651 | The Esplanade,
EX10 8RY

STRETE
The Laughing Monk
🏵 Modern British
01803 770639 | Totnes Road,
TQ6 0RN

TAVISTOCK
Bedford Hotel
🏵 British
01822 613221 | 1 Plymouth Road,
PL19 8BB

The Horn of Plenty
🏵🏵 Modern British V
01822 832528 | Gulworthy, PL19 8JD

THURLESTONE
Thurlestone Hotel
🏵🏵 British V
01548 560382 | TQ7 3NN

The Village Inn
🏵 Modern
01548 563525 & 560382
TQ7 3NN

TORQUAY
The Cary Arms
◉ British, Seafood
01803 327110 | Babbacombe Beach,
TQ1 3LX

Grand Hotel
◉ Modern European
01803 296677 | Torbay Road, TQ2 6NT

The Imperial Hotel
◉ Modern British
01803 294301 | Park Hill Road,
TQ1 2DG

John Burton-Race @ The Grosvenor
◉◉ Modern British
01803 294373 | The Grosvenor Hotel,
Belgrave Road, TQ2 5HG

Orestone Manor
◉◉ Modern, European **V**
01803 328098 | Rockhouse Lane,
Maidencombe, TQ1 4SX

Seasons
◉ Modern British
01803 226366 | Belgrave Road,
TQ2 5HF

TOTNES
The Riverford Field Kitchen
◉ Modern British, Organic
01803 762074 | Riverford, TQ11 0JU

The White Hart
◉◉ Modern British
01803 847150 | Dartington Hall,
The Darington Hall Trust, TQ9 6EL

TWO BRIDGES
Two Bridges Hotel
◉◉ Modern British **V**
01822 892300 | PL20 6SW

WOOLACOMBE
Watersmeet Hotel
◉◉ Traditional British, European
01271 870333 | Mortehoe, EX34 7EB

▶ Dorset

BEAMINSTER
Brassica Restaurant
◉ Modern European, Mediterranean
01308 538100 | 4 The Square, DT8 3AS

BridgeHouse
◉◉ Modern European
01308 862200 | 3 Prout Bridge,
DT8 3AY

BOURNEMOUTH
Best Western Plus
The Connaught Hotel
◉◉ Modern British
01202 298020 | 30 West Hill Road,
West Cliff, BH2 5PH

The Crab at Bournemouth
◉◉ Seafood
01202 203601 | Exeter Road, BH2 5AJ

Cumberland Hotel
◉◉ Traditional British
01202 290722 & 298350
27 East Overcliffe Drive, BH1 3AF

The Green House
◉◉ Modern British
01202 498900 | 4 Grove Road,
BH1 3AX

Hermitage Hotel
◉ Traditional British **V**
01202 557363 | Exeter Road, BH2 5AH

The Riviera Hotel
◉ Modern British, European
01202 763653 | Burnaby Road,
Alum Chine, BH4 8JF

West Beach
◉ Modern British, Seafood
01202 587785 | Pier Approach,
BH2 5AA

BRIDPORT
Riverside Restaurant
◉ Seafood, International
01308 422011 | West Bay, DT6 4EZ

CHRISTCHURCH
Captain's Club Hotel & Spa
◉◉ Modern European
01202 475111 | Wick Ferry,
Wick Lane, BH23 1HU

The Jetty
◉◉ Modern British **V ▼**
01202 400950 | 95 Mudeford,
BH23 3NT

The Lord Bute & Restaurant
◉◉ British, Mediterranean
01425 278884 | 179-181 Lymington
Road, Highcliffe on Sea, BH23 4JS

Upper Deck Bar & Restaurant
◉ Modern British **V ▼**
01202 400954 | 95 Mudeford,
BH23 3NT

Dorset

CORFE CASTLE
Mortons House Hotel
◉◉ Modern British
01929 480988 | 49 East Street,
BH20 5EE

EVERSHOT
The Acorn Inn
◉ British
01935 83228 | 28 Fore Street, DT2 0JW

George Albert Hotel
◉ Modern British
01935 483430 | Wardon Hill, DT2 9PW

FARNHAM
Museum Inn
◉◉ Modern & Traditional British
01725 516261 | DT11 8DE

MAIDEN NEWTON
Le Petit Canard
◉ Modern British, French
01300 320536 | Dorchester Road,
DT2 0BE

POOLE
Harbour Heights Hotel
◉◉ British, French
01202 707272 | 73 Haven Road,
Sandbanks, BH13 7LW

The Haven
◉◉ Modern British
01202 707333 | 161 Banks Road,
Sandbanks, BH13 7QL

Hotel du Vin Poole
◉ Modern British, French
01202 785578 | Mansion House,
Thames Street, BH15 1JN

Rick Stein Sandbanks
◉ Seafood V ♟
01202 283280 & 283000
10-14 Banks Road, BH13 7QB

SHAFTESBURY
La Fleur de Lys
Restaurant with Rooms
◉◉ Modern French
01747 853717 | Bleke Street,
SP7 8AW

SHERBORNE
Eastbury Hotel
◉◉ Modern British V
01935 813131 | Long Street, DT9 3BY

The Green
◉◉ Modern European
01935 813821 & 07969 264782
3 The Green, DT9 3HY

The Kings Arms
◉ Modern British
01963 220281 | Charlton Herethorne,
DT9 4NL

The Rose and Crown Inn, Trent
◉◉ Modern British
01935 850776 | Trent, DT9 4SL

STUDLAND
THE PIG on the Beach
◉◉ Modern British ♟
01929 450288 | The Manor House,
Manor Road, BH19 3AU

WEYMOUTH
Moonfleet Manor Hotel
◉ Mediterranean
01305 786948 | Fleet Road, DT3 4ED

WIMBORNE MINSTER
Les Bouviers Restaurant
with Rooms
◉◉ Mediterranean, French
01202 889555 | Arrowsmith Road,
Canford Magna, BH21 3BD

Number 9
◉◉ Modern British, Seafood
01202 887557 | West Borough,
BH21 1LT

WYKE REGIS
Crab House Café
◉ British, Seafood
01305 788867 | Ferrymans Way,
Portland Road, DT4 9YU

▶ County Durham

BARNARD CASTLE
The Morritt Country House Hotel
& Spa
◉◉ Modern French
01833 627232 | Greta Bridge,
DL12 9SE

BILLINGHAM
Wynyard Hall Hotel
◉◉ Modern British
01740 644811 | Wynyard, TS22 5NF

DARLINGTON
Headlam Hall
@@ Modern British, French
01325 730238 | Headlam,
Gainford, DL2 3HA

DURHAM
Fusion Restaurant
@ Pan Asian, Thai **V**
0191 386 5282 & 375 3088
Ramside Hall Hotel Golf & Spa,
Carrville, DH1 1TD

The Rib Room
@ International **V**
0191 386 5282 | Ramside Hall Hotel
Golf & Spa, Carrville, DH1 1TD

HUTTON MAGNA
The Oak Tree Inn
@@ Modern British
01833 627371 | DL11 7HH

ROMALDKIRK
The Rose & Crown
@@ Modern British, International
01833 650213 | DL12 9EB

SEAHAM
The Ozone Restaurant
@ Asian Fusion
0191 516 1400 | Seaham Hall Hotel,
Lord Byron's Walk, SR7 7AG

Seaham Hall - Byron's Restaurant
@@ Modern British ♀
0191 516 1400 | Seaham Hall Hotel,
Lord Byron's Walk, SR7 7AG
See advert below

▶ **Essex**
BRENTWOOD
Marygreen Manor Hotel
@@ Modern European **V**
01277 225252 | London Road,
CM14 4NR

Luxury Modern Dining, Byron's Restaurant

Seaham Hall, an 18th-Century Georgian mansion is home to Byron's

Restaurant in Seaham, which has an emphasis and commitment to using

only quality ingredients. Dine on fabulous menus using local ingredients,

we are sure will inspire you to return time and time again.

Opening Times: Sunday - Thursday 6.30pm - 9.00pm /

Friday - Saturday 6.30pm - 9.30pm

SEAHAM HALL

SEAHAM HALL HOTEL, LORD BYRON'S WALK, COUNTY DURHAM,
SR7 7AG TEL: 0191 516 1400
EMAIL: RESERVATIONS@SEAHAM-HALL.COM WWW.SEAHAMHALL.CO.UK

Essex

CHELMSFORD
County Hotel
◉ Modern European
01245 455700 | 29 Rainsford Road,
CM1 2PZ

COGGESHALL
Ranfield's Brasserie
◉◉ Modern British **V**
01376 561453 | 4-6 Stoneham Street,
CO6 1TT

COLCHESTER
**Stoke by Nayland Hotel,
Golf & Spa**
◉◉ Modern British
01206 262836 | Keepers Lane,
Leavenheath, CO6 4PZ

DEDHAM
milsoms
◉ Modern International
01206 322795 | Stratford Road,
CO7 6HN

The Sun Inn
◉◉ Rustic Italian, Modern British 🍷
01206 323351 | High Street, CO7 6DF

Le Talbooth
◉◉ Modern British, European **V** 🍷
01206 323150 | Stratford Road,
CO7 6HN

GESTINGTHORPE
The Pheasant
◉ British
01787 465010 | Audley End, CO9 3AU

GREAT TOTHAM
**The Bull & Willow Room
at Great Totham**
◉◉ Modern, Traditional British
01621 893385 | 2 Maldon Road,
CM9 8NH

GREAT YELDHAM
The White Hart
◉◉ British, European
01787 237250 | Poole Street,
CO9 4HJ

HARWICH
The Pier at Harwich
◉◉ Modern British, Seafood **V**
01255 241212 | The Quay, CO12 3HH

HOCKLEY
**The Anchor Riverside Pub
and Restaurant**
◉ Modern British **V**
01702 230777 | Ferry Road,
Hullbridge, SS5 6ND

MANNINGTREE
The Mistley Thorn
◉◉ Modern British, Seafood
01206 392821 | High Street,
Mistley, CO11 1HE

SOUTHEND-ON-SEA
Holiday Inn Southend
◉ Traditional British
01702 543001 | 77 Eastwoodbury
Crescent, SS2 6XG

The Roslin Beach Hotel
◉ British
01702 586375 | Thorpe Esplanade,
Thorpe Bay, SS1 3BG

STOCK
Ellis's Restaurant
◉ Modern British
01277 829990 | Greenwoods Hotel
& Spa, Stock Road, CM4 9BE

The Hoop
◉ Modern British
01277 841137 | High Street, CM4 9BD

THORPE-LE-SOKEN
Harry's Bar & Restaurant
◉ Modern British
01255 860250 | High Street,
CO16 0EA

▶ Gloucestershire

ALMONDSBURY
Aztec Hotel & Spa
◉ Modern British
01454 201090 | Aztec West, BS32 4TS

ALVESTON
Alveston House Hotel
◉ Modern European
01454 415050 | Davids Lane,
BS35 2LA

ARLINGHAM
The Old Passage Inn
◉◉ Seafood, Modern British
01452 740547 | Passage Road,
GL2 7JR

CHELTENHAM
Cotswold Grange Hotel
⬤ Modern British, European
01242 515119 | Pittville Circus Road,
GL52 2QH

The Curry Corner Est. 1977
⬤⬤ Bangladeshi, Indian
01242 528449 | 133 Fairview Road,
GL52 2EX

The Greenway Hotel & Spa
⬤⬤ Modern British, French **V**
01242 862352 | Shurdington,
GL51 4UG

Hotel du Vin Cheltenham
⬤ French, European
01242 588450 | Parabola Road,
GL50 3AQ

Monty's Brasserie
⬤⬤ Modern British **V**
01242 227678 | George Hotel,
41 St Georges Road, GL50 3DZ

CHIPPING CAMPDEN
Fig
⬤⬤ Modern British
01386 840330 & 848928 | Upper High
Street, The Square, GL55 6AN

The Kings
⬤⬤ Modern British **V**
01386 840256 | The Square,
High Street, GL55 6AW

The Seagrave Arms
⬤⬤ Modern British
01386 840192 | Friday Street, GL55 6QH

Three Ways House
⬤ Modern British
01386 438429 | Chapel Lane,
Mickleton, GL55 6SB

CIRENCESTER
Barnsley House
⬤⬤ Modern European
01285 740000 | GL7 5EE

Jesse's Bistro
⬤⬤ Modern British
01285 641497 | 14 Blackjack Street,
GL7 2AA

CLEARWELL
**Tudor Farmhouse Hotel
& Restaurant**
⬤⬤ Modern British **V** 🍷
01594 833046 | High Street,
GL16 8JS

COLEFORD
The Miners Country Inn
⬤ Modern British, Traditional **V**
01594 836632 | Chepstow Road,
Sling, GL16 8LH

CORSE LAWN
Corse Lawn House Hotel
⬤⬤ British, French **V** 🍷
01452 780771 | GL19 4LZ

DAYLESFORD
Daylesford Farm Café
⬤ Modern British
01608 731700 | GL56 0YG

EBRINGTON
The Ebrington Arms
⬤⬤ Modern British
01386 593223 | GL55 6NH

GLOUCESTER
Hatherley Manor
⬤ Traditional British
01452 730217 | Down Hatherley Lane,
GL2 9UA

Hatton Court
⬤ Classic British, French **V**
01452 617412 | Upton Hill,
Upton St Leonards, GL4 8DE

**The Wharf House
Restaurant with Rooms**
⬤ Contemporary British
01452 332900 | Over, GL2 8DB

LOWER SLAUGHTER
The Slaughters Country Inn
⬤⬤ Modern British
01451 822143 | GL54 2HS

MORETON-IN-MARSH
Manor House Hotel
⬤⬤ Modern British **V**
01608 650501 | High Street, GL56 0LJ

Redesdale Arms
⬤ Modern **V**
01608 650308 | High Street,
GL56 0AW

White Hart Royal Hotel
⬤ Traditional British
01608 650731 | High Street,
GL56 0BA

Gloucestershire

NAILSWORTH
Wilder
@@ Modern British **V**
01453 835483 | Market Street,
GL6 0BX

Wild Garlic Restaurant and Rooms
@@ Modern British
01453 832615 | 3 Cossack Square,
GL6 0DB

NEWENT
Three Choirs Vineyards
@ Modern British
01531 890223 | GL18 1LS

SELSLEY
The Bell Inn
@@ Modern British
01453 753801 | Bell Lane, GL5 5JY

STOW-ON-THE-WOLD
The Kings Head Inn
@ British
01608 658365 | The Green,
Bledington, OX7 6XQ

Old Stocks Inn
@ Modern British
01451 830666 | The Square, GL54 1AP

The Porch House
@@ Modern British
01451 870048 | Digbeth Street,
GL54 1BN

Wyck Hill House Hotel & Spa
@@ Modern British
01451 831936 | Burford Road,
GL54 1HY

STROUD
The Bear of Rodborough
@ British, International
01453 878522 | Rodborough Common,
GL5 5DE

Burleigh Court Hotel
@@ British, Mediterranean
01453 883804 | Burleigh,
Minchinhampton, GL5 2PF

TETBURY
Calcot
@@ Modern British
01666 890391 | Calcot, GL8 8YJ

The Close Hotel
@@ Modern British
01666 502272 | 8 Long Street,
GL8 8AQ

Hare & Hounds Hotel
@@ Modern British **V**
01666 881000 | Westonbirt, GL8 8QL

THORNBURY
Ronnie's of Thornbury
@@ Modern British
01454 411137 | 11 St Mary Street,
BS35 2AB

Thornbury Castle
@@ Modern British, European
01454 281182 | Castle Street,
BS35 1HH

WINCHCOMBE
The Lion Inn
@ British, French
01242 603300 | 37 North Street,
GL54 5PS

Wesley House
@@ Modern European
01242 602366 | High Street,
GL54 5LJ

▶ Greater Manchester

BURY
Red Hall Hotel
@ Modern British
01706 822476 | Manchester Road,
Walmersley, BL9 5NA

DELPH
The Old Bell Inn
@ Modern British
01457 870130 | 5 Huddersfield Road,
OL3 5EG

The Saddleworth Hotel
@ Modern European
01457 871888 | Huddersfield Road,
OL3 5LX

DIDSBURY
HISPI
@@ Contemporary Brasserie
0161 445 3996 | 1C School Lane,
M20 6RD

MANCHESTER
Brasserie ABode
@@ European Brasserie **V**
0161 247 7744 | ABode Manchester,
107 Piccadilly, M1 2DB

George's Dining Room & Bar
❀ Modern British
0161 794 5444 | 17-21 Barton Road,
Worsley, M28 2PD

Greens
❀ Modern Vegetarian **V**
0161 434 4259 | 43 Lapwing Lane,
West Didsbury, M20 2NT

**Harvey Nichols Second
Floor Brasserie**
❀ Modern European ♟
0161 828 8899
21 New Cathedral Street, M1 1AD

Hotel Gotham
❀❀ Modern European
0161 413 0000 | 100 King Street,
M2 4WU

The Lowry Hotel
❀❀ Modern British
0161 827 4000 | 50 Dearmans
Place, Chapel Wharf, Salford,
M3 5LH

Malmaison Manchester
❀ Modern British, International
0161 278 1000 | Piccadilly, M1 3AQ

Mr Cooper's House and Garden
❀❀ International
0161 932 4128 | The Midland Hotel,
Peter Street, M60 2DS

Sweet Mandarin
❀ Chinese **V**
0161 832 8848 | 19 Copperas Street,
M4 1HS

OLDHAM
The Dining Room at White Hart Inn
❀❀ Modern British **V** ♟
01457 872566 | 51 Stockport Road,
Lydgate, OL4 4JJ

ROCHDALE
Nutters
❀ Modern British **V** ♟
01706 650167 | Edenfield Road,
Norden, OL12 7TT

The Peacock Room
❀❀ Modern British
01706 368591 | Crimble Hotel,
Crimble Lane, Bamford, OL11 4AD

WIGAN
Wrightington Hotel & Country Club
❀ Modern International
01257 425803 | Moss Lane,
Wrightington, WN6 9PB

▶ Hampshire

ALRESFORD
Pulpo Negro
❀❀ Modern Spanish
01962 732262 | 28 Broad Street,
SO24 9AQ

ALTON
The Anchor Inn
❀❀ British
01420 23261 | Lower Froyle,
GU34 4NA

ANDOVER
Esseborne Manor
❀❀ Modern British **V**
01264 736444 | Hurstbourne Tarrant,
SP11 0ER

The George and Dragon
❀ British
01264 736277 | The Square,
Hurstbourne Tarrant, SP11 0AA

BARTON-ON-SEA
Pebble Beach
❀ British, French, Mediterranean
01425 627777 | Marine Drive,
BH25 7DZ

BASINGSTOKE
Audleys Wood Hotel
❀❀ Modern British
01256 817555 | Alton Road,
RG25 2JT

Oakley Hall Hotel
❀❀ Modern International
01256 783350 | Rectory Road,
Oakley, RG23 7EL

The Sun Inn
❀❀ Modern & Classic
01256 397234 | Winchester Road,
RG25 2DJ

BAUGHURST
The Wellington Arms
❀❀ Modern British
0118 982 0110 | Baughurst Road,
RG26 5LP

Hampshire

BEAULIEU
Beaulieu Hotel
◉ British
023 8029 3344 | Beaulieu Road,
SO42 7YQ

**The Master Builder's at
Buckler's Hard**
◉ Modern British
01590 616253 | Buckler's Hard,
SO42 7XB

Monty's Inn
◉ Traditional British
01590 614986 & 612324
Palace Lane, SO42 7ZL

BRANSGORE
The Three Tuns
◉ British, European
01425 672232 | Ringwood Road,
BH23 8JH

BROCKENHURST
The Balmer Lawn Hotel
◉◉ Modern British
01590 623116 | Lyndhurst Road,
SO42 7ZB

THE PIG
◉◉ British V ♟
01590 622354 | Beaulieu Road,
SO42 7QL

Rhinefield House Hotel
◉◉ Classic, Traditional British V
01590 622922 | Rhinefield Road,
SO42 7QB

The Zen Garden Restaurant
◉ Thai
01590 623219 | The SenSpa,
Careys Manor Hotel, Lyndhurst Road,
SO42 7RH

BROOK
The Bell Inn
◉ Modern British
023 8081 2214 | SO43 7HE

BURLEY
Burley Manor
◉ British, Mediterranean
01425 403522 | Ringwood Road,
BH24 4BS

Moorhill House Hotel
◉ Modern, Traditional British
01425 403285 | BH24 4AG

CADNAM
Bartley Lodge Hotel
◉ Modern British
023 8081 2248 | Lyndhurst Road,
SO40 2NR

DROXFORD
Bakers Arms
◉ Modern British
01489 877533 | High Street, SO32 3PA

EASTLEIGH
**The Redwood Bistro
at Bishopstoke Park**
◉ British
023 8064 5100 | 1 Garnier Drive,
Bishopstoke, SO50 6HE

EMSWORTH
Fat Olives
◉◉ Modern British, Mediterranean
01243 377914 | 30 South Street,
PO10 7EH

FAREHAM
Solent Hotel & Spa
◉ Modern British, European
01489 880000 | Rookery Avenue,
Whiteley, PO15 7AJ

FARNBOROUGH
Aviator
◉◉ Modern International V
01252 555890 | Farnborough Road,
GU14 6EL

HAMBLE-LE-RICE
The Bugle
◉ Modern British
023 8045 3000 | High Street, SO31 4HA

HAYLING ISLAND
Langstone Hotel
◉◉ Modern British
023 9246 5011 | Northney Road,
PO11 0NQ

HIGHCLERE
The Yew Tree
◉◉ Modern British
01635 253360 | Hollington Cross,
RG20 9SE

HURSLEY
The King's Head
◉ Classic British
01962 775208 | Main Road,
SO21 2JW

Hampshire

LYMINGTON

The Mayflower
🌸 Modern British
01590 672160 | King's Saltern Road,
SO41 3QD

Stanwell House Hotel
🌸🌸 Modern European
01590 677123 | 14-15 High Street,
SO41 9AA

LYNDHURST

The Crown Manor House Hotel
🌸 Modern British
023 8028 2922 | High Street,
SO43 7NF

The Glasshouse
🌸🌸 Modern British, Welsh
023 8028 6129 | Forest Lodge Hotel,
Pikes Hill, Romsey Road, SO43 7AS

MILFORD ON SEA

Verveine Fishmarket Restaurant
🌸🌸 Modern Seafood
01590 642176 | 98 High Street,
SO41 0QE

NEW MILTON

Chewton Glen
🌸🌸 Modern British **V** 🍷
01425 282212 | Christchurch Road,
BH25 6QS

See advert on page 358

The Kitchen
🌸 Modern, International
01425 275341 | Chewton Glen,
Christchurch Road, BH25 6QS

See advert on page 358

NORTHINGTON

The Woolpack Inn
🌸 Classic British
01962 734184 | Totford, SO24 9TJ

OLD BURGHCLERE

The Dew Pond Restaurant
🌸 British, European
01635 278408 | RG20 9LH

OTTERBOURNE

The White Horse
🌸 Modern & Traditional British
01962 712830 | Main Road,
SO21 2EQ

PETERSFIELD

Langrish House
🌸🌸 Traditional British
01730 266941 | Langrish, GU32 1RN

The Old Drum
🌸 Modern British
01730 300208 | 16 Chapel Street,
GU32 3DP

The Thomas Lord
🌸 Modern British
01730 829244 | High Street,
West Meon, GU32 1LN

PORTSMOUTH

Restaurant 27
🌸🌸 Modern European **V**
023 9287 6272 | 27a South Parade,
PO5 2JF

ROMSEY

The Three Tuns
🌸 Modern British
01794 512639 | 58 Middlebridge Street,
SO51 8HL

The White Horse Hotel & Brasserie
🌸🌸 Modern British
01794 512431 | 19 Market Place,
SO51 8ZJ

See advert on page 359

ROTHERWICK

The Oak Room Restaurant
🌸🌸 British, French **V**
01256 764881 | Tylney Hall Hotel,
Ridge Lane, RG27 9AZ

ST MARY BOURNE

Bourne Valley Inn
🌸 British
01264 738361 | SP11 6BT

SOUTHAMPTON

Best Western Chilworth Manor
🌸 Modern British
023 8076 7333 | Chilworth, SO16 7PT

Quay Fifteen
🌸 Modern International
023 8033 6615 | Shamrock Quay,
William Street, SO14 5QL

STOCKBRIDGE

The Greyhound on the Test
🌸🌸 Modern British
01264 810833 | 31 High Street,
SO20 6EY

357

CHEWTON GLEN

HAMPSHIRE

An English Original...

At Chewton Glen we are fortunate enough to have
two fantastic dining options, The Dining Room and The Kitchen.

The Dining Room, is a truly cosmopolitan and quintessentially
English restaurant. Offering a nexus of beautiful conservatories,
intimate dining spaces and a stunning open wine room, The
Dining Room is as formal or relaxed as the mood takes you.
An open format grill menu has been carefully created for you
to enjoy old Chewton Glen favourites as well as innovative
creations from our present kitchen brigade.

The Kitchen, a purpose-built cookery school and relaxed dining
space for enjoying and learning about food. An informal dining
experience with an open plan layout offers you the chance to
watch the Chefs at work. The à la carte menu features
wood-fired pizzas, gourmet burgers,
superfood salads and much more...

**Call 01425 282212 or email reservations@chewtonglen.com
to book your table...**

Chewton Glen | New Forest | Hampshire | BH25 6QS

chewtonglen.com

RELAIS &
CHATEAUX

STOCKBRIDGE *continued*

The Peat Spade Inn
◉ Modern British
01264 810612 | Village Street,
Longstock, SO20 6DR

The Three Cups Inn
◉ Modern & Traditional British
01264 810527 | High Street,
SO20 6HB

WINCHESTER
The Black Rat
◉ Modern British
01962 844465 | 88 Chesil Street,
SO23 0HX

The Chesil Rectory
◉◉ Modern British
01962 851555 | 1 Chesil Street,
SO23 0HU

Holiday Inn Winchester
◉◉ Modern British
01962 670700 | Telegraph Way,
Morn Hill, SO21 1HZ

Hotel du Vin Winchester
◉ Traditional British, French
01962 841414 | 14 Southgate Street,
SO23 9EF

Marwell Hotel
◉◉ Modern European
01962 777681 | Thompsons Lane,
Colden Common, Marwell,
SO21 1JY

Running Horse Inn
◉◉ Modern International, British
01962 880218 | 88 Main Road,
Littleton, SO22 6QS

The Wykeham Arms
◉◉ Modern British
01962 853834 | 75 Kingsgate Street,
SO23 9PE

WOODLANDS
Woodlands Lodge Hotel
◉ Modern British
023 8029 2257 | Bartley Road,
Woodlands, SO40 7GN

Herefordshire

YATELEY
Casa Hotel & Marco Pierre White Steakhouse, Bar & Grill
☖ French, British
01252 873275 | Handford Lane, GU46 6BT

▶ Herefordshire

AYMESTREY
The Riverside at Aymestrey
☖☖ Modern British
01568 708440 | The Riverside Inn, HR6 9ST

EWYAS HAROLD
The Temple Bar Inn
☖☖ Modern British
01981 240423 | HR2 0EU

HEREFORD
Castle House
☖☖ Modern British
01432 356321 | Castle Street, HR1 2NW

LEDBURY
Feathers Hotel
☖ Modern British
01531 635266 | High Street, HR8 1DS

LEINTWARDINE
The Lion
☖ Modern British
01547 540203 & 540747
High Street, SY7 0JZ

ROSS-ON-WYE
The Chase Hotel
☖ British, Modern European
01989 763161 | Gloucester Road, HR9 5LH

Glewstone Court Country House
☖☖ Modern British, European
01989 770367 | Glewstone, HR9 6AW

Wilton Court Restaurant with Rooms
☖☖ Modern British
01989 562569 | Wilton Lane, HR9 6AQ

SYMONDS YAT [EAST]
Saracens Head Inn
☖ Modern British
01600 890435 | HR9 6JL

UPPER SAPEY
The Baiting House
☖☖ Modern British
01886 853201 & 07825 232843
Stourport Road, WR6 6XT

▶ Hertfordshire

BERKHAMSTED
The Gatsby
☖ Modern British
01442 870403 | 97 High Street, HP4 2DG

Porters Restaurant
☖ British
01442 876 666 | 300 High Street, HP4 1ZZ

BISHOP'S STORTFORD
Down Hall Country House Hotel
☖ Contemporary British
01279 731441 | Hatfield Heath, CM22 7AS

CHANDLER'S CROSS
The Stables Restaurant at The Grove
☖ Modern British
01923 807807 | WD3 4TG

DATCHWORTH
The Tilbury
☖☖ Modern British ♟
01438 815550 | Watton Road, SG3 6TB

ELSTREE
Laura Ashley The Manor
☖☖ Modern British
020 8327 4700 | Barnet Lane, WD6 3RE

FLAUNDEN
Bricklayers Arms
☖ Traditional French
01442 833322 | Black Robin Lane, Hogpits Bottom, HP3 0PH

HATFIELD
Beales Hotel
☖ Modern British
01707 288500 | Comet Way, AL10 9NG

HEMEL HEMPSTEAD
Aubrey Park Hotel
☖ Modern European
01582 792105 | Hemel Hempstead Road, Redbourn, AL3 7AF

HITCHIN
Needham House Hotel
◉◉ Modern British
01462 417240 | Blakemore End Road,
Little Wymondley, SG4 7JJ

ST ALBANS
Chez Mumtaj
◉◉ French, Asian
01727 800033 | Centurian House,
136-142 London Road, AL1 1PQ

See advert on page 362

St Michael's Manor
◉◉ Modern British, European
01727 864444 | Fishpool Street,
AL3 4RY

The Restaurant at Sopwell House
◉ Modern British
01727 864477 | Cottonmill Lane,
Sopwell, AL1 2HQ

TRING
Pendley Manor Hotel
◉◉ Traditional British
01442 891891 | Cow Lane,
HP23 5QY

WELWYN
The Waggoners
◉ French
01707 324241 | Brickwall Close,
Ayot Green, AL6 9AA

The Wellington
◉ Modern British
01438 714036 | High Street,
AL6 9LZ

The White Hart
◉ Modern British
01438 715353 | 2 Prospect Place,
AL6 9EN

WELWYN GARDEN CITY
Tewin Bury Farm Hotel
◉◉ Modern British V
01438 717793 | Hertford Road
(B1000), AL6 0JB

WILLIAN
The Fox
◉◉ Modern British
01462 480233 | SG6 2AE

▶ **Isle of Wight**
NEWPORT
Thompsons
◉◉ Modern British
01983 526118 | 11 Town Lane,
PO30 1JU

SEAVIEW
Seaview Hotel
◉ British
01983 612711 | High Street,
PO34 5EX

SHANKLIN
The Nightingale Hotel
◉ International
01983 862742 | 3 Queens Road,
PO37 6AN

VENTNOR
The Leconfield
◉ Traditional British
01983 852196 | 85 Leeson Road,
Upper Bonchurch, PO38 1PU

The Royal Hotel
◉◉ Modern British V
01983 852186 | Belgrave Road,
PO38 1JJ

YARMOUTH
The George Hotel
◉◉ Modern British, Mediterranean
01983 760331 | Quay Street, PO41 0PE

▶ **Kent**
BOUGHTON MONCHELSEA
The Mulberry Tree
◉◉ Modern British
01622 749082 | Hermitage Lane,
ME17 4DA

CANTERBURY
ABode Canterbury
◉◉ Modern European V
01227 766266 | High Street, CT1 2RX

Best Western Abbots Barton Hotel
◉ Modern British
01227 760341 | New Dover Road,
CT1 3DU

Deeson's British Restaurant
◉ Modern British
01227 767854 | 25-26 Sun Street,
CT1 2HX

CANTERBURY *continued*
The Goods Shed Restaurant
◉ British
01227 459153 | Station Road West,
CT2 8AN

CRUNDALE
The Compasses Inn
◉◉ Modern British
01227 700300 | Sole Street, CT4 7ES

DARTFORD
**Rowhill Grange Hotel
& Utopia Spa**
◉◉ Modern European V
01322 615136 | Wilmington,
DA2 7QH

DEAL
Dunkerleys Hotel & Restaurant
◉◉ Modern British
01304 375016 | 19 Beach Street,
CT14 7AH

DOVER
The Marquis at Alkham
◉◉ Modern British
01304 873410 | Alkham Valley Road,
Alkham, CT15 7DF

EGERTON
Frasers
◉◉ Modern British
01233 756122 | Coldharbour Farm,
TN27 9DD

FAVERSHAM
**Faversham Creek
& Red Sails Restaurant**
◉ Modern British
01795 533535 | Conduit Street,
ME13 7BH

Read's Restaurant
◉◉ Modern British
01795 535344 | Macknade Manor,
Canterbury Road, ME13 8XE

FAWKHAM GREEN
Brandshatch Place Hotel & Spa
◉◉ Modern British
01474 875000 | Brands Hatch Road,
DA3 8NQ

FOLKESTONE
Rocksalt Rooms
◉◉ Modern British V
01303 212070 | 2 Back Street,
CT19 6NN

GRAFTY GREEN
Who'd A Thought It
◉◉ Seafood V
01622 858951 | Headcorn Road,
ME17 2AR

HYTHE
Hythe Imperial
◉ British V
01303 267441 | Princes Parade,
CT21 6AE

Saltwood on the Green
◉ Contemporary British
01303 237800 | The Green,
Saltwood, CT21 4PS

LENHAM
Chilston Park Hotel
◉◉ Modern British
01622 859803 | Sandway, ME17 2BE

LEYSDOWN-ON-SEA
The Ferry House Inn
◉ British
01795 510214 | Harty Ferry Road,
ME12 4BQ

MAIDSTONE
Fish on the Green
◉◉ British, French
01622 738300 | Church Lane,
Bearsted Green, ME14 4EJ

MARGATE
The Ambrette
◉ Modern Indian
01843 231504 | 44 King Street,
CT9 1QE

Sands Hotel
◉◉ Modern European
01843 228228 | 16 Marine Drive,
CT9 1DH

ROCHESTER
Topes Restaurant
◉◉ Modern British
01634 845270 | 60 High Street,
ME1 1JY

SANDWICH
The Lodge at Prince's
◉◉ Modern British
01304 611118 | Prince's Drive,
Sandwich Bay, CT13 9QB

Kent

STALISFIELD GREEN
The Plough Inn
◉ Modern British
01795 890256 | ME13 0HY

TENTERDEN
The Swan Wine Kitchen
◉◉ European
01580 761616 | Chapel Down Winery,
Small Hythe Road, TN30 7NG

TUNBRIDGE WELLS (ROYAL)
Hotel du Vin Tunbridge Wells
◉ Modern French
01892 526455 | Crescent Road, TN1 2LY

The Kentish Hare
◉◉ Modern British V
01892 525709 | 95 Bidborough Ridge,
Bidborough, TN3 0XB

The Spa Hotel
◉◉ Modern, Traditional British
01892 520331 | Mount Ephraim,
TN4 8XJ

The Twenty Six
◉◉ Modern British
01892 544607 | 15a Church Road,
Southborough, TN4 0RX

WEST MALLING
The Swan
◉◉ Modern British
01732 521910 & 521918
35 Swan Street, ME19 6JU

WHITSTABLE
The Sportsman
◉◉ Modern British
01227 273370 | Faversham Road,
Seasalter, CT5 4BP

WROTHAM
The Bull
◉◉ Modern British ♟
01732 789800 | Bull Lane, TN15 7RF

WYE
Wife of Bath
◉◉ Modern Spanish
01233 812232 | 4 Upper Bridge Street,
TN25 5AF

▶ Lancashire

BLACKBURN
The Clog & Billycock
◉ Traditional British V
01254 201163 | Billinge End Road,
Pleasington, BB2 6QB

The Millstone at Mellor
◉◉ Modern British
01254 813333 | Church Lane,
Mellor, BB2 7JR

BURNLEY
White Swan at Fence
◉◉ Modern British
01282 611773 | 300 Wheatley Lane
Road, BB12 9QA

BURROW
The Highwayman
◉ Traditional British
01524 273338 | LA6 2RJ

CLITHEROE
The Assheton Arms
◉ Contemporary, Seafood
01200 441227 | Downham, BB7 4BJ

The Parkers Arms
◉ Modern British
01200 446236 | BB7 3DY

GREAT ECCLESTON
The Cartford Inn
◉ Modern British
01995 670166 | Cartford Lane,
PR3 0YP

LANCASTER
Lancaster House
◉ Traditional British
01524 844822 | Green Lane, Ellel,
LA1 4GJ

LEYLAND
Hallmark Hotel Preston Leyland
◉ Modern British
01772 422922 | Leyland Way, PR25 4JX

LOWER BARTLE
Bartle Hall Hotel
◉ Modern British
01772 690506 | Lea Lane, PR4 0HA

LYTHAM ST ANNES
Bedford Hotel
◉ Modern British
01253 724636 | 307-313 Clifton
Drive South, FY8 1HN

Best Western Glendower Hotel
@ Traditional British
01253 723241 | North Promenade,
FY8 2NQ

Clifton Arms Hotel
@@ British
01253 739898 | West Beach,
Lytham, FY8 5QJ

Greens Bistro
@ Modern British
01253 789990 | 3-9 St Andrews Road
South, St Annes-on-Sea, FY8 1SX

MORECAMBE
Best Western Lothersdale Hotel
@ Modern British
01524 416404 | 320-323 Marine Road,
LA4 5AA

The Midland
@ Modern British
01524 424000 | Marine Road West,
LA4 4BU

RILEY GREEN
The Royal Oak
@ Traditional British V
01254 201445 | Blackburn Old Road,
PR5 0SL

THORNTON
Twelve Restaurant and Lounge Bar
@@ Modern British
01253 821212 | Marsh Mill Village,
Marsh Mill in-Wyre, Fleetwood Road
North, FY5 4JZ
See advert on page 366

WHALLEY
The Three Fishes
@ British
01254 826888 | Mitton Road, Mitton,
BB7 9PQ

WHITEWELL
The Inn at Whitewell
@ Modern British
01200 448222 | Forest of Bowland,
Clitheroe, BB7 3AT

WREA GREEN
The Spa Hotel at Ribby Hall Village
@@ Modern & Traditional
01772 674484 | Ribby Hall Village,
Ribby Road, PR4 2PR

The Villa Country House Hotel
@ Classic British
01772 804040 | Moss Side Lane,
PR4 2PE

WRIGHTINGTON
Corner House
@ Modern British
01257 451400 | Wrightington Bar,
WN6 9SE

▶ Leicestershire

EAST MIDLANDS AIRPORT
Best Western Premier
Yew Lodge Hotel & Spa
@ British
01509 672518 | Packington Hill,
DE74 2DF

LEICESTER
Belmont Hotel
@@ Modern British
0116 254 4773 | De Montfort Street,
LE1 7GR

Maiyango Restaurant
@ Modern International V
0116 251 8898 | 13-21 St Nicholas
Place, LE1 4LD

LONG WHATTON
The Royal Oak
@ Modern British
01509 843694 | 26 The Green, LE12 5DR

MARKET HARBOROUGH
Three Swans Hotel
@ Modern, International
01858 466644 | 21 High Street,
LE16 7NJ

MELTON MOWBRAY
Stapleford Park
@@ Modern International, British V ♛
01572 787000 | Stapleford, LE14 2EF

MOUNTSORREL
John's House
@@ Modern British
01509 415569
139-141 Loughborough Road, LE12 7AR

NORTH KILWORTH
Kilworth House Hotel & Theatre
@@ Modern British V
01858 880058 | Lutterworth Road,
LE17 6JE

TWELVE

RESTAURANT & LOUNGE BAR

for Culinary Excellence
2007 - 2017

Marsh Mill Village, Fleetwood Road North
Thornton Cleveleys, Lancashire, FY5 4JZ

T: **01253 82 12 12**
twelve-restaurant.co.uk
twelveeventmanagement.co.uk

OPENING HOURS:
Tuesday - Saturday for dinner | Sundays 12noon - 8.00pm

- Situated beneath a beautifully restored 18th century windmill
- 5 minute drive from Blackpool
- British cuisine with a modern twist

SHAWELL
The White Swan
⑳ Modern European **V**
01788 860357 | LE17 6AG

WYMESWOLD
Hammer & Pincers
⑳⑳ British, European **V**
01509 880735 | 5 East Road,
LE12 6ST

▶ Lincolnshire

GREAT LIMBER
The New Inn
⑳⑳ Modern British, International
01469 569998 & 560405
2 High Street, DN37 8JL

HORNCASTLE
Magpies Restaurant with Rooms
⑳⑳ Modern British
01507 527004 | 73 East Street,
LN9 6AA

HOUGH-ON-THE-HILL
The Brownlow Arms
⑳ British
01400 250234 | High Road, NG32 2AZ

LINCOLN
Branston Hall Hotel
⑳ Modern British **V**
01522 793305 | Branston Park,
Branston, LN4 1PD

The Lincoln Hotel
⑳ Modern British **V**
01522 520348 | Eastgate, LN2 1PN

The Old Bakery
⑳⑳ Modern International
01522 576057 | 26-28 Burton Road,
LN1 3LB

Tower Hotel
⑳ Modern British
01522 529999 | 38 Westgate,
LN1 3BD

Washingborough Hall Hotel
⑳⑳ Traditional British
01522 790340 | Church Hill,
Washingborough, LN4 1BE

The White Hart
⑳ British, French
01522 526222 & 563293
Bailgate, LN1 3AR

LOUTH
Brackenborough Hotel
⑳ Modern British
01507 609169 | Cordeaux Corner,
Brackenborough, LN11 0SZ

MARKET RASEN
The Advocate Arms
⑳⑳ Modern European, British
01673 842364 | 2 Queen Street,
LN8 3EH

SCOTTER
The White Swan
⑳ Modern British
01724 763061 | 9 The Green,
DN21 3UD

SCUNTHORPE
Forest Pines Hotel & Golf Resort
⑳ Modern British
01652 650770 | Ermine Street,
Broughton, DN20 0AQ

San Pietro Restaurant Rooms
⑳⑳ Modern Mediterranean
01724 277774 | 11 High Street East,
DN15 6UH

SLEAFORD
The Bustard Inn & Restaurant
⑳ Modern British
01529 488250 | 44 Main Street,
South Rauceby, NG34 8QG

SOUTH FERRIBY
The Hope and Anchor Pub
⑳⑳ Modern British
01652 635334 | Sluice Road,
DN18 6JQ

STALLINGBOROUGH
Stallingborough Grange Hotel
⑳ English, European **V**
01469 561302 | Riby Road, DN41 8BU

STAMFORD
The Bull & Swan at Burghley
⑳ Traditional British
01780 766412 | High Street, St Martins,
PE9 2LJ

STAMFORD *continued*
The George of Stamford
◉ Traditional British **V** 🍷
01780 750750 | 71 St Martins, PE9 2LB

No.3 The Yard
◉ British, European
01780 756080 | 3 Ironmonger Street,
PE9 1PL

The William Cecil
◉◉ Modern British
01780 750070 | High Street,
St Martins, PE9 2LJ

WOOLSTHORPE
Chequers Inn
◉ Modern British
01476 870701 | Main Street, NG32 1LU

▶ London
LONDON E1
Blanchette East
◉ Modern French, North African
020 7729 7939 | 204 Brick Lane, E1 6SA

Café Spice Namasté
◉ Indian
020 7488 9242 | 16 Prescot Street,
E1 8AZ

Canto Corvino
◉◉ Modern Italian
020 7655 0390 | 21 Artillery Lane,
E1 7HA

Galvin HOP
◉◉ Modern British, International
020 7299 0404 | 35 Spital Square,
E1 6DY

Lyle's
◉◉ Modern British **V**
020 3011 5911 | Tea Building,
56 Shoreditch High Street, E1 6JJ

Super Tuscan
◉ Italian
020 7247 8717 | 8a Artillery Passage,
E1 7LJ

Taberna do Mercado
◉◉ Mediterranean, Portuguese
020 7375 0649 | Old Spitalfields
Market, 107b Commercial Street,
E1 6BG

Wright Brothers Spitalfields
◉◉ Modern British, Seafood
020 7377 8706 | 8-9 Lamb Street,
Old Spitalfields Market, E1 6EA

LONDON E2
Brawn
◉◉ Traditional European 🍷
020 7729 5692 | 49 Columbia Road,
E2 7RG

Marksman
◉◉ Modern British
020 7739 7393 | 254 Hackney Road,
E2 7SJ

LONDON E8
Ellory
◉◉ Modern European **V**
020 3095 9455 | Netil House,
1 Westgate Street, Hackney, E8 3RL

LONDON E9
The Empress
◉◉ Modern British
020 8533 5123 | 130 Lauriston Road,
Victoria Park, E9 7LH

LONDON E14
Plateau
◉◉ Modern French 🍷
020 7715 7100 | 4th Floor,
Canada Place, Canada Square,
Canary Wharf, E14 5ER

Quadrato
◉ Italian
020 7510 1999 & 7510 1858
46 Westferry Circus, Canary Wharf,
E14 8RS

Roka Canary Wharf
◉◉ Japanese
020 7636 5228 | 1st Floor,
40 Canada Square, E14 5FW

LONDON EC1
The Bleeding Heart
◉◉ Modern French
020 7242 2056 | Bleeding Heart Yard,
Off Greville Street, EC1N 8SJ

Le Café du Marché
◉ French
020 7608 1609 | Charterhouse Mews,
Charterhouse Square, EC1M 6AH

Comptoir Gascon
◉ Traditional European
020 7608 0851 | 61-63 Charterhouse
Street, EC1M 6HJ

Hix Oyster & Chop House
◉ Modern British **V**
020 7017 1930 | 36-37 Greenhill Rents,
Cowcross Street, EC1M 6BN

Luca
⊚ Italian
020 3859 3000 | 88 St John Street,
EC1M 4EH

Malmaison Charterhouse Square
⊚ Modern French
020 3750 9402 | 18-21 Charterhouse
Square, Clerkenwell, EC1M 6AH

The Modern Pantry Clerkenwell
⊚⊚ Modern, Fusion
020 7553 9210 | 47-48 St John's
Square, Clerkenwell, EC1V 4JJ

**The Montcalm London City
at The Brewery**
⊚ Traditional British
020 7614 0100 | 52 Chiswell Street,
EC1Y 4SB

Moro
⊚ Mediterranean, North African
020 7833 8336 | 34-36 Exmouth Market,
EC1R 4QE

St John
⊚⊚ British
020 7251 0848 | 26 St John Street,
EC1M 4AY

Smiths of Smithfield, Top Floor
⊚⊚ Modern British
020 7251 7950 | 67-77 Charterhouse
Street, EC1M 6HJ

LONDON EC2
L'Anima
⊚⊚ Italian
020 7422 7000 | 1 Snowden Street,
Broadgate West, EC2A 2DQ

L'Anima Café
⊚ Italian
020 7422 7080 | 10 Appold Street,
EC2A 2AP

Boisdale of Bishopsgate
⊚ Traditional British, French, Scottish
020 7283 1763 | Swedeland Court,
202 Bishopsgate, EC2M 4NR

Coq d'Argent
⊚⊚ French V
020 7395 5000 | 1 Poultry, EC2R 8EJ

Duck & Waffle
⊚⊚ British, European
020 3640 7310 | 110 Bishopsgate,
EC2N 4AY

Eastway Brasserie
⊚ British
020 7618 7400 | ANdAZ Liverpool
Street, 40 Liverpool Street,
EC2M 7QN

Eyre Brothers
⊚⊚ Spanish, Portuguese
020 7613 5346 | 70 Leonard Street,
EC2A 4QX

Manicomio City
⊚ Modern Italian
020 7726 5010 | Gutter Lane, EC2V 8AS

Miyako
⊚ Japanese V
020 7618 7100 | ANdAZ London,
40 Liverpool Street, EC2M 7QN

Popolo Shoreditch
⊚⊚ Italian
020 7729 4299 | 26 Rivington Street,
EC2A 3DU

SUSHISAMBA London
⊚⊚ Japanese, Brazilian, Peruvian ♟
020 3640 7330 | 110 Bishopsgate,
EC2N 4AY

Temple and Sons
⊚⊚ Modern British
020 7877 7710 | 22 Old Broad Street,
EC2N 1HQ

LONDON EC3
Caravaggio
⊚ Modern Italian
020 7626 6206 | 107-112 Leadenhall
Street, EC3A 4AF

See advert on page 370

Chamberlain's Restaurant
⊚⊚ Modern British, Seafood V
020 7648 8690 & 7648 8694
23-25 Leadenhall Market, EC3V 1LR

James Cochran EC3
⊚⊚ Modern British, Caribbean
020 3302 0310 | 19 Bevis Marks,
Liverpool Street, EC3A 7JB

Restaurant Sauterelle
⊚⊚ Modern European, French V
020 7618 2483 | The Royal Exchange,
EC3V 3LR

LONDON EC4
28-50 Wine Workshop & Kitchen
⊚⊚ Modern European
020 7242 8877 | 140 Fetter Lane,
EC4A 1BT

London EC4–N1

LONDON EC4 *continued*
Barbecoa
◉ Modern
020 3005 8555 | 20 New Change
Passage, EC4M 9AG

Bread Street Kitchen
◉◉ British, European
020 3030 4050 | 10 Bread Street,
EC4M 9AJ

The Chancery
◉◉ Modern European
020 7831 4000 | 9 Cursitor Street,
EC4A 1LL

Chinese Cricket Club
◉ Chinese **V**
020 7438 8051 | Crowne Plaza London
- The City, 19 New Bridge Street,
EC4V 6DB

Diciannove
◉◉ Italian
020 7438 8052 | Crowne Plaza London
- The City, 19 New Bridge Street,
EC4V 6DB

Lutyens Restaurant
◉◉ Modern British ♟
020 7583 8385 | 85 Fleet Street,
EC4Y 1AE

Vanilla Black
◉◉ Modern Vegetarian **V**
020 7242 2622 | 17-18 Tooks Court,
EC4A 1LB

**The White Swan Pub
& Dining Room**
◉ Modern British
020 7242 9696 | 108 Fetter Lane,
EC4A 1ES

LONDON N1
The Drapers Arms
◉ British
020 7619 0348 | 44 Barnsbury Street,
N1 1ER

Frederick's Restaurant
◉ Modern British
020 7359 2888 | 106-110 Islington
High Street, Camden Passage, N1 8EG

Grain Store
◎◎ Modern, European
020 7324 4466 | Granary Square,
1-3 Stable Square, King's Cross,
N1C 4AB

Jamie Oliver's Fifteen
◎ Modern British
020 3375 1515 | 15 Westland Place,
N1 7LP

Searcys St Pancras Grand
◎ Modern, Northern European
020 7870 9900 | Grand Terrace,
Upper Concourse,
St Pancras International, N1C 4QL

Smokehouse
◎ Modern American
020 7354 1144 | 63-69 Canonbury Road,
Islington, N1 2DG

Trullo
◎◎ Italian
020 7226 2733 |
300-302 St Paul's Road, N1 2LH

LONDON NW1
Gilgamesh Restaurant Lounge
◎ Pan Asian
020 7428 5757 | The Stables Market,
Chalk Farm Road, NW1 8AH

Meliã White House
◎◎ Spanish, Mediterranean
020 7391 3000 | Albany Street,
Regent's Park, NW1 3UP

Michael Nadra Primrose Hill
◎◎ Modern European
020 7722 2800 | 42 Gloucester Avenue,
NW1 8JD

Pullman London St Pancras
◎ Modern European
020 7666 9000 | 100-110 Euston Road,
NW1 2AJ

The Winter Garden
◎◎ British, Mediterranean
020 7631 8000 | The Landmark
London, 222 Marylebone Road,
NW1 6JQ

LONDON NW3
Manna
◎ International, Vegan
020 7722 8028 | 4 Erskine Road,
Primrose Hill, NW3 3AJ

XO
◎ Pan Asian
020 7433 0888 | 29 Belsize Lane,
NW3 5AS

LONDON SE1
The Anchor & Hope
◎ British, European
020 7928 9898 | 36 The Cut, SE1 8LP

Chino Latino London
◎◎ Modern Pan Asian, Peruvian V
020 7769 2500 | Park Plaza London
Riverbank, 18 Albert Embankment,
SE1 7TJ

See advert on page 372

H10 London Waterloo Hotel
◎ European
020 7928 4062
284-302 Waterloo Road, SE1 8RQ

Hutong
◎◎ Northern Chinese V
020 3011 1257 | Level 33, The Shard,
31 St Thomas Street, SE1 9RY

Magdalen
◎◎ British, European
020 7403 1342 | 152 Tooley Street,
SE1 2TU

Oblix
◎ Modern International
020 7268 6700 | Level 32, The Shard,
31 St Thomas Street, SE1 9RY

The Oxo Tower Restaurant
◎◎ Modern British V ♥
020 7803 3888 | 8th Floor, Oxo Tower
Wharf, Barge House Street, SE1 9PH

Park Plaza County Hall London
◎ Modern Italian
020 7021 1919 | 1 Addington Street,
SE1 7RY

**Park Plaza Westminster Bridge
London**
◎◎ Modern French
020 7620 7200 | SE1 7UT

Pizarro
◎◎ Traditional Spanish
020 7378 9455 | 194 Bermondsey
Street, SE1 3TQ

LONDON SE1 *continued*
Le Pont de la Tour
◉◉ Modern French
020 7403 8403 | The Butlers Wharf
Building, 36d Shad Thames, SE1 2YE

Roast
◉ British V
020 300 6611 | The Floral Hall, Borough
Market, Stoney Street, SE1 1TL

**RSJ, The Restaurant
on the South Bank**
◉ Modern European
020 7928 4554 | 33 Coin Street,
SE1 9NR

Shangri-La Hotel at The Shard
◉ British, European,
Asian influences V ♟
020 7234 8008 | 31 St Thomas Street,
SE1 9QU

Skylon
◉ Modern British V
020 7654 7800 | Royal Festival Hall,
Southbank Centre, SE1 8XX

Union Street Café
◉◉ Italian, Mediterranean
020 7592 7977 | 47-51 Great Suffolk
Street, SE1 0BS

LONDON SE3
Chapters All Day Dining
◉◉ Modern British
020 8333 2666 | 43-45 Montpelier Vale,
Blackheath Village, SE3 0TJ

LONDON SE10
Craft London
◉◉ Modern British
020 8465 5910 | Peninsula Square,
SE10 0SQ

LONDON SE22
Franklins
◉ British
020 8299 9598 | 157 Lordship Lane,
East Dulwich, SE22 8HX

The Palmerston
◉ Modern British, European
020 8693 1629 | 91 Lordship Lane,
East Dulwich, SE22 8EP

LONDON SE23
Babur
◉◉ Modern Indian
020 8291 2400 | 119 Brockley Rise,
Forest Hill, SE23 1JP

See advert on page 374

Aquavit
◉◉ Nordic
020 7024 9848 | St James's Market,
1 Carlton Street, SW1Y 4QQ

LONDON SW1
Avenue
◉ Modern British, American
020 7321 2111 | 7-9 St James's Street,
SW1A 1EE

Bar Boulud
◉◉ French, American ♟
020 7201 3899 | Mandarin Oriental
Hyde Park, 66 Knightsbridge, SW1X 7LA

Boisdale of Belgravia
◉ Modern British
020 7730 6922 | 15 Eccleston Street,
SW1W 9LX

Café Murano
◉◉ Northern Italian
020 3371 5559 | 33 St James's Street,
SW1A 1HD

Le Caprice
◉ Modern European V
020 7629 2239 | Arlington House,
Arlington Street, SW1A 1RJ

Cavendish London
◉◉ Modern European
020 7930 2111 | 81 Jermyn Street,
SW1Y 6JF

Caxton Grill
◉ Modern European
020 7222 7888 | St Ermin's Hotel,
2 Caxton Street, SW1H 0QW

**Le Chinois at Millennium
Knightsbridge**
◉ Chinese
020 7201 6330 | 17 Sloane Street,
Knightsbridge, SW1X 9NU

Chutney Mary
◉◉ Modern Indian ♟
020 7629 6688 | 73 St James's Street,
SW1A 1PH

See advert on page 382

A smart,
comfortable,
space with
fantastic food
babur
119 Brockley Rise, Forest Hill, London SE23 1JP
020 8291 2400
www.babur.info mail@babur.info

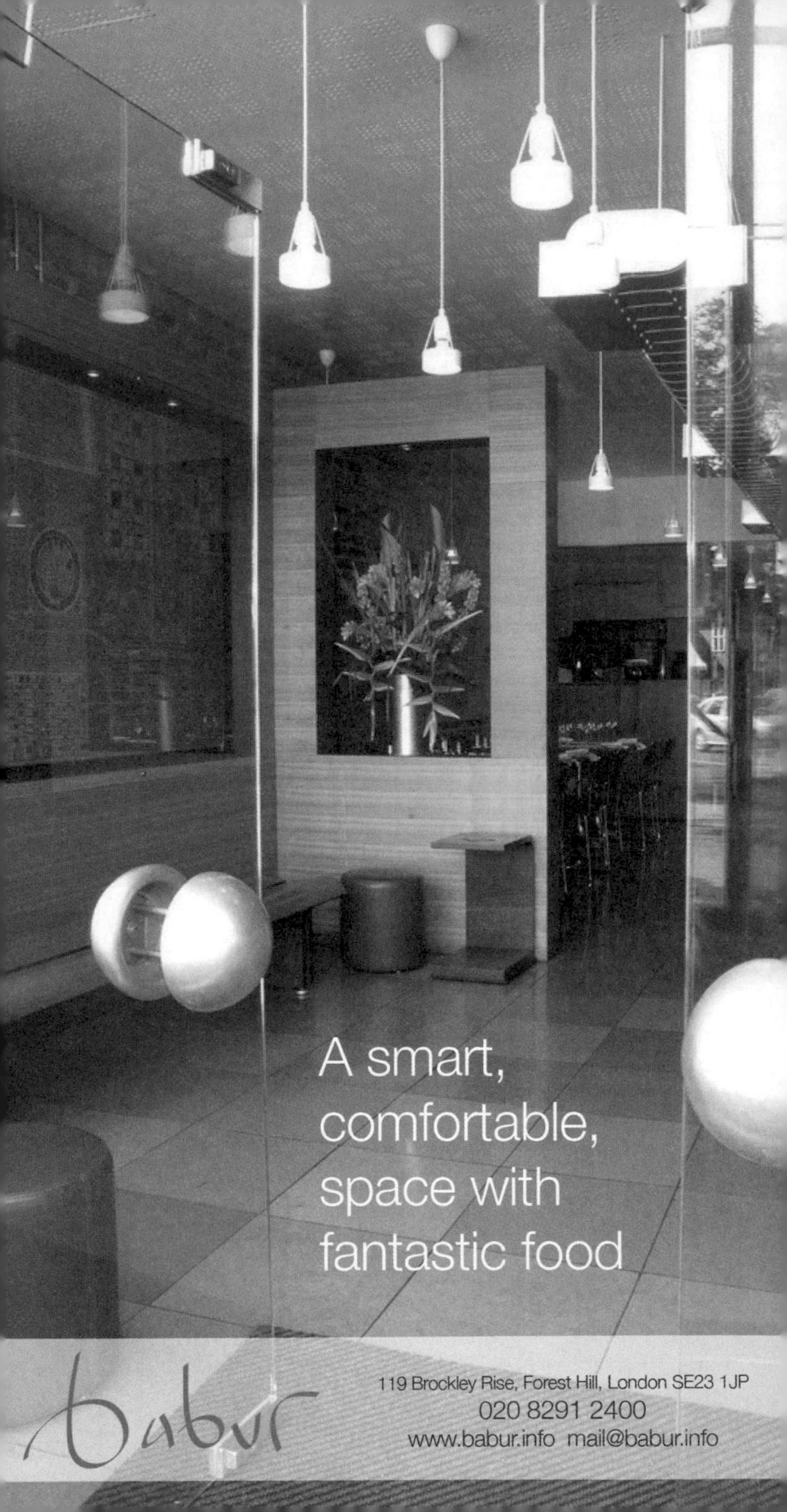

LONDON SW1 *continued*

The Cinnamon Club
◉◉ Modern Indian
020 7222 2555 | The Old Westminster Library, 30-32 Great Smith Street, SW1P 3BU

Colbert
◉ French V
020 7730 2804 | 50-52 Sloane Square, Chelsea, SW1W 8AX

Enoteca Turi
◉◉ Modern Italian ♥
020 7730 6327 | 87 Pimlico Road, SW1W 8PH

Estiatorio Milos
◉◉ Greek, Mediterranean, Seafood
020 7839 2080 | 1 Regent Street, St James's, SW1Y 4NR

**The Game Bird
at The Stafford London**
◉◉ Classic British
020 7518 1234 & 7518 1124
16-18 St James's Place, SW1A 1NJ

Grand Imperial London
◉ Cantonese, Chinese V
020 7821 8898 | The Grosvenor, 101 Buckingham Palace Road, SW1W 0SJ

Hai Cenato
◉◉ New York Italian
020 3816 9320 | Cardinal Place, 2 Sir Simon Milton Square, SW1E 5DJ

Il Convivio
◉◉ Modern Italian
020 7730 4099 | 143 Ebury Street, SW1W 9QN

See advert below

Ken Lo's Memories of China
◉ Chinese
020 7730 7734 | 65-69 Ebury Street, SW1W 0NZ

Lorne Restaurant
◉◉ Modern British & European
020 3327 0210 | 76 Wilton Road, SW1V 1DE

London SW1–SW5

LONDON SW1 *continued*
Osteria Dell'Angolo
◉ Italian
020 3268 1077 | 47 Marsham Street,
SW1P 3DR

Park Plaza Victoria London
◉◉ Italian
020 7769 9771 | 239 Vauxhall Bridge
Road, SW1V 1EQ

Quaglino's
◉◉ European
020 7930 6767 | 16 Bury Street,
SW1Y 6AJ

Quilon
◉◉ Indian ☻
020 7821 1899 | 41 Buckingham Gate,
SW1E 6AF

The Royal Horseguards
◉ Modern British
020 7451 9333 | 2 Whitehall Court,
SW1A 2EJ

The Rubens at the Palace
◉◉ Modern British
020 7834 6600 | 39 Buckingham
Palace Road, SW1W 0PS

Sake No Hana
◉◉ Modern Japanese **V** ☻
020 7925 8988 | 23 Saint James's
Street, SW1A 1HA

Salloos Restaurant
◉ Pakistani
020 7235 4444 | 62-64 Kinnerton
Street, SW1X 8ER

Santini Restaurant
◉ Traditional Italian
020 7730 4094 | 29 Ebury Street,
SW1W 0NZ

Sofitel London St James
◉◉ French
020 7968 2900 & 7747 2200
6 Waterloo Place, SW1Y 4AN

**Taj 51 Buckingham Gate,
Suites and Residences**
◉◉ Modern European
020 7769 7766 | SW1E 6AF

Veneta
◉◉ Northern Italian
020 3874 9100 | 3 Norris Street,
St James's Market, SW1Y 4RJ

Zafferano
◉◉ Modern Italian
020 7235 5800 | 15 Lowndes Street,
SW1X 9EY

LONDON SW3
Admiral Codrington
◉ British
020 7581 0005 | 17 Mossop Street,
SW3 2LY

Bo Lang Restaurant
◉ Chinese
020 7823 7887 | 100 Draycott Avenue,
SW3 3AD

Le Colombier
◉ Traditional French
020 7351 1155 | 145 Dovehouse Street,
SW3 6LB

Eight Over Eight
◉ Pan Asian
020 7349 9934 | 392 King's Road,
SW3 5UZ

Manicomio Chelsea
◉ Modern Italian
020 7730 3366 | 85 Duke of York
Square, Chelsea, SW3 4LY

Tom's Kitchen
◉◉ Modern British
020 7349 0202 | 27 Cale Street,
South Kensington, SW3 3QP

LONDON SW4
Bistro Union
◉◉ British
020 7042 6400 | 40 Abbeville Road,
Clapham, SW4 9NG

The Dairy
◉◉ Modern British **V**
020 7622 4165 | 15 The Pavement,
Clapham, SW4 0HY

The Manor
◉ Modern British **V**
020 7720 4662 | 148 Clapham Manor
Street, SW4 6BX

Tsunami
◉ Japanese
020 7978 1610 | 5-7 Voltaire Road,
SW4 6DQ

LONDON SW5
Cambio de Tercio
◉◉ Spanish **V**
020 7244 8970
163 Old Brompton Road, SW5 0LJ

Capote y Toros
🌑 Spanish **V**
020 7373 0567 | 157 Old Brompton
Road, SW5 0LJ

LONDON SW6
The Harwood Arms
🌑🌑 British **V**
020 7386 1847 | 27 Walham Grove,
Fulham, SW6 1QR

Marco Grill
🌑🌑 British
020 7915 2929 | M&C Hotels
at Chelsea FC, Stamford Bridge,
Fulham Road, SW6 1HS

LONDON SW7
Bombay Brasserie
🌑🌑 Indian
020 7370 4040 | Courtfield Close,
Courtfield Road, SW7 4QH

Brunello
🌑 Modern Italian
020 7368 5700 | Baglioni Hotel London,
60 Hyde Park Gate, Kensington Road
Kensington, SW7 5BB

Olive Restaurant
🌑 Italian
020 7331 6308 | Millennium Bailey's
Hotel London Kensington,
140 Gloucester Road, SW7 4QH

Zuma
🌑🌑 Modern Japanese
020 7584 1010 | 5 Raphael Street,
Knightsbridge, SW7 1DL

LONDON SW10
Maze Grill Park Walk
🌑 Modern American
020 7495 2211 | 11 Park Walk,
SW10 0AJ

The Painted Heron
🌑 Modern Indian
020 7351 5232 | 112 Cheyne Walk,
SW10 0DJ

LONDON SW11
London House
🌑🌑 Modern British
020 7592 8545 | 7-9 Battersea Square,
Battersea Village, SW11 3RA

LONDON SW13
Sonny's Kitchen
🌑🌑 Modern European
020 8748 0393 | 94 Church Road,
Barnes, SW13 0DQ

LONDON SW14
The Depot
🌑 Modern European, British
020 8878 9462 | Tideway Yard,
125 Mortlake High Street, Barnes,
SW14 8SN

The Victoria
🌑🌑 Modern British
020 8876 4238 | 10 West Temple Sheen,
SW14 7RT

LONDON SW15
Bibo
🌑 Modern Italian
020 8780 0592 | 146 Upper Richmond,
Putney, SW15 2SW

LONDON SW19
The Fox & Grapes
🌑 Traditional British
020 8619 1300 | 9 Camp Road,
Wimbledon, SW19 4UN

Hotel du Vin Wimbledon
🌑🌑 Modern British, European
020 8879 1464 | Cannizaro House,
West Side, Wimbledon Common,
SW19 4UE

The Light House Restaurant
🌑 Modern International
020 8944 6338 | 75-77 Ridgway,
Wimbledon, SW19 4ST

LONDON W1
Antidote
🌑 Modern European
020 7287 8488 | 12a Newburgh Street,
W1F 7RR

Aqua Kyoto
🌑🌑 Contemporary Japanese
020 7478 0540 | 240 Regent Street,
W1B 3BR

Aqua Nueva
🌑🌑 Modern Spanish
020 7478 0540 | 5th Floor,
240 Regent Street, W1B 3BR

The Arch London
🌑 Modern British
020 7725 4825 | 50 Great Cumberland
Place, W1H 7FD

London W1

LONDON W1 *continued*

Assunta Madre
◉ Italian, Seafood
020 3230 3032 | 9-10 Blenheim Street,
W1S 1LJ

Barrafina Dean Street
◉◉ Spanish
Reservations not taken
26-27 Dean Street, W1D 3LL

The Beaumont
◉ British, American **V**
020 7499 9499 | 8 Balderton Street,
Mayfair, W1K 6TF

Bellamy's
◉ French
020 7491 2727 | 18-18a Bruton Place,
W1J 6LY

Benares Restaurant
◉◉ Modern Indian **V** ♟
020 7629 8886 | 12a Berkeley Square,
W1J 6BS

Bentley's Oyster Bar & Grill
◉ British, Irish ♟
020 7734 4756 | 11-15 Swallow Street,
W1B 4DG

Berners Tavern
◉◉ Contemporary British ♟
020 7908 7979 | The London EDITION,
10 Berners Street, W1T 3NP

Blanchette
◉ Modern & Traditional French,
Tapas **V**
020 7439 8100 | 9 D'Arblay Street,
Soho, W1F 8DR

Bocca di Lupo
◉ Italian ♟
020 7734 2223 | 12 Archer Street,
W1D 7BB

Bó Drake
◉ Korean, Japanese, Modern Asian
020 7439 9989 | 6 Greek Street,
W1D 4DE

Casita Andina
◉ Peruvian
020 3327 9464 | 31 Great Windmill
Street, Soho, W1D 7LP

Cecconi's
◉◉ Traditional Italian
020 7434 1500 | 5a Burlington Gardens,
W1S 1EP

The Chesterfield Mayfair
◉◉ Traditional British
020 7491 2622 | 35 Charles Street,
Mayfair, W1J 5EB

China Tang at The Dorchester
◉◉ Classic Cantonese
020 7629 9988 | 53 Park Lane,
W1K 1QA

Clipstone
◉◉ Modern
020 7637 0871 | 2 Clipstone Street,
W1W 6BB

C London
◉◉ Italian
020 7399 0500 | 23-25 Davies Street,
W1K 3DE

Cocochan
◉ Pan Asian
020 7486 1000 | 38-40 James Street,
Marylebone, W1U 1EU

Coya
◉◉ Modern Peruvian
020 7042 7118 | 118 Piccadilly,
Mayfair, W1J 7NW

Dehesa
◉ Spanish, Italian
020 7494 4170 | 25 Ganton Street,
W1F 9BP

Dinings
◉◉ Japanese, European
020 7723 0666 | 22 Harcourt Street,
W1H 4HH

DSTRKT
◉◉ Modern American
020 7317 9120 | 9 Rupert Street,
W1D 6DG

Ember Yard
◉◉ Spanish, Italian ♟
020 7439 8057 | 60-61 Berwick Street,
W1F 8SU

L'Escargot
◉◉ French, Mediterranean
020 7439 7474 | 48 Greek Street,
W1D 4EF

**Four Seasons Hotel London
at Park Lane**
◉◉ Italian **V**
020 7319 5206 | Hamilton Place,
Park Lane, W1J 7DR

Galvin at The Athenaeum
@@ Modern & Classic British
020 7640 3333 | 116 Piccadilly,
W1J 7BJ

Galvin Bistrot de Luxe
@@ French ♈
020 7935 4007 | 66 Baker Street,
W1U 7DJ

Goodman
@ British, American ♈
020 7499 3776 | 26 Maddox Street,
W1S 1QH

The Grill at The Dorchester
@@ Modern British ♈
020 7317 6531 | Park Lane,
W1K 1QA

GYMKHANA
@@ Contemporary Indian V
020 3011 5900 | 42 Albermarle Street,
W1S 4JH

Hakkasan
@@ Modern Chinese
020 7927 7000 | 8 Hanway Place,
W1T 1HD

Heddon Street Kitchen
@ Modern British
020 7592 1212
3-9 Heddon Street,
Regent Street Food Quarter, W1B 4BD

HIX Mayfair
@@ Traditional British V ♈
020 7518 4004 | Brown's Hotel,
Albemarle Street, Mayfair, W1S 4BP

HIX Soho
@@ British V
020 7292 3518 | 66-70 Brewer Street,
W1F 9UP

JW Steakhouse
@ American
020 7399 8460 | Grosvenor House Hotel,
Park Lane, W1K 7TN

Kai Mayfair
@@ Modern Chinese V
020 7493 8988
65 South Audley Street, W1K 2QU

The Keeper's House
@ Modern British
020 7300 5881 | Royal Academy
of Arts, Burlington House, Piccadilly,
W1J 0BD

Kitty Fisher's
@@ Modern British
020 3302 1661 | 10 Shepherd Market,
W1J 7QF

Latium
@@ Italian ♈
020 7323 9123 | 21 Berners Street,
W1T 3LP

Levant
@ Lebanese, Middle Eastern V
020 7224 1111 | Jason Court,
76 Wigmore Street, W1U 2SJ

Lima
@@ Modern Peruvian
020 3002 2640 | 31 Rathbone Place,
Fitzrovia, W1T 1JH

The Mandeville Hotel
@ Modern British
020 7935 5599 | Mandeville Place,
W1U 2BE

The Mayfair Chippy
@ British
020 7741 2233 | North Audley Street,
W1K 6WE

Maze
@@ French, Asian V
020 7107 0000 | London Marriott
Hotel, 10-13 Grosvenor Square,
W1K 6JP

Mele e Pere
@ Italian
020 7096 2096 | 46 Brewer Street,
Soho, W1F 9TF

Le Meridien Piccadilly
@ Modern British V
020 7734 8000 | 21 Piccadilly, W1J 0BH

Mews of Mayfair
@ Modern British
020 7518 9388 | 10-11 Lancashire
Court, New Bond Street, Mayfair,
W1S 1EY

The Montagu
@@ Modern British
020 7299 2037 | Hyatt Regency
London, The Churchill, 30 Portman
Square, W1H 7BH

Nobu Berkeley ST
@@ Japanese, Peruvian ♈
020 7290 9222 | 15 Berkeley Street,
W1J 8DY

London W1

Nobu Old Park Lane
◉◉ Japanese
020 7447 4747 | COMO Metropolitan
London, Old Park Lane, W1K 1LB

NOPI
◉ Mediterranean
020 7494 9584 | 21-22 Warwick Street,
W1B 5NE

Novikov Asian Restaurant
◉ Chinese, Pan Asian
020 7399 4330 | 50a Berkeley Street,
W1J 8HA

Novikov Italian Restaurant
◉ Italian
020 7399 4330 | 50a Berkeley Street,
W1J 8HA

The Palomar
◉◉ Modern Jerusalem
020 7439 8777 | 34 Rupert Street,
W1D 6DN

Park Chinois
◉◉ Chinese
020 3327 8888 | 17 Berkeley Street,
Mayfair, W1J 8EA

La Petite Maison
◉◉ French, Mediterranean
020 7495 4774 | 54 Brooks Mews,
W1K 4EG

Peyote
◉ Mexican
020 7409 1300 | 13 Cork Street,
Mayfair, W1S 3NS

Picture
◉◉ Modern European **V**
020 7637 7892
110 Great Portland Street, W1W 6PQ

Plum Valley
◉ Chinese
020 7494 4366 | 20 Gerrard Street,
W1D 6JQ

Podium
◉ Modern European
020 7208 4022
London Hilton on Park Lane,
22 Park Lane, W1K 1BE

Polpo
◉ Italian
020 7734 4479 | 41 Beak Street,
W1F 9SB

The Providores and Tapa Room
◉ International, Fusion ♟
020 7935 6175 | 109 Marylebone
High Street, W1U 4RX

QP LDN
◉◉ Italian, Mediterranean
020 3096 1444 | 34 Dover Street,
W1S 4NG

Quo Vadis
◉◉ Modern British
020 7437 9585 | 26-29 Dean Street,
W1D 3LL

The Red Fort
◉ Indian
020 7437 2525 | 77 Dean Street,
Soho, W1D 3SH

The Riding House Café
◉ Modern European
020 7927 0840 | 43-51 Great
Titchfield Street, W1W 7PQ

Roti Chai
◉ Modern Indian
020 7408 0101 | 3 Portman Mews
South, W1H 6AY

Roux at The Landau
◉◉ Modern European, French **V** ♟
020 7636 1000 | The Langham London,
Portland Place, W1B 1JA

Salt Yard
◉◉ Italian, Spanish
020 7637 0657 | 54 Goodge Street,
W1T 4NA

Sartoria
◉ Italian **V**
020 7534 7000 | 20 Savile Row,
W1S 3PR

Scott's
◉◉ Seafood **V** ♟
020 7495 7309 & 7307 5784
20 Mount Street, W1K 2HE

Sexy Fish
◉◉ Asian, Seafood
020 3764 2000 | Berkeley Square
House, Berkeley Square, W1J 6BR

Sketch (The Parlour)
◉◉ Modern European
020 7659 4500 | 9 Conduit Street,
W1S 2XG

See advert opposite

Social Wine & Tapas
◉◉ Modern tapas
020 7993 3257 | 39 James Street,
W1U 1DL

Street XO
◉◉ Tapas
020 3096 7555 | 15 Old Burlington
Street, W1S 2JR

Tamarind
◉◉ Indian
020 7629 3561 | 20 Queen Street,
Mayfair, W1J 5PR

10 Greek Street
◉◉ Modern British, European
020 7734 4677 | W1D 4DH

Ten Room Restaurant
◉◉ Modern European
020 7406 3333 | Hotel Café Royal,
68 Regent Street, W1B 4DY

Trishna
◉◉ Indian V ♟
020 7935 5624 | 15-17 Blandford Street,
W1U 3DG

Twist
◉◉ Mediterranean Tapas
020 7723 3377 | 42 Crawford Street,
W1H 1JW

Vasco & Piero's Pavilion Restaurant
◉ Modern Italian
020 7437 8774 | 15 Poland Street,
W1F 8QE

Veeraswamy Restaurant
◉◉ Indian
020 7734 1401 | Mezzanine Floor,
Victory House, 99 Regent Street,
W1B 4RS

See advert on page 382

Villandry Great Portland Street
◉ French, Mediterranean
020 7631 3131 | 170 Great Portland
Street, W1W 5QB

Brunch 8am - 6pm
Cocktails 6pm - 2am (Sun - 12am)

9 Conduit Street, Mayfair, London
www.sketch.london

sketch PARLOUR

THREE OF THE VERY BEST INDIAN RESTAURANTS

Amaya

This award winning sophisticated Indian Grill offers intense flavours with an innovative twist, in a theatrical open kitchen setting. Michelin star.

Open for lunch and dinner seven days a week.

Halkin Arcade, Motcomb Street
Knightsbridge, London SW1X 8JT
T: 020 7823 1166
E: amaya@realindianfood.com

Private dining room seats 14

CHUTNEY MARY

The rich setting, interesting art and romantic candle lighting are secondary details in London's haven of great Indian contemporary food.

Open for lunch and dinner from Monday to Saturday.
Saturday Brunch with live jazz music.

73 St James's Street,
London SW1A 1PH
T: 020 7629 6688
E: chutneymary@realindianfood.com

Two private dining rooms seat 30 and 16

VEERASWAMY
1926

Classical dishes, lovingly prepared and beautifully served in sumptuous surroundings overlooking Regent Street. The oldest Indian restaurant in the world.

Open for lunch and dinner seven days a week.

Mezzanine Floor, Victory House, 1st floor
99 Regent Street, London W1B 4RS
T: 020 7734 1401
E: veeraswamy@realindianfood.com

Private dining room seats 24

LONDON W1 *continued*
The Wolseley
◉ Traditional European **V**
020 7499 6996 | 160 Piccadilly,
W1J 9EB

Yauatcha
◉◉ Modern Chinese
020 7494 8888 | 15 Broadwick Street,
W1F 0DL

Zoilo
◉◉ Argentine
020 7486 9699 | 9 Duke Street,
W1U 3EG

LONDON W2
Angelus Restaurant
◉◉ Modern French
020 7402 0083 | 4 Bathurst Street,
W2 2SD

Island Grill & Bar
◉◉ Modern European
020 7551 6070 | Lancaster London,
Lancaster Terrace, W2 2TY

Kurobuta
◉ Japanese
020 7920 6444 | 17-20 Kendal Street,
Marble Arch, W2 2AW

Nipa
◉◉ Traditional Thai
020 7551 6039 | Lancaster London
Hotel, Lancaster Terrace, W2 2TY

The Royal Park Hotel
◉ Modern British
020 7479 6600 | 3 Westbourne Terrace,
W2 3UL

Salt and Honey
◉ Modern European
020 7706 7900 | 28 Sussex Place,
W2 2TH

LONDON W4
Restaurant Michael Nadra
◉◉ Modern European
020 8742 0766 | 6-8 Elliott Road,
Chiswick, W4 1PE

La Trompette
◉◉ Modern European ♟
020 8747 1836 | 5-7 Devonshire Road,
Chiswick, W4 2EU

Le Vacherin
◉◉ French
020 8742 2121 | 76-77 South Parade,
W4 5LF

LONDON W5
Charlotte's Place
◉◉ Modern European, British
020 8567 7541 | 16 St Matthews Road,
Ealing Common, W5 3JT

The Grove
◉ Classic British, European
020 8567 2439 | The Green, Ealing,
W5 5QX

LONDON W6
L'Amorosa
◉ Italian, British
020 8563 0300 | 278 King Street,
Ravenscourt Park, W6 0SP

Anglesea Arms
◉ Modern British
020 8749 1291 | 35 Wingate Road,
Ravenscourt Park, W6 0UR

Novotel London West
◉ Modern British
020 8741 1555 | 1 Shortlands,
W6 8DR

Sagar
◉ Indian Vegetarian **V**
020 8741 8563 | 157 King Street,
Hammersmith, W6 9JT

LONDON W8
Babylon
◉◉ Contemporary British
020 7368 3993 | The Roof Gardens,
99 Kensington High Street, W8 5SA
See advert on page 384

Belvedere
◉◉ British, French
020 7602 1238 & 7493 9393
Abbotsbury Road, Holland House,
Holland Park, W8 6LU

Clarke's
◉◉ Modern British, Italian
020 7221 9225 | 124 Kensington
Church Street, W8 4BH

Kensington Place
◉◉ British
020 7727 3184 | 201-209 Kensington
Church St, W8 7LX

Launceston Place
◉◉ Modern European ♟
020 7937 6912 | 1a Launceston Place,
W8 5RL

LONDON W8 *continued*
The Milestone Hotel
◉◉ Modern British ♟
020 7917 1000 | 1 Kensington Court,
W8 5DL

Park Terrace Restaurant
◉◉ Modern British
020 7361 0602 | Royal Garden Hotel,
2-24 Kensington High Street, W8 4PT

See advert below

Zaika of Kensington
◉◉ Indian **V**
020 7795 6533
1 Kensington High Street, W8 5NP

LONDON W10
The Dock Kitchen
◉ Modern International
020 8962 1610 | Portobello Docks,
342/344 Ladbroke Grove,
W10 5BU

LONDON W11
E&O
◉ Pan Asian
020 7229 5454 | 14 Blenheim Crescent,
Notting Hill, W11 1NN

Edera
◉ Modern Italian
020 7221 6090 | 148 Holland Park
Avenue, W11 4UE

LONDON W14
Cibo
◉◉ Italian
020 7371 2085 | 3 Russell Gardens,
W14 8EZ

LONDON WC1
The Montague on the Gardens
◉ British
020 7612 8416 & 7637 1001
15 Montague Street, Bloomsbury,
WC1B 5BJ

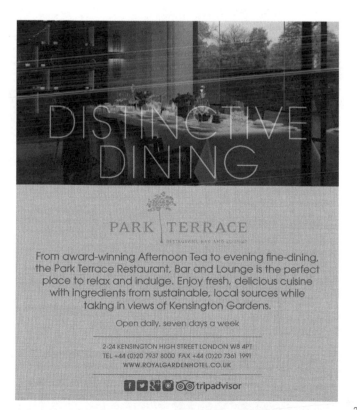

Otto's
◉◉ Classic French
020 7713 0107 | 182 Gray's Inn Road,
WC1X 8EW

Rosewood London
◉◉ Modern European
020 3747 8620 | 252 High Holborn,
WC1V 7EN

LONDON WC2
Balthazar
◉ French, European
020 3301 1155 | 4-6 Russell Street,
WC2B 5HZ

Barrafina Adelaide Street
◉◉ Modern Spanish
Reservations not taken
10 Adelaide Street, WC2N 4HZ

Barrafina Drury Lane
◉◉ Spanish
Reservations not taken
43 Drury Lane, WC2B 5AJ

Christopher's
◉ Contemporary American
020 7240 4222 | 18 Wellington Street,
Covent Garden, WC2E 7DD

Cigalon
◉ Mediterranean
020 7242 8373 | 115 Chancery Lane,
WC2A 1PP

The Delaunay
◉ European **V**
020 7499 8558 | 55 Aldwych,
WC2B 4BB

Les Deux Salons
◉◉ French
020 7420 2053 | 40-42 William IV
Street, WC2N 4DD

Frenchie Covent Garden
◉◉ French, Internatioanl
020 7836 4422 | 16 Henrietta Street,
WC2E 8QH

Great Queen Street
◉ British, European
020 7242 0622 | 32 Great Queen
Street, WC2B 5AA

The Ivy
◉ British, International **V**
020 7836 4751 & 7307 5784
1-5 West Street, Covent Garden,
WC2H 9NQ

J. Sheekey & J. Sheekey
Atlantic Bar
◉ Seafood **V**
020 7240 2565 | 32-34 St Martin's
Court, WC2N 4AL

Kaspar's Seafood Bar & Grill
◉ British, Japanese Seafood **V**
020 7836 4343 | The Savoy, Strand,
WC2R 0EU

Lima Floral
◉◉ Modern Peruvian
020 7240 5778 | 14 Garrick Street,
WC2E 9BJ

Margot
◉◉ Italian
020 3409 4777 | 45 Great Queen Street,
Covent Garden, WC2B 5AA

Massimo Restaurant & Bar
◉ Modern & Traditional Italian
020 7998 0555 | Corinthia Hotel
London, 10 Northumberland Avenue,
WC2N 5AE

Mon Plaisir
◉ Traditional French
020 7836 7243 | 19-21 Monmouth
Street, WC2H 9DD

The National Dining Rooms
◉ British
020 7747 2525 | Sainsbury Wing,
The National Gallery, Trafalgar Square,
WC2N 5DN

The Northall
◉◉ British
020 7321 3100 | Corinthia Hotel
London, 10a Northumberland Avenue,
WC2N 5AE

The Opera Tavern
◉◉ Spanish, Italian
020 7836 3680 | 23 Catherine Street,
Covent Garden, WC2B 5JS

Orso
◉ Modern Italian
020 7240 5269 | 27 Wellington Street,
WC2E 7DA

Roka Aldwych
◉◉ Contemporary Japanese
020 7294 7636 | 71 Aldwych,
WC2B 4HN

Savoy Grill
◉◉ British, French **V**
020 7592 1600 | 1 Savoy Hill,
Strand, WC2R 0EU

Spring
◎◎ European
020 3011 0115 | New Wing,
Somerset House, Lancaster Place,
WC2R 1LA

Terroirs
◎◎ Mediterranean, French
020 7036 0660 | 5 William IV Street,
Covent Garden, WC2N 4DW

Tredwells
◎◎ Modern British ♀
020 3764 0840 | 4a Upper St Martin's
Lane, Covent Garden, WC2H 9NY

▶ Greater London

BARNET
Savoro Restaurant with Rooms
◎ Modern European, British
020 8449 9888 | 206 High Street,
EN5 5SZ

CROYDON
Albert's Table
◎◎ Modern British **V**
020 8680 2010 | 49c Southend,
CR0 1BF

HADLEY WOOD
West Lodge Park Hotel
◎ Modern British
020 8216 3900 | Cockfosters Road,
EN4 0PY

HARROW ON THE HILL
Incanto Restaurant
◎ Modern Italian
020 8426 6767 | The Old Post Office,
41 High Street, HA1 3HT

HEATHROW AIRPORT
**Hilton London Heathrow Airport
Terminal 5**
◎ British, International
01753 686860 | Poyle Road,
Colnbrook, SL3 0FF

Mr Todiwala's Kitchen
◎◎ Modern Pan Asian
01753 686860 | Hilton London
Heathrow Airport Terminal 5,
Poyle Road, Colnbrook, SL3 0FF

Vivre Restaurant
◎ International
020 8757 5027 | Sofitel London
Heathrow, Terminal 5,
Wentworth Drive, TW6 2GD

KESTON
Herbert's
◎◎ British, International
01689 855501
6 Commonside, BR2 6BP

PINNER
Friends Restaurant
◎ British
020 8866 0286 | 11 High Street,
HA5 5PJ

RICHMOND UPON THAMES
Bacco Restaurant & Wine Bar
◎ Italian
020 8332 0348 | 39-41 Kew Road,
TW9 2NQ

La Buvette
◎ French, Mediterranean **V**
020 8940 6264 | 6 Church Walk,
TW9 1SN

The Dysart Petersham
◎◎ Modern British **V**
020 8940 8005 | 135 Petersham Road,
Petersham, TW10 7AA

The Petersham Hotel
◎◎ British, European **V**
020 8939 1084 | Nightingale Lane,
TW10 6UZ

Petersham Nurseries Café
◎ Modern British, Italian ♀
020 8940 5230 & 8332 0005
Church Lane, Petersham Road,
TW10 7AB

RUISLIP
The Barn Hotel
◎◎ Modern French **V**
01895 636057 | West End Road,
HA4 6JB

SURBITON
The French Table
◎◎ Modern European ♀
020 8399 2365 | 85 Maple Road,
KT6 4AW

TEDDINGTON
Retro
◎◎ French **V**
020 8977 2239 | 114-116 High Street,
TW11 8JB

London, Greater

TWICKENHAM
A Cena
◉ Modern Italian
020 8288 0108 | 418 Richmond Road,
TW1 2EB

▶ Merseyside
FRANKBY
Riviera at Hillbark
◉◉ French, Mediterranean
0151 625 2400 | Hillbark Hotel & Spa,
Royden Park, CH48 1NP

HESWALL
Burnt Truffle
◉ Modern British
0151 342 1111 | 106 Telegraph Road,
CH60 0AQ

LIVERPOOL
The Art School Restaurant, Liverpool
◉◉ Modern International **V** ⚱
0151 230 8600 | 1 Sugnall Street,
L7 7EB

The London Carriage Works
◉◉ Modern British ⚱
0151 705 2222 | Hope Street Hotel,
40 Hope Street, L1 9DA

Malmaison Liverpool
◉ Modern British
0151 229 5000 | 7 William Jessop Way,
Princes Dock, L3 1QZ

Mowgli
◉ Indian **V**
0151 708 9356 | 69 Bold Street, L1 4EZ

Panoramic 34
◉ Modern European
0151 236 5534 | 34th Floor, West Tower,
Brook Street, L3 9PJ

60 Hope Street Restaurant
◉ Modern British
0151 707 6060 | 60 Hope Street, L1 9BZ

PORT SUNLIGHT
Riviera at Leverhulme
◉◉ French, Mediterranean
0151 644 6655 | Leverhulme Hotel,
Central Road, CH62 5EZ

SOUTHPORT
Bistrot Vérité
◉◉ French, International
01704 564199 | 7 Liverpool Road,
Birkdale, PR8 4AR

Gusto Trattoria
◉ Modern Italian
01704 544255 | 58-62 Lord Street,
PR8 1QB

WALLASEY
Canteen
◉ Modern British, European
0151 639 6611 | 45 Wallasey Road,
CH45 4NN

▶ Norfolk
BAWBURGH
The Kings Head Bawburgh
◉◉ Modern British
01603 744977 | Harts Lane, NR9 3LS

BLAKENEY
The Blakeney Hotel
◉ Modern British **V**
01263 740797 | The Quay, NR25 7NE

BRANCASTER STAITHE
The White Horse
◉◉ Modern British
01485 210262 | PE31 8BY

COLTISHALL
Norfolk Mead Hotel
◉◉ Modern British
01603 737531 | Church Lane,
NR12 7DN

CROMER
The Grove Cromer
◉◉ British, Seafood
01263 512412 | 95 Overstrand Road,
NR27 0DJ

Sea Marge Hotel
◉◉ Modern British
01263 579579 | 16 High Street,
Overstrand, NR27 0AB

The White Horse Overstrand
◉◉ Modern European, British
01263 579237 | 34 High Street,
Overstrand, NR27 0AB

GREAT YARMOUTH
Andover House
◉◉ Modern British
01493 843490 | 27-30 Camperdown,
NR30 3JB

Imperial Hotel
◉ Modern British
01493 842000 | North Drive, NR30 1EQ

The Prom Hotel
◉ Contemporary British **V**
01493 842308 | 77 Marine Parade,
NR30 2DH

**Congham Hall Country
House Hotel**
◉◉ Modern British, European **V**
01485 600250 | Lynn Road,
PE32 1AH

Heacham Manor Hotel
◉ Mediterranean, European
01485 536030 | Hunstanton Road,
PE31 7JX

Park Farm Hotel
◉ Modern British
01603 810264 | NR9 3DL

The Lawns
◉ Modern European
01263 713390 | 26 Station Road,
NR25 6BS

The Pheasant Hotel & Restaurant
◉ British
01263 588382 | Coast Road, Kelling,
NR25 7EG

Caley Hall Hotel
◉ Modern British **V**
01485 533486 | Old Hunstanton Road,
PE36 6HH

Bank House
◉ Modern British
01553 660492 | King's Staithe Square,
PE30 1RD

The Duke's Head Hotel
◉ Modern British
01553 774996 | 5-6 Tuesday Market
Place, PE30 1JS

The Loddon Swan
◉◉ Modern British
01508 528039 | 23 Church Plain,
NR14 6LX

Beechwood Hotel
◉◉ Classic British **V**
01692 403231 | 20 Cromer Road,
NR28 0HD

Benedicts
◉◉ Modern British **V**
01603 926080 | 9 St Benedicts Street,
NR2 4PE

Best Western Annesley House Hotel
◉◉ Modern British
01603 624553 | 6 Newmarket Road,
NR2 2LA

Brasteds
◉◉ Modern European
01508 491112 | Manor Farm Barns,
Fox Road, Framingham Pigot,
NR14 7PZ

Maids Head Hotel
◉◉ Modern British
01603 209955 | Tombland,
NR3 1LB

The Old Rectory
◉◉ Modern British
01603 700772 | 103 Yarmouth Road,
Thorpe St Andrew, NR7 0HF

St Giles House Hotel
◉◉ Modern British
01603 275180 | 41-45 St Giles Street,
NR2 1JR

Stower Grange
◉ Modern British
01603 860210 | 40 School Road,
Drayton, NR8 6EF

Thailand Restaurant
◉ Thai **V**
01603 700444 | 9 Ring Road,
Thorpe St Andrew, NR7 0XJ

Dales Country House Hotel
◉◉ British, European
01263 824555 | Lodge Hill,
Upper Sheringham,
NR26 8TJ

The Rose & Crown
◉ Modern British
01485 541382 | Old Church Road,
PE31 7LX

Norfolk

STALHAM
The Ingham Swan
◉◉ Modern European
01692 581099 | Sea Palling Road,
Ingham, NR12 9AB

THETFORD
Elveden Courtyard Restaurant
◉ Traditional British
01842 898068 | London Road,
Elveden, IP24 3TQ

THORNHAM
The Chequers Inn
◉ Modern British
01485 512229 | High Street,
PE36 6LY

WIVETON
Wiveton Bell
◉ Modern British
01263 740101 | The Green,
Blakeney Road, NR25 7TL

WYMONDHAM
Kindreds Restaurant
◉ Modern French, British
01953 601872 | 2 Bridewell Street,
NR18 0AR

Number Twenty Four Restaurant
◉ Modern British
01953 607750 | 24 Middleton Street,
NR18 0AD

▶ Northamptonshire

DAVENTRY
Fawsley Hall Hotel & Spa
◉◉ Modern British
01327 892000 | Fawsley, NN11 3BA

KETTERING
Barton Hall Hotel
◉◉ Traditional British
01536 515505 | Barton Road,
Barton Seagrave, NN15 6SG

Kettering Park Hotel & Spa
◉ Modern British
01536 416666 | Kettering Parkway,
NN15 6XT

NASSINGTON
The Queens Head Inn
◉ Modern British
01780 784006 | 54 Station Road,
PE8 6QB

NORTHAMPTON
The Hopping Hare
◉◉ Modern British V
01604 580090 | 18 Hopping Hill
Gardens, Duston, NN5 6PF

OUNDLE
The Talbot Hotel
◉ British
01832 273621 | New Street,
PE8 4EA

WEEDON
Narrow Boat at Weedon
◉◉ Modern British
01327 340333 | Stowe Hill,
A5 Watling Street, NN7 4RZ

WHITTLEBURY
Whittlebury Hall
◉◉ Modern British, European
01327 857857 | NN12 8QH

▶ Northumberland

BAMBURGH
Waren House Hotel
◉◉ Modern & Traditional British
01668 214581 | Waren Mill,
NE70 7EE

BERWICK-UPON-TWEED
Magna
◉ Indian
01289 302736 | 39 Bridge Street,
TD15 1ES

Queens Head
◉ Modern British, European
01289 307852 | Sandgate,
TD15 1EP

BLANCHLAND
The Lord Crewe Arms Blanchland
◉ Traditional British
01434 675469 | The Square, DH8 9SP

CHATHILL
Doxford Hall Hotel & Spa
◉◉ Modern British V
01665 589700 | NE67 5DN

CORNHILL-ON-TWEED
**Tillmouth Park Country
House Hotel**
◉ Modern British
01890 882255 | TD12 4UU

HEXHAM
Barrasford Arms
🌸 Modern & Traditional British
01434 681237 | NE48 4AA

Langley Castle Hotel
🌸🌸 Contemporary British, French
01434 688888 | Langley,
NE47 5LU

LONGHORSLEY
**Macdonald Linden Hall,
Golf & Country Club**
🌸🌸 Modern British
01670 500000 | NE65 8XF

MATFEN
Matfen Hall
🌸🌸 Modern British V
01661 886500 | NE20 0RH

MORPETH
Eshott Hall
🌸🌸 British, European
01670 787454 | Eshott,
NE65 9EN

▶ Nottinghamshire

BARNBY MOOR
Restaurant Bar 1650
🌸 Modern European
01777 705121 | Ye Olde Bell Hotel,
DN22 8QS

BLIDWORTH
The Black Bull
🌸🌸 Classic British
01623 490222 | Main Street,
NG21 0QH

FARNDON
Farndon Boathouse
🌸 Modern British
01636 676578 | Off Wyke Road,
NG24 3SX

GUNTHORPE
Tom Browns Brasserie
🌸🌸 Modern International
0115 966 3642 | The Old School House,
Trentside, NG14 7FB

NOTTINGHAM
Hart's Restaurant
🌸🌸 Modern British
0115 988 1900 & 911 0666
Standard Hill, Park Row,
NG1 6GN

MemSaab Restaurant
🌸🌸 Indian
0115 957 0009
12-14 Maid Marian Way, NG1 6HS

See advert on page 392

Park Plaza Nottingham
🌸🌸 Pan Asian
0115 947 7444 | 41 Maid Marian Way,
NG1 6GD

World Service
🌸🌸 Modern British 🍷
0115 847 5587 | Newdigate House,
Castle Gate, NG1 6AF

OLLERTON
Thoresby Hall Hotel
🌸🌸 British, International
01623 821000 | Thoresby Park,
NG22 9WH

RETFORD
Blacksmiths
🌸🌸 Modern British
01777 818171 | Town Street,
Clayworth, DN22 9AD

▶ Oxfordshire

ASTON ROWANT
The Lambert
🌸 Modern British
01844 351496 | London Road,
OX49 5SN

BANBURY
**Best Western Plus
Wroxton House Hotel**
🌸🌸 Modern British
01295 730777 | Wroxton St Mary,
OX15 6QB

The Three Pigeons Inn
🌸 Contemporary British
01295 275220 | 3 Southam Road,
OX16 2ED

The White Horse
🌸🌸 Traditional British, French
01295 812440 & 07850 420844
2 The Square, Kings Sutton,
OX17 3RF

BURFORD
The Angel at Burford
🌸 Classic British
01993 822714 | 14 Witney Street,
OX18 4SN

MemSaab Nottingham is amongst the top three best Indian restaurants in the country

AA Gill, The Sunday Times

Best Indian Restaurant 2016

Nottinghamshire Food & Drink Awards

PRIVATE DINING • CANAPÉ & DRINKS RECEPTIONS
CELEBRATION DINNERS • OUTSIDE CATERING
£13.95 EARLY EVENING MENU AVAILABLE

BURFORD *continued*
The Bay Tree Hotel
⊚ Modern British
01993 822791 | Sheep Street,
OX18 4LW

The Bull at Burford
⊚⊚ Modern & Traditional
01993 822220 | 105 High Street,
OX18 4RG

CHECKENDON
The Highwayman
⊚ Modern & Traditional British
01491 682020 | Exlade Street,
RG8 0UA

CHINNOR
The Sir Charles Napier
⊚⊚ Modern British, European **V** ⏺
01494 483011 | Sprigg's Alley,
OX39 4BX

CHIPPING NORTON
The Chequers
⊚ Traditional British
01608 659393 | Church Road,
Churchill, OX7 6NJ

Wild Thyme Restaurant with Rooms
⊚⊚ Modern British
01608 645060 | 10 New Street,
OX7 5LJ

FARINGDON
The Eagle
⊚⊚ Modern European
01367 241879 | Little Coxwell,
SN7 7LW

Magnolia Brasserie
⊚⊚ Modern British
01367 241272 | 56 London Street,
SN7 7AA

The Trout Inn
⊚ Modern British
01367 870382 | Buckland Marsh,
SN7 8RF

FYFIELD
The White Hart
⊚⊚ Modern British
01865 390585 | Main Road,
OX13 5LW

GORING
The Miller of Mansfield
⊚⊚ British **V**
01491 872829 | High Street, RG8 9AW

HENLEY-ON-THAMES
The Baskerville
⊚ Modern British **V**
0118 940 3332 | Station Road,
Lower Shiplake, RG9 3NY

The Cherry Tree Inn
⊚ Modern British, European
01491 680430 | Main Street,
Stoke Row, RG9 5QA

Hotel du Vin Henley-on-Thames
⊚ European
01491 848400 | New Street, RG9 2BP

MILTON COMMON
The Oxfordshire
⊚ Modern British
01844 278300 | Rycote Lane, OX9 2PU

MURCOTT
The Nut Tree Inn
⊚⊚ Modern European **V** ⏺
01865 331253 | Main Street, OX5 2RE

OXFORD
Bear & Ragged Staff
⊚ Modern, & Classic British
01865 862329 | Appleton Road,
Cumnor, OX2 9QH

Cotswold Lodge Hotel
⊚ British, European
01865 512121 | 66a Banbury Road,
OX2 6JP

De Vere Oxford Thames
⊚ Modern International
01865 334444 | Henley Road,
Sandford-on-Thames, OX4 4GX

Gee's Restaurant
⊚ Mediterranean
01865 553540 | 61 Banbury Road,
OX2 6PE

Iffley Blue at Hawkwell House
⊚ British, European
01865 749988 | Church Way,
Iffley Village, OX4 4DZ

Malmaison Oxford
⊚ Modern British, French
01865 268400 | Oxford Castle,
3 New Road, OX1 1AY

The Oxford Kitchen
⊚⊚ Modern British **V**
01865 511149 | 215 Banbury Road,
Summertown, OX2 7HQ

Oxfordshire

STADHAMPTON
The Crazy Bear
◉◉ Modern British
01865 890714 | Bear Lane, OX44 7UR

Thai Thai at The Crazy Bear
◉◉ Modern Thai
01865 890714 | Bear Lane, OX44 7UR

SWINBROOK
The Swan Inn
◉◉ Modern British
01993 823339 | OX18 4DY

TOOT BALDON
The Mole Inn
◉ Modern European
01865 340001 | OX44 9NG

WANTAGE
The Star Inn
◉◉ Modern British
01235 751873 | Watery Lane,
Sparsholt, OX12 9PL

WATLINGTON
The Fat Fox Inn
◉ Modern British
01491 613040 | 13 Shirburn Street,
OX49 5BU

WITNEY
Hollybush Witney
◉ British
01993 708073 | 35 Corn Street,
OX28 6BT

Old Swan & Minster Mill
◉ Modern British
01993 774441 | Old Minster,
OX29 0RN

**The Restaurant at Witney
Lakes Resort**
◉ British, European
01993 893012 | Downs Road,
OX29 0SY

WOODSTOCK
The Feathers Hotel
◉◉ Modern British
01993 812291 | Market Street,
OX20 1SX

Macdonald Bear Hotel
◉◉ Modern, Traditional British
01993 811124 | Park Street, OX20 1SZ

WOOTTON
The Killingworth Castle
◉ Modern British
01993 811401 | Glympton Road,
OX20 1EJ

▶ Rutland

CLIPSHAM
The Olive Branch
◉◉ British, European **V**
01780 410355 | Beech House,
Main Street, LE15 7SH

LYDDINGTON
The Marquess of Exeter
◉ Classic & Modern European **V**
01572 822477 | 52 Main Street,
LE15 9LT

OAKHAM
Barnsdale Lodge Hotel
◉ Modern British
01572 724678 | The Avenue, Rutland
Water, North Shore, LE15 8AH

Fox & Hounds
◉◉ Modern British, European **V**
01572 812403 | 19 The Green, Exton,
LE15 8AP

UPPINGHAM
The Lake Isle
◉◉ British, French
01572 822951 | 16 High Street East,
LE15 9PZ

WING
Kings Arms Inn & Restaurant
◉◉ Traditional British
01572 737634 | 13 Top Street,
LE15 8SE

▶ Shropshire

BISHOP'S CASTLE
The Coach House
◉◉ Modern British
01588 650846 & 07930 694516
Norbury, SY9 5DX

IRONBRIDGE
Restaurant Severn
◉◉ British, French
01952 432233 | 33 High Street,
TF8 7AG

Shropshire

LUDLOW
The Charlton Arms
◉ Modern British
01584 872813 | Ludford Bridge, SY8 1PJ

The Cliffe at Dinham
◉◉ Modern British
01584 872063 & 873991 | Halton Lane, Dinham, SY8 2JE

The Clive Bar & Restaurant with Rooms
◉ Modern British
01584 856565 | Bromfield, SY8 2JR

The Feathers Hotel
◉ British, European
01584 875261 | The Bull Ring, SY8 1AA
See advert below

Overton Grange Hotel and Restaurant
◉◉ Modern British
01584 873500 | Old Hereford Road, SY8 4AD

MARKET DRAYTON
Goldstone Hall
◉◉ Modern British
01630 661202 | Goldstone Road, TF9 2NA

MUCH WENLOCK
Raven Hotel
◉◉ Modern British
01952 727251 | 30 Barrow Street, TF13 6EN

MUNSLOW
Crown Country Inn
◉◉ Modern British
01584 841205 | SY7 9ET
See advert on page 396

NORTON
The Hundred House
◉◉ British, French
01952 580240 | Bridgnorth Road, TF11 9EE

The Feathers Hotel of Ludlow

"The Most Handsome Inn in the World"

Fine Cuisine

Award Winning Restaurant

Exemplary service, in iconic surroundings for exceptional value

The Restaurant has been serving its AA Rosette standard food consistently for the last 15 years. Our chefs aim to combine locally sourced ingredients with their considerable expertise, so that when your dish arrives your palate will be in for a treat.

The Bull Ring
Ludlow
Shropshire
SY8 1AA
England

Telephone:
01584 875 261

enquiries@feathersatludlow.co.uk
www.feathersatludlow.co.uk

Shropshire

OSWESTRY
Pen-y-Dyffryn Country Hotel
◉◉ Modern British
01691 653700 | Rhydycroesau,
SY10 7JD

Sebastians
◉◉ French
01691 655444 | 45 Willow Street,
SY11 1AQ

Wynnstay Hotel
◉◉ British
01691 655261 | Church Street,
SY11 2SZ

SHREWSBURY
**Albright Hussey Manor Hotel
& Restaurant**
◉◉ Modern British
01939 290571 | Ellesmere Road,
Broad Oak, SY4 3AF

Drapers Hall
◉◉ Modern & Traditional
01743 344679 | 10 Saint Mary's Place,
SY1 1DZ

**Henry Tudor House
Restaurant and Bar**
◉ Modern British
01743 361666 | Henry Tudor House,
Barracks Passage, SY1 1XA

House of the Rising Sun
◉ Australian, Asian, Pacific Rim **V**
01743 588040 | 18 Butcher Row,
SY1 1UW

Lion & Pheasant Hotel
◉◉ British **V**
01743 770345 | 49-50 Wyle Cop,
SY1 1XJ

The Peach Tree Restaurant
◉ Modern British, Asian Fusion **V**
01743 355055 | 18-21 Abbey Foregate,
SY2 6AE

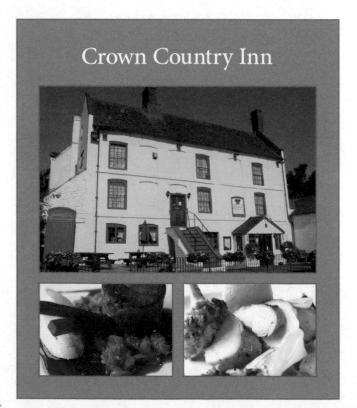

Crown Country Inn

Somerset

TELFORD
Chez Maw Restaurant
◉◉ Modern British **V**
01952 432247 | Ironbridge, TF8 7DW

Hadley Park House
◉ Modern British
01952 677269 | Hadley Park, TF1 6QJ

UPTON MAGNA
The Haughmond
◉◉ Modern British **V**
01743 709918 | Pelham Road, SY4 4TZ

▶ Somerset

AXBRIDGE
The Oak House
◉◉ Classic British
01934 732444 | The Square, BS26 2AP

BATH
Bailbrook House Hotel
◉◉ Modern British **V**
01225 855100 | Eveleigh Avenue,
London Road West, BA1 7JD

The Chequers
◉◉ Modern British
01225 360017 | 50 Rivers Street,
BA1 2QA

The Circus Restaurant
◉ Modern European
01225 466020 | 34 Brock Street,
BA1 2LN

The Hare & Hounds
◉ Modern British
01225 482682 | Lansdown Road,
BA1 5TJ

Jamie's Italian
◉ Modern Italian
01225 432340 | 10 Milsom Place,
BA1 1BZ

Macdonald Bath Spa
◉◉ Modern British **V**
01225 444424 | Sydney Road,
BA2 6JF

Marlborough Tavern
◉◉ Modern British
01225 423731 | 35 Marlborough
Buildings, BA1 2LY

Menu Gordon Jones
◉◉ Innovative British **V**
01225 480871 | 2 Wellsway, BA2 3AQ

Woods Restaurant
◉ Modern British, French
01225 314812 | 9-13 Alfred Street,
BA1 2QX

BRIDGWATER
Walnut Tree Hotel
◉ Modern British
01278 662255 | North Petherton,
TA6 6QA

CASTLE CARY
The Pilgrims
◉◉ Modern British
01963 240597 | Lovington, BA7 7PT

CHEW MAGNA
The Pony & Trap
◉◉ Modern British
01275 332627 | Knowle Hill,
BS40 8TQ

CORTON DENHAM
The Queens Arms
◉◉ Modern British
01963 220317 | DT9 4LR

DULVERTON
Woods Bar & Restaurant
◉ Modern British, French **V**
01398 324007 | 4 Banks Square,
TA22 9BU

DUNSTER
The Luttrell Arms Hotel
◉ British
01643 821555 | Exmoor National Park,
TA24 6SG

FIVEHEAD
Langford Fivehead
◉◉ Modern British **V**
01460 282020 | Lower Swell,
TA3 6PH

GLASTONBURY
The Sheppey Inn
◉ Modern Bistro
01458 831594 | Lower Godney,
BA5 1RN

HINTON CHARTERHOUSE
Homewood Park Hotel & Spa
◉◉ British **V**
01225 723731 | Abbey Lane,
BA2 7TB

Somerset

HOLCOMBE
The Holcombe Inn
◉ British, International, French **V**
01761 232478 | Stratton Road, BA3 5EB

HUNSTRETE
THE PIG near Bath
◉◉ Modern British 🍷
01761 490490 | Hunstrete House,
Pensford, BS39 4NS

LOWER VOBSTER
The Vobster Inn
◉◉ British, European
01373 812920 | BA3 5RJ

MIDSOMER NORTON
Best Western Plus Centurion Hotel
◉◉ Modern British **V**
01761 417711 | Charlton Lane, BA3 4BD

MILVERTON
The Globe
◉ Modern British
01823 400534 | Fore Street, TA4 1JX

MONKSILVER
The Notley Arms Inn
◉ Classic British
01984 656095 | Front Street, TA4 4JB

NORTH WOOTTON
Crossways
◉ Modern British
01749 899000 | Stocks Lane, BA4 4EU

OAKHILL
The Oakhill Inn
◉ Modern British
01749 840442 | Fosse Road, BA3 5HU

RADSTOCK
The Redan Inn
◉◉ Modern British
01761 258560 | Fry's Well,
Chilcompton, BA3 4HA

SHEPTON MALLET
Charlton House Spa Hotel
◉◉ Modern British
0344 248 3830 | Charlton Road,
BA4 4PR

SOMERTON
The Devonshire Arms
◉ Modern British
01458 241271 | Long Sutton, TA10 9LP

STON EASTON
Ston Easton Park Hotel
◉◉ Modern British **V**
01761 241631 | BA3 4DF

TAUNTON
Augustus
◉◉ European **V**
01823 324354 | 3 The Courtyard,
St James Street, TA1 1JR

Castle Bow Restaurant
◉◉ Modern British
01823 272671 | Castle Green, TA1 1NF

The Willow Tree Restaurant
◉◉ Modern British
01823 352835 | 3 Tower Lane,
Off Tower Street, TA1 4AR

TINTINHULL
Crown & Victoria
◉ British
01935 823341 | Farm Street, BA22 8PZ

WELLS
Best Western Plus Swan Hotel
◉◉ Modern British
01749 836300 | Sadler Street, BA5 2RX

Goodfellows
◉◉ Mediterranean, European
01749 673866 | 5 Sadler Street,
BA5 2RR

WESTON-SUPER-MARE
The Cove
◉ Modern British
01934 418217 | Marine Lake,
Birnbeck Road, BS23 2BX

WINCANTON
Holbrook House
◉◉ Modern British
01963 824466 | Holbrook, BA9 8BS

YEOVIL
The Yeovil Court Hotel & Restaurant
◉ Modern European
01935 863746 | West Coker Road,
BA20 2HE

▶ Staffordshire

LEEK
Three Horseshoes Country Inn & Spa
◉◉ Modern & Classic
01538 300296 | Buxton Road,
Blackshaw Moor, ST13 8TW

Suffolk

LICHFIELD
Netherstowe House
◉ Modern British **V**
01543 254270 | Netherstowe Lane, WS13 6AY

STAFFORD
The Moat House
◉◉ Modern British
01785 712217 | Lower Penkridge Road, Acton Trussell, ST17 0RJ

The Shropshire Inn
◉ Traditional British
01785 780904 | Newport Road, Haughton, ST18 9HB

▶ Suffolk

ALDEBURGH
Brudenell Hotel
◉◉ Modern British, European
01728 452071 | The Parade, IP15 5BU

Regatta Restaurant
◉ Modern British
01728 452011 | 171 High Street, IP15 5AN

The White Lion Hotel
◉ British, French
01728 452720 | Market Cross Place, IP15 5BJ

BILDESTON
The Bildeston Crown
◉◉ Modern British
01449 740510 | 104-106 High Street, IP7 7EB

BROME
Best Western Brome Grange Hotel
◉◉ Modern British
01379 870456 | Norwich Road, Nr Diss, IP23 8AP

BURY ST EDMUNDS
The Angel Hotel
◉◉ Modern British
01284 714000 | Angel Hill, IP33 1LT

The Bannatyne Spa
◉ Modern European
01284 705550 | Horringer Court, Horringer Road, IP29 5PH

Best Western Priory Hotel
◉ Modern British, International
01284 766181 | Mildenhall Road, IP32 6EH

The Grange Hotel
◉ Modern British
01359 231260 | Barton Road, Thurston, IP31 3PQ

The Leaping Hare Restaurant & Country Store
◉◉ Classic & Traditional
01359 250287 | Wyken Vineyards, Stanton, IP31 2DW

Maison Bleue
◉◉ Modern French
01284 760623
30-31 Churchgate Street, IP33 1RG

1921 Angel Hill
◉◉ British
01284 704870 | IP33 1UZ

Pea Porridge
◉◉ Modern Bistro
01284 700200 | 28-29 Cannon Street, IP33 1JR

The White Horse
◉ Modern British
01284 735760 | Rede Road, Whepstead, IP29 4SS

CAVENDISH
The George
◉◉ Modern British
01787 280248 | The Green, CO10 8BA

DUNWICH
The Ship at Dunwich
◉ Modern British
01728 648219 | St James Street, IP17 3DT

FRESSINGFIELD
Fox & Goose Inn
◉◉ Modern British
01379 586247 | Church Road, IP21 5PB

HINTLESHAM
Hintlesham Hall Hotel
◉◉ Modern European **V**
01473 652334 | George Street, IP8 3NS

HORRINGER
The Ickworth
◉◉ Modern Mediterranean **V**
01284 735350 | IP29 5QE

INGHAM
The Cadogan Arms
◉ Traditional British
01284 728443 | The Street, IP31 1NG

Suffolk

IPSWICH
Mariners
◉◉ French, Mediterranean **V**
01473 289748 | Neptune Quay,
IP4 1AX

milsoms Kesgrave Hall
◉ Modern International
01473 333741 | Hall Road, Kesgrave,
IP5 2PU

Salthouse Harbour Hotel
◉◉ Modern British
01473 226789 | No 1 Neptune Quay,
IP4 1AX

IXWORTH
Theobalds Restaurant
◉◉ Modern British
01359 231707 | 68 High Street,
IP31 2HJ

LAVENHAM
The Swan at Lavenham Hotel and Spa
◉◉ Modern & Traditional **V ☖**
01787 247477 | High Street, CO10 9QA

LONG MELFORD
Long Melford Swan
◉◉ Contemporary British **V**
01787 464545 | Hall Street, CO10 9JQ

LOWESTOFT
The Crooked Barn Restaurant
◉◉ Modern British
01502 501353 | Ivy House Country
Hotel, Ivy Lane, Beccles Road,
Oulton Broad, NR33 8HY

MILDENHALL
The Bull Inn
◉ Modern British
01638 711001 | The Street,
Barton Mills, IP28 6AA

NEWMARKET
Bedford Lodge Hotel & Spa
◉◉ British, Mediterranean
01638 663175 | Bury Road, CB8 7BX

The Packhorse Inn
◉◉ Modern British
01638 751818 | Bridge Street, Moulton,
CB8 8SP

ORFORD
The Crown & Castle
◉◉ Italian, British **V ☖**
01394 450205 | IP12 2LJ

SIBTON
Sibton White Horse Inn
◉◉ Modern British
01728 660337 | Halesworth Road,
IP17 2JJ

SOUTHWOLD
Sutherland House
◉◉ Modern British, Seafood
01502 724544 | 56 High Street,
IP18 6DN

STOKE-BY-NAYLAND
The Angel Inn
◉ Modern British
01206 263245 | Polstead Street,
CO6 4SA

The Crown
◉◉ Modern British
01206 262001 | CO6 4SE

SUDBURY
The Case Restaurant with Rooms
◉ Mediterranean
01787 210483 | Further Street,
Assington, CO10 5LD

The Mill Hotel
◉ Classic British
01787 375544 | Walnut Tree Lane,
CO10 1BD

THORPENESS
Thorpeness Golf Club & Hotel
◉ Modern British
01728 452176 | Lakeside Avenue,
IP16 4NH

WESTLETON
The Westleton Crown
◉◉ Modern British **V**
01728 648777 | The Street, IP17 3AD

WOODBRIDGE
The Crown at Woodbridge
◉◉ Modern European
01394 384242 | 2 Thoroughfare,
IP12 1AD

Seckford Hall Hotel
◉◉ Modern European, British
01394 385678 | IP13 6NU

YAXLEY
The Auberge
◉◉ Traditional, International
01379 783604 | Ipswich Road,
IP23 8BZ

▶ Surrey

BAGSHOT
The Brasserie at Pennyhill Park
◉◉ Modern British
01276 471774 | London Road,
GU19 5EU

CAMBERLEY
**Macdonald Frimley Hall Hotel
& Spa**
◉◉ British, European
01276 413100 | Lime Avenue,
GU15 2BG

DORKING
**Emlyn at The Mercure
Burford Bridge**
◉◉ Modern British
01306 884561 | Burford Bridge,
Box Hill, RH5 6BX

Two To Four
◉◉ Modern European V
01306 889923 | 2-4 West Street,
RH4 1BL

EAST MOLESEY
Petriti's Restaurant
◉◉ Modern European V
020 8979 5577 | 98 Walton Road,
KT8 0DL

EGHAM
**The Estate Grill
at Great Fosters**
◉◉ Modern British
01784 433822 | Stroude Road,
TW20 9UR

The Runnymede on Thames
◉ British
01784 220600 | Windsor Road,
TW20 0AG

GUILDFORD
The Mandolay Hotel
◉◉ Modern European
01483 303030 | 36-40 London Road,
GU1 2AE

MICKLEHAM
Running Horses
◉ Traditional British
01372 372279 | Old London Road,
RH5 6DU

OTTERSHAW
Foxhills Club & Resort
◉◉ Modern & Traditional British ♟
01932 704471 | Stonehill Road,
KT16 0EL

See advert on page 402

REDHILL
Nutfield Priory Hotel & Spa
◉◉ Modern British
01737 824400 | Nutfield, RH1 4EL

REIGATE
Tony Tobin @ The Dining Room
◉◉ Modern British V
01737 226650 | 59a High Street,
RH2 9AE

RIPLEY
The Anchor
◉◉ Modern British
01483 211866 | High Street,
GU23 6AE

STOKE D'ABERNON
Oak Room
◉◉ Modern British
01372 843933 | Woodlands Lane,
KT11 3QB

WARLINGHAM
India Dining
◉◉ Modern Indian
01883 625905 | 6 The Green,
CR6 9NA

WEYBRIDGE
Brooklands Hotel
◉◉ British, European
01932 335700 | Brooklands Drive,
KT13 0SL

WONERSH
Oak Room Restaurant
◉◉ Modern British
01483 893361 | Barnett Hill Country
House Hotel, Blackheath Lane, GU5 0RF

▶ East Sussex

ALFRISTON
Deans Place
◉◉ Modern British V
01323 870248 | Seaford Road,
BN26 5TW

Sussex, East

BATTLE
The Powder Mills Hotel
◉◉ Modern British **V**
01424 775511 | Powdermill Lane,
TN33 0SP

BODIAM
The Curlew Restaurant
◉◉ Modern British ♛
01580 861394 | Junction Road,
TN32 5UY

BRIGHTON & HOVE
Chilli Pickle
◉◉ Regional Indian
01273 900383 | 17 Jubilee Street,
BN1 1GE

etch. by Steven Edwards
◉◉ Modern British **V**
01273 227485 | 216 Church Road,
Hove, BN3 2DJ

GB1 Restaurant
◉◉ Modern British, Seafood
01273 224300 | The Grand Brighton,
97-99 King's Road, BN1 2FW

The Ginger Dog
◉ Modern British
01273 620990 | 12-13 College Place,
BN2 1HN

The Gingerman Restaurant
◉◉ Modern British
01273 326688 | 21a Norfolk Square,
BN1 2PD

Hotel du Vin Brighton
◉ Traditional British, French
01273 718588 | 2-6 Ship Street,
BN1 1AD

64 Degrees
◉◉ Modern British
01273 770115 | 53 Meeting House
Lane, BN1 1HB

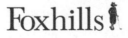

Terre à Terre
◉ Modern Vegetarian **V**
01273 729051 | 71 East Street,
BN1 1HQ

Twenty Four St Georges
◉◉ Modern European
01273 626060 | 24-25 St Georges Road,
Kemp Town Village, BN2 1ED

CAMBER
The Gallivant
◉◉ Modern British **V**
01797 225057 | New Lydd Road,
TN31 7RB

DITCHLING
The Bull
◉ Modern British
01273 843147 | 2 High Street, BN6 8TA

EASTBOURNE
Langham Hotel
◉ Modern British
01323 731451 | 43-49 Royal Parade,
BN22 7AH

The Mirabelle Restaurant
◉◉ Modern & Classic ♟
01323 412345 | The Grand Hotel,
King Edwards Parade, BN21 4EQ

FOREST ROW
The Anderida Restaurant
◉◉ Modern British
01342 824988 | Ashdown Park Hotel,
Wych Cross, RH18 5JR

LEWES
Jolly Sportsman
◉ Modern British, European
01273 890400 | Chapel Lane,
East Chiltington, BN7 3BA

RYE
Mermaid Inn
◉◉ British, Traditional French
01797 223065 | Mermaid Street,
TN31 7EY
See advert below

Sussex, East

RYE *continued*
Webbe's at The Fish Café
◉ Modern British
01797 222226 | 17 Tower Street,
TN31 7AT

TICEHURST
Dale Hill Hotel & Golf Club
◉ Modern European
01580 200112 | TN5 7DQ

UCKFIELD
Buxted Park Hotel
◉◉ Modern European V
01825 733333 & 0845 072 7412 *(calls
cost 7p per minute plus your phone company's
access charge)* | Buxted, TN22 4AY

**East Sussex National Golf
Resort & Spa**
◉◉ Modern British
01825 880088 | Little Horsted,
TN22 5ES

Horsted Place
◉◉ Modern British
01825 750581 | Little Horsted,
TN22 5TS

WESTFIELD
The Wild Mushroom Restaurant
◉◉ Modern British
01424 751137 | Woodgate House,
Westfield Lane, TN35 4SB

WILMINGTON
Crossways
◉◉ Modern British
01323 482455 | Lewes Road,
BN26 5SG

▶ West Sussex

ALBOURNE
The Ginger Fox
◉◉ Modern British, European
01273 857888 | Muddleswood Road,
BN6 9EA

ARUNDEL
The Parsons Table
◉◉ British, European
01903 883477 | 2 & 8 Castle Mews,
Tarrant Street, BN18 9DG

The Town House
◉◉ Modern V
01903 883847 | 65 High Street,
BN18 9AJ

BOSHAM
The Millstream Hotel & Restaurant
◉◉ Modern British
01243 573234 | Bosham Lane,
PO18 8HL

CHICHESTER
Chichester Harbour Hotel
◉ Modern British
01243 778000 | 57 North Street,
PO19 1NH

Crouchers Restaurant & Hotel
◉◉ Modern British V
01243 784995 | Birdham Road,
PO20 7EH

Earl of March
◉ Modern British
01243 533993 & 783991
Lavant Road, PO18 0BQ

Halliday's
◉◉ Modern British
01243 575331 | Watery Lane,
Funtington, PO18 9LF

Richmond Arms
◉ Eclectic
01243 572046 | Mill Road,
West Ashling, PO18 8EA

CHILGROVE
The White Horse
◉ British, European
01243 519444 | High Street,
PO18 9HX

GATWICK AIRPORT
Arora Hotel Gatwick
◉ Modern British
01293 597701 | Southgate Avenue,
Southgate, RH10 6LW

Sofitel London Gatwick
◉◉ British, International
01293 567070 | North Terminal,
RH6 0PH

GOODWOOD
The Goodwood Hotel
◉◉ Modern British
01243 775537 & 01243 755070
PO18 0QB

HAYWARDS HEATH
Jeremy's at Borde Hill
◉◉ Modern European, Mediterranean
01444 441102 | Balcombe Road,
RH16 1XP

HORSHAM
Wabi
◉◉ Modern Japanese
01403 788140 | 38 East Street,
RH12 1HL

LODSWORTH
The Halfway Bridge Inn
◉ Modern British
01798 861281 | Halfway Bridge,
GU28 9BP

LOWER BEEDING
**The Camellia Restaurant
at South Lodge**
◉◉ British **V** 🍷
01403 891711 | Brighton Road,
RH13 6PS

PETWORTH
The Leconfield
◉◉ Modern British
01798 345111 | New Street,
GU28 0AS

ROWHOOK
The Chequers Inn
◉ British
01403 790480 | RH12 3PY

RUSPER
Ghyll Manor
◉ Modern British
0330 123 0371 | High Street,
RH12 4PX

SIDLESHAM
The Crab & Lobster
◉◉ Modern British
01243 641233 | Mill Lane, PO20 7NB

TANGMERE
Cassons Restaurant
◉◉ Modern British
01243 773294 | Arundel Road,
PO18 0DU

TILLINGTON
The Horse Guards Inn
◉ Traditional British
01798 342332 | Upperton Road,
GU28 9AF

TURNERS HILL
Reflections at Alexander House
◉◉ Modern British **V**
01342 714914 | Alexander House Hotel,
East Street, RH10 4QD

▶ Tyne & Wear

GATESHEAD
Eslington Villa Hotel
◉ Modern British
0191 487 6017 | 8 Station Road,
Low Fell, NE9 6DR

NEWCASTLE UPON TYNE
artisan
◉ Modern British
0191 260 5411 | The Biscuit Factory,
16 Stoddart Street, Shieldfield,
NE2 1AN

Blackfriars Restaurant
◉ Modern & Traditional British
0191 261 5945 | Friars Street,
NE1 4XN

Horton Grange Country House Hotel
◉◉ Modern British
01661 860686 | Berwick Hill,
Ponteland, NE13 6BU

Hotel du Vin Newcastle
◉ British, French
0191 229 2200 | Allan House,
City Road, NE1 2BE

Malmaison Newcastle
◉ British, International
0191 245 5000 | 104 Quayside,
NE1 3DX

Peace and Loaf
◉◉ Modern British
0191 281 5222 | 217 Jesmond Road,
Jesmond, NE2 1LA

21
◉ Modern British **V**
0191 222 0755 | Trinity Gardens,
Quayside, NE1 2HH

Vujon
◉ Indian
0191 221 0601 | 29 Queen Street,
Quayside, NE1 3UG

NORTH SHIELDS
Staith House
◉ Modern British
0191 270 8441 | NE30 1JA

TYNEMOUTH
Buddha Lounge
◉ Pan Asian
0191 270 8990 | 76 Front Street,
NE30 4BP

Warwickshire

▶Warwickshire

ALDERMINSTER
The Bell at Alderminster
◉ British
01789 450414 | Shipston Rd, CV37 8NY

Ettington Park Hotel
◉◉ Modern & Traditional British **V**
01789 450123 & 0845 072 7454
*(calls cost 7p per minute plus your phone
company's access charge)* | CV37 8BU

ANSTY
Macdonald Ansty Hall
◉ British
024 7661 2888 | Main Road, CV7 9HZ

ARMSCOTE
The Fuzzy Duck
◉◉ Seasonal, Modern British
01608 682635 | Ilmington Road,
CV37 8DD

EDGEHILL
Castle at Edgehill
◉◉ Modern British
01295 670255 | Main Street, OX15 6DJ

HENLEY-IN-ARDEN
The Bluebell
◉◉ Modern & Classic
01564 793049 | 93 High Street, B95 5AT

ILMINGTON
The Howard Arms
◉ British
01608 682226 | Lower Green, CV36 4LT

KENILWORTH
The Cross at Kenilworth
◉◉ Modern British **V** ♆
01926 853840 | 16 New Steet, CV8 2EZ

LEA MARSTON
Lea Marston Hotel & Spa
◉◉ Modern British
01675 470468 | Haunch Lane, B76 0BY

LEAMINGTON SPA (ROYAL)
The Brasserie at Mallory Court Hotel
◉◉ Modern British **V**
01926 453939 | Harbury Lane,
Bishop's Tachbrook, CV33 9QB

Queans Restaurant
◉ Modern European
01926 315522 | 15 Dormer Place,
CV32 5AA

Restaurant 23 & Morgan's Bar
◉◉ Modern British, European
01926 422422 | 34 Hamilton Terrace,
CV32 4LY

The Tame Hare
◉ Modern British
01926 316191 | 97 Warwick Street,
CV32 4RJ

SHIPSTON ON STOUR
The Red Lion
◉ Traditional British
01608 684221 | Main Street,
Long Compton, CV36 5JS

STRATFORD-UPON-AVON
The Arden Hotel
◉◉ Modern British **V**
01789 298682 | Waterside, CV37 6BA

The Billesley Manor Hotel
◉ Modern British **V**
01789 279955 | Billesley, Alcester,
B49 6NF

Hallmark Hotel The Welcombe
◉ Modern British, French
0330 028 3422 | Warwick Road,
CV37 0NR

Macdonald Alveston Manor
◉ Modern British
01789 205478 | Clopton Bridge,
CV37 7HP

WARWICK
The Brasserie
◉ Modern British
01926 843111 | Ardencote,
The Cumsey, Lye Green Road,
Claverdon, CV35 8LT

Tailors Restaurant
◉◉ Modern British **V**
01926 410590 | 22 Market Place,
CV34 4SL

WISHAW
The Belfry
◉ Modern British, European
01675 238600 | B76 9PR

▶West Midlands

BALSALL COMMON
Nailcote Hall
◉ Traditional European
024 7646 6174 | Nailcote Lane,
Berkswell, CV7 7DE

BIRMINGHAM

Carters of Moseley
◉◉ Modern British **V**
0121 449 8885 | 2c Wake Green Road,
Moseley, B13 9EZ

Circle Restaurant
Birmingham Hippodrome
◉ Modern British
0844 338 9000 *(calls cost 7p per minute*
plus your phone company's access charge)
B5 4TB

Edmunds French Fine Dining
◉◉ French, Mediterranean **V**
0121 633 4944 | 6 Brindleyplace,
B1 2JB

Hotel du Vin & Bistro Birmingham
◉ British, French
0121 200 0600 | 25 Church Street,
B3 2NR

Lasan Restaurant
◉◉ Indian
0121 212 3664 | 3-4 Dakota Buildings,
James Street, St Paul's Square, B3 1SD

Malmaison Birmingham
◉ Modern& Traditional
0121 246 5000 | 1 Wharfside Street,
The Mailbox, B1 1RD

Opus Restaurant
◉◉ Modern British
0121 200 2323 | 54 Cornwall Street,
B3 2DE

DORRIDGE

Hogarths Hotel
◉◉ Modern British
01564 779988 | Four Ashes Road,
B93 8QE

HOCKLEY HEATH

Nuthurst Grange Hotel
◉◉ Modern British **V**
01564 783972 | Nuthurst Grange Lane,
B94 5NL

MERIDEN

Best Western Plus Manor
NEC Birmingham
◉◉ Modern British
01676 522735 | Main Road, CV7 7NH

Forest of Arden Marriott Hotel
& Country Club
◉ Modern British **V**
01676 522335 | Maxstoke Lane,
CV7 7HR

SUTTON COLDFIELD (ROYAL)

The Oak Room Restaurant
◉◉ Modern British
0121 308 3751 | Moor Hall Hotel
& Spa, Moor Hall Drive, Four Oaks,
B75 6LN

Restaurant at New Hall
◉◉ Modern British
0121 378 2442 | Walmley Road,
B76 1QX

See advert on page 408

WALSALL

Fairlawns Hotel & Spa
◉◉ Modern British **V**
01922 455122 | 178 Little Aston Road,
Aldridge, WS9 0NU

WOLVERHAMPTON

Bilash
◉ Indian, Bangladeshi
01902 427762 | 2 Cheapside, WV1 1TU

The Mount Hotel
and Conference Centre
◉◉ Modern European
01902 752055 | Mount Road,
Tettenhall Wood, WV6 8HL

▶ Wiltshire

BEANACRE

Beechfield House Restaurant
◉◉ Modern British
01225 703700 | SN12 7PU

BOX

The Northey Arms
◉ British, European
01225 742333 | Bath Road, SN13 8AE

BRADFORD-ON-AVON

The George
◉ Modern British
01225 865650 & 07511 662784
67 Woolley Street, BA15 1AQ

CALNE

Strand Room
◉◉ Modern British
01249 812488 | The Strand, SN11 0EH

COLERNE

The Brasserie
◉◉ Modern British
01225 742777 | Lucknam Park Hotel
& Spa, SN14 8AZ

Wiltshire

CORSHAM
Guyers House Hotel
◉◉ Modern European, British
01249 713399 | Pickwick,
SN13 0PS

The Methuen Arms
◉◉ British, Italian **V**
01249 717060 | 2 High Street,
SN13 0HB

CRICKLADE
The Red Lion Inn
◉ Modern British
01793 750776 | 74 High Street,
SN6 6DD

DEVIZES
The Peppermill
◉◉ British **V**
01380 710407 | 40 Saint
John's Street, SN10 1BL

EDINGTON
The Three Daggers
◉◉ Modern British
01380 830940 | Westbury Road,
BA13 4PG

FONTHILL BISHOP
The Riverbarn
◉◉ Modern British
01747 820232 | SP3 5SF

FOXHAM
The Foxham Inn
◉ Modern British
01249 740665 | SN15 4NQ

HORNINGSHAM
The Bath Arms at Longleat
◉ Modern British
01985 844308 | Longleat Estate,
BA12 7LY

Restaurant at New Hall
◉◉ Modern British

Tel: 0121 378 2442 **Address:** Walmley Road, B76 1QX
Email: newhall@handpicked.co.uk
Web: www.handpickedhotels.co.uk/newhall

**New Hall's gastronomic philosophy is to offer contemporary British
dishes where the flavour of the ingredients is given pride of place.**

There is no great secret to our food. In fact, we mirror the ethic handed
down by successive Earls of Warwick by living off the land, with menus
changing to match the season. We simply take the freshest regional
ingredients and construct quality British cuisine with creative passion
and flair. The 2 AA Rosette restaurant has an intimate atmosphere
where fine dining is an experience to truly savour. Here you will find
superb food and an extensive selection of wines to complement each
course: the perfect choice, whether you are looking for Sunday lunch,
elevenses or private dining in Birmingham

Head Chef: David Humphreys

LACOCK
Sign of the Angel
@@ British
01249 730230 | 6 Church Street,
SN15 2LB

MALMESBURY
Best Western Mayfield House Hotel
@ Traditional British **V**
01666 577409 | Crudwell, SN16 9EW

PURTON
The Pear Tree at Purton
@@ Modern British
01793 772100 | Church End, SN5 4ED

RAMSBURY
The Bell at Ramsbury
@@ Modern British, European
01672 520230 | The Square, SN8 2PE

ROWDE
The George & Dragon
@@ Modern British, Mediterranean **V**
01380 723053 | High Street, SN10 2PN

SALISBURY
Milano Italian Restaurant
@ Italian
01722 417411 | Milford Hall Hotel,
206 Castle Street, SP1 3TE

SOUTH WRAXALL
The Longs Arms
@@ Seasonal, Modern British
01225 864450 | BA15 2SB

SWINDON
The Angel
@ Modern British
01793 851161 | 47 High Street,
Royal Wootton Bassett, SN4 7AQ

Chiseldon House Hotel
@ Modern European, British
01793 741010 | New Road, Chiseldon,
SN4 0NE

TOLLARD ROYAL
King John Inn
@@ British
01725 516207 | SP5 5PS

WARMINSTER
The Bishopstrow Hotel & Spa
@@ Modern British **V**
01985 212312 | Borenam Road,
BA12 9HH

▶ Worcestershire

ABBERLEY
The Manor Arms
@@ Modern International **V**
01299 890300 | The Village, WR6 6BN

BEWDLEY
The Mug House Inn
@ Modern British
01299 402543 | 12 Severnside North,
DY12 2EE

Royal Forester Country Inn
@ Modern European
01299 266286 | Callow Hill,
DY14 9XW

BROADWAY
The Broadway Hotel
@@ Traditional British
01386 852401 | The Green,
High Street, WR12 7AA

Dormy House Hotel
@@ Modern **V** 🍷
01386 852711 | Willersey Hill,
WR12 7LF

The Fish
@ British
01386 858000 | Farncombe Estate,
WR12 7LJ

Russell's
@@ Modern British
01386 853555 | 20 High Street,
WR12 7DT

EVESHAM
Wood Norton Hotel
@@ Modern British
01386 765611 | Wood Norton,
WR11 4YB

KIDDERMINSTER
The Granary Hotel & Restaurant
@@ Modern British
01562 777535 | Heath Lane,
Shenstone, DY10 4BS

Stone Manor Hotel
@ Traditional
01562 777555 | Stone, DY10 4PJ

MALVERN
L'Amuse Bouche Restaurant
@@ Classic French **V**
01684 572427 | The Cotford Hotel,
51 Graham Road, WR14 2HU

Worcestershire

MALVERN *continued*
The Cottage in the Wood
☖☖ Modern British
01684 588860 | Holywell Road,
Malvern Wells, WR14 4LG

Holdfast Cottage Hotel
☖ Traditional, Modern British
01684 310288 | Marlbank Road,
Welland, WR13 6NA

The Malvern
☖ Modern British
01684 898290 | Grovewood Road,
WR14 1GD

OMBERSLEY
The Venture In Restaurant
☖☖ British, French
01905 620552 | Main Road, WR9 0EW

UPTON UPON SEVERN
White Lion Hotel
☖ Traditional British
01684 592551 | 21 High Street,
WR8 0HJ

▶ East Riding of Yorkshire

BEVERLEY
The Pipe and Glass Inn
☖☖ Modern British V ♟
01430 810246 | West End,
South Dalton, HU17 7PN

▶ North Yorkshire

ALDWARK
Aldwark Manor Golf & Spa Hotel
☖ Classic British
01347 838146 | YO61 1UF

ARKENGARTHDALE
Charles Bathurst Inn
☖ British
01748 884567 | DL11 6EN

ASENBY
Crab & Lobster Restaurant
☖☖ Modern British V
01845 577286 | Dishforth Road,
YO7 3QL

AUSTWICK
The Traddock
☖☖ Modern British
01524 251224 | Settle, LA2 8BY

AYSGARTH
The Aysgarth Falls
☖ Modern V
01969 663775 | DL8 3SR

BIRSTWITH
The Station Hotel
☖ Modern British, Seafood
01423 770254 | Station Road, HG3 3AG

BOLTON ABBEY
The Devonshire Brasserie & Bar
☖ Traditional British
01756 710710 & 718100
The Devonshire Arms Hotel, BD23 6AJ

BOROUGHBRIDGE
The Crown Inn
☖☖ Modern British V
01423 322300 | Roecliffe, YO51 9LY

BURNSALL
The Devonshire Fell
☖ Modern British V
01756 729000 & 718111
BD23 6BT

ESCRICK
The Parsonage Country House Hotel
☖ Modern British V
01904 728111 | York Road, YO19 6LF

GILLING EAST
The Fairfax Arms
☖ Classic British
01439 788212 | Main Street, YO62 4JH

GOATHLAND
Mallyan Spout Hotel
☖ Modern British
01947 896486 | YO22 5AN

GOLDSBOROUGH
Goldsborough Hall
☖ British
01423 867321 | Church Street, HG5 8NR

GRASSINGTON
Grassington House
☖☖ Modern British
01756 752406 | 5 The Square,
BD23 5AQ

GUISBOROUGH
Gisborough Hall
☖☖ Modern British V
01287 611500 | Whitby Lane, TS14 6PT

HAROME
The Star Inn
◉◉ Modern British **V**
01439 770397 | YO62 5JE

HARROGATE
Hotel du Vin & Bistro Harrogate
◉ British, French, European
01423 856800 | Prospect Place,
HG1 1LB

Nidd Hall Hotel
◉◉ Modern British **V**
01423 771598 | Nidd, HG3 3BN

Norse
◉◉ Modern North European
01423 313400 | 28A Swan Road,
HG1 2SA

Rudding Park Hotel, Spa & Golf
◉◉ Modern British
01423 871350 | Rudding Park,
Follifoot, HG3 1JH

Studley Hotel
◉◉ Pacific Rim
01423 560425 | 28 Swan Road,
HG1 2SE

West Park Hotel
◉ Modern British
01423 524471 | West Park, HG1 1BJ

White Hart Hotel
◉◉ Classic British
01423 505081 | 2 Cold Bath Road,
HG2 0NF

HAWES
The Simonstone Brasserie
◉ Modern British **V**
01969 667255 | Simonstone Hall Hotel,
Simonstone, DL8 3LY

HAWNBY
The Inn at Hawnby
◉ Modern European
01439 798202 | YO62 5QS

HELMSLEY
**Feversham Arms Hotel
& Verbena Spa**
◉◉ Modern British **V**
01439 770766 | 1-8 High Street,
YO62 5AG

The Pheasant Hotel
◉◉ Modern British **V**
01439 771241 | Mill Street,
Harome, YO62 5JG

HETTON
The Angel Inn
◉◉ British
01756 730263 | BD23 6LT

HOVINGHAM
The Worsley Arms Hotel
◉◉ Modern British
01653 628130 & 628130
High Street, YO62 4LA

KIRKBY FLEETHAM
Black Horse Inn
◉ Modern British
01609 749010 | 7 Lumley Lane, DL7 0SH

KNARESBOROUGH
General Tarleton Inn
◉◉ Modern British
01423 340284 | Boroughbridge Road,
Ferrensby, HG5 0PZ

MALTON
The Talbot Hotel
◉◉ British
01653 639096 | Yorkersgate, YO17 7AJ

MASHAM
Vennell's
◉◉ Modern British
01765 689000 | 7 Silver Street, HG4 4DX

MIDDLESBROUGH
Chadwicks Inn Maltby
◉◉ Modern British **V**
01642 590300 | High Lane, Maltby,
TS8 0BG

MONK FRYSTON
Monk Fryston Hall
◉ Modern British
01977 682369 | LS25 5DU

OSMOTHERLEY
The Cleveland Tontine
◉◉ Modern British
01609 882671 | Staddlebridge, DL6 3JB

PICKERING
Fox & Hounds Country Inn
◉ Modern British
01751 431577 | Main Street,
Sinnington, YO62 6SQ

The White Swan Inn
◉◉ Modern, Traditional
01751 472288 | Market Place,
YO18 7AA

Yorkshire, North

RICHMOND
The Frenchgate Restaurant and Hotel
◉◉ Modern British
01748 822087 | 59-61 Frenchgate, DL10 7AE

RIPON
The George at Wath
◉◉ Modern
01765 641324 | Main Street, Wath, HG4 5EN

SALTBURN-BY-THE-SEA
Brockley Hall Boutique Hotel & Fine Dining Restaurant
◉◉ Modern British
01287 622179 | TS12 1JS

SCARBOROUGH
Lanterna Ristorante
◉ Italian Seafood
01723 363616 | 33 Queen Street, YO11 1HQ

Palm Court Hotel
◉ Modern British
01723 368161 | St Nicholas Cliff, YO11 2ES

SELBY
Abbey House Restaurant
◉ Modern English
01757 290643 | 8 Park Street, YO8 4PW

WEST WITTON
The Wensleydale Heifer
◉ Modern British V
01969 622322 | Main Street, DL8 4LS

WHITBY
Estbek House
◉◉ Modern British
01947 893424 | East Row, Sandsend, YO21 3SU

YARM
Crathorne Hall Hotel
◉◉ Modern British
01642 700398 & 0845 072 7440 *(calls cost 7p per minute plus your phone company's access charge)* | Crathorne, TS15 0AR

YORK
The Churchill Hotel
◉◉ Modern British
01904 644456 | 65 Bootham, YO30 7DQ

Le Cochon Aveugle
◉◉ Modern French V
01904 640222 | 37 Walmgate, YO1 9TX

Dean Court Hotel
◉ Modern British
01904 625082 | Duncombe Place, YO1 7EF

The Grange Hotel
◉◉ Modern
01904 644744 | 1 Clifton, YO30 6AA

Guy Fawkes Inn
◉ British
01904 466674 | 25 High Petergate, YO1 7HP

Hotel du Vin & Bistro York
◉ European, French
01904 557350 | 89 The Mount, YO24 1AX

The Judge's Lodging
◉ Modern British
01904 638733 | 9 Lendal, YO1 8AQ

Lamb & Lion Inn
◉ Modern British
01904 654112 | 2-4 High Petergate, YO1 7EH

Middlethorpe Hall & Spa
◉◉ Traditional British ♟
01904 641241 | Bishopthorpe Road, Middlethorpe, YO23 2GB

Oxo's on The Mount
◉◉ Modern European V
01904 619444 | The Mount Royale Hotel, 119 The Mount, YO24 1GU

Skosh
◉◉ Contemporary British
01904 634849 | 98 Micklegate, YO1 6JX

▶ South Yorkshire

ROTHERHAM
Hellaby Hall Hotel
◉ Modern British
01709 702701 | Old Hellaby Lane, Hellaby, S66 8SN

SHEFFIELD
Best Western Plus Aston Hall Hotel
◉ Modern British V
0114 287 2309 | Worksop Road, Aston, S26 2EE

Jöro Restaurant
◉◉ British, Scandinavian **V**
0114 299 1539 | Krynkl, 294
Shalesmoor, S3 8UL

Nonnas
◉ Modern Italian
0114 268 6166 | 535-541 Ecclesall Road,
S11 8PR

Rafters Restaurant
◉◉ Modern British
0114 230 4819 | 220 Oakbrook Road,
Nethergreen, S11 7ED

See advert below

Whitley Hall Hotel
◉◉ Modern British
0114 245 4444 | Elliott Lane,
Grenoside, S35 8NR

WORTLEY
The Wortley Arms
◉ Modern British **V**
0114 288 8749 | Halifax Road,
S35 7DB

▶ **West Yorkshire**

BRADFORD
Prashad
◉◉ Indian Vegetarian **V**
0113 285 2037 | 137 Whitehall Road,
Drighlington, BD11 1AT

CLIFTON
The Black Horse Inn
Restaurant with Rooms
◉ Modern British, Mediterranean
01484 713862 | Westgate, HD6 4HJ

HALIFAX
Holdsworth House Hotel
◉◉ Traditional British
01422 240024 | Holdsworth Road,
Holmfield, HX2 9TG

Shibden Mill Inn
◉◉ Modern British **V**
01422 365840 | Shibden Mill Fold,
Shibden, HX3 7UL

See advert on page 414

220 Oakbrook Road,
Sheffield,
S11 7ED
01142 304819
bookings@raftersrestaurant.co.uk

www.shibdenmillinn.com

Nestling in the fold of West Yorkshire's picturesque Shibden Valley.

For over 350 years *The Shibden Mill Inn* has been at the heart of life in West Yorkshire's Shibden Valley. It's a magical place where generation after generation of locals have enjoyed time well spent with friends and family, sharing in life's special moments and shaping memories to last a life time.

The inn's reputation for warm hospitality, premier 2 Rosette gastro dining and 5 Star Inn accommodation draws people to the Shibden Valley from far and wide, and the Mill has naturally become a popular choice for those wishing to savour a sumptuous weekend break or mid-week stay.

Stunning countryside walks are in easy reach, as too are the bright lights and city centre shopping on offer in Leeds. From its unique location, Shibden Mill Inn offers easy access to the very best to be found in this delightful part of West Yorkshire.

Opening times for breakfast, morning coffee & cake, afternoon teas, lunch and dinner can be found on the food page of the website:
www. shibdenmillinn.com

Tel. 01422 365840
enquiries@shibdenmillinn.co.uk
www.shibdenmillinn.co.uk

HUDDERSFIELD
315 Bar and Restaurant
◉◉ Modern **V**
01484 602613 | 315 Wakefield Road,
Lepton, HD8 0LX

LEEDS
Fourth Floor Café
◉ British, Modern Mediterranean
0113 204 8888 & 204 8000
107-111 Briggate, LS1 6AZ

Malmaison Leeds
◉ Modern British
0113 398 1000 | 1 Swinegate, LS1 4AG

Salvo's Restaurant & Salumeria
◉ Italian
0113 275 5017 | 115 Otley Road,
Headingley, LS6 3PX

Thorpe Park Hotel & Spa
◉ British, French
0113 264 1000 | Century Way,
Thorpe Park, LS15 8ZB

Town Hall Tavern
◉ Modern British
0113 244 0765 | 17 Westgate,
LS1 2RA

LIVERSEDGE
Healds Hall Hotel & Restaurant
◉ Modern British
01924 409112 | Leeds Road,
WF15 6JA

PONTEFRACT
Wentbridge House Hotel
◉◉ Modern British **V** ⚑
01977 620444 | The Great North Road,
Wentbridge, WF8 3JJ

WAKEFIELD
Waterton Park Hotel
◉ Modern, Traditional British **V**
01924 257911 | Walton Hall, The Balk,
Walton, WF2 6PW

WETHERBY
Wood Hall Hotel & Spa
◉◉ Modern British **V**
01937 587271 & 0845 072 7564
*(calls cost 7p per minute plus your phone
company's access charge)* | Trip Lane,
Linton, LS22 4JA

CHANNEL ISLANDS

▶ **Guernsey**
ST MARTIN
The Auberge
◉◉ Modern British
01481 238485 | Jerbourg Road,
GY4 6BH

La Barbarie Hotel
◉ Traditional British
01481 235217 | Saints Road,
Saints Bay, GY4 6ES

**Bella Luce Hotel,
Restaurant & Spa**
◉◉ French, Mediterranean **V**
01481 238764 | La Fosse, GY4 6EB

ST PETER PORT
Best Western Hotel de Havelet
◉ Traditional British, International **V**
01481 722199 | Havelet, GY1 1BA

The Duke of Richmond Hotel
◉ Modern, British, French
01481 726221 & 740866
Cambridge Park, GY1 1UY

Mora Restaurant & Grill
◉ Modern Mediterranean
01481 715053 | The Quay, GY1 2LE

**The Old Government
House Hotel & Spa**
◉ Modern European **V**
01481 724921 | St Ann's Place,
GY1 2NU

▶ **Herm**
White House Hotel
◉◉ European, Traditional British **V**
01481 750000 & 750075 | GY1 3HR

▶ **Jersey**
GOREY
The Moorings Hotel & Restaurant
◉◉ Traditional
01534 853633 | Gorey Pier, JE3 6EW

Sumas
◉◉ Modern British **V**
01534 853291 | Gorey Hill, JE3 6ET

ROZEL
Château la Chaire
◉◉ Classic Traditional
01534 863354 | Rozel Bay, JE3 6AJ

Jersey

ST BRELADE
L'Horizon Beach Hotel and Spa
◉◉ Modern British
01534 743101 | JE3 8EF

Oyster Box
◉◉ Modern British
01534 850888 | JE3 8EF

ST CLEMENT
Green Island Restaurant
◉ Mediterranean, Seafood
01534 857787 | Green Island, JE2 6LS

ST HELIER
Best Western Royal Hotel
◉ Modern European
01534 726521 | David Place, JE2 4TD

Dorans
◉ British, French
01534 611111 | The Hotel Revere,
Kensington Place, JE2 3PA

Hampshire Hotel
◉ Mediterranean
01534 724115 | 53 Val Plaisant, JE2 4TB

ST PETER
Greenhills Country Hotel
◉ Mediterranean, British, French
01534 481042 | Mont de L'Ecole,
JE3 7EL

Mark Jordan at the Beach
◉◉ Anglo French
01534 780180 | La Plage,
La Route de la Haule, JE3 7YD

▶ Sark

La Sablonnerie
◉ International
01481 832061 | Little Sark, GY10 1SD
See advert below

Stocks Hotel
◉◉ Modern British
01481 832001 | GY10 1SD

La Sablonnerie Hotel

Enjoy the magical charm of La Sablonnerie, a hotel of rare quality situated in the southern part of Sark, even more beautiful, remote and romantic than the rest.

Unspoiled and scenic, it is a haven for lovers of peace and tranquillity.

Nestled in gorgeous gardens this oasis of hospitality has an enchanting air of simplicity and sophistication.

The bar is a convivial meeting place with roaring log fire. Savour a gourmet luncheon, or dine romantically by candlelight.

Excellent cuisine, including fresh Sark lobster and produce from our farm and gardens.

Own horses and carriages.

Chosen by the hotel guide 'Which?' as 'The place to stay in the Channel Islands' and also awarded 'Johansens Small Hotel of the Year'.

Don't leave the island without visiting Little Sark. It will be a truly amazing experience that will live with you forever.

Birds, Butterflies and Flowers – Sark – How could one not enjoy this beautiful paradise?

A stepping stone to heaven. A hotel with a real 'joie de vivre'.

SCOTLAND

▶Aberdeen

Fusion
◉ Modern European
01224 652959 | 10 North Silver Street,
AB10 1RL

IX Restaurant
◉◉ Modern Scottish
01244 327777 | The Chester Hotel,
59-63 Queens Road, AB15 4YP

Malmaison Aberdeen
◉ Modern French
01224 327370 | 49-53 Queens Road,
AB15 4YP

**Mercure Aberdeen Ardoe
House Hotel & Spa**
◉ Modern Scottish, French
01224 860600 | South Deeside Road,
Blairs, AB12 5YP

Moonfish Café
◉ Modern British
01224 644166 | 9 Correction Wynd,
AB10 1IIP

The Silver Darling
◉◉ French, Seafood
01224 576229 | Pocra Quay,
North Pier, AB11 5DQ

▶Aberdeenshire

BALLATER
Loch Kinord Hotel
◉ Traditional Scottish
01339 885229 | Ballater Road,
Dinnet, AB34 5JY

BALMEDIE
Cock & Bull
◉ Modern Scottish, British
01358 743249 | Ellon Road, Blairton,
AB23 8XY

BANCHORY
The Falls of Feugh Restaurant
◉ Modern British
01330 822123 | Bridge of Feugh,
AB31 6NL

ELLON
Eat on the Green
◉◉ British, Scottish, European
01651 842337 | Udny Green,
AB41 7RS

INVERURIE
The Green Lady
◉◉ Modern British
01467 621643 | Thainstone House,
AB51 5NT

Macdonald Pittodrie House
◉◉ Modern, Traditional Scottish
01467 622437 | Chapel of Garioch,
Pitcaple, AB51 5HS

KILDRUMMY
Kildrummy Inn
◉◉ Modern Scottish
01975 571227 | AB33 8QS

OLDMELDRUM
**Meldrum House Country Hotel
& Golf Course**
◉◉ Modern Scottish
01651 872294 | AB51 0AE

PETERHEAD
Buchan Braes Hotel
◉ Modern Scottish, European
01779 871471 | Boddam, AB42 3AR

STONEHAVEN
The Tolbooth Seafood Restaurant
◉ Modern British, Seafood
01569 762287 | Old Pier,
Stonehaven Harbour, AB39 2JU

▶Angus

CARNOUSTIE
Carnoustie Golf Hotel & Spa
◉ Bistro, Scottish, European
01241 411999 | The Links, DD7 7JE

FORFAR
Drovers
◉ Modern Scottish
01307 860322 | Memus By Forfar,
DD8 3TY

▶Argyll & Bute

ARDUAINE
Loch Melfort Hotel
◉◉ Modern British
01852 200233 | PA34 4XG

COVE
Knockderry House
◉◉ Modern Scottish
01436 842283 | Shore Road,
G84 0NX

417

Argyll & Bute

KILCHRENAN
The Ardanaiseig Hotel
◉◉ Modern British V
01866 833333 & 833337
by Loch Awe, PA35 1HE

Taychreggan Hotel
◉◉ Classic French, Seafood V
01866 833211 | PA35 1HQ

LUSS
The Lodge on Loch Lomond
◉◉ Modern British, International
01436 860201 | G83 8PA

OBAN
Coast
◉ Modern British
01631 569900 | 104 George Street,
PA34 5NT

The Hawthorn Restaurant
◉ Modern British
01631 720777 | 5 Keil Crofts,
Benderloch, PA37 1QS

Manor House Hotel
◉ Scottish, European
01631 562087 | Gallanach Road,
PA34 4LS

PORT APPIN
The Pierhouse Hotel
◉ Seafood
01631 730302 | PA38 4DE

RHU
Rosslea Hall Hotel
◉ Modern Scottish
01436 439955 | Ferry Road, G84 8NF

TARBERT
Stonefield Castle Hotel
◉ Scottish
01880 820836 | PA29 6YJ

TAYNUILT
Etive Restaurant
◉◉ Seasonal, Scottish
01866 822437 | The Taynuilt, PA35 1JN

▶ Ayrshire, South
AYR
Enterkine Country House
◉◉ Modern British V
01292 520580 | Annbank, KA6 5AL

Fairfield House Hotel
◉ Modern International
01292 267461 | 12 Fairfield Road,
KA7 2AS

TROON
MacCallums of Troon
◉ International, Seafood
01292 319339 | The Harbour,
KA10 6DH

TURNBERRY
Trump Turnberry
◉◉ Traditional French
01655 331000 | Maidens Road,
KA26 9LT

▶ Dumfries & Galloway
AUCHENCAIRN
Balcary Bay Hotel
◉◉ Modern European
01556 640217 & 640311
Shore Road, DG7 1QZ

GATEHOUSE OF FLEET
Cally Palace Hotel
◉ Traditional British V
01557 814341 | Cally Drive, DG7 2DL

GRETNA
Smiths at Gretna Green
◉◉ Modern British, International
01461 337007 | Gretna Green,
DG16 5EA

MOFFAT
Brodies
◉ Modern British
01683 222870 | Holm Street, DG10 9EB

SANQUHAR
Blackaddie House Hotel
◉◉ Modern British
01659 50270 | Blackaddie Road,
DG4 6JJ

THORNHILL
**The Buccleuch and Queensberry
Arms Hotel**
◉ Modern Scottish V
01848 323101 | 112 Drumlanrig Street,
DG3 5LU

▶ Dunbartonshire, West

BALLOCH
The Cameron Grill
◉◉ Modern British
01389 722582 | Cameron House on
Loch Lomond, G83 8QZ

CLYDEBANK
Golden Jubilee Conference Hotel
◉ Modern British
0141 951 6000 | Beardmore Street,
G81 4SA

▶ Dundee

Castlehill Restaurant
◉◉ Modern Scottish
01382 220008 | 22-26 Exchange Street,
DD1 3DL

Malmaison Dundee
◉ British, French
01382 339715 | 44 Whitehall Crescent,
DD1 4AY

The Tayberry
◉◉ Scottish V
01382 698280 | 594 Brook Street,
Broughty Ferry, DD5 2EA

▶ Edinburgh

The Atelier
◉◉ Modern European
0131 629 5040 | 159-161 Morrison
Street, EH3 8AG

Dia Distot
◉ British, French
0131 452 8453 | 19 Colinton Road,
EH10 5DP

The Bon Vivant
◉ Contemporary European
0131 225 3275 | 55 Thistle Street,
EH2 1DY

**The Brasserie –
Norton House Hotel & Spa**
◉ Modern British
0131 333 1275 | Ingliston, EH28 8LX

Britannia Spice
◉ Indian, Thai, Bangladeshi V
0131 555 2255 | 150 Commercial
Street, EH6 6LB

The Café Royal
◉ Modern Scottish
0131 556 1884 | 19 West Register
Street, EH2 2AA

Calistoga Restaurant
◉ Modern American ♛
0131 225 1233 | 70 Rose Street,
North Lane, EH2 3DX

Chop Chop
◉ Traditional Chinese
0131 221 1155 | 248 Morrison Street,
Haymarket, EH3 8DT

**AA Restaurant of the Year
for Scotland 2017-18
The Dining Room**
◉◉ Modern French, Scottish V
0131 220 2044 & 07496 146652
28 Queen Street, EH2 1JX

See page 271

Divino Enoteca
◉ Modern Italian, International
0131 225 1770 | 5 Merchant Street,
EH1 2QD

**The Dungeon Restaurant
at Dalhousie Castle**
◉◉ Traditional European
01875 820153 | Bonnyrigg, EH19 3JB

l'escargot blanc
◉ French
0131 226 1890 | 17 Queensferry
Street, EH2 4QW

l'escargot bleu
◉ French, Scottish
0131 557 1600 | 56 Broughton
Street, EH1 3SA

La Favorita
◉ Modern Italian, Mediterranean
0131 554 2430 | 325-331 Leith Walk,
EH6 8SA

Field
◉ Scottish
0131 667 7010 | 41 West Nicolson
Street, EH8 9DB

Galvin Brasserie de Luxe
◉ French
0131 222 8988 | The Caledonian,
Princes Street, EH1 2AB

The Gardener's Cottage
◉ British
0131 558 1221 | 1 Royal Terrace
Gardens, London Road, EH7 5DX

La Garrigue
◉◉ French, Mediterranean ♛
0131 557 3032 | 31 Jeffrey Street,
EH1 1DH

419

Edinburgh

Hadrian's Brasserie
⊛ Modern Scottish
0131 557 5000 | The Balmoral Hotel,
1 Princes Street, EH2 2EQ

Harajuku Kitchen
⊛ Japanese
0131 281 0526 | 10 Gillespie Place,
EH10 4HS

**Harvey Nichols Forth Floor
Restaurant**
⊛ British, European, International 🍷
0131 524 8350 | 30-34 St Andrew
Square, EH2 2AD

The Honours
⊛⊛ Modern French
0131 220 2513 | 58a North Castle
Street, EH2 3LU

Hotel du Vin Edinburgh
⊛ Modern British, French
0131 247 4900 | 11 Bristo Place,
EH1 1EZ

The Howard
⊛ Traditional British, French
0131 557 3500 | 34 Great King Street,
EH3 6QH

Kanpai Sushi
⊛ Japanese
0131 228 1602 | 8-10 Grindlay Street,
EH3 9AS

Locanda De Gusti
⊛⊛ Italian, Mediterranean, Seafood
0131 346 8800 | 102 Dalry Road,
EH11 2DW

Malmaison Edinburgh
⊛ British, French
0131 468 5000 | One Tower Place,
Leith, EH6 7BZ

Mother India's Cafe
⊛ Indian Tapas
0131 524 9801 | 3-5 Infirmary Street,
EH1 1LT

The Mumbai Mansion
⊛⊛ Modern Indian V
0131 229 7173 & 229 7886
250 Morrison Street, EH3 8DT

New Chapter
⊛ Scottish, European
0131 556 0006 & 07956 396806
18 Eyre Place, EH3 5EP

Ondine Restaurant
⊛⊛ Seafood 🍷
0131 226 1888 | 2 George IV Bridge,
EH1 1AD

One Square
⊛ Modern British
0131 221 6422 | Sheraton Grand Hotel
& Spa, 1 Festival Square, EH3 9SR

The Restaurant at The Bonham Hotel
⊛ Classic Scottish, British
0131 226 6050 | 35 Drumsheugh
Gardens, EH3 7RN

Rhubarb at Prestonfield House
⊛⊛ Traditional British 🍷
0131 225 1333 | Priestfield Road,
EH16 5UT

The Scran & Scallie
⊛ Traditional Scottish V
0131 332 6281 | 1 Comely Bank Road,
EH4 1DT

The Stockbridge Restaurant
⊛⊛ Scottish, European
0131 226 6766 | 54 Saint Stephen
Street, EH3 5AL

Taisteal
⊛ Modern Scottish
0131 332 9977 | 1-3 Raeburn Place,
Stockbridge, EH4 1HU

Ten Hill Place Hotel
⊛ Modern, Traditional British
0131 662 2080 | 10 Hill Place,
EH8 9DS

The Witchery by the Castle
⊛ Traditional Scottish 🍷
0131 225 5613 | Castlehill,
The Royal Mile, EH1 2NF

RATHO
The Bridge Inn at Ratho
⊛ Modern British
0131 333 1320 | 27 Baird Road,
EH28 8RA

▶ Falkirk

BANKNOCK
Glenskirlie House & Castle
◉◉ Modern British **V**
01324 840201 | Kilsyth Road, FK4 1UF

POLMONT
Macdonald Inchyra Hotel and Spa
◉ Modern & Traditional
01324 711911 | Grange Road, FK2 0YB

▶ Fife

CUPAR
Ostlers Close Restaurant
◉◉ Modern Scottish **V**
01334 655574 | Bonnygate, KY15 4BU

NEWPORT-ON-TAY
The Newport Restaurant
◉◉ Modern Scottish **V**
01382 541449 | 1 High Street, DD6 8AB

ST ANDREWS
The Adamson
◉◉ Modern British
01334 479191 | 127 South Street,
KY16 9UH

Ardgowan Hotel
◉ Steakhouse, Scottish
01334 472970 | 2 Playfair Terrace,
North Street, KY16 9HX

Hotel du Vin St Andrews
◉ French, British
01334 045313 | 40 The Scores,
KY16 9AS

Rufflets Hotel
◉◉ Modern British, European **♟**
01334 472594 | Strathkinness Low
Road, KY16 9TX

St Andrews Bar & Grill
◉ Scottish
01334 837000 | Fairmont St Andrews
Scotland, KY16 8PN

Sands Grill
◉ Modern Scottish
01334 474371 | The Old Course Hotel,
Golf Resort & Spa, KY16 9SP

ST MONANS
Craig Millar@16 West End
◉◉ Modern Scottish **♟**
01333 730327 | 16 West End,
KY10 2BX

▶ Glasgow

Blythswood Square
◉◉ Modern British **♟**
0141 248 8888 | 11 Blythswood Square,
G2 4AD

La Bonne Auberge
◉ French, Mediterranean
0141 352 8310 | Holiday Inn Glasgow,
161 West Nile Street, G1 2RL

The Fish People Café
◉ Modern Seafood
0141 429 8787 | 350a Scotland Street,
G5 8QF

Gamba
◉◉ Scottish, Seafood
0141 572 0899 | 225a West George
Street, G2 2ND

The Hanoi Bike Shop
◉ Vietnamese **V**
0141 334 7165 | 8 Ruthven Lane,
G12 9BG

See advert on page 422

Malmaison Glasgow
◉◉ Modern French
0141 572 1001
278 West George Street, G2 4LL

Mother India
◉ Indian
0141 221 1663
28 Westminster Terrace,
Sauchiehall Street, G3 7RU

Number Sixteen
◉◉ Modern International
0141 339 2544 | 16 Byres Road,
G11 5JY

111 by Nico
◉ Modern European **V**
0141 334 0111 | 111 Cleveden Road,
Kelvinside, G12 0JU

Opium
◉ Chinese, Oriental Fusion
0141 332 6668 | 191 Hope Street,
G2 2UL

Ox and Finch
◉◉ Modern British **V**
0141 339 8627 | 920 Sauchiehall Street,
G3 7TF

THE HANOI BIKE SHOP

VIETNAMESE CANTEEN

GLASGOW *continued*
La Parmigiana
Italian, Mediterranean
0141 334 0686 | 447 Great Western
Road, Kelvinbridge, G12 8HH

Shish Mahal
Indian
0141 339 8256 | 60-68 Park Road,
G4 9JF

Stravaigin
Modern International, Scottish V
0141 334 2665 | 28 Gibson Street,
Kelvinbridge, G12 8NX
See advert on page 424

Turnip & Enjoy Restaurant
Modern European V
0141 334 6622 | 393-395 Great Western
Road, Kelvinbridge, G4 9HY

Ubiquitous Chip Restaurant
Scottish V ♆
0141 334 5007 & 334 7109
12 Ashton Lane, G12 8SJ
See advert on page 425

Urban Bar and Brasserie
Modern British
0141 248 5636 | 23-25 St Vincent Place,
G1 2DT

Wee Lochan
Modern Scottish
0141 338 6606 | 340 Crow Road,
Broomhill, G11 7HT

▶ Highland

CROMARTY
The Factor's House
Modern British
01381 600394 | Denny Road, IV11 8YT

DORNOCH
Links House at Royal Dornoch
Classic Scottish
01862 810279 | Links House, Golf Road,
IV25 3LW

FORT AUGUSTUS
The Inch
Modern Scottish
01456 450900 | Inchnacardoch Bay,
PH32 4BL

GLENFINNAN
The Prince's House
Modern British
01397 722246 | PH37 4LT

INVERGARRY
Glengarry Castle Hotel
Scottish, International
01809 501254 | PH35 4HW

INVERGORDON
Kincraig Castle Hotel
Modern Scottish
01349 852587 | IV18 0LF

INVERNESS
Bunchrew House Hotel
Scottish
01463 234917 | Bunchrew, IV3 8TA

Contrast Brasserie
Scottish V
01463 223777 | Glenmoriston Town
House Hotel, 20 Ness Bank, IV2 4SF

Loch Ness Country House Hotel
Modern British
01463 230512 | Loch Ness Road,
IV3 8JN

The New Drumossie Hotel
Modern Scottish
01463 236451 | Old Perth Road,
IV2 5BE

Rocpool
Modern European
01463 717274 | 1 Ness Walk, IV3 5NE

Rocpool Reserve and Chez Roux
French, Scottish V
01463 240089 | 14 Culduthel Road,
IV2 4AG

LOCHALINE
The Whitehouse Restaurant
Modern Scottish V
01967 421777 | PA80 5XT

LOCHINVER
Inver Lodge and Chez Roux
French V
01571 844496 | Iolaire Road, IV27 4LU

MUIR OF ORD
Ord House Hotel
British, French
01463 870492 | Ord Drive, IV6 7UH

NAIRN
Golf View Hotel & Spa
Modern Scottish V
01667 452301 | Seabank Road,
IV12 4HD

THINK GLOBAL

Stravaigin

WANDERING
SINCE 1994

EAT LOCAL

28 GIBSON ST KELVINBRIDGE GLASGOW G12 8NX
STRAVAIGIN.CO.UK f 🐦 📷 0141 334 2665

Ubiquitous Chip

UBIQUITOUS CHIP 12 ASHTON LANE GLASGOW G12 8SJ
0141 334 5007 🅕 🅣 🅨 🅞 UBIQUITOUSCHIP.CO.UK

Highland

SPEAN BRIDGE
Russell's at Smiddy House
◎◎ Modern Scottish
01397 712335 | Roy Bridge Road,
PH34 4EU

STRONTIAN
Kilcamb Lodge Hotel
◎◎ Modern Seafood V ♉
01967 402257 | PH36 4HY

TAIN
**The Glenmorangie Highland Home
at Cadboll**
◎◎ British, French
01862 871671 | Cadboll, Fearn,
IV20 1XP

THURSO
Forss House Hotel
◎◎ Modern Scottish
01847 861201 | Forss, KW14 7XY

WICK
Mackay's Hotel
◎ Modern Scottish V
01955 602323 | Union Street,
KW1 5ED

▶ Lanarkshire, North

CUMBERNAULD
**The Westerwood Hotel
& Golf Resort**
◎ Modern Scottish
01236 457171 | 1 St Andrews Drive,
Westerwood, G68 0EW

▶ Lanarkshire, South

EAST KILBRIDE
Macdonald Crutherland House
◎◎ British
01355 577000 | Strathaven Road,
G75 0QZ

STRATHAVEN
Rissons at Springvale
◎ Modern Scottish V
01357 520234 | 18 Lethame Road,
ML10 6AD

▶ Lothian, East

ABERLADY
Ducks Inn
◎◎ Modern British
01875 870682 | Main Street, EH32 0RE

GULLANE
Greywalls and Chez Roux
◎◎ Modern French V
01620 842144 | Muirfield, EH31 2EG

La Potinière
◎◎ Modern British
01620 843214 | Main Street,
EH31 2AA

NORTH BERWICK
Macdonald Marine Hotel & Spa
◎◎ European
01620 897300 | Cromwell Road,
EH39 4LZ

▶ Lothian, West

LINLITHGOW
Champany Inn
◎◎ Traditional British
01506 834532 | Champany Corner,
EH49 7LU

UPHALL
Macdonald Houstoun House
◎◎ Traditional British,
Modern Scottish
01506 853831 | EH52 6JS

▶ Midlothian

DALKEITH
The Sun Inn
◎ Modern & Traditional
0131 663 2456 | Lothian Bridge,
EH22 4TR

▶ Moray

ELGIN
Mansion House Hotel
◎ Traditional Scottish
01343 548811 | The Haugh, IV30 1AW

FORRES
Cluny Bank
◎ Traditional European
01309 674304 | 69 St Leonards Road,
IV36 1DW

▶ Perth & Kinross

AUCHTERARDER
The Strathearn
◉◉ British, French
01764 694270 | The Gleneagles Hotel,
PH3 1NF

COMRIE
Royal Hotel
◉ Traditional Scottish
01764 679200 | Melville Square,
PH6 2DN

FORTINGALL
Fortingall Hotel
◉ Modern Scottish
01887 830367 | PH15 2NQ

KILLIECRANKIE
Killiecrankie Hotel
◉◉ Modern British V
01796 473220 | PH16 5LG

KINCLAVEN
Ballathie House Hotel
◉◉ Classic V
01250 883268 | PH1 4QN

PERTH
Deans Restaurant
◉◉ Modern Scottish
01738 643377 | 77 79 Kinnoull Street,
PH1 5EZ

Murrayshall House Hotel
& Golf Course
◉ Modern British
01738 551171 | New Scone, PH2 7PH

Pig'Halle
◉ French
01738 248784 | 38 South Street,
PH2 8PG

The Roost Restaurant
◉◉ British, Modern French
01738 812111 | Forgandenny Road,
Bridge of Earn, PH2 9AZ

63@Parklands
◉◉ Modern European V 01738
622451 | Parklands Hotel,
2 St Leonards Bank, PH2 8EB

63 Tay Street Restaurant
◉◉ Modern Scottish V ▾
01738 441451 | 63 Tay Street, PH2 8NN

Tabla
◉ Indian V
01738 444630 | 173 South Street,
PH2 8NY

PITLOCHRY
Knockendarroch
◉◉ Modern Scottish
01796 473473 | Higher Oakfield,
PH16 5HT

ST FILLANS
The Four Seasons Hotel
◉◉ Modern British V
01764 685333 | Loch Earn, PH6 2NF

SPITTAL OF GLENSHEE
Dalmunzie Castle Hotel
◉ Modern British V
01250 885224 | PH10 7QG

▶ Scottish Borders

KELSO
The Cobbles Freehouse & Dining
◉ Modern British
01573 223548 | 7 Bowmont Street,
TD5 7JH

The Roxburghe Hotel, Golf Course
and Chez Roux
◉◉ British, French V
01573 229250 | Heiton, TD5 8JZ

MELROSE
Burts Hotel
◉◉ Modern Scottish, British
01896 822285 | Market Square, TD6 9PL

▶ Stirling

ABERFOYLE
Macdonald Forest Hills Hotel
& Resort
◉ Modern Scottish
01877 389500 | Kinlochard, FK8 3TL

FINTRY
Culcreuch Castle Hotel & Estate
◉◉ Traditional Scottish V
01360 860555 | Kippen Road, G63 0LW

STIRLING
The Stirling Highland Hotel
◉ British, European
01786 272727 | Spittal Street, FK8 1DU

SCOTTISH ISLANDS

▶ Isle of Harris
TARBERT (TAIRBEART)
Hotel Hebrides
◉ Modern Scottish, Seafood
01859 502364 | Pier Road, HS3 3DG

▶ Isle of Mull
FIONNPHORT
Ninth Wave Restaurant
◉ Modern, Pacific Rim V
01681 700757 | PA66 6BL

TOBERMORY
Highland Cottage
◉◉ Modern Scottish, International
01688 302030 | 24 Breadalbane Street,
PA75 6PD

▶ Shetland
SCALLOWAY
Scalloway Hotel
◉◉ Scottish, Seafood V
01595 880444 | Main Street, ZE1 0TR

▶ Isle of Skye
ISLEORNSAY
Duisdale House Hotel
◉◉ Modern Scottish
01471 833202 | Sleat, IV43 8QW

Hotel Eilean Iarmain
◉ Modern & Traditional Scottish
01471 833332 | Sleat, IV43 8QR

Toravaig House Hotel
◉◉ Modern Scottish
01471 820200 | Knock Bay, Sleat,
IV44 8RE

PORTREE
Dulse & Brose
◉◉ Scottish, Seafood
01478 612846 | Bosville Hotel,
9-11 Bosville Terrace, IV51 9DG

STEIN
Loch Bay Restaurant
◉ Seafood, Traditional Scottish, French
01470 592235 | Macleods Terrace,
IV55 8GA

WALES

▶ Isle of Anglesey
BEAUMARIS
Bishopsgate House Hotel
◉ Traditional Welsh V
01248 810302 | 54 Castle Street,
LL58 8BB

The Bull - Beaumaris
◉◉ Modern British
01248 810329 | Castle Street,
LL58 8AP

Château Rhianfa
◉ Modern French
01248 713656 | LL59 5NS

LLANFACHRAETH
Black Lion Inn
◉ Modern, Traditional British
01407 730718 | Llanfaethlu, LL65 4NL

▶ Cardiff
CARDIFF
Bully's
◉◉ French, European
029 2022 1905 | 5 Romilly Crescent,
CF11 9NP

Moksh
◉◉ Indian V
029 2049 8120 | Ocean Building,
Bute Crescent, CF10 5AN

Park House Restaurant
◉◉ British, International V ♆
029 2022 4343 | 20 Park Place,
CF10 3DQ

▶ Carmarthenshire
LAUGHARNE
The Corran Resort & Spa
◉◉ Modern British, Welsh
01994 427417 | East Marsh, SA33 4RS

LLANELLI
Sosban Restaurant
◉◉ British, French
01554 270020 | The Pumphouse,
North Dock, SA15 2LF

LLANSTEFFAN
Mansion House Llansteffan
◉◉ Modern British
01267 241515 | Pantyrathro, SA33 5AJ

NANTGAREDIG
Y Polyn
◉◉ Classic European
01267 290000 | SA32 7LH

Ceredigion

CARDIGAN
Caemorgan Mansion
◉ Modern European
01239 613297 | Caemorgan Road,
SA43 1QU

LAMPETER
The Falcondale Hotel & Restaurant
◉◉ Modern British
01570 422910 | Falcondale Drive,
SA48 7RX

LLECHRYD
Hammet House
◉◉ Modern British **V**
01239 682382 & 07866 682451
SA43 2QA

TREGARON
Y Talbot
◉◉ Modern British
01974 298208 | The Square, SY25 6JL

Conwy

ABERGELE
Brasserie 1786
◉ Modern British
01745 832014 | The Kinmel,
St George's Road, LL22 9AS

The Kinmel Arms
◉◉ Modern British, French
01745 832207 | The Village, St George,
LL22 9BP

BETWS-Y-COED
Craig-y-Dderwen Riverside Hotel
◉ Traditional, International
01690 710293 | LL24 0AS

Llugwy River
Restaurant@Royal Oak Hotel
◉ Modern British, Welsh
01690 710219 | Holyhead Road,
LL24 0AY

See advert on page 430

CAPEL CURIG
Bryn Tyrch Inn
◉ Modern Welsh
01690 720223 | LL24 0EL

COLWYN BAY
Bryn Williams at Porth Eirias
◉◉ Modern, Seasonal
01492 577525 | The Promenade,
LL29 8HH

CONWY
Castle Hotel Conwy
◉◉ Modern British
01492 582800 | High Street,
LL32 8DB

Signatures Restaurant
◉◉ Modern British **V**
01492 583513 & 07738 275814
Aberconwy Resort & Spa,
Aberconwy Park, LL32 8GA

DEGANWY
Quay Hotel & Spa
◉ Modern European **V**
01492 564100 | Deganwy Quay,
LL31 9DJ

LLANDUDNO
Dunoon Hotel
◉◉ Classic British
01492 860787 | Gloddaeth Street,
LL30 2DW

Imperial Hotel
◉◉ Modern & Traditional British
01492 877466 | The Promenade,
Vaughan Street, LL30 1AP

The Lilly Restaurant with Rooms
◉ Modern Welsh
01492 876513 | West Parade,
West Shore, LL30 2BD

St George's Hotel
◉ Modern, Traditional, Welsh
01492 877544 | The Promenade,
LL30 2LG

LLANDUDNO JUNCTION
Queens Head
◉ Traditional British, Seafood
01492 546570 | Glanwydden,
LL31 9JP

Denbighshire

RUTHIN
Ruthin Castle Hotel
◉ Modern British
01824 702664 | Castle Street,
LL15 2NU

▶ Gwynedd

ABERDYFI
Penhelig Arms
® British
01654 767215 | Terrace Road,
LL35 0LT

ABERSOCH
The Dining Room
® British Bistro
01758 740709 | 4 High Street,
LL53 7DY

Porth Tocyn Hotel
®® Modern British ⬤
01758 713303 & 07789 9994942
Bwlchtocyn, LL53 7BU

CRICCIETH
Bron Eifion Country House Hotel
® Modern British, Welsh
01766 522385 | LL52 0SA

DOLGELLAU
Bwyty Mawddach Restaurant
® European
01341 421752 | Pen Y Garnedd,
Llanelltyd, LL40 2TA

Penmaenuchaf Hall Hotel
® Modern British ⬤
01341 422129 | Penmaenpool,
LL40 1YB

PORTMEIRION
The Hotel Portmeirion
®® Modern Welsh
01766 770000 & 772440
Minffordd, LL48 6ET

PWLLHELI
Plas Bodegroes
®® Modern British ⬤
01758 612363 | Nefyn Road,
LL53 5TH

▶ Monmouthshire

ABERGAVENNY
Angel Hotel
® British, International
01873 857121 | 15 Cross Street,
NP7 5EN

The Hardwick
®® Modern British
01873 854220 | Old Raglan Road,
NP7 9AA

Llansantffraed Court Hotel
®® Modern British, Welsh V ⬤
01873 840678 | Old Raglan Road,
Llanvihangel Gobion, Clytha,
NP7 9BA

Restaurant 1861
®® Modern British, European V
01873 821297 | Cross Ash, NP7 8PB

MONMOUTH
#7 Church Street
◉◉ Modern British
01600 712600 | 7 Church Street,
NP25 3BX

ROCKFIELD
**The Stonemill & Steppes
Farm Cottages**
◉◉ Modern British
01600 716273 | NP25 5SW

USK
Newbridge on Usk
◉◉ Traditional British
01633 451000 | Tredunnock,
NP15 1LY

See advert below

The Raglan Arms
◉ Modern British
01291 690800 | Llandenny,
NP15 1DL

The Three Salmons Hotel
◉ Modern Welsh
01291 672133 | Bridge Street,
NP15 1RY

▶ Newport

NEWPORT
Rafters
◉ Modern British
01633 413000 | The Celtic Manor
Resort, Coldra Woods, NP18 1HQ

See advert on page 432

Steak on Six
◉◉ Modern British
01633 413000 | The Celtic Manor
Resort, Coldra Woods, NP18 1HQ

See advert on page 432

▶ Pembrokeshire

HAVERFORDWEST
Slebech Park Estate
◉◉ Modern British V
01437 752000 | SA62 4AX

NEWPORT
Llys Meddyg
◉◉ Classic
01239 820008 | East Street,
SA42 0SY

Newbridge on Usk
By Celtic Manor

An idyllic riverside inn offering lovingly cooked seasonal British
dishes featuring home-grown ingredients from our kitchen garden.

DISCOVER MORE AND BOOK ONLINE AT
CELTIC-MANOR.COM OR CALL 01633 410262

PORTHGAIN
The Shed
◉ Fish, Traditional British, Mediterranean
01348 831518 | SA62 5BN

ST DAVIDS
Cwtch
◉ Modern British
01437 720491 | 22 High Street, SA62 6SD

Twr Y Felin Hotel
◉◉ Modern British, French
01437 725555 | Caerfai Road, SA62 6QT

SAUNDERSFOOT
Coast Restaurant
◉◉ Modern British V
01834 810800 | Coppet Hall Beach, SA69 9AJ

St Brides Spa Hotel
◉ Modern British
01834 812304 | St Brides Hill, SA69 9NH

SOLVA
Crug Glâs Country House
◉ Modern British
01348 831302 | Abereiddy, SA62 6XX

TENBY
The Salt Cellar
◉◉ Modern British V
01834 044005 | The Esplanade, SA70 7DU

Trefloyne Manor
◉ Classic British
01834 842165 & 844429
Trefloyne Lane, Penally, SA70 7RG

WOLF'S CASTLE
Wolfscastle Country Hotel
◉◉ Modern & Traditional
01437 741225 | SA62 5LZ

▶ Powys
BRECON
Peterstone Court
◉ Modern British, European
01874 665387 | Llanhamlach, LD3 7YB

BUILTH WELLS
Caer Beris Manor Hotel
◉◉ Modern European
01982 552601 | LD2 3NP

CRICKHOWELL
The Bear
◉ Modern British, International
01873 810408 | High Street, NP8 1BW

Manor Hotel
◉ Modern British
01873 810212 | Brecon Road, NP8 1SE

HAY-ON-WYE
Old Black Lion Inn
◉ Modern British, Italian
01497 820841 | 26 Lion Street, HR3 5AD

The Swan at Hay
◉◉ Modern British, Welsh
01497 821188 | Church Street, HR3 5DQ

KNIGHTON
Milebrook House Hotel
◉ Modern, Traditional V
01547 528632 | Milebrook, LD7 1LT

LLANDRINDOD WELLS
Metropole Hotel & Spa
◉ Modern British V
01597 823700 | Temple Street, LD1 5DY

LLANFYLLIN
Seeds
◉ Modern British
01691 648604 | 5-6 Penybryn Cottages, High Street, SY22 5AP

LLANWDDYN
Lake Vyrnwy Hotel & Spa
◉ Modern British
01691 870692 | Lake Vyrnwy, SY10 0LY

LLANWRTYD WELLS
Carlton Riverside
◉◉ Modern British
01591 610248 & 07795 259849
Irfon Crescent, LD5 4SP

Lasswade Country House
◉◉ Modern British
01591 610515 | Station Road, LD5 4RW

MONTGOMERY
The Nags Head Inn
◉ Traditional British
01686 640600 | Garthmyl, SY15 6RS

▶ Rhondda Cynon Taff

PONTYCLUN
La Luna
◉ Modern International
01443 239600 | 79-81 Talbot Road,
Talbot Green, CF72 8AE

PONTYPRIDD
Llechwen Hall Hotel
◉ Modern Welsh
01443 742050 | Llanfabon, CF37 4HP

▶ Swansea

OXWICH
**AA Restaurant of the Year
for Wales 2017-18**
**Beach House Restaurant
at Oxwich Beach**
◉◉ Modern British V
01792 390965 | SA3 1LS
See page 315

REYNOLDSTON
Fairyhill
◉ Modern British
01792 390139 | SA3 1BS

SWANSEA
Hanson at the Chelsea Restaurant
◉ Modern Welsh, French
01792 464068 | 17 St Mary Street,
SA1 3LH

▶ Torfaen

CWMBRAN
The Parkway Hotel & Spa
◉◉ Modern European
01633 871199 | Cwmbran Drive,
NP44 3UW

▶ Vale of Glamorgan

HENSOL
Llanerch Vineyard
◉ Modern British
01443 222716 | CF72 8GG

The Red Lion at Pendoylan
◉ Modern & Classic British
01446 760690 | Pendoylan,
CF71 7UJ

The Vale Resort
◉ Modern British
01443 667800 & 667950
Hensol Park, CF72 8JY

LLANCARFAN
The Fox & Hounds
◉ Modern British
01446 781287 | CF62 3AD

▶ Wrexham

LLANARMON DYFFRYN CEIRIOG
The Hand at Llanarmon
◉◉ Modern European
01691 600666 | Ceiriog Valley,
LL20 7LD

ROSSETT
Hallmark Hotel Chester Llyndir Hall
◉ Traditional British
01244 571648 | Llyndir Lane,
LL12 0AY

NORTHERN IRELAND

▶ County Antrim

BUSHMILLS
Bushmills Inn Hotel
◉ Modern, Traditional V
028 2073 3000 | 9 Dunluce Road,
BT57 8QG

NEWTOWNABBEY
Sleepy Hollow
◉ Modern Irish
028 9083 8672 | 15 Kiln Road,
BT36 4SU

▶ Belfast

BELFAST
Deanes at Queens
◉◉ Modern British V
028 9038 2111 | 1 College Gardens,
BT9 6BQ

James Street South Restaurant
◉◉ Modern & Classic
028 9043 4310 | 21 James Street South,
BT2 7GA

The Merchant Hotel
◉◉ Modern European V �
028 9023 4888 | 16 Skipper Street,
Cathedral Quarter, BT1 2DZ

Shu
◉◉ Modern Irish
028 9038 1655 | 253-255 Lisburn Road,
BT9 7EN

▶ County Down

COMBER
The Old Schoolhouse Inn
◉◉ Modern British **V**
028 9754 1182 | 100 Ballydrain Road,
BT23 6EA

CRAWFORDSBURN
The Old Inn
◉◉ Modern European
028 9185 3255 | 15 Main Street,
BT19 1JH

DUNDRUM
Mourne Seafood Bar
◉ Seafood
028 4375 1377 | 10 Main Street,
BT33 0LU

NEWCASTLE
**Brunel's Restaurant at
The Anchor Bar**
◉ Modern Irish
028 4372 3951 | 9 Bryansford Road,
BT33 0HJ

NEWTOWNARDS
Balloo House
◉ Modern British
028 9754 1210 | 1 Comber Road,
Killinchy, BT23 6PA

▶ County Fermanagh

ENNISKILLEN
Manor House Country Hotel
◉ Irish, European
028 6862 2200 | Killadeas,
BT94 1NY

▶ County Londonderry

LIMAVADY
The Lime Tree
◉ Classic Mediterranean
028 7776 4300 | 60 Catherine Street,
BT49 9DB

LONDONDERRY
**Browns Restaurant
and Champagne Lounge**
◉ Modern Irish **V**
028 7134 5180 | 1 Bonds Hill,
Waterside, BT47 6DW

MAGHERA
Ardtara Country House
◉◉ Modern Irish **V**
028 7964 4490 | 8 Gorteade Road,
BT46 5SA

REPUBLIC
OF IRELAND

▶ County Carlow

BORRIS
1808 Brasserie
◉ Modern British
059 9773209 | Step House Hotel,
Main Street

LEIGHLINBRIDGE
Lord Bagenal Inn
◉ Modern Irish ♟
059 9774000 | Main Street

TULLOW
**Mount Wolseley Hotel,
Spa & Country Club**
◉ Modern Irish **V**
059 9180100

▶ County Cavan

CAVAN
Cavan Crystal Hotel
◉ Modern Irish
049 4360600 | Dublin Road

Radisson Blu Farnham Estate Hotel
◉ European, Modern International **V**
049 4377700 | Farnham Estate

▶ County Clare

DOOLIN
**Cullinan's Seafood Restaurant
& Guest House**
◉◉ Modern French
065 7074183

ENNIS
Legends Restaurant
◉ Modern International **V**
065 6823300 | Temple Gate Hotel,
The Square

LAHINCH
Moy House
◉◉ Modern French **V**
065 7082800

County Clare

LAHINCH *continued*
VL Restaurant
⊛⊛ Modern, Seafood
065 7081111 | Ennistymon Road

LISDOONVARNA
Sheedy's Country House Hotel
⊛⊛ Modern Irish
065 7074026

Wild Honey Inn
⊛⊛ French Bistro
065 7074300 | Kincora

NEWMARKET-ON-FERGUS
Dromoland Castle Hotel
⊛⊛ Traditional Irish, European **V**
061 368144

▶ County Cork

BALLINGEARY
Gougane Barra Hotel
⊛ Classic & Traditional
026 47069 | Gougane Barra

BALLYLICKEY
Seaview House Hotel
⊛⊛ Traditional **V**
027 50073

BALTIMORE
Rolfs Country House
⊛ French, European
028 20289

CORK
Bellini's Restaurant
⊛⊛ Modern International **V**
021 4365555 | Maryborough Hill, Douglas

The Springboard Restaurant
⊛ Classic & Traditional
021 4800500 | Victoria Cross

DURRUS
Blairscove House & Restaurant
⊛⊛ Modern European
027 61127

GOLEEN
The Heron's Cove
⊛ Traditional Irish
028 35225 | The Harbour

KINSALE
The White House
⊛ Traditional, International
021 4772125 | Pearse Street, The Glen

MALLOW
Springfort Hall Country House Hotel
⊛ Modern Irish
022 21278

ROSSCARBERY
Kingfisher Bistro
⊛ Seafood **V**
023 8848722 | The Celtic Ross Hotel

SHANAGARRY
Ballymaloe House
⊛⊛ Modern & Traditional ♟
021 4652531

SKIBBEREEN
Kennedy Restaurant
⊛ Modern & Traditional Irish
028 21277 | West Cork Hotel, Ilen Street

▶ County Donegal

BALLYLIFFIN
Jacks Restaurant
⊛ Modern European
074 9378146 | Ballyliffin Lodge & Spa, Shore Road

DONEGAL
Harvey's Point Hotel
⊛⊛ Modern Irish
074 9722208 | Lough Eske

The Red Door Country House
⊛ Modern & Traditional European
074 9360289 | Fahan, Inishowen

DUNFANAGHY
Arnolds Hotel
⊛ Traditional
074 9136208 | Main Street

MOVILLE
Redcastle Hotel, Golf & Spa Resort
⊛ Modern, International
074 9385555 | Inishowen Peninsula

▶ Dublin

DUBLIN
Ashling Hotel, Dublin
⊛ Irish, European
01 6772324 | Parkgate Street

Balfes at The Westbury
⊛ Contemporary Irish
01 6463353 | Grafton Street

Bang Restaurant
⊛⊛ Modern International V
01 4004229 | 11 Merrion Row

Castleknock Hotel & Country Club
⊛ European, International
01 6406300 | Porterstown Road,
Castleknock

Coppinger Row Restaurant
⊛⊛ Mediterranean, Modern Irish
01 6729884 | off South William Street

Crowne Plaza Dublin Northwood
⊛ Asian Fusion
01 8628888 | Northwood Park,
Santry Demesne, Santry

**Crowne Plaza Hotel Dublin -
Blanchardstown**
⊛ Italian, European, International
01 8977777 | The Blanchardstown
Centre

Fahrenheit Restaurant
⊛⊛ Modern Irish
01 8332321 | Clontarf Castle Hotel,
Castle Avenue, Clontarf

The Marker
⊛⊛ Modern International
01 687 5100 | Grand Canal Square

Pichet
⊛⊛ French
01 6771060 | 14-15 Trinity Street

Radisson Blu St Helens Hotel
⊛ Italian
01 2186000 & 2186032
Stillorgan Road

Roganstown Hotel and Country Club
⊛ European
01 8433118 | Naul Road, Sword

**The Shelbourne Dublin,
a Renaissance Hotel**
⊛⊛ Traditional Irish, European V
01 6634500 | 27 St Stephen's Green

Talbot Hotel Stillorgan
⊛ Modern Fusion
01 2001800 & 2001822
Stillorgan Road

The Westbury
⊛⊛ Modern Irish
01 6791122 | Grafton Street

▶ County Dublin

KILLINEY
Fitzpatrick Castle Hotel
⊛ Modern European
01 2305400

PORTMARNOCK
The 1780
⊛⊛ Modern Irish
01 8666533 | Portpatrick Hotel
and Golf Links

▶ County Galway

BARNA
The Pins Gastro Bar
⊛ International, Modern Irish
091 597000 & 597011 | Barna Village

Upstairs@West, The Twelve
⊛⊛ Modern Irish ♟
091 597000 | Barna Village

CASHEL
Cashel House Hotel
⊛⊛ Traditional Irish
095 31001

GALWAY
Ardilaun Bistro
⊛ Modern Irish
091 521433 | Taylor's Hill

Park House Hotel & Restaurant
⊛ Modern Irish, International
091 564924 | Forster Street,
Eyre Square

Pullman Restaurant
⊛⊛ Modern French
091 519600 | Kentfield, Bushypark

**Restaurant gigi's
at the g Hotel & Spa**
⊛⊛ Modern Irish
091 865200 | Wellpark, Dublin Road

County Galway

GALWAY *continued*
Screebe House
◉◉ Irish, Seafood
091 574110 | Rosmuc

ORANMORE
Basilico Restaurant
◉ Italian
091 788367 & 483693
Main Street

RECESS (SRAITH SALACH)
Lough Inagh Lodge Hotel
◉◉ Irish, French
095 34706 | Inagh Valley

The Owenmore Restaurant
◉◉ Modern Irish
095 31006 | Ballynahinch Castle

County Kerry

DINGLE (AN DAINGEAN)
Coastguard Restaurant
◉ Modern Irish
066 9150200 | Dingle Skellig Hotel

**Gormans Clifftop House
& Restaurant**
◉ Modern & Traditional
Irish, Seafood
066 9155162 & 083 0033133
Glaise Bheag, Ballydavid
(Baile na nGall)

KENMARE
Park Hotel Kenmare
◉◉ Classic Irish
064 6641200

Sheen Falls Lodge
◉◉ Modern European V
064 6641600 | Sheen Falls Lodge

KILLARNEY
Cahernane House Hotel
◉◉ Classic & Traditional
064 6631895 | Muckross Road

Danu at The Brehon
◉◉ Modern European V
064 6630700 | The Brehon Hotel,
Muckross Road

The Lake Hotel
◉◉ Traditional European V
064 6631035 | On the Shore,
Muckross Road

The Park Restaurant
◉◉ Irish V
064 6635555 | The Killarney
Park Hotel, Kenmare Place

KILLORGLIN
**Carrig House Country House
& Restaurant**
◉◉ Modern Irish, European
066 9769100 | Caragh Lake

TRALEE
Ballyseede Castle
◉◉ Traditional European
066 7125799

County Kildare

STRAFFAN
The K Club
◉◉ Traditional French
01 6017200 | River Room

County Kilkenny

KILKENNY
Lyrath Estate
◉ Modern Irish, European V
056 7760088 | Old Dublin Road

THOMASTOWN
The Restaurant @ Hunters Yard
◉ French, European
056 7773000 | Mount Juliet Hotel

County Laois

BALLYFIN
Ballyfin Demesne
◉◉ Traditional European V
057 8755866

County Limerick

LIMERICK
Limerick Strand Hotel
◉ Contemporary Irish
061 421800 | Ennis Street

County Louth

CARLINGFORD
Ghan House
◉◉ Modern Irish
042 9373682

DROGHEDA
Scholars Townhouse Hotel
🏵🏵 Modern Irish
041 9835410 | King Street

County Mayo

BALLINA
Belleek Castle
🏵🏵 International V
096 22400 | Belleek

Mount Falcon Estate
🏵🏵 Traditional
096 74472 | Foxford Road

BELMULLET
The Talbot Hotel
🏵🏵 Modern Irish
097 20484 | Barrack Street

CONG
The George V Dining Room
🏵🏵 Traditional European,
International V 🍷
094 9546003 | Ashford Castle

The Lodge at Ashford Castle
🏵 Contemporary Irish V
094 9545400 | Ashford Estate

MULRANY
Mulranny Park Hotel
🏵🏵 Modern Irish
098 36000

WESTPORT
Hotel Westport Leisure,
Spa & Conference
🏵 Modern Irish, British, European
098 25122 | Newport Road

Knockranny House Hotel
🏵🏵 Modern Irish
098 28600

County Meath

DUNBOYNE
Dunboyne Castle Hotel & Spa
🏵🏵 Modern European
01 8013500

KILMESSAN
The Signal Restaurant
🏵 Modern Irish
046 9025239

NAVAN
Bellinter House
🏵🏵 Modern European V
046 9030900

SLANE
Conyngham Arms Hotel
🏵 Modern International
041 9884444 | Main Street

Tankardstown –
Brabazon Restaurant
🏵🏵 Classic International
041 9824621

County Monaghan

CARRICKMACROSS
Shirley Arms Hotel
🏵 Modern Irish V
042 9673100 | Main Street

GLASLOUGH
Snaffles Restaurant
🏵🏵 Traditional Irish, International
047 88100 | The Lodge,
Castle Leslie Estate

County Roscommon

ROSCOMMON
Kilronan Castle Estate & Spa
🏵🏵 Modern European V
071 9618000 | Ballyfarnon

County Sligo

ENNISCRONE
Waterfront House
🏵 Modern European
096 37120 | Sea Front, Cliff Road

SLIGO
The Hall Door Restaurant
🏵 Modern Irish
071 9118080 | Castle Dargan Hotel,
Ballygawley

Radisson Blu Hotel & Spa Sligo
🏵 Modern Irish, Mediterranean
071 9140008 | Rosses Point Road,
Ballincar

Sligo Park Hotel & Leisure Club
🏵 Modern Irish
071 9190400 | Pearse Road

County Tipperary

▶ County Tipperary

CLONMEL
Hotel Minella
◉ Traditional V
052 6122388

▶ County Waterford

WATERFORD
Bianconi Restaurant
◉ Traditional Irish
051 305555 | Granville Hotel,
The Quay

**Faithlegg House Hotel
& Golf Resort**
◉◉ Modern Irish, French
051 382000 | Faithlegg

The Munster Room Restaurant
◉◉ Irish, International V
051 878203 | Waterford Castle Hotel,
The Island

▶ County Wexford

GOREY
Amber Springs Hotel
◉ Irish
053 9484000 | Wexford Road

Ashdown Park Hotel
◉ Mediterranean, European
053 9480500 | Station Road

Clonganny House
◉◉ Contemporary Irish, French
053 9482111 | Ballygarrett

Marlfield House Hotel
◉◉ Classic
053 9421124 | Courtown Road

Seafield Hotel & Spa Resort
◉◉ Modern Irish, French
053 9424000 | Ballymoney

ROSSLARE
**Beaches Restaurant
at Kelly's Resort Hotel**
◉◉ Traditional European
053 9132114

La Marine Bistro
◉ Modern French V
053 9132114
Kelly's Resort Hotel & Spa

WEXFORD
**Aldridge Lodge Restaurant
and Guesthouse**
◉◉ Modern Irish V
051 389116 | Duncannon

▶ County Wicklow

DELGANY
Glenview Hotel
◉◉ Modern Irish, European V
01 2873399 | Glen O' the Downs

ENNISKERRY
Powerscourt Hotel
◉◉ Modern European V
01 2748888 | Powerscourt Estate

MACREDDIN
BrookLodge & Macreddin Village
◉◉ Modern Irish, Organic
0402 36444
See advert opposite

NEWTOWNMOUNTKENNEDY
Druids Glen Hotel & Golf Resort
◉◉ Modern European
01 2870800

RATHNEW
Hunter's Hotel
◉ Traditional Irish, French
0404 40106 | Newrath Bridge

Tinakilly Country House
◉◉ Modern Irish
0404 69274

Maps

Maps 1 to 29 in this section correspond to the map references given in the 3, 4 and 5-Rosette section of the guide (pages 20–328). See also the London maps on pages 104–115.

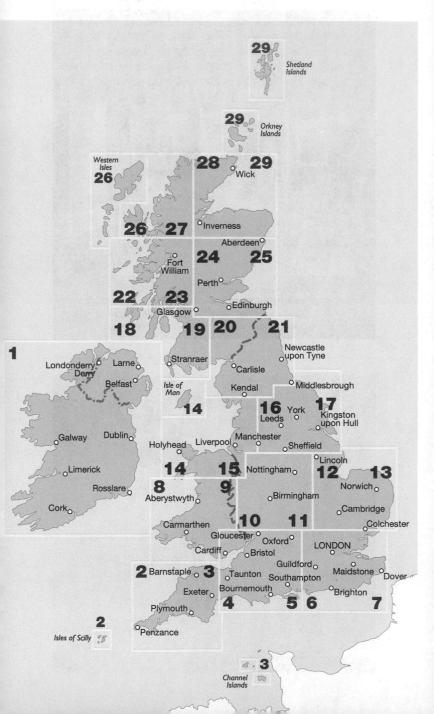

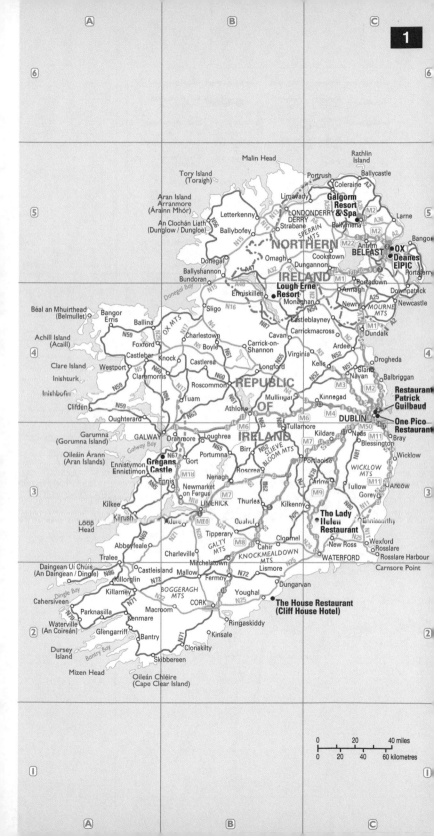

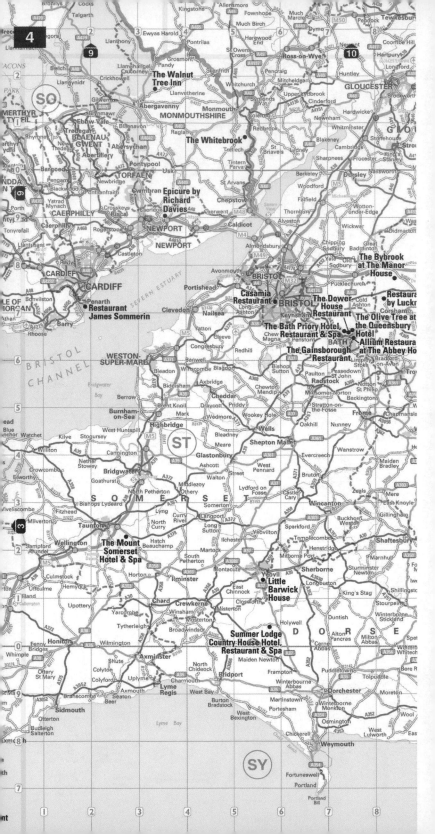

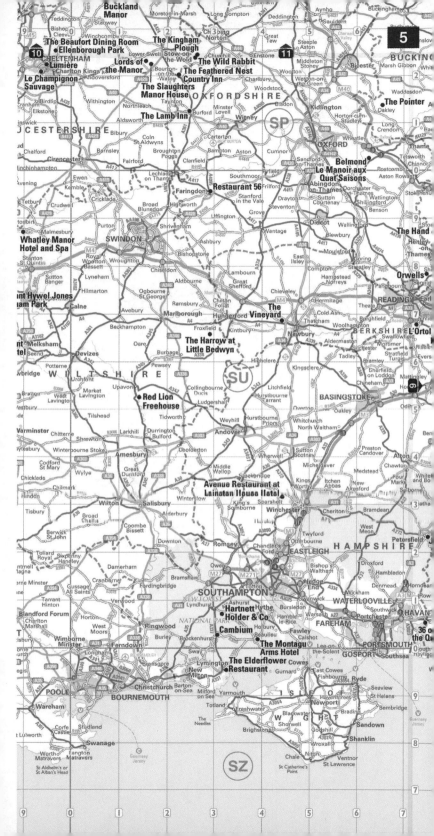

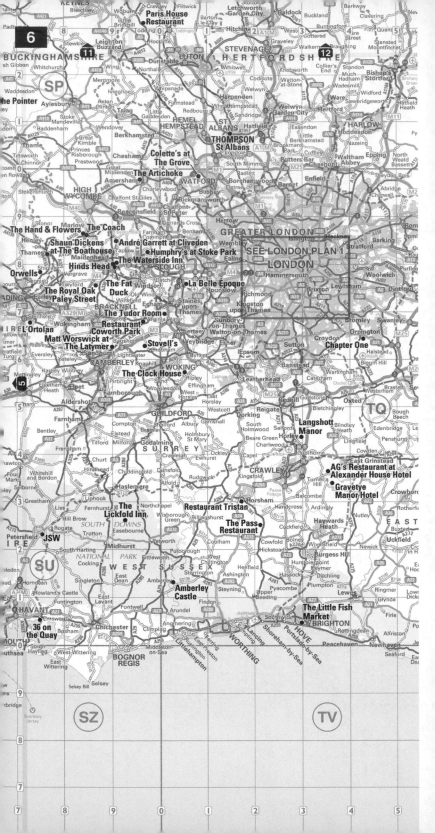

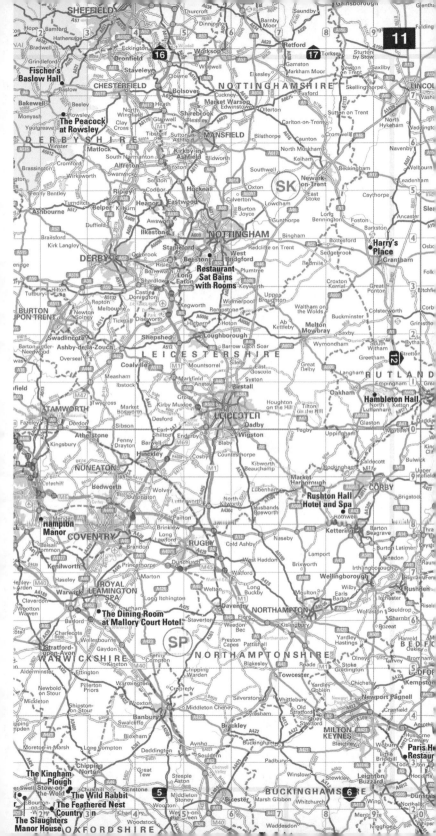

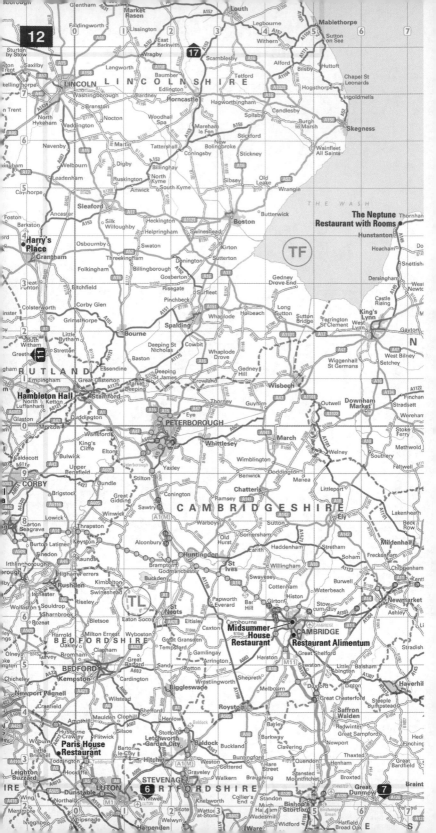

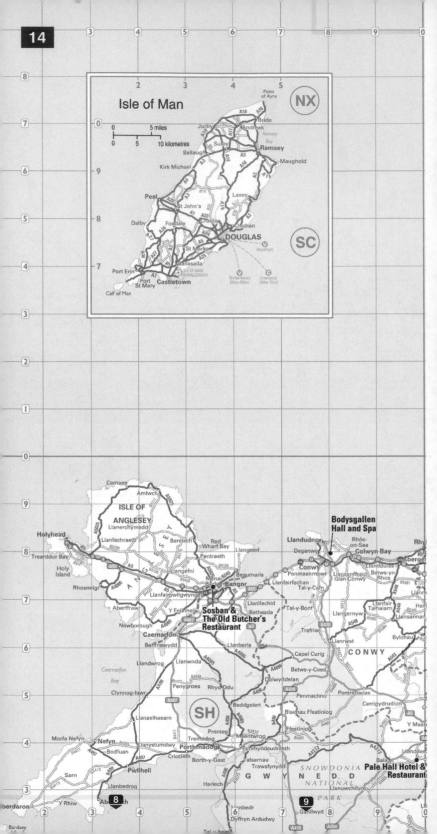

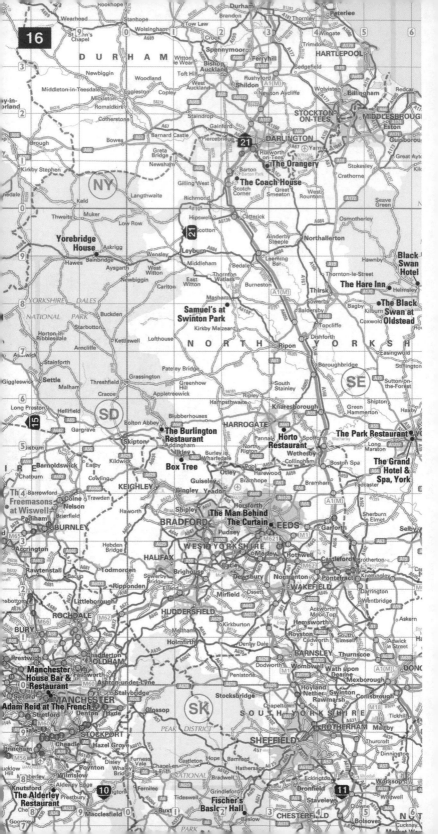

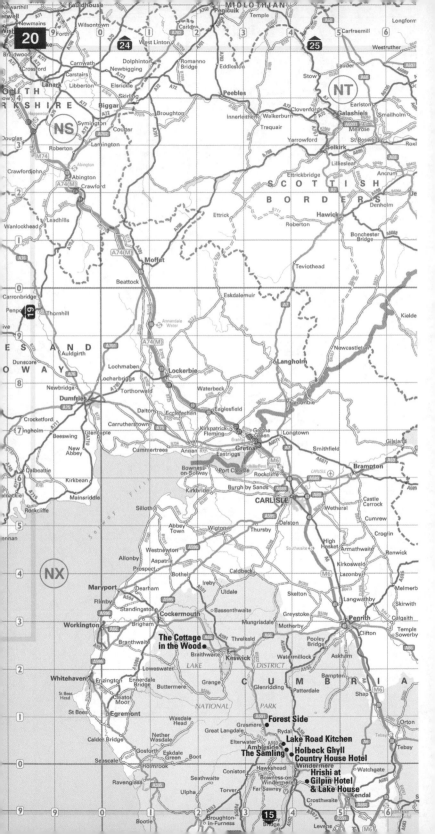

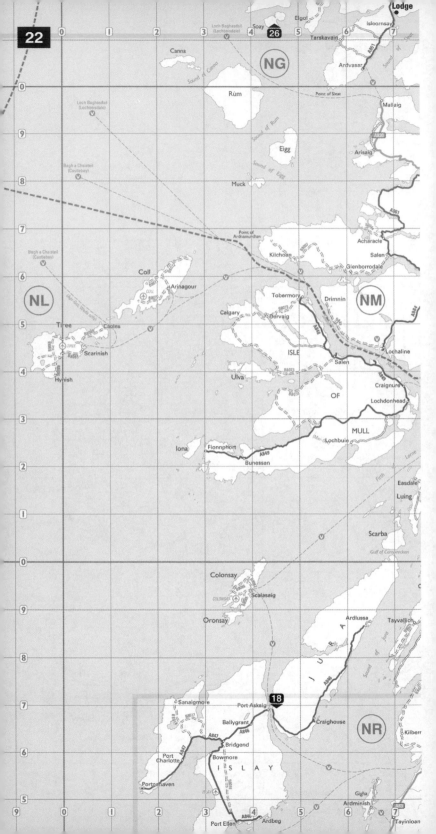

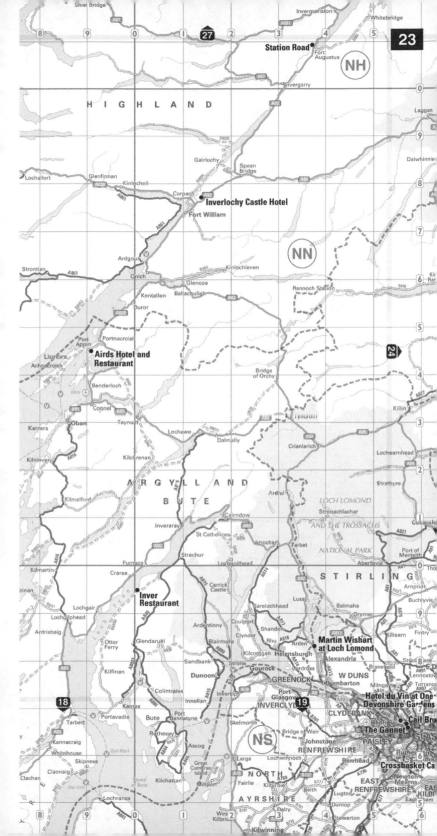

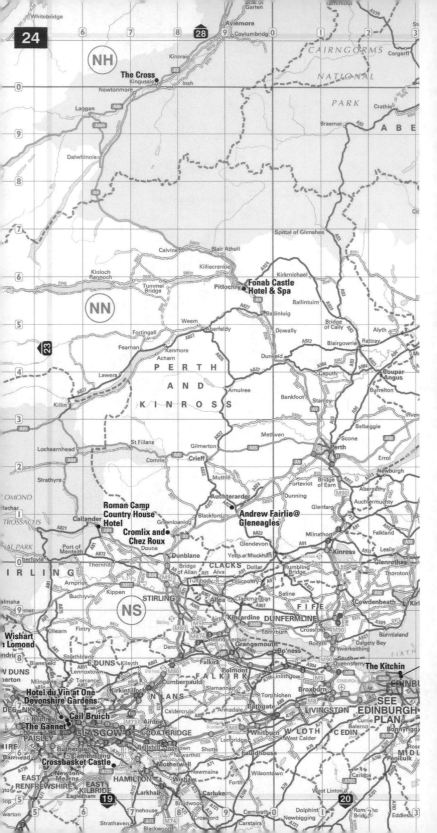

NJ

Douneside
House

RDEENSHIRE

Stonehaven

NO

ANGUS

Montrose

Gordon's

Arbroath

DUNDEE

Road Hole Restaurant
Rocca Restaurant
St Andrews

The Peat Inn

The Cellar

Restaurant
-Martin
Wishart
URGH

NT

EAST LOTHIAN

Berwick-
upon-Tweed

20

21

29

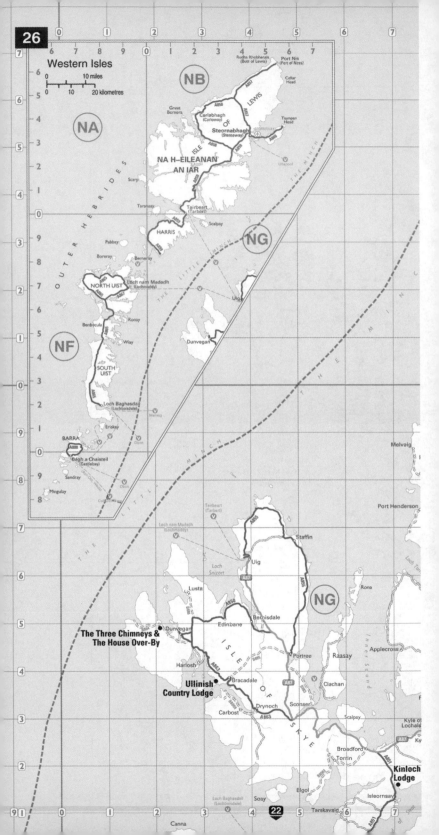

26

Western Isles

0   10 miles
0   10   20 kilometres

NA

NB

Rudha Rhobhanais (Butt of Lewis)
Port Nis (Port of Ness)

LEWIS

Great Bernera

Cellar Head

Carlabhagh (Carloway)

Tiumpan Head

ISLE

Steornabhagh (Stornoway)

NA H–EILEANAN AN IAR

Ullapool

Scarp

OUTER HEBRIDES

THE MINCH

Taransay

Tairbeart (Tarbert)

Scalpay

NG

HARRIS

Pabbay

Boreray

Berneray

NORTH UIST
Loch nam Madadh (Lochmaddy)

Uig

NF

Benbecula

Ronay

Wiay

Dunvegan

SOUTH UIST

THE LITTLE MINCH

Loch Baghasdail (Lochboisdale)

Eriskay

Malraig

THE MINCH

BARRA

Doun

Bàgh a Chaisteil (Castlebay)

Sandray

Oban

Mingulay

Castlebay

Melvaig

Tairbeart (Tarbert)

Port Henderson

Loch nam Madadh (Lochmaddy)

Staffin

Loch Snizort

Uig

Loch Torridon

Lusta

NG

Rona

Dunvegan

Bernisdale

Applecross

The Three Chimneys & The House Over-By ● Dunvegan

Edinbane

Portree

Raasay

ISLE

Harlosh

Bracadale

SOUND OF RAASAY

Clachan

Ullinish Country Lodge

Drynoch

Sconser

OF

Carbost

Kyle of Lochalsh

SKYE

Scalpay

Broadford

22

Torrin

Kinloch Lodge

Elgol

Isleornsay

Kyle

Canna

Soay

Loch Baghasdail (Lochboisdale)

Tarskavaig

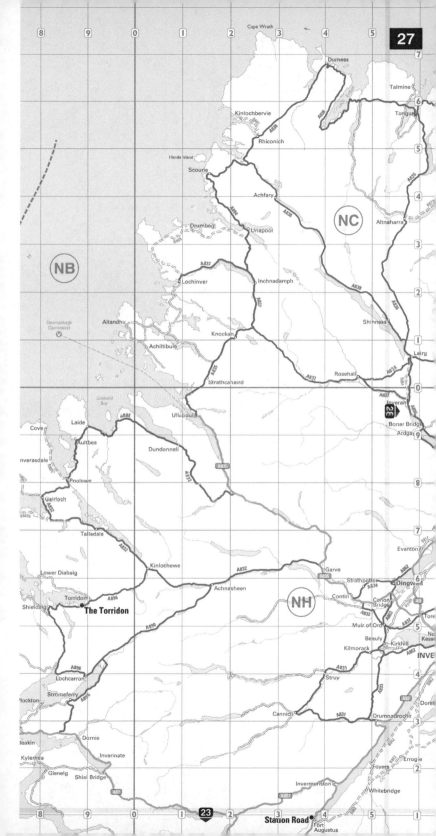

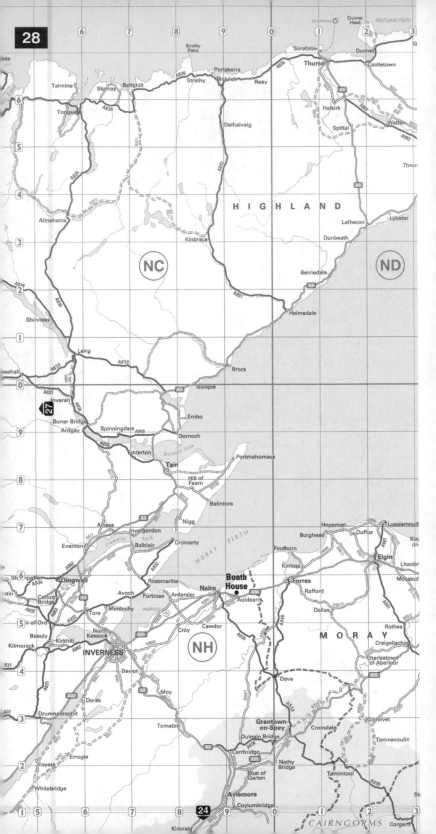

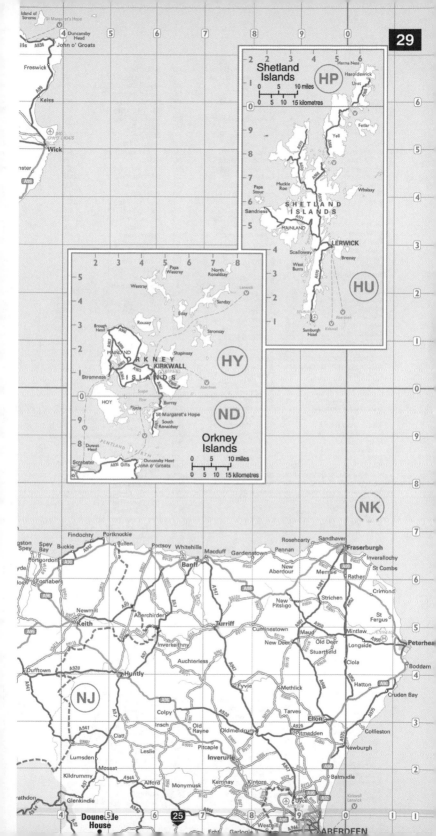

Shetland Islands

0 5 10 miles
0 5 10 15 kilometres

HP

Herma Ness

Haroldswick

Unst

Fetlar

Yell

Papa
Stour

Muckle
Roe

Whalsay

Sandness

SHETLAND
ISLANDS

MAINLAND

Scalloway

West
Burra

LERWICK

Bressay

HU

SUMBURGH

Aberdeen
Kirkwall

Sumburgh
Head

Papa
Westray

North
Ronaldsay

Westray

Sanday

Lerwick

Eday

Rousay

Brough
Head

Stronsay

MAINLAND

ORKNEY
KIRKWALL

Shapinsay

HY

Stromness

ISLANDS

Scapa

Aberdeen

HOY

Flotta

Burray

ND

St Margaret's Hope

South
Ronaldsay

Orkney Islands

0 5 10 miles
0 5 10 15 kilometres

Dunnet
Head

PENTLAND

FIRTH

Scrabster

Gills

Duncansby Head
John o' Groats

Island of
Stroma

St Margaret's Hope

Duncansby
Head

John o' Groats

Freswick

Keiss

ills

AB36

MO
JOHN O GROATS

Wick

nster

A99

NK

Findochty Portknockie

gston Spey Buckie Cullen

Spey Bay

Portsoy Whitehills Macduff Gardenstown

Rosehearty Sandhaven

Fraserburgh

rgordon

A98

Banff

Pannan

New
Aberdour

Inverallochy

St Combs

yde

A96

loch Fochabers

A98

Memsie

Rathen

A90

A95

Newmill

Aberchirder

New
Pitsligo

Strichen

Crimond

Keith

Turriff

St
Fergus

Dufftown

A941

Inverkeithny

Cuminestown

Maud

Mintlaw

PETERHEAD

A950

New Deer

Old Deer

Longside

Peterhea

Auchterless

Stuartfield

A97

A90

H

A920

Huntly

Fyvie

Methlick

Clola

Boddam

Lumsden

Colpy

A947

Tarves

Hatton

Cruden Bay

Kildrummy

Mossat

Insch

Old
Rayne

Oldmeldrum

Elon

A90

Colieston

Clatt

Leslie

Pitcaple

A920

Pitmedden

Newburgh

Alford

Monymusk

Kemnay

Inverurie

Kintore

A96

Balmedie

Glenkindie

Echt

Dyce

Kirkwall
Lerwick

**Doune
House**

25

Westhill

ABERDEEN

Index

Index

Index

Index

Index

Index

Index

Index